W0082554

BEFORE THE MYTH

THE EARLIEST
FOOTPRINT OF JESUS

What We Have Heard

— BOOK I —

Daniel G. Slawter

PUBLISHER

PeggySue-Bluesky2 Associates

Copyright © 2022 Daniel G. Slawter
All rights reserved.

Before the Myth
The Earliest Footprint of Jesus
Book 1: What We Have Heard

ISBN 978-1-66781-840-5
eBook ISBN 978-1-66781-841-2

Where indicated by the abbreviation "RSV" Scripture quotations are from Revised Standard Version of the Bible, copyright © 1946, 1952, and 1971 National Council of the Churches of Christ in the United States of America. Used by permission. All rights reserved worldwide.

All rights reserved. No part of this publication may be reproduced, stored in a retrieval system, distributed, or transmitted in any form or by any means without the prior written permission of the publisher, except in the case of brief quotations embodied in critical reviews and certain other noncommercial uses permitted by copyright law.

Front cover image by Danita Delimont, "Detail of Arch of Titus in Roman Forum, Rome, Italy." Image appears courtesy of Getty Images.

Printed by PeggySue-Bluesky2 Associates, in the United States of America.

First printing edition 2022.

DEDICATION

To Urban C. Von Wahlde, PhD,
Professor Emeritus,
New Testament Studies,
Loyola University of Chicago

Who has believed what we have heard?

(Is 53.1, RSV)

CONTENTS

WRITER'S NOTE

Research for these works commenced in the fall of 1973 and continued off and on to the present day. While citing experts throughout (many hundreds), the author is not a scholar. Or affiliated with any scholar(s). All arguments and conclusions drawn herein (i.e. across all related works and venues) are his own unless otherwise indicated.

PREFACE

Approaching 50 years. Autumn of 1973. Sitting in a library at Harvard University. Many volumes in neat stacks packed the cubicle. That is when and where the author began researching the historical Jesus.

He actually never attended Harvard. In between semesters at a small college on the banks of the Mississippi, the author spent a fall and winter working in Boston's Fenway district.

On days off, he would depart his tiny apartment situated in the infamous "combat zone." If memory serves, he would head for a nearby "T" station. He vaguely recalls that the commuter rail passed a drop-off point within easy reach of the famous university.

Without any doubt, he cannot remember specifics anymore. Apparently, his college student card got him through the door. Or maybe the public was freely admitted. A mystery today with everyone focused on security, identity, and formal procedures. But back then, if memory serves, you just walked in.

This research pattern repeated for decades. Other libraries at other destination points around the country. Places like Ann Arbor, Detroit, Chicago, Portland, Los Angeles, Costa Mesa, Irvine, San Diego. Visiting local and university libraries. Trying to find answers to the historical Jesus. Until some point late in the 1990s. When the internet took off. And for some who had shunned the implicit boredom of formal education, intellectual life started over. In a very big way.

Within that general timeframe – in other words, within a year or so of the new millennium – the author discovered a study by a professor from the upper Midwest. As to the author's research, after encountering this work, the book became essential reading. The little book was called *The*

Earliest Version of John's Gospel: Recovering the Gospel of Signs by Urban C. von Wahlde (Wilmington, DE: Michael Glazier, Inc, 1989).

Around the turn of the century, too, the author had begun researching the oral origins of gospel tradition. Digging into ideas and formulations from experts on orality. Studies by specialists like Kelber, Ong, Bailey, Gerhardsson, J. Dewey, Byrskog, and others affected the author in a strange way.

He became intrigued with the idea that people named Matthew, Mark, Luke, and John, or (more popularly depicted) communities in their name, had not produced the canonical stories. Had not in any way been associated with original development behind the written sources.

This revelation, along with von Wahlde's moving thesis, induced a kind of epiphany in the author's intellectual life. For the first time the historical Jesus was not so far away. The author had one last time sifted the dust. And uncovered faint traces of an ancient path that would, very possibly, finally lead him home.

If they are curious about history, these several books may assist most readers. Spanning fifty years or so the author has made measurable progress moving past worn out platitudes that have no chance of retaining historical connections to early first-century Palestine. And, conversely, solidified links to the authentic figure.

Thus, the author insists that this study does, in fact, offer valuable insights into a truthful understanding of Jesus the Nazarene. Though due to space limits, most of the time painted in broad brushstrokes. Who he was. What he believed. His accomplishments. His destiny.

Chapter endnotes are stocked with citations from reliable institutional scholars, cultural experts, sociologists, as well as archeologists and niche specialists. Specific bibliographical references are also included.

After nearly half a century of determined effort the author herein puts forth that this little two book study offers viable answers to the long-standing mystery of Jesus the Nazarene.

What We Have Heard

INTRODUCTION
Athens and Dionysus

On the morning of February 17, 2011, within the Athenian public sector, the debt-driven economic woes of the Euro Zone flittered away. Many locals were taken by the hand to revisit a hallowed memory all but forgotten sometime in the long ago.

The historical Athens narrative spans more than 7,000 years.[1] This archaic geographical zone is one of the oldest continuously inhabited urban settings on Earth. For historians, its extraordinary timetable recorded some of the most sacrosanct and influential moments in the chronicles of Western man.

Here the non-aristocrat *Themistokles* battled the Persian hordes (and Athenian political elites) to save democracy.[2]

Here the ancient Parthenon (Western classical architecture in perfect mathematical expression[3]) rose above the Acropolis like the stirrings of a second Olympus.[4]

Here, in 404 BCE, while warrior-stateman Pericles, son of Xanthippus, may have delivered the most famous speech ever uttered in defense of warfare, his real focus was the innate virtue of his audience and of Athens itself.[5]

And here on this hallowed ground the likes of Plato (our greatest Western philosopher[6]), Aristotle (discoverer of logic and tutor to Alexander[7]), and Socrates (father of the dialectic or Socratic method[8]) midst the centuries-traversed pathways of the ancient Agora chiseled out the rudiments of original Western thought.

In short, it is impossible to overstate the influence of one southeastern Mediterranean city on the social and intellectual DNA of Western man.

All that said, there is not a shadow of a doubt that February 17, 2011 marked a special day in the history of the ancient metropolis. More than 100 newspapers and news outlets announced the rare archeological find. In fact, in the early morning hours many sleepy Athenians cast uncertain glances at the ethereal caption tempting their eyes. The spectral banner read:

"Altar of the Twelve Gods Sees the Light"[9]

Audiences eventually learned that the rather provocative discovery seamlessly confirmed very ancient literary tradition.[10] Quite simply, the banner headline effectively revealed a small piece of Athenian history. The newly discovered altar was in fact *real*!

While resurrected in the twenty-first century, we cannot overestimate the role of the Altar of the Twelve Gods in the original ancient landscape. The monument was formerly constructed at the orders of a member of the then ruling family. A grandson of the tyrant Peisistratos, while serving as "Archōn" or chief magistrate, established the altar (Thucydides 6.54)[11] around the year 522 BCE.

Strangely, similar headlines might have been disclosed across various eras and in contrasting geographical environs across the world. As strange as it seems, this idea of "twelve gods" somehow connects to our common genetic pool. A brief tour of antiquity reveals that the concept of a pantheon of "twelve gods" was multicultural, crossed most continents, and spanned many thousands of years.

In North America, the Lenape people in the Susquehanna River Valley (mid-Atlantic region) worshipped twelve gods.[12]

In India, Hindis believed that the Lord Brahma created twelve Jayas or Gods to assist him in the ordering of creation.[13]

During the first millennium BCE, the Babylonian Chaldeans inhabited a broad region from Mesopotamia and Arabia across to the Turkish region of Anatolia in the Armenian highland. They, too, held traditions revolving around 12 gods associated with signs of the zodiac.[14]

In the Norse tradition, Odin was said to have organized twelve gods called "Aesir."[15]

In China in 1934, south of the Yangtse River near Ch'ang-sha grave-robbers discovered the silk manuscript of Ch'u, dated to 400 BCE. As of 1994 this find represented the oldest written script yet discovered in all of China (other than writing on bones or stone stele). On the manuscript twelve entities were depicted as representative of twelve spirits or gods.[16]

In the land of the Pharaohs, from the fourteenth century BCE onward, the month deities were twelve in number.[17]

And in ancient Greece, the twelve Olympians led by Zeus in splendid victory over the primeval Titans, were permanently etched into collective memory sometime during the Classical Age. By 350 BCE Plato had dictated that twelve festivals would be celebrated in honor of these twelve primary gods.[18]

With many centuries in-between, a generous plurality of Athenian readers that February morning could well have forgotten their twelve celebrated luminaries keeping a watchful eye from the heights of Olympus. However, the sensational news story reminded all that the ancient Altar of the Twelve Gods was advantageously placed at the northwest entrance of the Agora at the epicenter of the city.

The altar's location was not only a real historic landmark. Just as importantly, it literally defined the very heart of the Athens metropolis. In ancient times, the Altar became the central marker for calculating point-to-point distances from the ancient city.[19]

Just as important, from roughly the fifth century BCE onward, the Altar of the Twelve Gods emerged as a protective "sanctuary" for the persecuted. This site was considered a sacred place of refuge. Conceptually, experts think of this tradition in a similar way to the sanctuary church interiors provided throughout medieval Europe.[20]

We hear from the aforementioned historian Herodotus that in 519 BCE the Plataeans, besieged by neighboring Thebes, put their lives in the hands of the Athenians by literally depositing themselves on the altar while Athenians were at worship. According to the account, the Athenians were forced to honor the "sacred sanctuary" tradition. They extended an alliance to the besieged Plataeans saving their lives.[21]

We know, too, that the Plataeans under Aëimnestus later repaid this kindness at the Battle of Marathon in 490 BCE. A band of soldiers arrived just in time to cover the Athenian left flank against overwhelming Persian forces.[22]

Due to the clash of separate cultures and the massive disparities in troop strength, the battle has sometimes been characterized in symbolic terms. Some specialists feel this confrontation marked "a turning point in the history of Western civilization."[23]

Tiny Plataea was the only Greek city-state to answer the Athenian call for help in the first of a number of Persian invasions (Greco-Persian Wars). At the Battle of Marathon, the Hellenes defeated the Persians in a rout. After the battle, it is impossible imagining that the Athenians would not have laid sacrifices at the foot of the Altar of the Twelve Gods giving thanks for deliverance and victory.

We do know for certain, however, that "[f]rom the time of this battle, when the Athenians perform sacrifices at their quadrennial festivals, the Athenian herald prays that there be 'good things' for both the Athenians and the Plataeans" (Herodotus 6.111.2).

Archeology has revealed that the Altar of the Twelve Gods was actively worshipped by Athenians even into the second century of the common era.[24]

For those readers who follow history and archaeology, a few background particulars can be noted. Previous excavations had uncovered the actual remains of the *peribolos* (enclosure) of the altar but not the altar landmark itself. We have to understand that locations in the immediate vicinity of the Athenian Agora (spanning some thirty acres) have been nearly continuously occupied for more than 5,000 years.[25]

From what archeologists can reasonably discern, all or most of the Agora destination site was built on top of ancient burial grounds known as the *Kerameikos* (Potters Quarter).[26] A trivia factoid: the Athenian *Kerameikos* became the most popular potters location in the Grecian geographical region,[27] having been active from the 12th century BCE to the 6th century BCE.[28]

Associating burial grounds with potters' activity in the archaeological record seems to be quite common throughout the ancient Greek world.[29] In Greek antiquity, where there was a common burial ground, there was often a pottery workshop nearby. Perhaps a place of worship such as the famous Altar would not be a surprise.

The Altar of the Twelve Gods, dating to the 6th century BCE, along with the *Pististratids* fountain were the first public monuments to occupy the Athenian Agora.[30] Apparently (as stated), the altar was established by a grandson of Peisistratos (Thucydides 6.54) around 522-521 BCE.[31]

Over time the historical Athenian Agora was transformed into a place for the living from a place for the dead. Its significance and impact on Western civilization is truly uncanny. For within the geographical limits of this thirty-acre parcel *democracy itself was born.*[32]

Within the perimeters of this former burial ground, the likes of Themistocles, Herodotus, Pericles, Cleisthenes, Aristotle, Plato, Socrates, Plutarch (and many more dignitaries and original thinkers) walked the Earth and lived their lives. Once upon a time in the span of antediluvian history commerce, government, entertainment, philosophy, social interchange (the nuts-n-bolts of everyday life) by and large replaced death, burial, and remembrance on these few acres of hallowed ground in sight of the ancient Acropolis.

Who knows, maybe popular and unbroken worship at the Altar of the Twelve Gods (across centuries) really had something to do with the unprecedented Athenian influence on Western progress. For what comes next may sound trivially embroidered. But from a historical standpoint what follows happens to be one hundred percent true.

In one rather sensational, longwinded pronouncement we are able to deduce today that nowhere else at any time in recorded history would humanity be introduced from one generation to the next, literally, for hundreds of years to such a uniquely versatile, often multi-skilled collection of original thinkers and doers occupying one relatively meager parcel of earth as could be found at the geographical site of the Agora marketplace in pre-Roman Athens.

How important was Athens to the ancient world? Alexander of Macedon, better known as "Alexander the Great," is probably one of a small handful of historical figures who actually earned the title. In his time Alexander was first to conquer most of the known world.

Not only did he conquer "most of the known world." But he accomplished this feat with military forces that were often far outnumbered. Alexander was an exceptionally brilliant, inspirational leader. He repeatedly demonstrated an enormous gift for improvisation and exploiting enemy vulnerabilities that is uncanny in the chronicles of warfare. Alexander of Macedon was just smarter and more proficient than anyone else.[33]

Pupil of Aristotle, he is widely recognized as the greatest military genius of antiquity (arguably of all time). He is famously quoted asking: "How great are the dangers I face to win a good name in Athens?" A self-proclaimed god, in history Alexander did not often concern himself over the opinions of conquered domains.

His court historian, Callisthenes of Olynthus, said in the *Deeds of Alexander* that in early 333 BCE, while Alexander's army passed through the coast of Pamphylia, the very sea "receded, doing obeisance to the conqueror" (*Fragments of the Greek Historians* 124 F 31). Lesson learned: Even gods gave pause to the mystique of ancient Athens.

By the first century of the Common Era, the direct impact of Athens on the Western world was entering its twilight years.[34] Imperial Rome had effectively taken the stage. However, visitors to the ancient city would not have guessed by the vast accumulation of cultic statues besieging the ancient metropolis.

Probably impossible for us today to surmise, inside the ancient landscape, the visual chaos created by the overwhelming number of cultic representatives populating the whole Athenian geography inundated the senses. Myriad numbers of statues gazed upon the human population from virtually every niche and recess around the city.

The highest concentrations were represented around the Acropolis and the slopes of the Are-op'agus as well as the Agora below.[35] The primary reason for such an unusual number of statues in one wide-ranging geographical zone lies in a happenstance phenomenon: once approved by local authorities, the gods had a habit of never going away. In the Athenian cultural world, populations customarily introduced new cults without eliminating the old ones.[36]

What moderns describe as "cult statues" were critically necessary to represent, in each instance, the cultic deity's presence on Earth. This practice was a fundamental rite of their belief system. What's more, ancient Athenians truly accepted this claim. Their statues were treated just as the gods themselves would be if present in human form. So lacking an accompanying statue each cultic dignitary would not be properly represented. Thus the requirement of visible proof.

For a single, relatively unified religious culture that spanned many centuries, the mathematical implications cannot be ignored. As one century transitioned to the next, the old cults would not be replaced. They would simply be forgotten.

Decade after decade new statues kept appearing beside the forgotten ones. On and on. Thus, by the time of the first century CE, the overabundance of cultic deities virtually occupied the entire available landscape. Turns out that casual remarks from a certain first-century visitor to that time and place setting happened to coincide with the historical narrative.

> "Men of Athens, I perceive that in every way you are very religious. For as I passed along, and observed the objects of your worship …" (Acts 17.22-23, RSV).

"Objects of your worship," of course, was a way of depicting their devotional statuary. It is virtually certain that no one short of the blind could have missed the layers upon layers of amassed cultic representatives. The Apostle Paul from Tarsus, a pagan Asia Minor regional capital, surely didn't.

For antiquarian Athenian locals at times the amassed statuary must have taken on aspects of a live sci fi thriller. Right out of H. G. Wells. Or one of our contemporary scary movies. For everyone encountering this locale, the Athenian geographical landscape represented an alternate reality frozen in time.

Down the centuries, history has recorded numerous instances when visitors to Athens would comment on the vast cultic population. Again, Paul's *Acts* reading happened to fit snugly into the ancient historical setting.

We know that as a rule people calling on Athens would arrive from the sea. They would access the city from one of three serviceable harbors along the southwestern peninsula of Piraeus a few miles away.[37]

From the Piraeus peninsula, they would take the *hamaxitos* road (Xenophon) and arrive at the double-arched Dipylon Gate flanked by towers and leading directly into the heart of the city.

During Greek antiquity, the northeastern Dipylon Gate,[38] with its bath houses on either side for the benefit of weary travelers,[39] was the most imposing of the fifteen entry gates to the metropolis.

Hinted at above, in 404 BCE, just outside the Dipylon Gate, Pericles had delivered his "Funeral Oration" praising fellow Athenians who had fought and died in the recently declared Peloponnesian Wars. A series of extremely violent encounters extended across an inordinate timeframe would last a devastatingly long 27 years. Some consider the Pericles oratory as "the most famous" speech recited in ancient times.[40]

The Dipylon Gate was known throughout the Mediterranean region for cultural celebrations, athletic competitions, and religious festivals. For example, it was cast as the traditional starting point of the quadrennial, regionwide "Panathenaic" games. This sporting competition was popular for more than a *millennium*.[41] They were never canceled even once due to war, pestilence, or any other reason. As some of us today may know, the Panathenaic Games has been recognized as the forerunner of our modern-day Olympic games.

For our purposes, on a spring day around the year 50 CE, a certain weary traveler, wearing physical signs of an unfed vagabond, entered the famous gate. This individual was no typical first-century tourist lingering just to gape at the dominating Parthenon. No, this conclusion is virtually certain. Armed with the force of will of a miniature dervish, Saul of Tarsus, also known as the Apostle Paul, was there to confront the pagans. All of them! Or so it seemed.

But for nearly all readers today, something rather mindboggling escapes the eye. Doubtless Paul would have stood out from the rest of the dusty trekkers surrounding him at the famous gate. Paul would stand out not for his imposing reserves of energy. Probably not for any unusual attire. And certainly not for the weary attitude. Many would have mirrored his worn countenance. Unfortunately, the naked truth was far less flattering.

Behind the historical counterpoint to Paul's mythological persona as Christian *superhero* lurked an ugly reality. Bereft of his religious-crusader "cape," in person Paul would stand out not for fantastical and charismatic spiritual gifts. In person the Apostle Paul would stick out – if even marked by passersby – due to his unusually *diminutive height*.

Such a determination is not creative license from an overzealous biographer. There is some reliable evidence that comes down to us from antiquity. We know that during this period average male height ranged from 5'4" to 5'7." In the past, people were much smaller than today. But certainly not to the extent of Paul's alleged petite dimensions.

The dependable *Pseudo-Chrysostom* (347-407 CE) reported that Paul was "the man of three cubits"[42] (*anthropos tripechys*). For those of us who need translating, three cubits came to **four-and-a-half feet tall**.

There was no deriding or condemnation in John Chrysostom's claim. Paul's height bordered on what many people today would solicitously characterize with a popular slang. In everyday conversation we often call such individuals *midgets*. The little people.

In reference to Paul, there is trustworthy backup to this assertion. We have only to look at the meaning of the name "Paul" (or *Paulus*) in Latin to learn that it reliably translates to "small." The ancient record wants us to know that the Apostle Paul was the runt of the litter. There is almost no doubt about that.

What else do we know about this endlessly mythologized Christian crusader? His letters are revealing. By his own admission, Paul was made an apostle by divine intervention: "Paul an apostle – not from men nor through man, but through Jesus Christ and God the Father" (Gal 1.1, RSV).

Truly *significant* self-endorsements. A singular calling card that would allow Paul, despite his diminutive size, to muscle his way into most any devotional or philosophical debate across the hellenistic world. Pagans loved to champion their gods. For the Christian crusader it was the other way around. Paul's credentials were *personally* endorsed. From above.

All things were lawful for this chosen advocate appointed from on high. From Paul's point of view the Ineffable definitely had his back: "'All things are lawful for me,' but not all things are helpful" (1 Cor 6.12, RSV), once observed this ambassador for the otherworldly.

Perhaps offering support in such pronouncements was, according to Paul's thinking, the fact that the Mosaic law honored by the Jews had been abolished. Forgotten. Abandoned.

Christos, a former village rabbi and faith healer from Nazareth in Galilee, had suffered the ultimate penalty on a Roman cross. The penalty reserved for violent criminals and insurrectionists. Amazingly, for Paul and his followers, such an utterly humiliating, utterly catastrophic turn of events had somehow ushered in a new world order.

> Likewise, my brethren, you have died to the law through the body of Christ, so that you may belong to another, to him who has been raised from the dead in order that we may bear fruit for God. While we were living in the flesh, our sinful passions, aroused by the law, were at work in our members to bear fruit for death. But now we are discharged from the law, dead to that which held us captive, so that we serve not under the old written code but in the new life of the Spirit (Rom 7.4-6, RSV).

During the first century, pulling off this remarkable turn of events would have seriously challenged most practicing Jews. Inside Jerusalem, regardless of divine connections, Paul's following probably would have been cited by a higher court both for idolatry *and* blasphemy. At the least, they would have been *strangled to death*. Quite literally.

> One who prophesies in the name of idol worship and says: This is what the idol said, even if he approximated the correct halakha in the name of the idol to deem ritually impure that which is ritually impure and to deem ritually pure that which is ritually pure, is executed by strangulation (*Mishnah Sanhedrin* 11).

Word games aside, Paul and his congregations definitely qualified. In the pagan, hellenized world, when practicing newfound faith in Christos, somehow Paul's alleged connections to native Judaism seemed to vanish.

Replaced by a higher calling. Mere incidentals like Sinai and laws in stone were meticulously allocated to the back burner.

For Paul and his gentile followers, the former Mosaic law had been transformed into a theological union now celebrated as divine *grace*: "For sin will have no dominion over you, since you are not under law but under grace" (Rom 6.14, RSV), Paul would utter more than once.

Said another way utilizing this apostle's unique doctrinal lexicon, "by abolishing in his flesh the law of commandments and ordinances, that he might create in himself one new man in place of the two, so making peace" (Eph 2.15, RSV). For us today, this epic Christological "revelation," unique to, and originally laid out by, Paul from Tarsus appeared to be in direct opposition to the canonical teachings once attributed to a local village rabbi, *Yeshu ha-Notzri*.[43]

The gospels acknowledged their Christian Savior preaching: "Think not that I have come to abolish the law and the prophets; I have come not to abolish them but to fulfil them" (Matt 5.17, RSV). The Lukan version was more specific: "But it is easier for heaven and earth to pass away, than for one dot of the law to become void" (Lk 6.17, RSV). The "law," of course, was the law of Moses. The Nazarene's first followers, in fact, loved their Judaism.

After one particularly unseemly confrontation, we have to expect that Paul's unusually eccentric personality would have left at least some believers scratching their heads. At some point in the historical record the little man took it upon himself to further insult one of the *original* disciples. Not only that but St Peter himself. "But when Cephas came to Antioch I opposed him to his face, because he stood condemned" (Gal 2.11, RSV).

In a literal sense, without a helping hand from one of the faithful lifting the little dynamo to eye level, such *opposition* probably would have been difficult to assay. Before Antioch, Peter had been regularly seen casting nets on the Kinneret. We have to believe that his upper torso would have been inordinately strong. Even in late middle age.

So even in Paul's time the former Galilean fisherman was probably still physically vigorous. It is difficult imagining that the Nazarene's "Rock" would *stand* condemned as he peered down at the miniature dervish. Especially considering the *opposition*. One thing is certain. The Apostle Paul was a focused man.

Probably many original Palestinian followers had not received the news that, when all was said and done, Paul was equal to (or greater than) the initial disciples: "I think that I am not in the least inferior to these superlative apostles" (2 Cor 11.5, RSV), he once grandly boasted. We can almost imagine the little figure strutting around some anonymous house church like a rooster intoning those fighting words.

Apparently, Paul took his own self-importance even further. Congregations were instructed to literally follow his Christly example: "I urge you, then, be imitators of me" (1 Cor 4.16, RSV).

These words were not for "shock" value. They were fighting words. As torchbearer and archetype, the self-appointed apostle from Tarsus was adamant among his diverse gentile flocks: "I beseech you, become as I am" (Gal 4.12, RSV) he would intone to backsliders at Galatia. And again, "Be imitators of me, as I am of Christ" (1 Cor 11.1, RSV) for the Corinthian faithful.

Today, no offense to any religious cause, but for the less doctrinally inclined, one has to wonder what this guy was really about.

From the erratic behaviors alone, at least some of us can better understand why former followers would reject both Paul's teachings and his ministry. From his own lips: "You are aware that all who are in Asia turned away from me" (2 Tim 1.15, RSV).

Paul's undersized physical presence, added to a raging propensity for confrontation and violence, establishes for us a solid theory. Across the timeframe of his public life, we begin to sense a near omnipresent "chip" on Paul's shoulder. According to many details in his extensive correspondence, this behavioral trait seemed to shadow many of his thoughts and movements.

From confrontations with Jewish synagogues to confrontations with former disciples to confrontations with his own congregations. Paul's personal insecurities were never far away. One has to wonder what his god-man *Christos* had to say about all of that.

The profile suggests that in modern parlance, the Apostle Paul was a victim of the male neurological disorder we informally call "small man's disease." In more official jargon, this condition is sometimes described as *Napoleon Complex.*

From Paul's extensive writings, it isn't difficult to recognize his perceived subconscious inferiorities assuaged in zealous, righteous fervor. In his own words ...

> Whatever anyone else dares to boast about – I am speaking as a fool – I also dare to boast about. Are they Hebrews? So am I. Are they Israelites? So am I. Are they Abraham's descendants? So am I. Are they servants of Christ? (I am out of my mind to talk like this.) I am more. I have worked much harder, been in prison more frequently, been flogged more severely, and been exposed to death again and again. Five times I received from the Jews the forty lashes minus one. Three times I was beaten with rods, once I was pelted with stones, three times I was shipwrecked, I spent a night and a day in the open sea, I have been constantly on the move. I have been in danger from rivers, in danger from bandits, in danger from my fellow Jews, in danger from Gentiles; in danger in the city, in danger in the country, in danger at sea; and in danger from false believers. I have labored and toiled and have often gone without sleep; I have known hunger and thirst and have often gone without food; I have been cold and naked. Besides everything else, I face daily the pressure of my concern for all the churches. Who is weak, and I do not feel weak? Who is led into sin, and I do not inwardly burn? (2 Cor 11.21-29, RSV).

Wind him up and the preaching missionary transformed to a walking dynamo. Before their very eyes. Does this unbroken, braggadocios rant sound like the utterance of a balanced mind, much less a spiritual role model to the early Eastern Mediterranean gentile churches?

Laying aside periodic one-on-one interviews with the Risen Lord as beyond our scope,[44] without delving into complex psychoanalysis, we don't have far to venture to easily conclude that, in all his sufferings and in all his quarrels, the Apostle Paul was utterly convinced he had something to prove.

What individual could have survived this life of perpetual hostility and violence? Who in their right mind would elect to live this way? No wonder Paul had otherworldly visions. His was a mental world of extreme, emotion-filled anguish. Not only that. But back on Earth *serious* temperament issues. Major temperament issues. The kind today where people are forced to get help. Whether they like it or not.

Not all serious thinkers of the first several centuries sympathized with Paul's distinctive demeanor. Porphyry of Tyre (234-305 CE), a Greek Neoplatonic philosopher who studied under Plotinus in Rome, wrote many books on many contemporary topics. Porphyry didn't much like the writings of Paul. His *Against the Christians* was a trendsetter for active resistance against Pauline Christianity.[45]

Notably, Porphyry's fifteen volume corpus was later banned by the Roman emperor Constantine the Great.[46] Regarding Paul's teachings and reported actions, Porphyry did not mince words. In serious tones Porphyry got directly to the point questioning Paul's mental acuity.[47]

While the Apostle Paul no doubt had critics and no doubt at times exhibited problematic behavior, it is important not to make the common mistake of demonizing this early Christian church father. No doubt at times he might have been seen as a little out of whack. But Paul was totally sincere in his religious beliefs. And would literally die for his patented vision of what he considered a supernatural figure. In the end, despite the giant-size disposition, we might fairly characterize Paul as a not-so-flawed missionary crusader who intoned boundless energy, courage, and faith.

Importantly, we don't have all the facts regarding Paul's numerous outbursts. We have no access to underlying details that – if we had – may at times (at least) tamped down our gut responses to some of the more mercurial outbursts.

What we can confidently say is that in his time and place the Apostle Paul had the respect and esteem of many, many people from diverse political, economic, and social strata. From lowest peasantry to powerful movers and shakers.

Surely, there may be a legitimate defense behind many of Paul's more extravagant actions that justifiably pointed in the direction of an undying love for an otherworldly vision. Paul from Tarsus put everything on the line for his faith.

As we come closer to Paul's imminent Athenian address allegedly preserved in the *Book of Acts*, introducing his views of Christ and resurrection to the various philosophical schools, in advance some readers may be interested reflecting upon a measurable change in tone and tactic.

Many will be familiar with Paul's famous Athens speech. The group gathered at the Are-op'agus hill (literal: "Rocky Hill of Ares") represented the leading philosophical thinkers of Paul's day. There is little doubt that even Paul from Tarsus would have strived mightily to be on his best behavior. Within intellectual circles numerous individuals inside this group would have been widely admired across the ancient world.

Once past the Dipylon Gate, entering the illustrious city, it isn't difficult imagining where Paul ventured next. The *Book of Acts* can be called upon to offer assistance: "While Paul was waiting for them in Athens, he was greatly distressed to see that the city was full of idols. So he reasoned in the synagogue with both Jews and God-fearing Greeks" (Acts 17.16-17, RSV). In history, this observation is entirely plausible. We have already touched upon *statuary*. We may wish to underline the term "reasoned."

Nevertheless, even before the first century, in main population centers diasporan synagogues offered wayfaring Jews food and shelter.[48] Whether or not the full definition was sustainable, as a self-identified "practicing" Jew crisscrossing the Eastern Mediterranean region, no doubt, the apostle Paul often took full advantage of a generous attitude of Judaic hospitality.

When visiting Athens, we can feel confident that engaging the local synagogue would have logically comprised Paul's first move in the city. *Acts* mentioned both before and after this strategic stopover that Paul preached in local synagogues.[49] However, if this source can be further trusted, while in the great city, reaching out to Judaic believers was not Paul's true objective. His sights were set on the Are-op'agus hill.

As tradition has it, northwest of the Acropolis at the Are-op'agus hill, Ares (the Greek God of War) had been put on trial by the gods for murdering Poseidon's son. The word "Are-op'agus" in Greek is the combined "aerios" and "pagos" or "Ares Rock." This traditional response most likely relates to an original artifact, the hill's authentic name.

Even today, on one's way on foot up the hill, a path bears left. Alongside the path, a bronze tablet is set in stone. The bronze tablet memorializes (in Greek) the Apostle Paul's famous speech to Athenian dignitaries. Further on past the plaque is the Are-op'agus (Romanized: "Mars Hill").

Where exactly on the hill Paul delivered his famous speech is unknown. In any sensible way, most likely on the lower, gentler slopes where the intelligentsia of Athens regularly gathered.[50]

In the Acts 17 account Paul allegedly addressed the Athenian Council. Is the story credible? Or not? Either way, the written stream left to us certainly *isn't incredible*. Various reasons defend this thinking.

Comprised of thirty members, for centuries the governmental body depicted in the *Acts* story had been active on behalf of the local populace. A ruling "elder" presided over deliberations.[51] So we are talking about a real, historical legislative body responsible for lawmaking and governmental affairs. And quite active during Athenian antiquity.

So we look back now two thousand years or so on a certain spring day around mid-century to a certain hill in plain sight of the Acropolis. The first thing we see is frowning faces clad in their customary brightly colored chitons. These governing legislators are loitering around the hill. Uncertainty permeates the setting.

In their midst their attention is riveted on an ugly little figure. He is wildly shouting judgments and praises, waving hands for dramatic effect. Our undersized "dervish" is hard at work.

If we look more closely, however, we witness something not often seen on the hill of the Are-op′agus. Glazed eyes. Creased brows. Arms folding, slowly refolding. Again and again. Solemn deliberation. They are listening.

On the minds of all present a single derisive articulation creeps in. So what exactly is this little puffed-up rooster getting at? What does upstart Tarsus have to do with Athens anyway? They may have learning in Tarsus. But this is *Athens*!

In truth, this collection of Greek thinkers doesn't quite know what to think. Let the record state (and it cannot be overstated), in the tradition of Socrates and Plato, these individuals represent the brightest intelligentsia of the hellenistic world. They are extravagantly mystified by the presence of one of the little people defending a crucified insurrectionist on the grounds that a divinity had blessed his labors. How could that be? Didn't he know the punishment? Crucifixion was reserved for derelicts. Pariahs. Outcasts. Subversives. Murderers!

For official Athens, the occasion was an oratory from a wee bantam the world has since come to know as the Apostle Paul. He had just arrived from the outer reaches (Beroe′a or Berea[52]), huffing and puffing his way toward the Agora (at the foot of the Acropolis).

They discovered him there, having gathered a crowd and breathing fire. The crackpot was complaining about *idols*. Did he know where he was, home to the Altar of the Twelve Gods – the Twelve Gods that defined the very heart of Athens itself!?[53] And now the firey cock was babbling nonsense about "resurrection"[54] as if someone named *Christos* was another Asclepius or Achilles.

So when the shouting had ceased and with all possible options cast aside, we are told the quorum of Athenian intellectuals were still at odds. Some ridiculed; others just laughed (Acts 17.32).

For readers' benefit, in Greek religion both characters, Asclepius and Achilles, preserved resurrection stories attached to their names.[55] Paul was accused by some among local Athenians for being a *spermolog* or babbler (Acts 17.18). An individual who knows just enough in public to get himself into trouble.[56]

So they had shepherded the bandy-legged fireball up the hill where the Council of the Are-op'agus, the first Athenian supreme court and main legislative body, met.

The account we read today is almost definitively NOT all apocryphal. There are just too many *legitimate* details preserved between the lines. Certain historical connections actually serve as an effective backdrop to the story's residual plot and setting. We should not discount Paul's encounter out of hand.

During the long reign of Caesar Augustus (31 BCE – 14 CE) in Rome, and even after, a herald of the Are-op'agus would announce to the city of Athens the presence of a *new deity*. This detail is *historically* recalled. The herald's announcement would typically come at a gathering place for Athenians such as the Agora. The reason for a common meeting place was to secure popular support.

The Council of the Are-op'agus would be responsible for examining and passing judgment on evidence the herald produced hoping to prove or disprove if the new deity was legit.[57]

So in a historical light, we should bear in mind that it is quite possible Are-op'agus officials were reasonably looking upon Paul as a "herald" attempting to announce a new god to the transnational pagan capital.[58]

This tradition has obvious implications confirming at least certain aspects of the *Book of Acts* story. Speculatively, Are-op'agus council members were questioning whether Paul was heralding a new deity in the form of the cited "Unknown God" (17.23). In early Christian circles, a core Pauline devotional plank, the *Unknown God* represented the same God who had allegedly raised a crucified village rabbi back to life.

According to the *Book of Acts*, the following preserves Paul's participation in the scene:

> So Paul, standing in the middle of the Are-op'agus, said: "Men of Athens, I perceive that in every way you are very religious. For as I passed along, and observed the objects of your worship, I found also an altar with this inscription, 'To an unknown god.' What therefore you worship as unknown, this I proclaim to you. The God who made the world and everything in it, being Lord of heaven and earth, does not live in shrines made by man (Acts 17:23-24, RSV).

By custom the Council would review the claims announced by the herald. If the council accepted the claims then several outcomes followed.

The deity would be admitted to the Parthenon.

A temple honoring the deity would be erected.

The deity's name would be added to the Greek calendar as a feast day and celebrated on the given annual day.

Other Greek municipalities would usually follow suit.[59]

By Paul's time, two very important aspects of its relationship with Rome to some extent preserved Athenian autonomy. First, Rome allowed special tax-exempt privileges to Athens. Second, the Athenians were extended rights to govern their citizens.[60]

History informs us that turn-of-the-era Roman elites were truly fixated on Athens and its traditions. Augustus Caesar donated funds in 19

BCE for the Roman Agora, the first commercial center in Athens. He was an enormous patron.[61]

So deeply embedded was the Athens mystique that the famous (Roman) orator and statesman, Cicero, made his will to be buried there.

By the next century, the Roman emperor Hadrian added monuments and building projects. More specifically, Hadrian donated a library on the north side of the Acropolis (132 CE) which included a public square and cultural center.[62]

It is safe to say: In the western world, as far as culture, government, art, mathematics, and science is concerned, during antiquity everything Athenian was in vogue. But every rule has its limits.

Which brings us back to the little man whining about statues and Christos. Having arrived from Beroe'a, the Apostle Paul had eluded Thessalonican Jews who previously rallied the locals against the future saint (Acts 17.13). As far as we know, they were by no means impressed with Paul's "divine-man" talk interlaced with "resurrection" claims. In fact, this much is firm: they were beyond-control enraged. Enraged to murder.

Apparently, Paul had somehow departed Beroe'a unscathed. In Athens, prior to visiting the Are-op'agus, he had already argued in the local synagogue.[63] Among the Gentiles, Paul could be found debating daily in the Agora with any unfortunate soul who would listen (Acts 17.17). If anything, such behavior would lead most anyone to believe that the Apostle Paul was a determined man.

Following is the full text of his famous Athens speech on Are-op'agus hill:

So Paul, standing in the middle of the Are-op'agus, said: "Men of Athens, I perceive that in every way you are very religious. For as I passed along, and observed the objects of your worship, I found also an altar with this inscription, 'To an unknown god.' What therefore you worship as unknown, this I proclaim to you. The God who made the world and everything in it, being Lord of heaven and earth, does not live in shrines made by man, nor is he served by human hands, as though he needed anything, since he himself gives to all men life and breath and everything. And he made from one every nation of men to live on all the face of the earth, having determined allotted periods and the boundaries of their habitation, that they should seek God, in the hope that they might feel after him and find him. Yet he is not far from each one of us, for ...

> 'In him we live
>
> and move
>
> and have our being';
>
> as even some of your poets have said,
>
> 'For we are indeed his offspring.'

Being then God's offspring, we ought not to think that the Deity is like gold, or silver, or stone, a representation by the art and imagination of man. The times of ignorance God overlooked, but now he commands all men everywhere to repent, because he has fixed a day on which he will judge the world in righteousness by a man whom he has appointed, and of this he has given assurance to all men by raising him from the dead (Acts 17.22-31, RSV).

As far as outcome ...

Those who heard were divided in opinion. Some simply indulged in ribaldry and gave this teacher no further attention. Others apparently thought the matter might be worthy of further consideration. A few accepted, but there was not, so far as we know, an Athenian church as the outcome of Paul's brief activity there.[64]

In fact, beyond Paul's time, with the assistance of an early church father, it is currently thought that there was no Athens Christian presence till the *late second century*.

Moreover, already suggested, we rather surprisingly uncover plausible historical threads behind at least some of the Athens Lukan-Pauline details.[65] Quite credibly, the lens could be focused on a number of points of interest:

> The whole episode was unflattering as it produced only a couple of named converts ("Dionys'ius the Are-op'agite and a woman named Dam'aris" – Acts 17.34, RSV). This trend certainly supports the scholarly idea of the "criterion of embarrassment." These internal comments added plausibility to at least some related thematic development.

> Athenians unabashedly <u>laughed</u> at Paul – the only time in the entire New Testament such extreme ridicule was displayed on a perceived Christian apologetic figure. While Jesus was "mocked" during passion week, within the narrative the specific instances appeared "stage-managed" for dramatic effect.

> Lending an authentic hue, the name "Damaris" as Pauline convert (again, Acts 17.34) was extremely rare across the region.[66] It appears the nomenclature was not made up.

> Jesus and/or Christ was hardly mentioned in the speech. For us this is a rather shocking development, especially coming from Paul. Nearly his entire literary corpus celebrated the Nazarene's (apparent) varied personas and otherworldly aspects.

> In the speech's text there were few specifically identified Pauline "Christian" terms and thought-streams. When stated, they were rather "generically" delivered.

> Quite uncharacteristically, the speech was sympathetic to hellenized "Stoic-Platonic" views. Otherwise, across the scope of

his considerable literary correspondence, (already mentioned) Paul devoted nearly all of his attention to Christological themes.

The tone and rhythm of the Are-op'agus speech was truly impromptu strongly resisting the idea of a carefully laid out religious tome.

The philosophers' ridicule of Paul's arguments and attempted logic threw mud on the Christian religious establishment's "apostolic" image of their trailblazing, gentile-preaching crusader.

In early religious circles preserving the speech would have been considered problematic as evangelists did not plant a Christian flag on Athenian soil till 179 CE (Eusebius, *Ecclesiastical History*, 4.23.2-3). If accurate, this date was more than a century past Paul's historical timeline. From a missionary standpoint Paul had utterly failed.

In this type of conversation, something further needs airing. If some enterprising post-Jewish-War, Christian convert had decided to place the Apostle Paul in mid-first-century Athens, and write about it, they sure managed to tie loose ends.

To arrive at the story we read today, they would have been required to look at historical Athens in detail. They would have been required to investigate how the bureaucratic side was instituted in everyday life. This aspect of the *Acts* story does coincide with our knowledge of the historical place and related social behaviors.

Without the benefit of the internet, or even horseback, such a likelihood is slim to none. The strong probability is someone in Luke's immediate circle preserved snapshots of an authentic witness to a confrontation on the famous Are-op'agus hill. Then developed related (sympathetic) scenes supporting the original imagery. Probably in light of Paul's known behaviors elsewhere. But not necessarily. There is no historical reason for rejecting much of the Are-op'agus confrontation. Various aspects of the story are clearly plausible.

In short, the Lukan-Acts tradition depicting Paul's Athens stopover got many things *right*. Including (at the top of the list), in plain language, his propensity to *piss* people off. However, this was Athens, no fleabag layover. Literally *worshiped* in the ancient world. Even by Rome.

The more sophisticated and tolerant Athenians merely accused Paul of being a "babbler." No assaults. No arrests. No stonings. This contrasts strikingly with other regions across the Eastern Mediterranean. Preserved in *Acts*, these are authentically re-enacted responses we might expect from this ancient population. Responses that intuit echoes of "real-world" behavior.

Bible students today will tell us that consistently across his missionary journeys Paul and his companions were harassed and sometimes physically assaulted by local populations. Not so in Athens.

Finally, we opened this series about the real-life Jesus with Paul's Athens memory for a calculated reason. That is, to perhaps afford us future opportunities to gauge mighty contrasts represented at multiple thematic levels between the historical figures of Jesus and Paul.

When we move into the Nazarene's story, the differences in character and witness will become easier to articulate contrasted against the Athens memory. A rather modest affair in Paul's history of hostility and confrontation across the Eastern Mediterranean.

So this chapter offers us the opportunity to introduce their differences utilizing historically laden background behind the scriptural text. In the end this approach should enable us to flesh out more truthful images for readers. The clearest, unbiased pictures we can reasonably ascertain.

In pursuit of historical figures, it is impossible to ignore legitimate perspectives, attitudes, and worldviews. Comparing the profile of a village rabbi with his cosmopolitan counterpart, a former Pharisee from Tarsus, allows a breath of true insight. At the top of the study, beginning with

Paul, as we proceed even casual readers will have an opportunity to contrast clear disparities in personality, character, religious beliefs, and social attitudes.

As we move forward, a few introductory bullet points readers might wish to store away:

> During his lifetime, Jesus the Nazarene would never address a group of gentile officials. For any reason. Even Athenians.

> He would never depart his beloved Israel for pagan surroundings.

> For whatever reasons, Jesus would never even venture into a cosmopolitan environment (other than Jerusalem).

> The historical Jesus was a rural "rabbi" who loved the local peasantry and honored Torah. Those local demographic populations, composed exclusively of worshipping Jews, constituted his *entire* "missionary" program. As historical reflection, witnessed alongside John the Baptist (see Jn 3.22-30), emphasizing his exclusive *Judaic* baptizing outreach makes this outcome virtually certain.

> In reference to the Hebrew *Holy One*, Jesus would never address this topic couched in terms like "Unknown God." Especially in exchanges with gentiles. Just the sound of the words would set him off as utterly offensive. Not to mention the objectionable audience taking part in such a religiously restrictive topic.

> Finally, from the Nazarene's standpoint, to imagine an open discussion focused on admitting the Judaic divinity into a polytheistic pantheon inside the Parthenon,[67] centerpiece of the Mediterranean pagan world, *Yeshu ha-Notzri* would have found perverse and obscene. If rebutted by practicing Jews, an offense probably deemed worthy of stoning.

In pursuit of the historical Jesus, we are investigating a human profile. Not a divine or semi-divine figure. We are investigating a human being who happened to be – by any proper measure – a devout Jew.[68] Even after these few pages, readers may wish to appreciate the rather conspicuous differences in identities. *Dramatically stark* differences.

This series is not aimed at either invoking religious fervor. Or denouncing it. Nevertheless, at the beginning of our journey we must note the mistake of accepting religious beliefs for *historical recall*. A "mistake" routinely encountered in New Testament scholarship.

The gospel stories are filled with accounts intended to summon doctrinal faith. Many featuring mythologized details of preconceived events. Nevertheless, some of the narrative streams plausibly contained fragments of historically inspired memories. This inherent contradiction cannot be discounted. And should not be discounted. But carefully negotiated.

Regardless of the challenges, the "earliest footprint" (as it pertains to Jesus) is unobtainable without venturing into more historically palatable territory. That means pursuing, to the extent possible, more reliably showcased Judaic themes. Such themes cast in authentically portrayed, early-first-century, *Palestinian* geographies.

Along those lines, can we know the distant past? Or are we just speaking to myth and legend? These questions certainly fit into a search for the historical Jesus. If the past is lost, then obviously, so is the flesh and blood Jesus.

Mentioned above, perhaps one of the best remembered examples of a distant "historical" past is Alexander from Macedon (aka "Alexander the Great"). What do we know about Alexander? What do we *really* know?

A good start on this preserved larger-than-life figure might focus on one remarkable ancient Roman: *Titus Livius Patavinus* from the northern Roman *municipium* or "town" of *Patavium* (modern "Padua") in Italy. Most scholars today just call him Livy (59 BCE – 17 CE). For Roman times, Livy lived a long life – a very long 76 years.

As far as death rates go – to our Western sensibilities the statistical results of numerous first-century mortality studies really are difficult to believe. Nearly every formal study concludes that life expectancy was between 20 and 30 years.[69] Astoundingly, some studies indicate 50% of children died before the age of 10.[70]

Nowadays there are virtually no qualified experts who dispute conclusions pointing at very high early mortality rates within the ancient setting. Those rates underline poor diet and lack of proper hygiene among other obvious indicators. As well as inadequate remediation against infection and disease.

Thus, near the end, Livy's extreme old age must have appealed to the *credulous* in many fellow Romans. In an era of limited sanitation and less hygiene, he lived more than *double* the then average lifespan.

Today in the U.S. men on *average* live to about 76,[71] the age Livy died. However, to match Livy's *relative* lifespan the math tells us someone would have to live beyond *152 years old*,[72] obviously an impossible feat. Even with workouts, supplements, regular checkups, healthy food, and organ replacements.

Known to us as "the greatest Roman narrator of historical events"[73] Livy had *many* stories to tell. His *muse*, however, was an ambitious history of the Roman Republic. The history was called *Ab Urbe Cóndita* or "From the Foundation of the City."

The literary effort covered the period from 753 BCE to 9 BCE. It produced 142 "books"[74] and totaled about 6,000 of our modern pages.[75] Though the full text is lost, enough survives to know that by any standard *Titus Livius* was a major literary figure of the Roman period.

As some might guess, Livy's history spoke also to the life of Alexander. While several centuries removed from Livy's time, Romans still idolized the Macedonian conqueror. "Idolized" for many of us today is probably an understatement.

Livy recounted a (probably) apocryphal interview[76] between the great Roman general, Africanus (*Scipio Africanus Major* or Scipio the Elder), and another great general in his own right, *Hannibal Barca,*[77] from the North African urban center of Carthage.[78]

> Africanus asked who, in Hannibal's opinion, was the greatest general of all time. Hannibal replied: "Alexander, King of the Macedonians, because with a small force he routed armies of countless numbers, and because he traversed the remotest lands. Merely to visit such lands transcended human expectation" (Titus Livius, *The History of Rome,* 35.14.6-7).

Livy was not the only ancient historian that remembered Alexander: Arrian, Plutarch, Polybius, Diodorus, Justin, Curtius – probably more – offered an enormous catalog of detailed memories of the Macedonian commander.[79]

In his *Bibliotheca historica,* Diodorus covered a "universal history" in 40 books. As expected, the *historica* provided details of Alexander's mercurial career. Here is a brief extract:

> Alexander accomplished great things in a short space of time, and by his acumen and courage surpassed in the magnitude of his achievements all kings whose memory is recorded from the beginning of time. In twelve years he conquered no small part of Europe and practically all of Asia, and so acquired a fabulous reputation like that of the heroes and demigods of old. But there is really no need to anticipate in the introduction any of the accomplishments of this king; his deeds reported one by one will attest sufficiently the greatness of his glory (Diodorus Siculus, *The Library of History,* 17.1.3-4).

What do the biographical works – no doubt brimming with apocryphal stories – in the end still manage to tell us? That even with thousands of years of separation, and even without modern technology to record live events, Alexander the Great's detailed legacy overshadowed all notables of Western antiquity. That list even included *Caesar.* On that score there is little doubt: "The myth of the undefeated hero inspired Julius Caesar to weep when he saw a statue of the young Alexander."[80] One can hardly imagine Alexander offering the same show of respect.

Covering an extensive timeframe that even encompassed the life of Jesus, Romans toyed with an unhealthy fascination for the Macedonian king.[81] By Livy's time, from the coifed hairstyle to the popular designation "the Great,"[82] even battle-hardened warriors idolized Alexander from Macedon. Not surprisingly, both Caesar and later Octavian[83] made separate pilgrimages to Egypt in part to pay homage at Alexander's tomb.[84]

Ironically, we are indebted to ancient Rome, not Greece, for the popular appellation: *Alexander the Great*.[85] A self-proclaimed god, Alexander even among his troops behaved as such. Mentioned above, his court historian *Callisthenes of Olynthus* stated in the *Deeds of Alexander* that in early 333 BCE while passing through the coast of Pamphylia (the modern-day province of Antalya in Turkey), apparently the sea moved away from the shoreline in a way that suggested nonhuman interference. Observers interpreted the phenomenon as divine intercession in praise of Alexander.[86]

Complementing the mythically-charged *receding sea*, during this period the tradition asserting Alexander's divinity was apparently taken seriously. In evidence archeology has preserved deific features superimposed with his likeness imprinted on coins.[87] While most of the recovered coins were minted after his passing, throughout his short life (we are on solid ground concluding that) at some turning point Alexander was increasingly compared to the immortals.[88]

Despite all of that, the real takeaway, however, is that the *historical* aspects of Alexander's life and career dominated the majority of serious biographers' accounts.

Undeniably, many of our memories of Alexander are plausibly historical. Besides the sources referenced above, we have fragments recovered from an unearthed Babylonian diary that offer incidental, though authentic, memories of the incomparable war leader.[89]

Our credible historical knowledge of Alexander from Macedon demonstrates that the modern era is not so handcuffed from distant memories as some would have us believe. That is why signal flares rise overhead at mention of one Jesus, ostensibly from the lower Galilean village of Nazareth, in ancient Palestine. From his reported miraculous birth to his untimely, gruesome death, mythologies and theologies doggedly snap at the heels of historical reflection.

Just like Alexander's "receding sea," in modern times some traditions preserved in the canonical Gospels might be viewed on a matching scale:

The birth of Jesus is foretold (Lk 1.26-38).

The virgin Mary conceives Jesus by the Holy Spirit (Mt 1.18-19).

An angel in a dream appears to Joseph affirming Mary's virginity (Mt 1.19-21).

Thus the "Word" becomes flesh (Jn 1.14).

A star rises in the eastern sky (Mt 2.9-10).

Wise men approach and worship the baby Jesus (Mt 2.1).

They offer costly gifts to the destitute parents (Mt 2.11).

A heavenly host populates the star-filled sky (Lk 2.13).

A celestial choir sings praises (Lk 2.14).

The angels fly back to Heaven from whence they came (Lk 2.15).

Herod hatches a plan to massacre Bethlehem's infants (Mt 2.16-18).

Jesus survives and as a twelve year-old sits for three days with teachers of the law inside the Jerusalem temple (Lk 2.41-46).

At his baptism the Spirit of G-d perches on his shoulder like a dove (Mt 3.16; Mk 1.17; Lk 3.22).

Then in the wilderness Jesus is interviewed by Satan; wild beasts provide entertainment (Mk 1.12-13; Lk 4.1-13).

Christ defeats the Devil and angels flock to succor him (Mt 4.11).

Jesus commences his ministry routinely casting out demons (a tradition many scholars claim dignifies the legitimacy of his ministry – ex. Mt 8.16, 28-33; Mk 5.1-20; Lk 8:26-38).

Demons recognize and address Jesus the Nazarene (Mt 8.28-29; Mk 1.24; 3.11; Lk 4.34, 41).

The Father loves the Jews so much he offers Jesus as a sacrifice (Jn 3.16).

Jesus bestows eternal life on those who believe (Jn 5.24).

In turn the faithful are asked to eat the flesh of Jesus and drink his blood (Jn 6.56).

Nearing the story's climax, he enters Jerusalem riding an ass (a colt in Luke) (Mt 21.1-11; Mk 11.1-10; Lk 19.28-40; Jn 12.12-15) drawing parallels with existent Hebraic scripture (1 Kgs 1:33-44).

He cleanses the Jerusalem Temple of moneychangers (Mt 21.12-17; Mk 11.15-19; Lk 19.45-48; Jn 2.13-24).

He foretells the destruction of the Jerusalem Temple (Mt 24.1-2; Mk 13.1-8; Lk 21.20-24).

He foretells his death and resurrection (Mt 16.21-23, 17.22-23, 20.17-19; Mk 8.31-38, 9.30-32; 10.32-34; Lk 18.31-34; Jn 16.16-18).

He foretells his return to Earth (Lk 21.25-28; Jn 14.18).

After the Resurrection, in a fitting postscript, the former village rabbi, by now mysteriously reawakened in an other-worldly form as the Pauline "Christ," ascends to Heaven (Mk 16.19-20; Lk 24:50-53).

The accounts just mentioned were far more familiar inside Hellenistic culture beyond ancient Israel. For example, the infancy accounts of Matthew and Luke were probably based on well-known Mediterranean stories depicting the birth scenes of important figures.[90] The Hebrew Bible preserved no such ideas even approaching the supernatural influences contained in most of the synoptic tales noted above.

There is no way avoiding the suspicion that many familiar images used by the synoptic editors were – at one time or other – probably borrowed from Greek and Roman sources. Arguably, they had no place in ancient Palestine. One such image connected to supernatural events was the familiar Christian "dove."

Located in all four of the canonical stories, at the baptism of Jesus the Spirit of God descended upon him "like a dove" (Mt 3.16; Mk 1.10; Lk 3.22; Jn 1.32). The dove symbol in the Mediterranean world often represented the "soul" or similar imagery.[91]

In the archaeological record we witness such ideas in the Roman catacombs. The dead saints were sometimes visually depicted with doves flying to and fro. In the Hellenistic world, pictures of doves used in a religious sense were fairly common.[92]

In Judaic tradition the dove was "a symbol of innocence in the midst of wickedness."[93] This visual metaphor did not take on otherworldly or otherwise supernatural imagery.

Along the same vein, from time to time scholarship has noted numerous suspect parallels between the pagan cult of Dionysus[94] matched against the traditional story of Jesus. The similarities between the two figures are, at least, extremely suspicious.

Following is a list of Dionysian themes familiar to the Christian Testament:

Conceived by virgin (Mt 1.23; Lk 1.27)

Descended from heaven (1 Cor 15.47; Eph 4.10; 1 Thess 4.16; 2 Thess 1.7)

Divine and human (Phil 2.6-8)

Rejected by intimates (Mk 8.31; Lk 9.22; 17.25; Jn 7.3-7; Rom 9-11)

Performed miracles (numerous attestations in Matthew, Mark, Luke, John)

Resistance from authorities (Mt 21.45-46; Mk 12.12; 14.1; Jn 7.30, 32, 44; 10.39; 11.57)

Stoned by hostiles (Jn 8.59; 10.31)

Eluded enemies (Lk 4.28-30; Jn 8.58-59)

Triumphal procession on an ass (Mt 21.1-11; Mk 11.1-10; Lk 19.28-40 (colt); Jn 12.12-15)

Blood and wine (Mt 26.26-28; Mk 14.23-24; Lk 22.17-20; 1 Cor 10.16)

Women depicted as loyal followers (Mt 27.55-56, 61; 28.1-2; Mk 5.25-34; 7.24-30; 14.3-9; 15.40, 47; Lk 7.37-38; 23.49; 24.10; Jn 2.3-5; 4.13-19; 11.25-27; 19.25-26; 12.2-3; 20.1, 11-18).

Arrested by local authorities (Mt 26.47-56; Mk 14.43-52; Lk 22.47-53; Jn 18.1-11)

Intense suffering (Mt 27.26; Mk 15.15; Lk 22.63-65; Jn 19.1)

Crucifixion (Mt 27.32-43; Mk 15.21-32; Lk 23.26-43; Jn 19.17-37)

Death location key religious center (Mt 27.32-33; Mk 15.21-22; Lk 23.33; Jn 19.17)

Resurrection (Mt 28.1-10; Mk 16.1-11; Lk 24.1-11; Jn 20.1-18)

Ascension (Mk 16.19-20; Lk 24.50-53)

Worshipped by followers (Mt; 2.8-11; 14.33; 15.25; 28.9, 17; Mk 5.6; 14.61-62; Lk 1.23, 35; 22.69; Jn 20.28; Acts 2.33-34; 7.56; Rom 8.34; Eph 1.20; Col 3.1; Heb 1.3; 8.1; 1 Pet 3.22)

Salvation promised beyond the grave (Rom 1.16-17; Eph 1.3-14; 5.9-10; 2 Thess 2.13-15; 2 Tim 2.8-10)

Notably, such modern comparisons are drawn from *reliable* experts.[95] By that not from what many people would deem "fringe" scholars.

The above bullet points matching the Dionysus tradition with the Christian Testament coincidentally represent a balanced nuts-n-bolts summary of the later, post-Palestine, *Christ* tradition envisioned by Paul and the canonical editors.

Most experts believe the underlying ideas behind Pauline-Christian religious doctrine, as one can imagine, were heavily influenced in the initial stages by the Apostle Paul. His own correspondence circumstantially confirms such suspicions.

Dionysus was well known across the Mediterranean.[96] We have to reasonably consider the possibility that the numerous thematic resemblances with later Christianity are at least in part the result of Paul's originating time and place setting so absorbed in the popular Dionysian cultic environment. There are just too many examples to unconsciously skirt inevitable conclusions:

We meet a Dionysian godman (Phil 2.6-8), Jesus the *Christ*, who is specifically referenced 319 times by that appellation in the collective correspondence attributed to Paul.

This divine entity descends from heaven, (1 Cor 15.47; Eph 4.10; 1 Thess 4.16; 2 Thess 1.7), a metaphor consistent with the traditions behind the centuries earlier Greek Dionysian hero. Only in the earlier account, Dionysus, son of Zeus, is protected by his father from the wiles of Hera who intended to remove the infant forcibly from the heavenly setting.[97] She does so for good cause. Hera is not the natural mother. Like the virgin Mary of later Pauline-Christian tradition, a mortal (who is claimed to have been a virgin) is the mother of Dionysus.

This human-divine, deific figure, while rejected by his people (Rom 9-11), while nailed to a cross (1 Cor 1.18), in supernatural acts of religious glory transcends the lives of mere mortals: "For to this end Christ died and lived again, that he might be Lord both of the dead and of the living" (Rom 14:9, RSV).

Of course, that is the very reason why Christ is worshipped by followers of, what might be considered, Paul's colorful adaptational twist on the Dionysus, son of Zeus myth. At Paul's theological core was the godman Christ, "who died for us so that whether we wake or sleep we might live with him" (1 Thess 5:10, RSV). Dionysus died violently but was brought back to life as well.[98]

Paul from Tarsus was raised and later thrived in a pagan Hellenic setting. His hometown rivaled both Athens and Alexandria as a Hellenistic cultural and academic hotspot in the Eastern Mediterranean. Paul was extremely intelligent. That he would have avoided the gentile educational setting isn't a realistic proposal.

Probably news to casual readers, in Paul's day no other Greek god was as popular as *Diónysos*.[99] That in Paul's dogmatic world there would have been parallels between the popular Greek deity and his divine godman Christos is almost a predictable outcome.

Following is a more comprehensive bullet point summary of primary thematic similarities shared between the two:

Both were born of virgin mothers.

A star appeared at their births.

In teaching both entertained vivid allusions involving blood and wine.

Performed miracles specifically to inspire believers.

Returned to their ancestral homes to meet rejection.

Utilized imagery of the *true vine*.

Battled forces of evil.

Promoted intense religious experience.

Suffered painful deaths.

Were resurrected from the dead.

Cultivated memories that perpetuated their own cults.

Were considered mortal and immortal.

Promised believers salvation after death.

In Paul's case, was this all by accident? Did so many of his religious themes just happen to directly intertwine with earlier Dionysian theology? Certainly, with no ill intent, perhaps this theory is hard for impartial reviewers to justify.

Nevertheless, the idea that an authentically remembered village rabbi named *Yeshu-ha-Notzri*,[100] whose ultimate purpose was absolute adherence to Y-H-V-H's sacred word, would someday hear hymns sung in his praise is (in a historical context) *shocking*! Most scholars consider the following text from the *Epistle to the Colossians* as a hymn, ostensibly intended from Paul (or one of his devotees) to the divine Christ:

He is the image of the invisible God, the first-born of all creation;

for in him all things were created, in heaven and on earth, visible and invisible,

whether thrones or dominions

or principalities or authorities—

all things were created through him and for him.

He is before all things, and in him all things hold together.

He is the head of the body, the church;

he is the beginning, the first-born from the dead,

that in everything he might be pre-eminent.

For in him all the fullness of God was pleased to dwell,

and through him to reconcile to himself all things,

whether on earth or in heaven,

making peace by the blood of his cross (Col 1.15-20, RSV).

Again, this quote stems from (allegedly) Paul's letter to the church at Colossae, situated in the Lycus Valley, southwestern Phrygia (in the interior of Asia Minor). The Christ is the "first-born of all creation," and "all things were created through him and for him."

Not only is Christ "the head of the body, the church," he is "the first-born from the dead." These images, whether or not authored by Paul, are narrowly related to longstanding Pauline religious doctrine.

Arguably, placed upon an original foundation of legitimate pre-gospel oral tradition, the pagan world of Paul produced a flurry of later ideas collated into the final texts we refer to as the "Synoptic Gospels."[101] In the modern era, scholarship has explicitly identified *more than a hundred* specific passages in these texts that suspiciously mirror Pauline themes.[102]

In a historical context, what the Christ hymn above suggested is the Judaic religious ideas promoted by James and Peter were eventually swallowed up in the popular spread of Paul's gentile-dominated, devotional proclamation. This new hellenist-influenced religious doctrine was exclusively formed and expanded beyond the limits of territorial Palestine. And, as suggested, beyond the purview of the original disciples.

In terms of circumstantial evidence, it is notable that the scriptural *James Epistle* preserved nothing from the later Johannine Literature. Or even *Mark*. Strikingly, influences from the numerous Pauline discourses were entirely absent.[103] The whole Jamesian reference point was Judaically inspired, most likely, from the original teachings of Jesus.[104]

What is known about first-century Palestine confidently assessed that the Pauline religious program, for various reasons at least in part covered in this multivolume study, would never have had a lifecycle in territorial Israel. Certainly not in the lower Galilee, the home region of Jesus and the original disciples.

Encompassing the Nazarene's life and beyond, during the historical period between Herod from Idumea and the Jewish revolt most of Galilee was furiously loyal to the Mosaic traditions symbolized in Jerusalem temple worship.[105]

Thus, prior to the First Jewish War, it is inconceivable to imagine that Paul's followers could have recruited new devotees from inside the Galilean region. At least in the lower half where Jesus and the disciples originated.

In remembrance of the original healing ministry pacing itself across the local countryside, we have to reasonably conclude that many Galilean families would have once known Jesus, James, and numerous original disciples by name. With extremely high mortality rates, couples tended to have numerous offspring. That is, if mothers lived long enough. Initially, new Jesus believers were probably more often than naught recruited from their own extended families. Galilean village units were generally formed on the basis of family relations.

This leads to a rather astonishing, reliable, and decisive conclusion. While we never think about it this way, despite later Pauline-Christian claims, inside the Land of Israel authentic Jesus groups substantially preceded hellenistic Christianity. *Probably by many years*.

Whatever specific ideas were first represented in these rather tightly-knit groups of Judaic believers, their tenets radically contrasted with later hellenized worship.[106] That is almost a certainty. All of these individuals were devotional Jews wedded to late second-temple cultic worship. Despite his alleged upbringing, Paul's religious platform was not. By a very wide margin.

What these initial Jesus groups focused on is an important aspect of this study. As a summary statement, we might consider: people who followed Jesus in Palestine witnessed a village rabbi whose prayers to Y-H-V-H healed the sick. They did not witness a divine *godman* figure. A supernatural agent come down to earth. Day-to-day living was too cruel to put forth such extreme claims. Heroic ideas surrounding the original Jesus were wrapped around Mosaic imagery. And other Judaically related cultic ideals.

To some Galileans the Nazarene was probably considered a prophet-figure like Hebrew prophets of old. Due to his special calling in light of the original cultic setting, it isn't out of the question that the Nazarene's more remarkable feats would have reminded some villagers of *Mosaic signs.* Entirely absent, however, would have been later divine elements painted by post-Palestine gentile followers of Paul.[107]

How do we conceptualize this initial originating understanding? In pursuit of the earliest footprint, the oldest scriptural document available to us happens to be the *Letter of James.* As far as written sources, this rather primitive artifact represents the closest we come to the actual thought processes originally imbibed in the life of Jesus.

That the Jamesian text actually derived from the Nazarene's own kin adds enormous weight to this claim. The James letter probably preceded the canonical texts by at least *three* decades. Maybe more.

Let's take a minute to note a couple of key ideas presented in this document. First off, we should underline the treatment James received by later religious editors responsible for compiling the various New Testament materials familiar to us. Other than Paul, James was mentioned only several times in the entire Christian Testament. All references were isolated to the *Book of Acts.*[108]

This very credible statistical observation should send us a cut and dry message that the Jamesian testimony did not strike a harmonious chord for movers and shakers representing post-Palestine Christianity. If this comment is accurate, there is no way to miss the self-conscious effort performed by editorial interests to downplay his role in the early Jerusalem

Jesus community. Lukan-Acts editorial interests made their intentions patently clear.

Be that as it may, following is a citation from the mid-first-century (possibly a decade earlier) *Epistle of James*. Particularly, we cannot fail to detect the heated exclamation of this Nazareth son at the perceived comportment of the well to do:

> Come now, you rich, weep and howl for the miseries that are coming upon you. Your riches have rotted and your garments are moth-eaten. Your gold and silver have rusted, and their rust will be evidence against you and will eat your flesh like fire. You have laid up treasure for the last days. Behold, the wages of the laborers who mowed your fields, which you kept back by fraud, cry out; and the cries of the harvesters have reached the ears of the Lord of hosts. You have lived on the earth in luxury and in pleasure; you have fattened your hearts in a day of slaughter. You have condemned, you have killed the righteous man; he does not resist you (Ja 5.1-6, RSV).

Some of us will observe that James did not mince words. This ardent, intense testimony contrasted directly with details preserved from Paul's hellenized ministry. From the Pauline perspective, the focus was the world to come. Not remediation in the present environment. Even for those who suffered.[109]

Such an attitude seemed to lean alarmingly on the edge of *existential nihilism*. This philosophy probably began during the time of Aristippus of Cyrene (4th century BCE) who migrated to Athens from Cyrene, Libya to become a pupil of Socrates. In a nutshell, the philosophy of "existential nihilism" taught that "life has no intrinsic meaning or value."[110]

There really are arguments from Paul's own correspondence that support this position. Two brief examples follow.

The first citation, from the second letter to the Corinthian church, Paul claimed: "For we know that if the earthly tent we live in is destroyed, we have a building from God, a house not made with hands, eternal in the heavens" (2 Cor 5.1, RSV).

Hmm. From an outsider's point of view it is remarkable that this ideology caught on. One really must consider the audience. How many, demographically, were successful enough among Paul's congregations not to have to worry about hunger and a roof over their heads?

Who in their right minds, left homeless and alone, would cry out, hysterically, that while their "earthly tent" had been destroyed, everything was still running smoothly ... right on course? Paul had promised "a building from God." Not only that, but "a house not made with hands." In fact, this house was "eternal in the heavens." Wow! Would that really make sense to the homeless poor? The abandoned? The indigent wanderer?

The Pauline *Letter to the Romans* follow up started with, "I consider that the sufferings of this present time are not worth comparing with the glory that is to be revealed to us" (Rom 8.18, RSV). Really? That is, if one were not in chains or starving to death. Under those circumstances future "glory" was a bit problematic. At least in the moment. At least to everyday human beings.

In defiant contrast to Paul's largely listless here-and-now worldview harkening to future glory (in the beyond), Palestinian faithful with James at their head cried out against the appalling, oppressive policies of the elite Jewish ruling class.[111]

This strident, conscious effort was symbolized in the wake of a systematic, temple-for-profit, economic apparatus controlled by Judaic elites. As well as direct cooperation and financial participation from outside Roman entrepreneurial interests deeply engaged in the Jerusalem establishment's power scheme.[112]

Again, from the unambiguous, declarative language of his epistle, we cannot avoid speculating that James was energetically involved (at some meaningful level) in disrupting the political-economic machinations of Palestinian elites.

Further, in a broad textual comparison of James and Paul, it would have been impossible to ignore the unambiguous and vigorous active-tense descriptors behind the *James Epistle* dead-set against Paul's extensive Christological thesis. It would have been impossible eluding the fiery prov-ocation of James's righteous call for action, demanding and challenging his flock to faithfully observe Mosaic principles: "For whoever keeps the whole law but fails in one point has become guilty of all of it" (Ja 2.10, RSV).

This simple, concrete logic informed believers that true observance involved active participation as "doers of the law" (Ja 1.22, RSV). For this true Jesus disciple late second-temple Judaism in its purest form announced to the world that "faith apart from works is dead" (Ja 2.26, RSV).

Paul, on the other hand, advised *in direct contradiction* that his former pagan flock was *free from the law*: "But now we are discharged from the law, dead to that which held us captive, so that we serve not under the old writ-ten code but in the new life of the Spirit" (Rom 7.6, RSV).

As a practical matter, Paul counseled widows that they were free of the law upon the decease of their husbands (Rom 7.2). Scholarship argues that thru this verse the Apostle Paul clearly preached that Mosaic law had been discarded for a higher revelation centered in Paul's divine, supernat-ural Christos.[113]

Whatever scholars want to say about Paul from Tarsus, unmistak-ably, a massive theological gulf divided his religious views from James and other Palestinian faithful. Depending on how we wish to interpret, this gulf may have been textually evidenced in Paul's letter to followers in Galatia.

But because of false brethren secretly brought in, who slipped in to spy out our freedom which we have in Christ Jesus, that they might bring us into bondage—to them we did not yield submission even for a moment, that the truth of the gospel might be preserved for you. And from those who were reputed to be something (what they were makes no difference to me; God shows no partiality)—those, I say, who were of repute added nothing to me; but on the contrary, when they saw that I had been entrusted with the gospel to the uncircumcised, just as Peter had been entrusted with the gospel to the circumcised (for he who worked through Peter for the mission to the circumcised worked through me also for the Gentiles), and when they perceived the grace that was given to me, James and Cephas and John, who were reputed to be pillars, gave to me and Barnabas the right hand of fellowship, that we should go to the Gentiles and they to the circumcised; only they would have us remember the poor, which very thing I was eager to do. But when Cephas came to Antioch I opposed him to his face, because he stood condemned. For before certain men came from James, he ate with the Gentiles; but when they came he drew back and separated himself, fearing the circumcision party. And with him the rest of the Jews acted insincerely, so that even Barnabas was carried away by their insincerity. But when I saw that they were not straightforward about the truth of the gospel, I said to Cephas before them all, "If you, though a Jew, live like a Gentile and not like a Jew, how can you compel the Gentiles to live like Jews?" (Gal 2.4-14, RSV).

As leader of the Jerusalem Jesus movement, James was stridently opposed to the elite political-economic status quo. From the use of ruthlessly violent descriptors in his apostolic verse, James evidently firsthand witnessed this economic and social class effectively enslaving their own people. "Come now, you rich, weep and howl for the miseries that are coming upon you!" (Ja 5.1, RSV). There is just nothing like this violently explicit phrasing in all of gospel literature. A truly fearless leader of his tiny Judaic offshoot, devotional flock was James the Just.

The vitriolic speech condemning Judaic elites was so transparent that its sense of urgency was unparalleled in early Christian literature. The differences in tone and tenor on these very issues contrasted vividly against Paul's doctrinal program. To say the least.

There is evidence to suggest that James was identified as "The Just" probably even within the Judaic temple establishment.[114] We are on firmer ground declaring that he was looked up to by fellow Jerusalem peasant Jews, followers of Jesus or otherwise. That his outspoken views in defense of his people reached the highest layer of the Jerusalem ruling hierarchy is a matter of record.

The early church father Eusebius narrated an alternative account of the assassination of James learned from Hegesippus, an early church father. The significance in the Hegesippus account was that the people "gloried in the testimony of James, and said, 'Hosanna to the Son of David'" (Eusebius, *Church History* 2.23.14).

Presumably, they were referring to James. As the brother of Jesus, James was said to have been a descendant of David (i.e. "the Son of David") like his older sibling. As such, there was no doubt that late second-temple officials would have been resentful of James and his reputation among the common people.

Surely, there is little doubt that the honorific proclaimed by his countrymen was indeed intended for James. In the Hegesippus account, after the proclamation, James was first thrown from the steps of the Temple by scribal priests. Then stoned and clubbed to death.[115]

What makes this version believable is that, at the time, the ruling priestly family of Ananus was indeed from the house of Seth. Jesus and James were said to be from the house of David. In the Hebrew Bible, *Numbers* 24.17 (RSV) reads:

> I see him, but not now;
>
> I behold him, but not nigh:
>
> a star shall come forth out of Jacob,
>
> and a scepter shall rise out of Israel;
>
> it shall crush the forehead of Moab,
>
> and break down all the sons of Sheth [Seth].

In first-century Palestine, it was commonly held that such utterances were reflective of David and his rule: "A star shall come forth out of Jacob, and a scepter shall rise out of Israel ... ."[116] This whole scenario is enormously significant for gaining a deeper awareness of the more credible aspects of originating Jesus tradition. Not only that but recognizing the accompanying historical factors looming just in the background.

Annas (more properly "Ananus") had been high priest in Israel from 6-15 CE. His son-in-law Ca'iaphas reigned from 18-36 CE and presided over the crucifixion of Jesus. His blood son, Ananus the Younger, presided during the time while James shepherded early Judaic believers in Jerusalem.

Focusing the lens more closely on the first-century historical drama, Ananus the Younger and previous high priests of his blood would have had a particular sensitivity to Messianic claimants from the house of David. Why? According to sacred tradition, the "scepter" out of Israel would rise and destroy the sons of Seth.

In reflection, we would be remiss by ignoring that the high priest presiding over the deaths of both Jesus and James was none other *than a son of Seth*.[117]

INTRODUCTION
References

Adams, Samuel L. *Social and Economic Life in Second Temple* (Louisville, KY: Westminster John Knox Press, 2014). (Abbr. "Social-Economic Life")

Arrian, *The Landmark Arrian: The Campaigns of Alexander*, Romm, James, ed., Mensch, Pamela, trans. (New York, NY: Anchor Books, 2010). (Abbr. "The Landmark Arrian")

Beard, Mary. *SPQR: A History of Ancient Rome* (New York: NY: Liveright Publishing Corporation, 2015). (Abbr. "SPQR")

Becker, Eve-Marie, et al., eds. *Mark and Paul: Comparative Essays Part II. For and Against Pauline Influence on Mark* (Berlin, Germany: Walter de Gruyter, 2014). (Abbr. "Mark and Paul")

Bilby, Mark G. "The First Dionysian Gospel: Imitational and Redactional Layers in Luke and John," in *Classical Greek Models of the Gospels and Acts: Studies in Mimesis Criticism*, Bilby, Mark G., et al., eds. (Claremont, CA: Claremont Press, 2018), pp. 49-68. (Abbr. "The First Dionysian Gospel")

Bird, Michael F. and Willitts, Joel, eds. *Paul and the Gospels: Christologies, Conflicts and Convergences* (New York, NY: T&T Clark International, 2011). (Abbr. "Paul and the Gospels")

Bond, Helen K. *The Historical Jesus: A Guide for the Perplexed* (New York, NY: T&T Clark International, 2012). (Abbr. "Guide for the Perplexed")

Boucher, Esther Diane. *Yeshua, The Jewish Messiah* (Bloomington, IN: AuthorHouse, 2008). (Abbr. "Yeshua")

Bowden, Hugh. *Alexander the Great: A Very Short Introduction* (Oxford, UK: Oxford University Press, 2014). (Abbr. "Alexander the Great")

Bradley, Pamela. *The Ancient World Transformed: Societies, Personalities, and Historical Periods From Egypt, Greece, and Rome* (Cambridge, Great Britain: Cambridge University Press, 2014). (Abbr. "The Ancient World Transformed")

Bruce, F. F. *Paul: Apostle of the Heart Set Free* (Grand Rapids, MI: William B. Eerdmans Publishing Company, 1977). (Abbr. "Apostle Heart Set Free")

Bryant, Clifton D. and Peck, Dennis L., eds. *Encyclopedia of Death and the Human Experience* (Thousand Oaks, CA: Sage Publications, Inc., 2009). (Abbr. "Death and Human Experience")

Caldwell, John C. Demographic Transition Theory (Dordrecht, The Netherlands: Springer, 2006). (Abbr. "Demographic Transition Theory")

Camp, John M. *The Archaeology of Athens* (New Haven, CT: Yale University Press, 2001). (Abbr. "The Archaeology of Athens")

Camp II, John McK. *The Athenian Agora: A Short Guide to the Excavations* (Athens, Greece: The American School of Classical Studies at Athens, 2003). (Abbr. "The Athenian Agora")

Casey, Maurice. *Jesus of Nazareth: An Independent Historian's Account of his Life and Teaching* (New York, NY: T&T Clark International, 2010). (Abbr. "Independent Historian Account")

Chancey, Mark A. *The Myth of a Gentile Galilee* (New York, NY: Cambridge University Press, 2002). (Abbr. "Myth of Gentile Galilee")

Charles, J. Daryl. *Retrieving the Natural Law: A Return to Moral First Things* (Grand Rapids, MI: William B. Eerdmans Publishing Company, 2008). (Abbr. "Retrieving the Natural Law")

Charlesworth, James H. *The Historical Jesus: An Essential Guide* (Nashville, TN: Abingdon Press, 2008). (Abbr. "Historical Jesus Essential Guide")

Charlesworth, James H. "The Temple and Jesus' Followers," in *Jesus and Temple: Textual and Archaeological Explorations*, Charlesworth, James H., ed. (Minneapolis, MN: Fortress Press, 2014), pp. 183-212. (Abbr. "Temple and Jesus' Followers")

Chilton, Bruce. "Getting It Right: Jesus, James, and Questions of Sanctity" in *The Missing Jesus: Rabbinic Judaism and the New Testament*, Chilton, Bruce, et al., eds. (Boston, MA: Brill Academic Publishers, 2002), pp. 107-124. (Abbr. "Getting It Right")

Chilton, Bruce. "Jesus and James: Martyrs of the Temple," in *James The Just and Christian Origins*, Chilton, Bruce and Evans, Craig A., eds. (Leiden, The Netherlands: Brill, 1999). (Abbr. "Martyrs of the Temple")

Chilton, Bruce. *Rabbi Jesus: An Intimate Biography* (New York, NY: Doubleday, 2000). (Abbr. "Rabbi Jesus")

Clackson, James. *Language and Society in the Greek and Roman Worlds* (Cambridge, UK: Cambridge University Press, 2015). (Abbr. "Language and Society")

Clark, Gillian, trans. *On the Pythagorean Life* (Liverpool, Great Britain: Liverpool University Press, 1989). (Abbr. "On the Pythagorean Life")

Connelly, Joan Breton. The Parthenon Enigma: A New Understanding of the West's Most Iconic Building and the People Who Made It (New York, NY: Vintage Books, 2014). (Abbr. "The Parthenon Enigma")

Conwell, David H. *Connecting a City to the Sea: The History of the Athenian Long Walls* (Leiden, The Netherlands: Brill, 2008). (Abbr. "Connecting City to Sea")

Coulter, Charles Russell and Turner, Patricia, eds. *Encyclopedia of Ancient Deities* (New York, NY: Routledge, Taylor and Francis Group, 2012). (Abbr. "Encyclopedia of Ancient Deities")

Croy, N. Clayton. "Disrespecting Dionysus: 3 Maccabees as Narrative Satire of the God of Wine," in *Scripture and Traditions: Essays on Early*

Judaism and Christianity in Honor of Carl R. Holladay, Gray, Patrick and O'Day, Gail R., eds. (Leiden, The Netherlands: Brill, 2008). (Abbr. "Disrespecting Dionysus")

Dahmen, Karsten. *The Legend of Alexander the Great on Greek and Roman Coins* (New York, NY: Routledge, 2007). (Abbr. "Legend of Alexander")

Davies, Paul E. "Jesus and the Role of the Prophet," *Journal of Biblical Literature*, Vol. 64, No. 2 (Jun., 1945), pp. 241-254. (Abbr. "Role Prophet")

Deines, Roland. "Galilee and the Historical Jesus in Recent Research," in *Galilee in Late Second Temple and Mishnaic Periods: Volume 1, Life, Culture, and Society*, Fiensy, David A. and Strange, James Riley, eds. (Minneapolis, MN: Fortress Press, 2014), pp. 11-50. (Abbr. "Jesus Recent Research")

Donnelly, Ignatius. *Atlantis: The Antediluvian World*, Sykes, Egerton, ed. (San Diego, CA: The Book Tree, 2006). (Abbr. "Atlantis: The Antediluvian World")

Eck, Ernest van. *The Parables of Jesus the Galilean: Stories of a Social Prophet* (Eugene, OR: Cascade Books, 2016). (Abbr. "Parables of Jesus")

Endsjø, Dag Øistein. *Greek Resurrection Beliefs and the Success of Christianity* (New York, NY: Palgrave MacMillan, 2009). (Abbr. "Greek Resurrection Beliefs")

Fairbairn, Donald. *Grace and Christology in the Early Church* (Oxford, Great Britain: Oxford University Press, 2003). (Abbr. "Grace and Christology")

Falk, Harvey. *Jesus the Pharisee: A New Look at the Jewishness of Jesus* (Mahwah, NJ: Paulist Press, 1985). (Abbr. "Jewishness Jesus")

Fant, Clyde E. and Reddish, Mitchell G. *A Guide to Biblical Sites in Greece and Turkey* (New York, NY: Oxford University Press, 2003). (Abbr. "Guide to Biblical Sites")

Feldman, Louis H. "How Much Hellenism in Jewish Palestine?", *Hebrew Union College Annual*, Vol. 57 (1986), pp. 83-111. (Abbr. "Hellenism in Jewish Palestine")

Feldman, Louis H. *Jew and Gentile in the Ancient World: Attitudes and Interactions from Alexander to Justinian* (Princeton, NJ: Princeton University Press, 1993). (Abbr. "Jew and Gentile")

Ferguson, Everett, ed. *Encyclopedia of Early Christianity*, Second Edition (New York, NY: Routledge, 1999). (Abbr. "Encyclopedia of Early Christianity")

Finney, Mark T. Resurrection, Hell and the Afterlife: Body and Soul in Antiquity, Judaism and Early Christianity (New York, NY: Routledge, 2016). (Abbr. "Resurrection, Hell, and Afterlife")

Francis, Arthur Morius. *Nihilism: Philosophy of Nothingness* (lulu.com, 2015). (Abbr. "Nihilism Philosophy of Nothingness")

Frankel, Ellen and Teutsch, Betsy Platkin. *The Encyclopedia of Jewish Symbols* (New York, NY: Rowman & Littlefield Publishers, Inc., 1992). (Abbr. "Encyclopedia of Jewish Symbols")

Friesen, Courtney J. P. "Dionysus as Jesus: The Incongruity of a Love Feast in Achilles Tatius's 'Leucippe and Clitophon 2.2'," *The Harvard Theological Review*, Vol. 107, No. 2 (APRIL 2014), pp. 222-240. (Abbr. "Dionysus as Jesus")

Gadbery, Laura M. "The Sanctuary of the Twelve Gods in the Athenian Agora: A Revised View," *Hesperia: The Journal of the American School of Classical Studies at Athens* (Oct 1, 1992), Vol 61, Issue 4, pp. 447-489. (Abbr. "Sanctuary of Twelve Gods")

Gagarin, Michael, ed., *The Oxford Encyclopedia of Ancient Greece and Rome*, Volume 1 (New York, NY: University Press, 2010). (Abbr. "Ancient Greece and Rome")

Gardner, Percy. *The Types of Greek Coins: An Archaeological Essay* (Cambridge, England: University of Cambridge Press, 1883). (Abbr. "Types of Greek Coins")

Garland, Robert. Introducing New Gods: The Politics of Athenian Religion (Cornell University Press, 1992). (Abbr. "Introducing New Gods")

Goodman, Martin. "Galilean Judaism and Judaean Judaism," in *The Cambridge History of Judaism*, vol. III, Horbury, William, et al., eds. (Cambridge: Cambridge University Press, 1999), 596-617. (Abbr. "Galilean Judaism, Judean Judaism")

Green, Joel B., gen. ed. *Dictionary of Jesus and the Gospels*, Second Edition (Downers Grove, IL: InterVarsity Press, 2013). (Abbr. "Dictionary of Jesus")

Green, Peter. *The Shadow of the Parthenon: Studies in Ancient History and Literature* (Berkeley, CA: University of California Press, 1972). (Abbr. "Shadow of the Parthenon")

Grossman, Janet Burnett. *Greek Funerary Sculpture: Catalogue of the Collections at the Getty Villa* (Los Angeles, CA: The J. Paul Getty Trust, 2002). (Abbr. "Greek Funerary Sculpture")

Gruen, Erich S. *The Hellenistic World and the Coming of Rome*, Volume 1 (Berkeley, CA: University of California Press, 1984). (Abbr. "Hellenistic World and Rome")

Hammond, N. G. L. *Three Historians of Alexander the Great* (New York, NY: Cambridge University Press, 1983). (Abbr. "Three Historians of Alexander")

Harrill, J. Albert. *Paul the Apostle: His Life and Legacy in their Roman Context* (New York, NY: Cambridge University Press, 2012). (Abbr. "Paul the Apostle")

Harrison, Jane Ellen. *Mythology and Monuments of Ancient Athens: Being a Translation of a Portion of the 'Attica' of Pausanias* (London, England: Macmillan and Company, 1890). (Abbr. "Mythology, Monuments Ancient Athens")

Hengel, Martin. *Between Jesus and Paul: Studies in the Earliest History of Christianity* (Eugene, OR: Wipf & Stock Publishers, 2003). (Abbr. "Between Jesus and Paul")

Hoff, Michael C. "Augustus, Apollo, and Athens," *Museum Helveticum*, Vol. 49, No. 4 (1992), pp. 223-232. (Abbr. "Augustus, Apollo, Athens")

Homolka, Walter. *Jewish Jesus Research and its Challenge to Christology Today* (Leiden, The Netherlands: Brill, 2017). (Abbr. "Jewish Research")

Horn, Cornelia B. and Martens, John W. *"Let the Little Children Come to Me": Childhood and Children in Early Christianity* (Washington, D.C: The Catholic University of America Press, 2009). (Abbr. "Let the Children Come")

Instone-Brewer, David. "Jesus of Nazareth's Trial in the Uncensored Talmud," *Tyndale Bulletin* 62.2 (2011), pp. 269-294. (Abbr. "Uncensored Talmud")

Jeffrey, David Lyle. "The Legacy of Paul: Literature," in *The Blackwell Campanion to Paul*, Westerholdm, Stephen, ed. (Malden, MA: Wiley-Blackwell, 2014), pp. 531-545. (Abbr. "Legacy of Paul: Literature")

Kauppi, Lynn Allan. *Foreign But Familiar Gods: Greco-Romans Read Religion in Acts* (New York, NY: T&T Clark, 2006). (Abbr. "Foreign But Familiar Gods")

Klausner, Joseph. *From Jesus to Paul*, Stinespring, William F., trans. (New York, NY: The Macmillan Co., 1943). (Abbr. "From Jesus to Paul")

Korab-Karpowicz, W. Julian. *On the History of Political Philosophy: Great Political Thinkers from Thucydides to Locke* (New York, NY: Routledge, 2016). (Abbr. "History of Political Philosophy")

Köstenberger, Andreas J. "Jesus as Rabbi in the Fourth Gospel," *Bulletin for Biblical Research* 8 (1998): 97-128. (Abbr. "Jesus as Rabbi")

Lawson, Russell M. *Science in the Ancient World: An Encyclopedia* (Santa Barbara, CA: ABC-CLIO, Inc., 2004). (Abbr. "Science in Ancient World")

Lee, Bernard J. *The Galilean Jewishness of Jesus: Retrieving the Jewish Origins of Christianity* (Mahwah, NJ: Paulist Press, 1988). (Abbr. "Galilean Jewishness")

Lemos, Irene S. *The Protogeometric Aegean: The Archaeology of the Late Eleventh and Tenth Centuries BC.*, Bennet, John, et al., eds. (New York, NY: Oxford University Press, 2002). (Abbr. "The Protogeometric Aegean")

Levine, Lee I. *The Ancient Synagogue: The First Thousand Years* (New Haven, CT: Yale University Press, 2000). (Abbr. "The Ancient Synagogue")

Levine, Amy-Jill. *The Misunderstood Jew: The Church and the Scandal of the Jewish Jesus* (New York, NY: HarperCollins Publishers, 2006). (Abbr. "Misunderstood Jew").

Litwa, M. David. *How the Gospels Became History: Jesus and Mediterranean Myths* (New Haven, CT: Yale University Press, 2019). (Abbr. "Jesus and Mediterranean Myths")

Lizorkin-Eyzenberg, Eli. *The Jewish Gospel of John: Discovering Jesus, King of All Israel* (Tel Aviv, Israel: Jewish Studies for Christians, 2015). (Abbr. "Jewish Gospel")

Loader, William. "What Happened to "Good News for the Poor" in the Johannine Tradition?" in *John, Jesus, and History, Volume 3: Glimpses of Jesus Through the Johannine Lens*, Anderson, Paul N., et al., eds. (Atlanta, GA: SBL Press, 2016), pp. 469-480. (Abbr. "What Happened Good News")

Long, Charlotte R. *The Twelve Gods of Greece and Rome* (Leiden, The Netherlands: Brill, 1987). (Abbr. "Twelve Gods, Greece, Rome")

Loewe, Michael. *Divination, Mythology and Monarchy in Han China* (Cambridge, UK: Cambridge University Press, 1994). (Abbr. "Divination, Mythology, Han China")

Lüdemann, Gerd. *Paul: The Founder of Christianity* (Amherst, NY: Prometheus Books, 2002). (Abbr. "Founder of Christianity")

Maccoby, Hyam. "The Jewishness of Jesus," *European Judaism: A Journal for the New Europe*, Vol. 28, No. 1 (Spring '95), pp. 52-62. (Abbr. "Jewishness of Jesus")

Maccoby, Hyam. *The Mythmaker: Paul and the Invention of Christianity* (New York, NY: Barnes and Noble, Inc., 1986). (Abbr. "The Mythmaker Paul")

Malamed, Stanley F. *Medical Emergencies in the Dental Office* (St. Louis, MO: Elsevier Mosby, 2015). (Abbr. "Medical Emergencies Dental Office")

Malina, Bruce J. and Rohrbaugh, Richard L. *Social-Science Commentary on the Synoptic Gospels* (Minneapolis, MN: Fortress Press, 2003). (Abbr. "Social-Science Commentary Synoptics")

Malinowski, Francis Xavier. *Galilean Judaism in the Writings of Flavius Josephus* (Ph.D. Diss., Duke University, 1973). (Abbr. "Galilean Judaism")

Mauzy, Craig A. and Camp, John McK. *Agora Excavations, 1931-2006: A Pictorial History* (Athens, Greece: The American School of Classical Studies at Athens, 2006). (Abbr. "Agora Excavations, 1931-2006")

Maynard-Reed, Pedrito U. *Poverty and Wealth in James* (Eugene, OR: Wipf and Stock Publishers, 2004). (Abbr. "Poverty and Wealth")

Mikalson, Jon D. *Religion in Hellenistic Athens* (Berkeley, CA: University of California Press, 1998). (Abbr. "Religion in Hellenistic Athens")

Millar, Fergus. *The Roman Near East: 31 B.C.-A.D. 337* (Cambridge, MA: Harvard University Press, 1993). (Abbr. "Roman Near East")

Minderhout, David J. *Native Americans in the Susquehanna River Valley Past and Present* (Lewisburg, PA: Bucknell University Press, 2013). (Abbr. "Native Americans in Susquehanna")

Mishkin, David. *Jewish Scholarship on the Resurrection of Jesus* (Eugene, OR: Pickwick Publications, 2017). (Abbr. "Jewish Scholarship")

Moles, John. "Jesus and Dionysus in 'The Acts of the Apostles' and Early Christianity," *Hermathena*, No. 180 (Summer 2006), pp. 65-104. (Abbr. "Jesus and Dionysus")

Moore, Daniel F. "Jesus, An Emerging Jewish Mosaic," in *Jesus Research – New Methodologies and Perceptions: The Second Princeton-Prague Symposium on Jesus Research*, Charlesworth, James H., ed. With Rhea, Brian and Pokorny, Petr (Grand Rapids, MI: William B. Erdmans Publishing Company, 2014), pp. 58-81. (Abbr. "Jewish Mosaic")

Nicholls, Matthew. "Roman Libraries as Public Buildings in the Cities of the Empire," in Ancient Libraries (Cambridge, UK: Cambridge University Press, 2013), pp. 261-276. (Abbr. "Roman Libraries Public Buildings")

Ogden, Daniel, ed.. *A Companion to Greek Religion* (Malden, MA: Wiley-Blackwell, 2010). (Abbr. "Companion to Greek Religion")

Otto, Walter Fredrich. *Dionysus: Myth and Cult*, Palmer, Robert B., trans. (Bloomington, IN: Indiana University Press, 1965). (Abbr. "Dionysus: Myth and Cult")

Paga, Jessica. *Building Democracy in Late Archaic Athens* (New York, NY: Oxford University Press, 2021). (Abbr. "Building Democracy Late Athens")

Palagia, Olga and Spetsieri-Choremi, Alkestis, eds. *The Panathenaic Games: Proceedings of an International Conference held at the University of Athens, May 11-12, 2004* (Oxford, UK: Oxbow Books, 2007). (Abbr. "The Panathenaic Games")

Papadopoulos, John K. Ceramicus *Redivivus: The Early Iron Age Potters' Field in the Area of the Classical Athenian Agora* (Athens, Greece: American School of Classical Studies, 2003). (Abbr. "Iron Age Potters' Field")

Phillips, Christopher. *Socrates Café: A Fresh Taste of Philosophy* (New York, NY: W. W. Norton and Company, Inc., 2000). (Abbr. "Socrates Café")

Plutarch, *The Life of Alexander the Great*, Clough, Hugh, Arthur, ed., Dryden, John, trans. (New York, NY: The Modern Library, 2004). (Abbr. "The Life of Alexander")

Reyes, E. Christopher. *In His Name* (Bloomington, IN: AuthorHouse, 2010). (Abbr. "In His Name")

Reynolds, John Mark. *When Athens Met Jerusalem: An Introduction to Classical and Christian Thought* (Downers Grove, IL: InterVarsity Press, 2009). (Abbr. "When Athens Met Jerusalem")

Richard, Carl J. *Greeks and Romans Bearing Gifts: How the Ancients Inspired the Founding Fathers* (Lanham, MD: Rowman and Littlefield Publishers, Inc., 2008). (Abbr. "Greeks and Romans Gifts")

Rigoglioso, Marguerite. *The Cult of Divine Birth in Ancient Greece* (New York, NY: Palgrave MacMillan, 2009). (Abbr. "Cult of Divine Birth")

Roberts, J.W. *City of Sokrates: An Introduction to Classical Athens*, Second Edition (New York, NY: Routledge & Kegan Paul plc, 1984). (Abbr. "City of Sokrates")

Robinson, James M. *The Gospel of Jesus: A Historical Search for the Good News* (San Francisco, CA: HarperSanFrancisco, 2006). (Abbr. "Historical Search")

Rock, Ian E. Paul's Letter to the Romans and Roman Imperialism: An Ideological Analysis of the Exordium (Romans 1:1-17) (Eugene, OR: Pickwick Publications, 2012). (Abbr. "Paul's Letter")

Rothschild, Clare K. *Paul in Athens: The Popular Religious Context of Acts 17* (Tübingen, Germany: Mohr Siebeck, 2014). (Abbr. "Paul in Athens")

Rutherford, Ian. "Canonizing the Pantheon: the Dodekatheon in Greek Religion and its Origins," in *The Gods of Ancient Greece: Identities and Transformations*. Bremmer, Jan N. and Erskine, Andrew, eds. (Edinburgh: Scotland: Edinburgh University, 2010), pp. 43-54. (Abbr. "Canonizing the Pantheon")

Saldarini, Anthony J. *Matthew's Christian-Jewish Community* (Chicago, IL: The University of Chicago Press, 1994). (Abbr. "Matthew's Christian-Jewish Community")

Salier, Willis Hedley. *The Rhetorical Impact of the Sēmeia in the Gospel of John* (Tübingen, Germany: Mohr Siebeck, 2004). (Abbr. "Rhetorical Impact Sēmeia")

Sanders, E. P. *Jesus and Judaism* (Philadelphia, PA: Fortress Press, 1985). (Abbr. "Jesus and Judaism")

Scodel, Ruth. "Euripides, The Derveni Papyrus, and the Smoke of Many Writings," in *Sacred Words: Orality, Literacy and Religion: Orality and Literacy in the Ancient World*, Vol. 8, Lardinois, André, et al., eds. (Leiden, The Netherlands: Brill, 2011), pp. 79-100. (Abbr. "Euripides, Derveni Papyrus")

Shoemaker, Karl. *Sanctuary and Crime in the Middle Ages, 400-1500* (Bronx, NY: Fordham University Press, 2011). (Abbr. "Sanctuary and Crime")

Sivertsen, Barbara J. *The Three Pillars: How Family Politics Shaped the Earliest Church and the Gospel of Mark* (Eugene, OR: Wipf and Stock Publishers, 2010). (Abbr. "The Three Pillars")

Skelton, Debra and Dell, Pamela. *Empire of Alexander the Great*, Lee, John W. I., Historical Consultant (New York, NY: Chelsea House Publishers, 2009). (Abbr. "Empire Alexander the Great")

Smith, David Oliver. *Matthew, Mark, Luke, and Paul: The Influence of the Epistles on the Synoptic Gospels* (Eugene, OR: Resource Publications, 2011). (Abbr. "Matthew, Mark, Luke, Paul")

Smith, Mark D. The Final Days of Jesus: The Thrill of Defeat, The Agony of Victory – A Classical Historian Explores Jesus's Arrest, Trial and Execution (Cambridge, UK: The Lutterworth Press, 2018). (Abbr. "Final Days of Jesus")

Spielvogel, Jackson. *Western Civilization: A Brief History – Volume I: To 1715*, Fourth Edition (Belmont, CA: Thomson Wadsworth, 2008). (Abbr. "Western Civilization – Brief History")

Stearns, Wallace N. "The Apostle Paul in Athens," *The Biblical World*, Jun., 1911, Vol. 37, No. 6 (Jun., 1911), pp. 411-419. (Abbr. "Apostle Paul in Athens")

Steinbock, Bernd. *Social Memory in Athenian Public Discourse: Uses and Meanings of the Past* (Ann Arbor, MI: The University of Michigan Press, 2013). (Abbr. "Social Memory Athenian Discourse")

Stibbe, Mark W. G. *John As Storyteller: Narrative Criticism and the Fourth Gospel* (New York, NY: Cambridge University Press, 1992). (Abbr. "John as Storyteller")

Stock, Augustine. *The Method and Message of Matthew* (Collegeville, MN: The Liturgical Press, 1989). (Abbr. "Method and Message Matthew")

Stocks, Claire. *The Roman Hannibal: Remembering the Enemy in Silius Italicus' Punica* (Liverpool, UK: Liverpool University Press, 2014). (Abbr. "The Roman Hannibal")

Tabor, James D. *Paul and Jesus: How the Apostle Transformed Christianity* (New York, NY: Simon & Schuster Paperbacks, 2012). (Abbr. "Paul and Jesus")

Tondo, Douglas J. Del. *Jesus' Words Only Or Was Paul the Apostle Jesus Condemns in Revelation 2:2?* (W. Conshohocken, PA: Infinity Publishing, 2006). (Abbr. "Jesus' Words Only")

Timayenis, Telemachus Thomas. *A History of Greece from the Earliest Times to the Present*, Volume 1 (New York, NY: D. Appleton and Company, 1881). (Abbr. "A History of Greece")

Tung, Anthony. *Preserving the World's Great Cities: The Destruction and Renewal of the Historic Metropolis* (New York: Three Rivers Press, 2002). (Abbr. "Preserving World's Great Cities")

Valavanēs, Panos. *Great Moments in Greek Archaeology* (Los Angeles, CA: J. Paul Getty Museum, 2007). (Abbr. "Great Moments Greek Archaeology")

Vermès, Géza. *Christian Beginnings: From Nazareth to Nicaea* (New Haven, CT: Yale University Press, 2013). (Abbr. "Christian Beginnings")

Vermès, Géza. *Jesus in His Jewish Context* (Minneapolis, MN: Fortress Press, 2003). (Abbr. "Jewish Context")

Vermès, Géza. *Jesus the Jew: A Historian's Reading of the Gospels* (Philadelphia, PA: Fortress Press, 1981). (Abbr. "Historian's Reading")

Vermès, Géza, *The Religion of Jesus the Jew* (Minneapolis, MN: Fortress Press, 1993). (Abbr. "Jesus the Jew")

Wassen, Cecilia. "The Jewishness of Jesus and Ritual Purity," *Jewish Studies in the Nordic Countries Today*, Vol 27 (2016), pp. 11-36. (Abbr. "Jewishness of Jesus")

Westermann, William Linn. *The Slave Systems of Greek and Roman Antiquity* (Philadelphia, PA: The American Philosophical Society, 1955). (Abbr. "Slave System of Greeks")

Wilkins, W. J. *Hindu Mythology, Vedic and Purānic* (London, England: W. Thacker and Company, Ltd., 1882). (Abbr. "Hindu Mythology")

Winter, Bruce W. "Introducing the Athenians to God: Paul's failed apologetic in Acts 17," *Themelios: An International Journal for Pastors and Students of Theological and Religious Studies*, Volume 31, Issue 1, October 2005, pp. 40-41. (Abbr. "Introducing Athenians to God")

Witherington, III, Ben. *The Jesus Quest: The Third Search for the Jew of Nazareth*, Second Edition (Downers Grove, IL: InterVarsity Press, 1997). (Abbr. "Jesus Quest")

Woodruff, Paul (Thucydides). *On Justice, Power, and Human Nature: Selections from The History of the Peloponnesian War*, trans with intro and notes, Woodruff, Paul (Indianapolis, IN: Hackett Publishing Company, 1993). (Abbr. "Justice, Power, Human Nature")

Wycherley, R. E. *Literary and Epigraphical Testimonia: The Athenian Agora*, Volume 3 (Princeton, NJ: The Princeton School of Classical Studies at Athens, 1957). (Abbr. "The Athenian Agora")

Yenne, Bill. *Alexander the Great: Lessons from History's Undefeated General* (New York, NY: St. Martin's Press, 2010). (Abbr. "Alexander the Great")

Young, Brad H. *Jesus the Jewish Theologian* (Grand Rapids, MI: Baker Academic, 1995). (Abbr. "Jewish Theologian")

Zaslow, David. *Jesus: First-Century Rabbi* (Brewster, MA: Paraclete Press, 2014). (Abbr. "First-Century Rabbi")

Zetterholm, Magnus. The Formation of Christianity in Antioch: A Sociological Approach to the Separation Between Judaism and Christianity (New York, NY: Routledge, 2003). (Abbr. "Formation of Early Christianity")

Zilioli, Ugo. *The Cyrenaics* (New York, NY: Routledge, 2014). (Abbr. "The Cyrenaics")

Chapter Endnotes

1 See Tung 2002, Preserving World's Great Cities, 266.

2 See Garland 1992, Introducing New Gods, 80.

3 See Green 1972, Shadow of the Parthenon, 43.

4 For a superbly informative study, see Joan Breton Connelly, The Parthenon Enigma: A New Understanding of the West's Most Iconic Building and the People Who Made It (New York, NY: Vintage Books, 2014).

5 Korab-Karpowicz, History of Political Philosophy, 4.

6 See Spielvogel 2008, Western Civilization – Brief History, 91.

7 See Reynolds 2009, When Athens Met Jerusalem, 185-186.

8 See Phillips 2000, Socrates Café, 18-19.

9 Paga 2021, Building Democracy Late Athens, 83, note 12.

10 Long 1987, Twelve Gods, Greece, Rome, 160.

11 Camp 2001, The Archaeology of Athens, 32.

12 Minderhout 2013, Native Americans in Susquehanna, 97.

13 Wilkins 1882, Hindu Mythology, 307.

14 Donnelly 2006, Atlantis: The Antediluvian World, 154.

15 Coulter and Turner, eds. 2012, Encyclopedia of Ancient Deities, 233.

16 Loewe 1994, Divination, Mythology, Han China, 42.

17 Rutherford 2010, Canonizing the Pantheon, 50.

18 Ogden, ed. 2010, Companion to Greek Religion, 44.

19 Wycherley 1957, The Athenian Agora, 121; Camp II 2003, The Athe-

nian Agora, 8; Rutherford 2010, Canonizing the Pantheon, 43.

20 See Shoemaker 2011, Sanctuary and Crime, 9-28.

21 Steinbock 2013, Social Memory Athenian Public Discourse, 174-177.

22 Timayenis 1881, A History of Greece, 151.

23 Camp 2001, The Archaeology of Athens, 47.

24 See Gadbery 1992, Sanctuary Twelve Gods, 485.

25 Mauzy and Camp 2006, Agora Excavations, 1931-2006, 10.

26 See Lemos 2002, The Protogeometric Aegean, 18; Papadopoulos 2003, Iron Age Potters' Field, 288.

27 Bryant and Peck, eds. 2009, Death and Human Experience, 174.

28 Grossman 2002, Greek Funerary Sculpture, 1.

29 Papadopoulos 2003, Iron Age Potters' Field, 276.

30 Gagarin, ed. 2010, Ancient Greece and Rome, 307.

31 Camp 2001, The Archaeology of Athens, 32.

32 See Valavanēs 2007, Great Moments Greek Archaeology, 202.

33 Skelton and Dell, Empire of Alexander, 8.

34 See Rothschild 2014, Paul in Athens, 90, note 51.

35 Garland 1992, Introducing New Gods, 9.

36 Mikalson 1998, Religion in Hellenistic Athens, 5.

37 See Conwell 2008, Connecting City to Sea, 13.

38 The Dipylon Gate was renamed probably around 350 BCE from the previous "Thriasian Gate." See Harrison 1890, Mythology, Monuments Ancient Athens, 9.

39 Roberts 1984, City of Sokrates, 20.

40 Woodruff (Thucydides) 1993, Justice, Power, Human Nature, 39.

41 For an insightful perspective, see Palagia and Spetsieri-Choremi, eds. 2007, The Panathenaic Games.

42 Jeffrey 2014, Legacy of Paul: Literature, 532.

43 For a sympathetic reading in defense of Paul's proposals, see Fairbairn 2003, Grace and Christology.

44 For example, "Paul, an apostle – sent not from men nor by a man, but by Jesus Christ and God the Father, who raised him from the dead" (Gal 1.1, RSV). Also, "For Christ did not send me to baptize, but to preach the gospel – not with wisdom and eloquence, lest the cross of Christ be emptied of its power" (1 Cor 1.17, RSV). More specifically, "One night the Lord spoke to Paul in a vision: Do not be afraid; keep on speaking, do not be silent'" (Acts 18.9, RSV).

45 Harrill 2012, Paul the Apostle, 117.

46 Clark, trans. 1989, On the Pythagorean Life.

47 Lüdemann 2002, Founder of Christianity, 127.

48 For background, see L. Levine 2000, The Ancient Synagogue, 132.

49 "When Paul and his companions had passed through Amphipolis and Apollonia, they came to Thessalonica, where there was a Jewish synagogue. As was his custom, Paul went into the synagogue, and on three Sabbath days he reasoned with them from the Scriptures" (Acts 17:1-2, RSV). "After this, Paul left Athens and went to Corinth. ... Every Sabbath he reasoned in the synagogue, trying to persuade Jews and Greeks" (Acts 18:1, 4, RSV).

50 Fant and Reddish 2003, Guide to Biblical Sites, 23-24.

51 Charles 2008, Retrieving the Natural Law, 49.

52 Present day Veria or Veroia in southwestern Macedonia, 250 Roman miles from Athens, 3 days by sea or 12 days by land. In Cicero's writings – In Pisonem 89 — he calls Berea oppidum deuium which means "an out of the way town." Historically, Berea surrendered to Rome in 168 B.C. See Bruce 1977, Apostle Heart Set Free, 235 and f1; Fant and Reddish 2003, Guide to Biblical Sites, 38-40.

53 For an archeological survey, see Gadbery 1992, Sanctuary of Twelve

Gods, 447-489.

54 From the Latin "resurrectio", in Greek, "anastasis"; according to both Strong's Concordance and NAS Exhaustive Concordance meaning literally "a standing up" or "a raising up" or "rising."

55 See Finney 2016, Resurrection, Hell, and Afterlife, 13-14.

56 Stearns 1911, Apostle Paul in Athens, 415.

57 Winter 2005, Introducing Athenians to God, 40-41.

58 Kauppi 2006, Foreign But Familiar Gods, 90.

59 Garland 1992, Introducing New Gods, 18-19.

60 See Fant and Reddish, Guide to Biblical Sites, 14.

61 Hoff 1992, Augustus, Apollo, and Athens, 223.

62 Nicholls, Roman Libraries Public Buildings, 272-273.

63 See Vermes 2013, Christian Beginnings, 88.

64 Stearns 1911, Apostle Paul in Athens, 419.

65 Lüdemann 2002, Founder of Christianity, 125-126.

66 Rothschild, Paul in Athens, 94, note 74.

67 Garland 1992, Introducing New Gods, 18-19.

68 Klausner 1943, From Jesus to Paul, 441, 528-536, 580-590; Davies 1945, Role Prophet, 241-254; Malinowski 1973, Galilean Judaism, esp. 66-71; Vermès 1981, Historian's Reading, 19-41; Sanders 1985, Jesus and Judaism, 3-12, 19; Falk 1985, Jewishness Jesus, 148-161; Feldman 1986, Hellenism in Jewish Palestine, 83-111; Lee 1988, Galilean Jewishness, 96-147; Stock 1989, Method and Message Matthew, 57; Feldman 1993, Jew and Gentile, 24-25; Millar 1993, Roman Near East, 347; Vermès 1993, Jesus the Jew, 11-45, 223-224; Saldarini 1994, Matthew's Christian-Jew Community, 75-76; Maccoby 1995, Jewishness of Jesus, 52-62; Young 1995, Jewish Theologian, 49-224; Witherington III 1997, Jesus Quest, 38; Köstenberger 1998, Jesus as Rabbi, 97-128; Goodman 1999, Galilean Judaism, Judaean Judaism, 596-617; Chilton 2000, Rabbi Jesus,

3-22; Chancey 2002, Myth of Gentile Galilee, 26; Zetterholm 2003, Formation of Early Christianity, 3; Vermès 2003, Jewish Context, 1-52; A. Levine 2006, Misunderstood Jew, 17-51; Robinson 2006, Historical Search, 55-88; Charlesworth 2008, Historical Jesus Essential Guide, 17; Casey 2010, Independent Historian Account, 164; Bond 2012, Guide for the Perplexed, 80; Moore 2014, Jewish Mosaic, 58-81; Zaslow 2014, First-Century Rabbi, 12-32; Lizorkin-Eyzenberg 2015, Jewish Gospel; Homolka 2017, Jewish Research, 9-104; Wassen 2016, Jewishness of Jesus, 11-36; Mishkin 2017, Jewish Scholarship, 143.

69 See Salier 2004, Rhetorical Impact Sēmeia, 135; Caldwell 2006, Demographic Transition Theory, 120-121.

70 Horn and Martens 2009, Let the Little Children Come, 21, note 63.

71 Malamed 2015, Medical Emergencies Dental Office, 425.

72 Twice the average male mortality rate in contemporary society is 76 + 76 = 152.

73 Lawson 2004, Science in Ancient World, 114.

74 Closer in length to our modern bound chapters. See Richard 2008, Greeks and Romans Gifts, 13.

75 Lawson 2004, Science in Ancient World, 114.

76 Gruen 1984, Hellenistic World and Rome, 629, note 81.

77 Stocks 2014, The Roman Hannibal, 46.

78 Barca means "thunderbolt" in Punic. The Punic language has Semitic origins shared by the ancient Hebrew language. See Clackson 2015, Language and Society, 147.

79 See Hammond 1983, Three Historians of Alexander; Arrian 2010, The Landmark Arrian; Plutarch 2004, The Life of Alexander.

80 Bradley 2014, The Ancient World Transformed, 201.

81 Yenne 2010, Alexander the Great, 198.

82 Beard 2015, SPQR, 161.

83 Octavian was renamed Augustus – Caesar's adopted son and the first Roman emperor.

84 Beard 2015, SPQR, 161.

85 Plautus, Mostellaria, 775.

86 Litwa 2019, Jesus and Mediterranean Myths, 136.

87 Gardner 1883, Types of Greek Coins, 51.

88 Dahmen 2007, Legend of Alexander, 6.

89 Bowden 2014, Alexander the Great, 93.

90 Malina and Rohrbaugh 2003, Social-Science Commentary Synoptics, 25.

91 See Ferguson, ed. 1999, Encyclopedia of Early Christianity, 348.

92 Rigoglioso 2009, Cult of Divine Birth, 150.

93 Frankel and Teutsch 1992, Encyclopedia of Jewish Symbols, 42.

94 A useful reference to our understanding of Dionysus: Walter Fredrich Otto, Dionysus: Myth and Cult, Robert B. Palmer, trans. (Bloomington, IN: Indiana University Press, 1965).

95 Stibbe 1992, John As Storyteller, 131-147; Moles 2006, Jesus and Dionysus, 65-104; Green, gen. ed. 2013, Dictionary of Jesus, 331; Friesen 2014, Dionysus as Jesus, 222-240; Bilby 2018, The First Dionysian Gospel, 49-68.

96 Croy 2008, Disrespecting Dionysus, 7.

97 Ruth Scodel, Euripides, Derveni Papyrus, 87.

98 Endsjø 2009, Greek Resurrection Beliefs, 77.

99 Green, gen. ed. 2013, Dictionary of Jesus, 331.

100 Restated in another volume of this series, in its most accurate form, his true name was along the lines of "Yeshu ha-Notzri" ("Jesus the Nazarene") (Chilton 2002, Getting It Right, 121-122; Reyes 2010, Name, 349; M. Smith 2018, Final Days of Jesus, 4, 105). "Yeshu" in Galilee.

"Yeshua" in the southerly territory of Judea (Flusser with Notley, Sage from Galilee, 6). From the geography most likely he was known by family and friends pronouncing the former. The Yeshu ha-Notzri epithet is cited in Talmud b.Sanhedrin.43a. from older oral tradition. Such memories were probably codified sometime around the early part of the third century. The Jewish Talmud excerpt revolved around the passion trial. Apparently, the only surviving source behind this claim is the Munich Talmud (Instone-Brewer 2011, Uncensored Talmud, 272). The name does not appear anymore in other older Talmud manuscripts. In some the unique nomenclature may have been erased. Nevertheless, consistent with very early origins, some experts suppose an oral source behind the account surfaced prior to the First Jewish War (Ibid. 274).

101 For lively discussions from leading scholars, see Bird and Willits, eds. 2011, Paul and the Gospels; Becker, et al. eds. 2014, Mark and Paul. For a more controversial, though certainly relevant critique, see Maccoby 1986, The Mythmaker Paul.

102 Smith 2011, Matthew, Mark, Luke, Paul, 1.

103 Tabor 2012, Paul and Jesus, 44.

104 Tabor 2012, Paul and Jesus, 6.

105 Hengel 2003, Between Jesus and Paul, 7.

106 Tabor 2012, Paul and Jesus, xvi.

107 Vermès 2013, Christian Beginnings, 99.

108 Tabor 2012, Paul and Jesus, 34.

109 Westermann 1955, Slave Systems of Greeks, 156-157.

110 Francis 2015, Nihilism Philosophy of Nothingness, 27. Also, Zilioli 2014, The Cyrenaics.

111 Maynard-Reid 2004, Poverty and Wealth, 87; Rock 2012, Paul's Letter, 222; Van Eck 2016, Parables of Jesus, 238.

112 Adams 2014, Social-Economic Life, 78-79; Deines 2014, Jesus Recent Research, 29; Loader 2016, What Happened Good News, 469.

113 Del Tondo 2006, Jesus' Words Only, 78.

114 See Chilton 1999, Martyrs of the Temple, 248.

115 See Charlesworth 2014, Temple and Jesus' Followers, 200-201.

116 Boucher 2008, Yeshua, 25.

117 Sivertsen 2010, The Three Pillars, 49.

1

Desert Oasis

If we intend to unravel a hidden truth. If we care to glimpse an *iconic figure*. If our purpose is to surpass hackneyed metaphors. Credulous visions. Anachronistic recall. Then we open with determined effort setting our sights on a distant past. Across desert sands. To an isolated oasis of human construction. An obscure setting. Once re-envisioned by a madman. Though completed decades beyond his passing. Then shortly thereafter razed beyond recovery. For a breath of time, however, eternity had visited the earth.

So to locate the real figure, flesh and blood, we have to go back. Back to the original framing. Back to David's City. We must kneel down. Run our fingers along meandering, twisting, cobblestone lanes. For they all lead to a singular destination. To a massive stone structure.[1] To an archaic place of worship housing the anatomy of an unearthly, invisible presence. Hidden. Unnamable.

Safe inside the holy city's protective gates we are forced down to our hands and knees. We find ourselves situated among a breathless convergence of Near Eastern pilgrims. We are facing a colossal, manmade structure of incalculable proportions. The dimensions both ways move far beyond our line of vision. A great convergence of sights and sounds roars all around us.

Inside our own heads, cacophonous shouts of religious ecstasy batter our senses: "O come, let us worship and bow down, let us kneel before the Lord, our Maker!" (Ps. 95.6, RSV). For, "By myself I have sworn, from my mouth has gone forth in righteousness a word that shall not return: 'To me every knee shall bow, every tongue shall swear'" (Is 45.23, RSV).[2] By heart long ago we learned the holy words. On and on the shouts crescendo past us.

Eventually they echo away. Back on our feet, once inside the hallowed sanctuary carved of giant, many-ton stones, again, we hear unearthly tones and tenors unrecognizable in the day-to-day drama of first-century cultic life. Nuanced, filtered pleadings take form in many-voiced chants echoing through cloister halls.[3]

We have never breathed such sacred sounds in our lives. We smell burning incense seeping through hallowed enclosures.[4] Feel an essence of desert wastelands paying silent homage to this mysterious, enigmatic oasis. Whispered secrets once carried inside desert winds. Deep, cultic images permeate our senses.

Flitting images of familiar sacred scenes engulf our inner world. Our senses seamlessly transition to another place and time. The focus narrows. Limitless, open expanses. Limitless, silent spaces. The great Sinai is listening. Low whistling winds shift sand and anonymous desert debris across our vision. It is lonely here. No signs of habitation. No sounds but wind whistling in hot desert air.

Then off in the distance our senses converge on a great mass of humanity. A slow-moving caravan of no particular distinction. Then comes to a halt in restless uncertainty. Fear and uncertainty. Tribal leaders in clearly identifiable woven markings move from one group to another.

We intuit worry in ancient blood-red tribal alliances. Maybe running scared. Risking all on a dream of "milk and honey" somewhere in a vast oasis beyond the hot, naked desert. Is it true? Is it really true?

Our inner senses dig deeper into various patterns of human behavior. The caravan comprises a massive spread of humanity. A few existent forms take on new hues. Their body language coalesces into synchronized displays of appeasement. Passivity. This mass of humanity has been at last … placated. Somehow. Some way. Spared. *Cloud by day. Fire by night.* All preserved in visually stark, unutterably sacrosanct, mental brushstrokes. The caravan begins to crawl away. But for the low, whistling wind, the mass of humanity has left the desert sands once again breathlessly, stiflingly silent.

Our vision slowly returns to the vast, humming space among countless groups of pilgrims. We are once again inside the temple enclosure. The physical length and breadth of this enormous chamber seems to somehow echo the natural pitch of those vast desert sands.

Tuned more closely to the unfolding scene, an entire melodrama of archaic cultic images flits past our inner vision. A great shout splits our senses ...

> But will God indeed dwell on the earth? Behold, heaven and the highest heaven cannot contain thee; how much less this house which I have built! Yet have regard to the prayer of thy servant and to his supplication, O Lord my God, hearkening to the cry and to the prayer which thy servant prays before thee this day (1 Kgs 8.27-28, RSV).

Maybe the madman-tyrant from Idumea uttered this sanctified prayer. Probably he didn't. But one thing is very certain. In the ancient setting, in the temple proper, each and every devotee who enters the sanctum has already intoned unselfconscious awareness of a mysterious, invisible presence. A still, small voice. The unknowable. The nameless. The eternal. The primordial. The limitless Maker.

For devotees: so holy, so inviolable, the mere notion to even guess its inexplicable nature somehow disappears beyond any conceivable inclination. Of existence. Or reality. One senses to his toes that this divine presence, so deserving of its majestic setting, is truly awesome. Beyond any form of human trope. Or praise.

We ponder the notion that the Chosen People's sacred temple had been initially formed to house this invisible, deific force.[5] Now inside the crammed vestibule every waiting pilgrim senses Its fastened gaze. Saint and sinner. Rich and poor. Guilt-filled and blameless. And one deftly intuits that each in their own turn humbly begs forbearance. The invisible divine presence is here in our midst. He is here to peel away the moments of our lives.

One senses that the priestly establishment, too, feels an awesome load. They are not exempt. This decidedly privileged (in many ways) sectarian class has taken measurable safeguards to ward the sacred spot. Rock slabs in plain sight warn pagans not to enter the holy Sanctuary. Upon pain of death.[6] Of course, at this level of cultic scrutiny, such religious authorities – whether political opportunists, humdrum clerics, or sure-fired fanatics – really mean it!

As an aside, one interesting, related incident. The *Book of Acts* memorialized that the Apostle Paul on happenstance once escorted Greek gentiles from beyond Palestine into the temple structure. Remembering our just-mentioned citation, *Acts* confirmed that he came within one protective width of a Roman *scutum* from losing his life (Acts 21.27-36, RSV). In any historical context, only Roman henchmen could have saved him.

So now, if we mean to assimilate certain findings assiduously preserved in the following essays, we must turn to first-century Israel. To a cultic setting where, for many, fastidious temple worship dominated every breath, every decibel, every heartbeat of human existence. Most certainly, including our "iconic figure" mentioned at the opening.

If we intend to encounter history, the "earliest footprint," then there is no other plan or reckoning. For the Jerusalem temple truly constituted "the focal point of every aspect of Jewish national life."[7]

The remodeled Zerubbabel complex[8] had preserved sacrosanct traditions from the experiential lessons of its revered, mythic lawgiver. Lessons learned in the shadow of, in many ways, a mysterious deific force.

Across the centuries, at the temple complex worshipping Jews paid their respects and celebrated their gratitude in various cyclical festivals. Traditionally, for devotional Jews the Jerusalem religious feasts measured the seasons of the year.

The festivals were commemorated on the temple grounds inside the Holy City. And nowhere else on Earth. Amongst the faithful, Jerusalem was remembered more as the place where the temple was situated than the site of ongoing political intrigue.[9] For worshipping Jews, set against the vast temple architecture, the importance of the Jerusalem governing council ran an almost forgotten distant second.

Near the time of the first Judaic revolt (approx. 68-73 CE), a Roman army advancing on the capital entered the city of Lydda, about 11 miles southeast of Joppa. But for some 50 people, the Roman force encountered a deserted district. The bulk of the city's inhabitants had abandoned their homes for the road to Jerusalem. They were off to celebrate the periodic Sukkot holiday.[10]

Contemporaries of Jesus and his disciples believed that their feast traditions had emerged out of the shared memories of distant forebears. Nowhere is this conclusion more highlighted than in the Mosaic stories originally preserved in the *Book of Exodus*.

> Three times in the year you shall keep a feast to me. You shall keep the feast of unleavened bread [Pesach]; as I commanded you, you shall eat unleavened bread for seven days at the appointed time in the month of Abib, for in it you came out of Egypt. None shall appear before me empty-handed. You shall keep the feast of harvest [Shavu'ot], of the first fruits of your labor, of what you sow in the field. You shall keep the feast of ingathering [Sukkot] at the end of the year, when you gather in from the field the fruit of your labor. Three times in the year shall all your males appear before the Lord God (Ex 23.14-17, RSV).

For late second-temple worshippers the exodus myth was still considered "foundational" to their cultural heritage.[11]

As to the Exodus itself, when we talk *foundational*, first-century Judaic populations would have pictured certain visceral, poetic images etched prominently as shared awareness. Such poetic images would have incorporated vivid cultic imagery envisioning an ancient tribal past.

All who shared this vision at one point or other would picture in their mind's eye the scene of a lonely mountain located somewhere in the stark Sinai desert. The mountain would be infused with flashpoints of thunder and lightning. A din roaring of trumpets would shake the earth. Courage and despair. Mystery and yearning.

Atop the mountain, a lone pilgrim didn't seem fazed. He was bent over. Studying a gnarled wasteland bush. Burning brightly. Unconsumed. Courage and despair. Mystery and yearning.

All Hebraic believers at one time or other viewed such cultic flashpoints in their mind's eye. From the filthiest rich to the lowliest poor. All actively observed the nurturing of *Israelite shared awareness*.[12]

By the first century the seasonal Jerusalem cultic festivals were so popular that at some point their mass attendance required widened streets and added water sources.[13]

Perhaps this observation helps readers to assess that memories of ancient seasonal festivals still voiced in various chronicles today are distinctively *historical*. These preserved snapshots were not representative of hackneyed mythologies synthesized into history. They were real. They echoed the vast cultic support of adherents.

The festivals were conducted by *kohanim* ("priests") at the Jerusalem temple structure. Most Palestinian (and some foreign) Jews joined the swelling masses at least once per year. They came to offer sacrifices to the deific presence.[14] They came to demonstrate cultic solidarity. They came to participate in ritual worship before the Holy One of Israel.

Across the centuries the three pilgrimage festivals (Heb. שלושה רגלים , *shalosh regalim*) retained the following labels:

Tabernacles or Booths (*Sukkot* – 7 days)

Passover or Unleavened Bread (*Pesach* – 7 days)

Pentecost or Weeks (*Shavuot* – 1 day)

The Judaist festivals (or feasts) comprised elaborately ritualistic displays filled with symbolic cultic pageantry and nationalistic fervor. If we want to be honest, these ancient socio-cultural events probably have no adequate comparisons in modern times.

Across the centuries leading up to the First Jewish War, this common and intimately familiar cultural legacy routinely re-enacted on periodic dates each year. Without exception. Even in times of war. Feast days served to unite Israelites against, what many perceived as, an unreceptive world.[15]

During the first century, annual reminders of Rome's direct rule would have been a persistent source of nationalistic tensions and religious fire. It is natural to expect that tempers would have flared during these communal, religiously invoked, occasions.

We should not be surprised at all to learn that such cultically accessible festivities "became a flashpoint for potential protest against Roman domination."[16] During the Roman era nearly "all the riots we know of took place at festivals, particularly Passover."[17]

Along similar lines, we should not be surprised by the strong-armed reaction of Judaic and Roman authorities to a certain early first-century passover visit from one charismatic Galilean rabbi. A compelling religious figure who was rumored in the territories by groups of rural peasants to be none other than the rightful, long-awaited *King of the Jews*.

Even when transferred to foreign lands and placed in the hands of decades later Christian scribal editors, numerous canonical snapshots still preserved this wholly Judaic originating viewpoint.

Now when Jesus was born in Bethlehem of Judea in the days
of Herod the king, behold, wise men from the East came to
Jerusalem, saying, "Where is he who has been born king of

the Jews? For we have seen his star in the East, and have come to worship him." When Herod the king heard this, he was troubled, and all Jerusalem with him (Mt 2.1-3, RSV).

And as soon as it was morning the chief priests, with the elders and scribes, and the whole council held a consultation; and they bound Jesus and led him away and delivered him to Pilate. And Pilate asked him, "Are you the King of the Jews?" And he answered him, "You have said so" (Mk 15.1-2, RSV).

Then the whole company of them arose, and brought him before Pilate. And they began to accuse him, saying, "We found this man perverting our nation, and forbidding us to give tribute to Caesar, and saying that he himself is Christ a king." And Pilate asked him, "Are you the King of the Jews?" And he answered him, "You have said so" (Lk 23.1-3, RSV).

Pilate entered the praetorium again and called Jesus, and said to him, "Are you the King of the Jews?" Jesus answered, "Do you say this of your own accord, or did others say it to you about me?" (Jn 18.33-34, RSV).

So they took Jesus, and he went out, bearing his own cross, to the place called the place of a skull, which is called in Hebrew Gol'gotha. There they crucified him, and with him two others, one on either side, and Jesus between them. Pilate also wrote a title and put it on the cross; it read, "Jesus of Nazareth, the King of the Jews" (Jn 19.17-19, RSV).

Oh yes, the profile of *Yeshu ha-Notzri* in real life had closely matched the cultic template of a living, breathing, devotional Jew. Quite correctly, not in name only. Historically remembered threads within the ancient narrative were adamant.

We are still able to observe that through humble obedience Jesus the Nazarene conscientiously followed various temple observances in everyday life. Primitive fragments found only in *John's Gospel* attempted to retrace thin historical threads eloquently articulated in this authentically envisioned portrait.

We can still see for ourselves. Yeshu's original cultically imbued connections are still unmistakable. The quite consistent pattern unmistakably links to conscientious Judaic worship:

> The Passover of the Jews was at hand, and Jesus went up to Jerusalem (Jn 2.13, RSV). FIRST PASSOVER

> After this there was a feast of the Jews, and Jesus went up to Jerusalem (Jn 5.1, RSV).

> After this Jesus went to the other side of the Sea of Galilee, which is the Sea of Tibe'ri-as. And a multitude followed him, because they saw the signs which he did on those who were diseased. Jesus went up on the mountain, and there sat down with his disciples. Now the Passover, the feast of the Jews, was at hand (Jn 6.1-4, RSV). SECOND PASSOVER

> After this Jesus went about in Galilee; he would not go about in Judea, because the Jews [i.e. Sanhedrin authorities] sought to kill him. Now the Jews' feast of Tabernacles was at hand. … [A]fter his brothers had gone up to the feast, then he also went up, not publicly but in private (Jn 7.1-2, 10, RSV).

> It was the feast of the Dedication [i.e. Feast of the Maccabees or Hanukkah – 8 days] at Jerusalem; it was winter, and Jesus was walking in the temple, in the portico of Solomon (Jn 10.22-23, RSV).

> Six days before the Passover, Jesus came to Bethany, where Laz'arus was, whom Jesus had raised from the dead. There they made him a supper. … The next day a great crowd who had come to the feast heard that Jesus was coming to Jerusalem. So they took branches of palm trees and went out to meet him, crying, "Hosanna! Blessed is he who comes in

the name of the Lord, even the King of Israel!" (Jn 12.1-2, 12-13, RSV). THIRD PASSOVER

As explained, passover season was a time of traditional, impassioned tribal loyalties. Visually reframed from mythically-charged, shared memories of cultic origins and fierce social separatism.

We have to reasonably conclude that with the Judaic festivals seasoned Roman overseers would be on hyperalert for any signs of (potential) trouble. During these times their military presence inside the capital was outnumbered by male devotional Jews hundreds to one.[18]

Reinforced by undermanned support troops, prior to such feast days, Roman officials would understandably order their forces to blanket the capital. Notably, in advance of festival proceedings. They would be searching for troublemakers. The gospel passion accounts, by implication, plausibly defended this narrative.[19]

The reality for our search: pre-empting the Judaic passover, an invisible net would have been cast along the Jerusalem perimeter for just the demographic profile demonstrated in the figure of Jesus and his immediate disciples.

Rome was famous for operating by rigorous military code. There were no exceptions in foreign lands. They had conquered most of the known world. Their methods were unutterably efficient. Even an auxiliary advance guard recruited in Palestine, within certain numerical limits, would methodically pursue and easily restrain the most rowdy among Israelite troublemakers.

In gospel tradition, this statement reasonably explains the Nazarene's competent detention. He had been labeled an agitator by governing officials. Again, memories of a pre-passover arrest, trial, execution, and burial – roughly patterned in all four canonical gospels – adequately replies to a legitimate, if imprecise, framing of the historical narrative.

All of this activity would have been accomplished within historically and culturally permissible time limits: by the end of the Judaic "Preparation

Day."[20] This term represented the official calendar day before the Jewish Passover. For observant believers: when all non-essential human activity would have been quelled.

We should not forget that for years Israel had by then been occupied by a foreign interloper – Rome. Not "an" enemy. But "the" enemy of a free, jealously religious culture.[21] This attitude would have especially rung true among common, rural Judeans and Galileans.

The historical context tells us even the elderly would routinely walk a hundred miles (and back) to participate in the temple's cyclical cultic activities. The festivals were open to all worshipping Israelites. By the cited figures from antiquity, we can safely conclude that most Hebrews, whether in Judea or outlying areas, truly cherished their shared religious life.

We should further drilldown on this simplification. Casual readers may wish to consider that eventually war was declared by this tiny speck of a Semitic people upon the world's only reigning superpower. A megalithic war machine holding vast, virtually limitless, resources to conduct the most advanced forms of killing against any independent state in the known world. In contrast, the Jews had their mysterious cultic divinity ceremoniously housed beyond immediate purview, their massive Jerusalem temple, and no standing militia. *Not even a ceremonial honor guard.*

In a far more historically palatable context, during the era, the Jewish historian Josephus recorded instances where "several leaders are said to have assumed kingly power."[22] This running theme was certainly visited inside the earliest fragments of Jesus tradition. These shared aspects of the collective gospel story, remembering Jesus as a kingly figure, are truly plausible.

Given this very reliable synthesis, during the first century a new Israelite *king* would have been visualized by most Jews as a traditional Hebrew <u>war leader</u>. Not a meek shepherd figure leading the lambs homeward. In other words, not a traditional *wisdom teacher* passing time distilling inspirational messages portrayed time and again by the post-Palestine gospel editors. These late religious snapshots *radically* defied the original historical backdrop.

All four canonical Gospels displayed a titulus above the cross that read: "The King of the Jews" (Mt 27.37; Mk 15.26; Lk 23.38; Jn 19.19, RSV). In the historical setting, in simple language the Roman titulus described why individuals were executed. In the case of Jesus, numerous forms of reliable evidence *all* "support the historicity of the inscription at Golgotha."[23]

Jesus was executed by Rome utilizing the cruelest method then available to ancient populations: *crucifixion*. So he wasn't tormented by the world's foremost imperialistic superpower for passing along proverbs and sayings on idyllic hillsides. That scenario just isn't real.

The combined canonical narrative strongly suggested the twelve disciples were anything but passivists. The likelihood is some were originally characterized by controversy and violence.

This "outsider" profile is supported by brief flashes in *Luke's* surviving unredacted snapshot that real-life followers were armed in the Garden of Gethsemane.

> And let him who has no sword sell his mantle and buy one.
> For I tell you that this scripture must be fulfilled in me, 'And
> he was reckoned with transgressors'; for what is written about
> me has its fulfilment." And they said, "Look, Lord, here are
> two swords." And he said to them, "It is enough" (Lk 22.35-
> 38, RSV).

We should probably remind ourselves that during this whole period the numerous reactionary causes that erupted across Palestine were often motivated by "political aims that they hoped to achieve by violent means."[24] Many authoritative experts would defend this suggestively explosive reading.[25]

Engrained in the early Jesus cult's prophetic vision, like many religious sects in the ancient setting, Providence would eventually deal *violently* with naysayers. To demonstrate, two scriptural citations from the *Gospel of Matthew* follow:

> Just as the weeds are gathered and burned with fire, so will it be at the close of the age. The Son of man will send his angels, and they will gather out of his kingdom all causes of sin and all evildoers, and throw them into the furnace of fire; there men will weep and gnash their teeth. Then the righteous will shine like the sun in the kingdom of their Father. He who has ears, let him hear. ... So it will be at the close of the age. The angels will come out and separate the evil from the righteous, and throw them into the furnace of fire; there men will weep and gnash their teeth. (Mt 13.40-43, 49-50, RSV).

> And the King will answer them, 'Truly, I say to you, as you did it to one of the least of these my brethren, you did it to me.' Then he will say to those at his left hand, 'Depart from me, you cursed, into the eternal fire prepared for the devil and his angels; for I was hungry and you gave me no food, I was thirsty and you gave me no drink, I was a stranger and you did not welcome me, naked and you did not clothe me, sick and in prison and you did not visit me.' Then they also will answer, 'Lord, when did we see thee hungry or thirsty or a stranger or naked or sick or in prison, and did not minister to thee?' Then he will answer them, 'Truly, I say to you, as you did it not to one of the least of these, you did it not to me.' And they will go away into eternal punishment, but the righteous into eternal life" (Mt 25.40-46, RSV).

With all of the *turning the other cheek* we see in modern religious doctrine, real *righteous indignation* was never too far away from the hearts and minds of early Jesus believers. Prior to migration to hellenized lands, we should be persuaded to accept that the original gospel story favored traditional Israelite *nationalistic* themes.

Themes like Mosaic signs and religiously invoked cultic *renewal* demonstrated in various *ritual* and *moral* purity forms. Such as Jesus and John's mutual baptizing activities. Such uniquely Judaic cultic symbology openly *defied* the outside world. Given the radical cultural and social disparities between Hellenism and Judaism, we should not be surprised that related narrative development was either watered down or totally eliminated from the final gospel drafts.

There is little doubt that their teacher's prophetic spirit envisioning Y-H-V-H invoking judgment on the age fit aspirations of at least some of the original disciples. Or at least certain profiles drawn from early sources. This study suggests core ideas behind the Matthean citations above probably originated from earlier fragments echoing longer and more in-depth memories of the original setting.

Whether at this late date we can defend the Judaic Passover's historical underpinnings, Jews in first century Palestine certainly did. They literally flooded Jerusalem's city streets with humanity. All were Judaic worshippers. At some point, there were so many people present for the Passover festival that for religious reasons the term "evening" had to be *redefined*.

Temple acolytes needed sufficient time between Preparation Day and Passover to kill the inconceivable quantities of lambs necessary to cover the proceedings. Thousands and thousands of lambs had to be slaughtered. There was no other choice but to "rejig" the definition of *evening* "to begin at noon so that the necessary work could be completed before the Passover feast began at sundown."[26]

As far as the Judaic Jerusalem temple structure itself, with undisguised pride, *Philo Judaeus* (aka "Philo of Alexandria") described this mammoth piece of Turonian and Cenomanian limestone architecture "as the most beautiful and notable temple anywhere (Embassy 191, 198)."[27]

As described herein, the temple was at the nexus of Judaic worship and celebration. Immense numbers, both from Palestine and the diaspora, came to worship. Pliny the Elder told his Roman friends that during this period Jerusalem was "easily the most outstanding city in the East."[28]

According to the historian Suetonius, the elder Pliny held several procuratorships and other related official positions throughout the Roman Empire. Such a statement from a bonafide Roman aristocrat who had traveled extensively throughout the Mediterranean world revealed high praise indeed.[29]

Pliny's conclusion would have been primarily drawn from the vast redesigned Jerusalem temple structure. From historical research modern scholarship describes the ancient complex as "one of the most overpowering buildings of the ancient world."[30]

The whole compound easily spanned the length of several modern-day *football fields*.[31] Just taking in the framed dimensions – the stone structure must have taken most people's breath away. And inner equilibrium. For many, to some other alternate vision of reality (representationally depicted above).

Herod from Idumea had begun major upgrades about 18 years into his long reign. They were inaugurated around 19 BCE. As a testimonial to the vast scope of work, the building project was not completed till 63 CE, more than *80 years* after groundbreaking. So decades after the tyrant's death.

To offer a plausible backstory to the enormous architectural and physical achievement ascribed to the temple redesign, a little should be said about the man: *Herod from Idumea*. In all fairness, though quite ironically, without him the story of the redesigned temple would never have been told.

It began, as it often did during antiquity, with the Romans. Just prior to the first century, adventurer warlords such as Pompey, Crassus, Cassius, and Caesar shared three driving goals: 1) create and maintain supply lines to Rome; 2) acquire influence, prestige, and power especially with the Roman Senate; 3) proliferate personal wealth via conquest.[32]

Our experts tell us that historically Julius Caesar was indebted to one Antipater from Idumea. Antipater was Herod's father. In Rome's civil war, Antipater provided crucial aid that produced Pompey's ultimate defeat. During the Alexandrian campaign, at the battle of Pelusium, Caesar had received critical military support from Antipater. At just the right time. Dare it be said: on behalf of the future Herodian line as well.[33]

By 40 BCE, to appoint a head of state, swayed by the likes of Mark Antony and Octavian (Augustus), the Roman Senate subsequently installed the Herodian dynasty in Palestine. This was accomplished in the figure of *Herodus Magnus* ("Herod the Great"). Herod was appointed by the Romans as their "client-king."[34] Herod was Antipater's second (after Phasael) blood son.

We are informed by Jewish historian, Flavius Josephus, that while still in Rome, immediately following senatorial confirmation, "flanked by Antonius and Octavian, [Herod] went to the grand Jupiter temple to sacrifice and to place the decree before the eyes of the Roman Capitol gods (J.W. 1.285; Ant. 14.388)."[35]

Herod from Idumea was not a practicing Jew. While during his lifetime he promoted the idea that his family was of Babylonian Jewish descent, this claim was entirely false.[36] From the Jews' viewpoint Herod was considered a foreigner. This was due to his Idumaean/Nabataean bloodline. A "half-Jew" at most.[37]

Roman authorities had concluded that as an outsider ruling the Jews, he would most likely be unpopular with the people. Therefore, from an oversight standpoint Herod would remain loyal to Rome. He would be dependent on Roman might to underline his authority.[38] Thus, installation of Herod as Palestine's ruler "was to be an attempted fusion between the incompatible worlds of Judaism and Hellenism."[39]

Herodus Magnus, though pre-first-century and despite a general ignorance by religious scholars today, cast a giant shadow over the ancient Palestinian historical stage. Such influence included the Nazarene's time-frame through the period of the second-temple revolt (CE 66-73).

First-century Palestinian social, political, economic, cultural, and religious affairs – virtually all elements in society – were touched (sometimes in profound ways) by the very complicated figure of Herod, second son of Antipater of Idumea.

Fortunately, we needn't argue for lack of available historical data (as many scholars claim in the case of Jesus). "There is no figure in antiquity about whom we have more detailed information than Herod."[40] The Idumean's reign over Palestine was an unusually long thirty-six years – 40 thru 4 BCE.

Historians of Palestinian antiquity apprise us that Herod from Idumea (73-4 BCE) was a prolific builder on a grand scale. His most remembered project would likely be the reconstruction of the Judaic temple in Jerusalem. As we can expect, the complex was so enormous that its completion resulted in serious unemployment problems within the city (see Josephus, *Ant* 20.9.7).

"According to a Jewish proverbial saying preserved in the Babylonian Talmud, 'He who has not seen the [Jerusalem Jewish] Temple of Herod has not seen a beautiful building in his life.'"[41] This ancient commentary is well-known among scholars. To add color to this citation, the Jerusalem temple redesign explicitly followed "the traditional plan and dimensions of Solomon's Temple ... to make the new Temple acceptable to Jewish conservatism."[42] Such attention to detail would have been overwhelmingly popular among devotional Jews.

Nevertheless, in the modern era Herod is often flatly described as "a madman."[43] It is certain that he murdered many family members as well as a number of contemporary rabbis.[44] From a summary standpoint we should probably consider that Herod the Great was "extremely ambitious and blindly jealous of and savagely cruel to anyone whom he suspected as being a threat to him or his position."[45]

In the final analysis, even the elitist Josephus, an undisputed child of the dwindling Jewish Hasmonean aristocracy, came to recognize the monstrous, contemptuous personal traits lurking behind the profoundly flawed and complicated character of *Herodes Magnus*.

Through his written memoirs, however, the aristocratic Josephus could only express this recognition in abbreviated form.

> Now some there are who stand amazed at the diversity of Herod's nature and purposes; for when we have respect to his magnificence, and the benefits which he bestowed on all mankind, there is no possibility for even those that had the least respect for him to deny, or not openly to confess, that he had a nature vastly beneficent; but when any one looks upon the punishments he inflicted, and the injuries he did, not only to his subjects, but to his nearest relations, and takes notice of his severe and unrelenting disposition there, he will be forced to allow that he was brutish, and a stranger to all humanity. (Josephus, *Ant* 16.5.4)

Herod's influence on the temple renovations was so pronounced that many modern commentators have erroneously referred to the completed structure as the "Herodian Temple." We should probably take note that this reference was, in fact, an unrecognizable term in Yeshu's day.

Our focus here is resurrecting authentic paths to history. For real memories we must go back. Back to the Land of Israel. Back to the sacred Promised Land. Concentrated on a tighter focus, we are led to return to the region's only true metropolis – David's City.

Turning to the story of Jesus, certain gospel streams managed to preserve a general outlook that was still in place many decades after original oral memories had first been formed. Even after collected traditions had relocated to pagan lands and prepared for scribal transmutation.

The following citations offer brief glimpses into a more primitive narrative track:

And when he entered the temple, the chief priests and the elders of the people came up to him as he was teaching, and said, "By what authority are you doing these things, and who gave you this authority?" (Mt 21.23, RSV).

"You blind fools! For which is greater, the gold or the temple that has made the gold sacred?" (Mt 23.17, RSV).

At that hour Jesus said to the crowds, "Have you come out as against a robber, with swords and clubs to capture me? Day after day I sat in the temple teaching, and you did not seize me" (Mt 26.55, RSV).

And they came again to Jerusalem. And as he was walking in the temple, the chief priests and the scribes and the elders came to him (Mk 11.27, RSV).

One day, as he was teaching the people in the temple and preaching the gospel, the chief priests and the scribes with the elders came up (Lk 20.1, RSV).

So Jesus proclaimed, as he taught in the temple, "You know me, and you know where I come from? But I have not come of my own accord; he who sent me is true, and him you do not know" (Jn 7.28, RSV).

These words he spoke in the treasury, as he taught in the temple (Jn 8.20, RSV).

It was winter, and Jesus was walking in the temple, in the portico of Solomon (Jn 10.23, RSV).

They were looking for Jesus and saying to one another as they stood in the temple, "What do you think? That he will not come to the feast?" (Jn 11.56, RSV).

Jesus answered him, "I have spoken openly to the world; I have always taught in synagogues and in the temple, where all

Jews come together; I have said nothing secretly" (Jn 18.20, RSV).

We should take special note that couched in inoffensive scriptural language an early conclusion is beyond dispute. Jesus the Nazarene loved his religious life centered in the Jerusalem temple. And he loved its underlying message to the outside world: absolute sovereignty of Judaism's invisible, divine presence.

We probably won't get very far unless we drill down to structural foundations. Preserved stories depicting activities conducted in the Jerusalem temple constitute graphically accurate, real-life impressions. They comprise a critical piece of the narrative architecture available to us. This awareness naturally transitions to a second realization.

Without much effort we appreciate that worship inside this Judaically sacred spot was a critical aspect of the Nazarene's temporal existence. Again and again he was located inside this extensive, hallowed space.

So, if we are to properly engage historical streams framing the life of a rural village rabbi, we cannot avoid focus on the Jerusalem temple of his day. This enormous religious monument set upon many ton stone foundations represented not only "the shrine of the people of Judaea, but the spiritual center of all the Jews regardless of where they lived."[46]

CHAPTER ONE
References

Akenson, Donald Harman. *Surpassing Wonder: The Invention of the Bible and the Talmuds* (Chicago, IL: The University of Chicago Press, 2001). (Abbr. "Surpassing Wonder")

Asano, Atsuhiro. Community-Identity Construction in Galatians: Exegetical, Social-Anthropological and Socio-Historical Studies (New York, NY: T&T Clark International, 2005). (Abbr. "Community-Identity Construction")

Bond, Helen Katharine. *Caiaphas: Friend of Rome and Judge of Jesus?* (Louisville, KY: Westminster John Knox Press, 2004). (Abbr. "Caiaphas")

Canfora, Luciano. *Julius Caesar: The Life and Times of the People's Dictator.* Hill, Marian and Windle, Kevin, trans. (Berkley, CA: University of California Press, 1999). (Abbr. "Caesar – Life and Times")

Chancey, Mark A. *Greco-Roman Culture and the Galilee of Jesus* (New York, NY: Cambridge University Press, 2005). (Abbr. "Greco-Roman Culture")

Cohen, Shaye J. D. *The Beginning of Jewishness: Boundaries, Varieties, Uncertainties* (Berkeley, CA: University of California Press, 1999). (Abbr. "The Beginning of Jewishness")

Dowley, Tim (author) and Poole, Peter (illustrator). *Solomon's Temple Model* (Grand Rapids, MI: Kregel Publications, 2003). (Abbr. "Solomon's Temple Model")

Feldman, Louis H. *Jew and Gentile in the Ancient World: Attitudes and Interactions from Alexander to Justinian* (Princeton, NJ: Princeton University Press, 1993). (Abbr. "Jew and Gentile")

Flinn, Frank K. *Encyclopedia of Catholicism* (New York, NY: Facts on File, Inc., 2007). (Abbr. "Encyclopedia of Catholicism")

Fredriksen, Paula. "The Historical Jesus, The Scene in the Temple, and the Gospel of John," in *John, Jesus, and History, Volume 1: Critical Appraisals of Critical Views*, Anderson, Paul N., et al., eds. (Atlanta, GA: Society of Biblical Literature, 2007), pp. 249-276. (Abbr. "Scene in the Temple")

Goldberg, David J. and Rayner, John D. *The Jewish People: Their History and Their Religion* (New York, NY: Penguin Books, 1989). (Abbr. "The Jewish People")

Goldhill, Simon. *The Temple of Jerusalem* (London, UK: Profile Books Ltd, 2004). (Abbr. "Temple of Jerusalem")

Goodman, Martin. *Rome and Jerusalem: The Clash of Ancient Civilizations* (New York, NY: First Vantage Books, 2008). (Abbr. "Rome and Jerusalem")

Goodman, Martin. *The Ruling Class of Judaea: The Origins of the Jewish Revolt Against Rome A.D. 66 – 70* (New York, NY: Cambridge University Press, 1987). (Abbr. "Ruling Class")

Han, Kyu Sam. *Jerusalem and the Early Jesus Movement: The Q Community's Attitude Toward the Temple* (London, UK: Sheffield Academic Press Ltd, 2002). (Abbr. "Jerusalem and Jesus Movement")

Hayward, C. T. R. *The Jewish Temple: A Non-Biblical Sourcebook* (New York, NY: Routledge, 1996). (Abbr. "The Jewish Temple")

Henty, G. A. *For the Temple: A Tale of Jerusalem* (Tucson, AZ: Fireship Press, 2008). (Abbr. "For the Temple")

Horsley, Richard A. *Revolt of the Scribes: Resistance and Apocalypse Origins* (Minneapolis, MN: Fortress Press, 2010). (Abbr. "Revolt of the Scribes")

Horsley, Richard. *The Prophet Jesus and the Renewal of Israel: Moving Beyond a Diversionary Debate* (Grand Rapids, MI: William B. Eerdmans Publishing Company, 2012). (Abbr. "Prophet Jesus")

Jensen, Morten Hørning. "The Political History in Galilee from the First Century BCE to the End of the Second Century CE," in *Galilee in the Late Second Temple and Mishnaic Periods, Volume I, Life, Culture, and Society*, Fiensy, David A. and Strange, James Riley, eds. (Minneapolis, MN: Fortress Press, 2014), pp. 51-77. (Abbr. "Political History Galilee")

Jeremias, Joachim. Jerusalem in the Time of Jesus: An Investigation Into Economic and Social Conditions During the New Testament Period (Philadelphia, PA: Fortress Press, 1969). (Abbr. "Economic and Social Conditions")

Kasher, Aryeh. *King Herod: A Persecuted Persecutor: a Case Study in Psychohistory and Psychobiography*, Gold, Karen, trans. (Berlin, Germany: Walter de Gruyter, 2007). (Abbr. "Persecuted Persecutor")

Leonhardt, Jutta. *Jewish Worship in Philo of Alexandria* (Tübingen, Germany: Mohr Siebeck, 2001). (Abbr. "Jewish Worship in Philo")

Levine, *Lee I. Jerusalem: Portrait of the City in the Second Temple Period (538 B.C.E. – 70 C.E.)* (Philadelphia, PA: The Jewish Publication Society, 2002). (Abbr. "Jerusalem, Portrait of City")

Lynch. Melissa. Parables of the Kingdom: A Curricular Unit for Language Arts on the New Testament Parables (Bloomington, IN: AuthorHouse, 2012). (Abbr. "Parables of the Kingdom")

Maier, Paul L. "The Inscription on the Cross of Jesus of Nazareth," *Hermes*, 124. Bd., H. 1 (1996), pp. 58-75. (Abbr. "Inscription on the Cross")

Maimonides, Moses. *The Guide for the Perplexed*, Unabridged Edition, Friedländer, Michael, trans. (New York, NY: Cosimo, 2007). (Abbr. "Guide for the Perplexed")

Malamat, Abraham. *A History of the Jewish People*, Ben-Sasson, H. H., ed. (Cambridge, MA: Harvard University Press, 1976). (Abbr. "History Jewish People")

Marshak, Adam Kolman. *The Many Faces of Herod the Great* (Grand Rapids, MI: William B. Eerdmans Publishing Company, 2015). (Abbr. "Many Faces of Herod")

Reed, Jonathan L. *Archaeology and the Galilean Jesus: A Re-examination of the Evidence* (Harrisburg, PA: Trinity Press International, 2001). (Abbr. "Re-Examination")

Ribbens, Benjamin J. *Levitical Sacrifice and Heavenly Cult in Hebrews* (Berlin, Germany: Walter de Gruyter, 2016). (Abbr. "Levitical Sacrifice")

Rocca, Samuel. *Herod's Judaea: A Mediterranean State in the Classical World* (Tübingen, Germany: Mohr Siebeck, 2008). (Abbr. Herod's Judaea")

Rogers, Cleon L., Jr. *The Topical Josephus: Historical Accounts that Shed Light on the Bible* (Grand Rapids, MI: Zondervan Publishing House, 1992). (Abbr. "The Topical Josephus")

Sandmel, Samuel. *Herod: Profile of a Tyrant* (Philadelphia, PA: J. B. Lippincott Company, 1967). (Abbr. "Herod Profile of Tyrant")

Schiffman, Lawrence H. *Who Was a Jew?: Rabbinic and Halakhic Perspectives on the Jewish-Christian Schism* (Hoboken, NJ: KTAV Publishing House, Inc., 1985). (Abbr. "Who Was a Jew")

Senior, Donald. *The Passion of Jesus in the Gospel of John* (Collegeville, MN: The Liturgical Press, 1991). (Abbr. "Passon of Jesus")

Smallwood, E. Mary. *The Jews Under Roman Rule: From Pompeii to Diocletian – A Study in Political Relations* (Leiden, The Netherlands: Brill Academic Publishers, Inc., 2001). (Abbr. "Jews Under Roman Rule")

Taylor, Joan E. *Christians and the Holy Places: The Myth of Jewish-Christian Origins* (New York, NY: Oxford University Press, 1993). (Abbr. "Christians and Holy Places")

Tranquillus, Gaius Suetonius. *Pliny's Defense of Empire*, (New York, NY: Routledge, 2013). (Abbr. "Pliny's Defense of Empire")

Vaux, Roland de. *Ancient Israel: Its Life and Instructions*, McHugh, John, trans. (Grand Rapids, MI: William B. Eerdmans Publishing Company, 1997). (Abbr. "Ancient Israel")

Vermès, Géza, *The True Herod* (New York, NY: T&T Clark, 2014). (Abbr. "The True Herod")

Wahlde, Urban C. von. "The First Edition of John's Gospel in Light of Archaeology and Contemporary Literature," in *The Gospel of John in Historical Research*, Charlesworth, James H. and Pruszinski, Jolyon G. R., eds. (New York, NY: T&T Clark, 2019), pp. 99-141. (Abbr. "First Edition John's Gospel")

Weitzman, Steven. "From Feasts into Mourning: The Violence of Early Jewish Festivals," *The Journal of Religion*, Vol. 79, No. 4 (Oct., 1999), pp. 545-565. (Abbr. "From Feasts into Mourning")

Wright, N. T. *The New Testament and the People of God* (Minneapolis, MN: Fortress Press, 1992). (Abbr. "People of God")

Zeitlin, Solomon. "Herod: A Malevolent Maniac," *The Jewish Quarterly Review*, Vol. 54, No. 1 (Jul., 1963), pp. 1-27. (Abbr. "Herod a Malevolent Maniac")

Zeitlin, Solomon. "The Temple and Worship: A Study of the Development of Judaism: A Chapter in the History of the Second Jewish Commonwealth," *The Jewish Quarterly Review*, Vol. 51, No. 3 (Jan., 1961), pp. 209-241. (Abbr. "The Temple and Worship")

CHAPTER ONE

Endnotes

1 The "walls [were] up to 16 feet deep" (Henty 2008, For the Temple, 313). The stones were originally dragged by oxen from a nearby quarry.

2 See Vaux 1997, Ancient Israel, 459.

3 "Jewish Temple worship included choral singing of psalms and employed many musical instruments" (Flinn 2007, Encyclopedia of Catholicism, 467).

4 The Book of Exodus describes the makeup of incense (Ex 30.34). Ben Sira (Praise of Wisdom, 24.25) repeated the 7 main ingredients to temple incense (Hayward 1996, The Jewish Temple, 98). It was said that the temple incense could be smelled by the sages located in Jericho 25 kilometers or 15.5 miles away (Maimonides 2007, Guide for the Perplexed, 358).

5 Akenson 2001, Surpassing Wonder, 406.

6 Zeitlin 1961, The Temple and Worship, 210.

7 Wright 1992, People of God, 224. Also, Han 2002, Jerusalem and Jesus Movement, 15.

8 Zerubbabel was a governor of Judah (appointed by the Persians) who had returned with the first wave of freed Jewish captives around 538 BCE. Work on the original Jerusalem Second Temple structure was completed in 515 BCE. The first Jewish temple built by Solomon had been destroyed by Babylon in 587 BCE. Traditionally, by the time of Zerubbabel, the Ark of the Covenant was not in the possession of the Jews. See Dowley and Pohle 2003, Solomon's Temple Model; Goldhill 2004, Temple of Jerusalem, 1-18.

9 Jeremias 1969, Economic and Social Conditions, 29.

10 L. Levine 2002, Jerusalem, Portrait of City, 249.

11 Four clear examples of ancient Israelite "foundation" stories are: Judges 6; Judges 13; Genesis 32; Exodus 3-4 (M. S. Smith, Collective Memory Israelite Religion, 631-651).

12 See Ex 19.1-25.

13 Weitzman 1999, From Feasts into Mourning, 548.

14 Leonhardt 2001, Jewish Worship in Philo, 224.

15 Goodman 1987, Ruling Class, 97; Goldberg and Rayner 1989, The Jewish People, 278-279; Feldman 1993, Jew and Gentile, 227.

16 Horsley 2012, Prophet Jesus, 89.

17 Bond 2004, Caiaphas, 46.

18 "Ant. 19.9.2, 20.6.1; War 2.3.4. Recruitment of auxiliaries from the provinces was typical throughout the empire" (Chancey 2005, Greco-Roman Culture, 49, note 37). Most of Rome's troops in Palestine were comprised of local recruits. For obvious reasons they would have hailed from pagan strongholds like Caesarea Maritima and Sebaste (Malamat 1976, History Jewish People, 297). As far as numbers, about a decade after Jesus the full Palestinian Roman presence measured about "one ala and five cohorts, or approximately three thousand men" (Chancey 2005, Greco-Roman Culture, 49). This is a miniscule figure in relation to the full Israelite male population. Based on estimates from Tacitus and Josephus, the Jerusalem population alone at the time of the First Jewish War was somewhere between 300,000-500,000 (Rocca 2008, Herod's Judaea, 333, note 19).

19 Mt 26.47-56; Mk 14.43-50; Lk 22.47-54; Jn 18.1-11.

20 Mt 27.62; Mk 15.42; Lk 23.54; Jn 19.14, 31, 42.

21 Goodman 1987, Ruling Class, 9-11.

22 Von Wahlde 2019, First Edition John's Gospel, 106.

23 Maier 1996, Inscription on the Cross, 62.

24 Mt 27.38 (robbers); Mk 15.27 (robbers); Lk 23.32-33 (criminals); Jn 19.18 (anonymous).

25 Horsley 2012, Prophet Jesus, 83.

26 Senior 1991, Passion of Jesus, 96-97.

27 Ribbens 2016, Levitical Sacrifice, 35.

28 Smallwood 2001, Jews Under Roman Rule, 94.

29 Tranquillus 2013, Pliny's Defense of Empire, 1.

30 Akenson 2001, Surpassing Wonder, 406.

31 Fredriksen 2007, Scene in the Temple, 206.

32 Horsley 2010, Revolt of the Scribes, 112.

33 Canfora 1999, Caesar – Life and Times, 209.

34 Marshak 2015, Many Faces of Herod, 104.

35 Jensen 2014, Political History Galilee, 59-60.

36 Smallwood 2001, Jews Under Roman Rule, 19.

37 Sandmel 1967, Herod Profile of Tyrant, 33; Schiffman 1985, Who Was a Jew, 12-13; Kasher 1988, Jews, Idumaeans, Ancient Arabs, 126-127; Cohen 1999, The Beginning of Jewishness, 18-19; Asano 2005, Community-Identity Construction, 79.

38 Goodman 2008, Rome and Jerusalem, 53-54.

39 Smallwood 2001, Jews Under Roman Rule, 55-56.

40 Vermès 2014, The True Herod, 42.

41 Vermès 2014, The True Herod, 103.

42 Smallwood 2001, Jews Under Roman Rule, 92.

43 Zeitlin 1963, Herod a Malevolent Maniac, 1-27; Kasher 2007, Persecuted Persecutor, 12-17; Vermès 2014, The True Herod, 99.

44 Lynch 2012, Parables of the Kingdom, 231.

45 Rogers 1992, The Topical Josephus, 31. Also, Kasher 2007, Persecuted Persecutor, 403; Vermès 2014, The True Herod, 99.

46 Zeitlin 1961, The Temple and Worship, 209.

2

Secret Name

If our interest is Jesus in history, then probably a little datamining goes a long way. After all is said and done, perhaps one crucial data bit is quite necessary and quite simply put: Y-H-V-H, Y-H-V-H, Y-H-V-H. In ancient times, below the surface, this repetition was continuously reset. Not only for Jesus. But for his earliest followers and rural village audiences as well. Y-H-V-H, Y-H-V-H, Y-H-V-H.

So we must seriously consider that the message of the first story-tellers was in certain ways consistent and uncompromising: the Hebraic divine presence, housed deep within the Jerusalem temple, dominated Israelite existence. Including that of *Yeshu ha-Notzri*.

As far as Jesus is concerned, if we are interested in authentic impressions secured in literary evidence, the following track moves us forward.

> Now after John was arrested, Jesus came into Galilee, preaching the gospel of God (Mk 1.14, RSV).
>
> "Whoever does the will of God is my brother, and sister, and mother" (Mk 3.35, RSV).
>
> And Jesus said to him, "Why do you call me good? No one is good but God alone" (Mk 10.18; Lk 18.19, RSV).
>
> "Teacher, which is the great commandment in the law?" And he said to him, "You shall love the Lord your God with all your heart, and with all your soul, and with all your mind. This is the great and first commandment. And a second is like it, You shall love your neighbor as yourself. On these two

commandments depend all the law and the prophets" (Mt 22.36-40; Mk 12.28-31; Lk 10.27, RSV).

"No one can serve two masters; for either he will hate the one and love the other, or he will be devoted to the one and despise the other. You cannot serve God and mammon" (Mt 6.24; Lk 16.13, RSV).

In these days he went out to the mountain to pray; and all night he continued in prayer to God (Lk 6.12, RSV).

They asked him, "Teacher, we know that you speak and teach rightly, and show no partiality, but truly teach the way of God" (Lk 20.21, RSV).

"Rabbi, we know that you are a teacher come from God; for no one can do these signs that you do, unless God is with him" (Jn 3.2, RSV).

"If this man were not from God, he could do nothing" (Jn 9.33, RSV).

Truly, in any historical rendering, Jesus the Nazarene had his own emphasis. The object of his devotion was the Holy One of Israel. Not his own Pauline inspired mystical role in the cosmos. Or other theologically interwoven Hellenic streams. The citations above suggest that the earliest storytellers attempted to convey this thrust of Y-H-V-H, Y-H-V-H, Y-H-V-H … almost to the point of the *irrational*.

Those who do Y-H-V-H's will is brother, sister, mother? Is that a rational statement? Maybe nay. Maybe yea. Either way, there is no questioning the focus. It certainly wasn't Jesus. The focus in Judaic life was the dominating divine presence: "Why do you call me good? No one is good but God alone" (Mk 10.18; Lk 18.19).

This brief piece of historically suggestive datum blended pure cultic assimilation. For us today, a Judaically inspired focus, with great emphasis on the deific source, was *entirely real*. What we observe in the Markan/

Lukan comment represented an accurate reflection of the social milieu preserved inside rural villages.

Again, Jesus did not on *this* day continue all night in prayer. But in "these" days. For a time all night in prayer was clearly *habitual* behavior.

We witness the life work of *Yeshu ha-Notzri* in numerous related passages to the same effect. Believers were instructed to love the divine presence with everything they had (i.e. all your heart, soul, mind, strength, etc.). Sources for these stories wanted their audiences to consider that from the Nazarene's range of thinking **all else** was *secondary*.

For casual readers today, inside scriptural tradition, Jesus was not alone. Numerous early figures had experienced lifechanging events resulting from a *heightened awareness* of an eternal, divine presence. Recognition of an ethereal figure that came to dominate their lives.

ENOCH

Enoch walked with God; and he was not, for God took him (Gen 5.24, RSV).

NOAH

Noah was a righteous man, blameless in his generation; Noah walked with God (Gen 6.9, RSV).

JACOB

God appeared to Jacob again, when he came from Paddan-aram, and blessed him. And God said to him, "Your name is Jacob; no longer shall your name be called Jacob, but Israel shall be your name" (Gen 35.9-10, RSV).

MOSES

But Moses said to the Lord, "Oh, my Lord, I am not eloquent, either heretofore or since thou hast spoken to thy servant; but

I am slow of speech and of tongue." Then the Lord said to him, "Who has made man's mouth? ... Now therefore go, and I will be with your mouth and teach you what you shall speak" (Ex 4.10-11, 12, RSV).

ELIJAH

And there he came to a cave, and lodged there; and behold, the word of the Lord came to him, and he said to him, "What are you doing here, Elijah?" He said, "I have been very jealous for the Lord, the God of hosts; for the people of Israel have forsaken thy covenant, thrown down thy altars, and slain thy prophets with the sword; and I, even I only, am left; and they seek my life, to take it away." And he said, "Go forth, and stand upon the mount before the Lord." And behold, the Lord passed by, and a great and strong wind rent the mountains, and broke in pieces the rocks before the Lord, but the Lord was not in the wind; and after the wind an earthquake, but the Lord was not in the earthquake; and after the earthquake a fire, but the Lord was not in the fire; and after the fire a still small voice (1 Kgs 19.9-12, RSV).

DAVID

And David inquired of God, "Shall I go up against the Philistines? Wilt thou give them into my hand?" And the Lord said to him, "Go up, and I will give them into your hand." And he went up to Ba'al-pera'zim, and David defeated them there; and David said, "God has broken through my enemies by my hand, like a bursting flood" (1 Chron 14.10-11, RSV).

EZRA

This Ezra went up from Babylonia. He was a scribe skilled in the law of Moses which the Lord the God of Israel had given;

and the king granted him all that he asked, for the hand of the Lord his God was upon him (Ezra 7.6, RSV).

DANIEL

Then the king was exceedingly glad, and commanded that Daniel be taken up out of the den. So Daniel was taken up out of the den, and no kind of hurt was found upon him, because he had trusted in his God (Dan 6.23, RSV).

And in the later Christian Testament …

There was a man sent from God, whose name was John (Jn 1.6, RSV).

These citations are only samples. They reveal a pure Hebraic synthesis. In Jewish tradition, regardless of personalities, physical threats, or evolving cultic forms, a substantial topical emphasis was consistently drawn. In so many words, Y-H-V-H's will was made practical in the lives of those who obeyed. G-d was with them. His presence was *irrefutably* revealed.

Taking this in full stride, to really appreciate the life of Jesus, we need to drilldown on the late second-temple cultic setting. We need to gauge the Nazarene's devotional grasp on the ineffable. One initial consideration: that he was deeply informed by second-temple Judaism is beyond any doubt *historical*.

In order of priority, what does this really mean? There are so many ways to approach this problem. So many reliable nuances and crisscrossing thematic placements to properly gauge a reply. In the end, probably the best approach in some sensible way takes measure of gaining access to a somewhat reliable awareness of the Judaic divinity. Who was this secret "divine presence" anyway? What was He about? What message to humanity did He appear to convey?

So, bottom line, just whom did the historical *Yeshu ha-Notzri* serve? In these few words we face an important question. After all, we are led to believe that he put his life on the line for belief in this deific entity. Such a focus in the end should come together in a deeper awareness of our protagonist. And his, in many ways, *unfathomable* inner life.

As a historical figure, many experts today would call rabbi Jesus an observant Jew (an insight that is repeated many times throughout this study). From all that we know, it is clear that he lived as a devoted supplicant within the uniquely Judaic second-temple experience. Then how did Jews of his era typically approach the indefinable? More important for this discussion, how did he – *Yeshu ha-Notzri?*

Across the spectrum of biblical tradition, perhaps a few readers have noticed something odd. Something inconsistent in the connected scriptural story. To avoid confusion, this peculiarity is probably better illustrated by direct examples rather than layered explanations. Or obscure definitions. Or longwinded, scholarly, circular rhetoric.

Quite frankly, without numerous citations for backup, many readers would probably <u>not</u> accept what follows. In this area of the discussion, unfortunately, advanced degrees in religious studies amount to zilch. For most in this category intellectual prowess probably just increases the confusion.

Given that brief admonition, within the ancient Hebraic texts we uncover a significant trend that does not want to go away. And, peculiarly, this repetitive tendency has received little notice from professional circles.

However, such an inexplicable penchant among ancient sources seemed to be self-sustaining. For us today, there is no guesswork involved. Such a consistent predilection is directly accessible in the Hebrew Testament:

> Abram journeyed to a mountain east of Bethel and pitched his tent. There he "built an altar to the Lord and called on the name of the Lord" (Gen 12.8, RSV).

In Beer-sheba, again, Abraham (same individual) planted a tamarisk tree and "called on the name of the Lord, the Everlasting God" (Gen 21.33, RSV).

Also in Beer-sheba, Isaac (only son of Abraham and Sarah) built a well and "called upon the name of the Lord" (Gen 26.25, RSV).

Elijah demanded of the prophets of Ba'al: "'You call on the name of your god and I will call on the name of the Lord; and the God who answers by fire, he is God" (1 Kgs 18.24, RSV).

Na'aman, a gentile leper, was commander of the army of the king of Syria. He visited Elisha in Israel, beseeching him to heal the great pagan war leader. Elisha merely told him to wash in the Jordan River seven times. Na'aman went away angry: "'Behold, I thought that he would surely come out to me, and stand, and call on the name of the Lord his God, and wave his hand over the place, and cure the leper'" (2 Kgs 5.11, RSV).

Traditionally, King David "called on the name of the Lord: 'O Lord, I beseech thee, save my life!'" (Ps 116.4, RSV). This phrase "on the name of the Lord" is repeated *three times* in the same psalm.

Zephaniah, son of Cushi, in the days of King Josiah of Judah, was determined to "'change the speech of the peoples to a pure speech, that all of them may call on the name of the Lord and serve him with one accord'" (Zeph 3.9, RSV).

So we get the idea here. But beyond the Hebrew Bible, in direct contrast, according to some New Testament scholars, "'calling on the name of the Lord Jesus' characterized the earliest Christian movement."[1] Emphasis on thematic linkage between "Jesus" and "Lord."

In actuality, that the Nazarene, a publicly proclaimed Jewish rabbi, would agree to such notions is inconsistent with historically-driven expectations. Based on all that we can reliably ascertain, Jesus worshipped the hidden Judaic *divine presence*. At the time, all worshipping Jews believed this invisible deity was ceremoniously housed at a physical site within the Jerusalem second-temple religious complex.

Interestingly, early in the Hebrew Testament, Jacob wrestled with the Judaic divinity and *asked His name*. "'Tell me, I pray, your name.' But He said, 'Why is it that you ask my name?'" (Gen 32.29, RSV). The entity refused to answer. Jacob later claimed that he had seen G-d "face to face" (Gen 32.30; see also Gen 35.15).

Past the *Book of Genesis* to *Exodus*, Moses was confronted with: "'If I come to the people of Israel and say to them, The God of your fathers has sent me to you, and they ask me, What is his name? what shall I say to them?'" (Ex 3.13, RSV).

From this now famous query we are able to identify a key (and quite mysterious) narrative clue. Apparently, in reference to *calling on the name of the Lord*, in the interim a critical piece of the puzzle was sorely missing. **Ancient common memories failed to offer an answer**.

Those familiar with the Hebrew Testament might wish to remind themselves that the character of Moses was forced to *ask the name* of this deific figure. Apparently, the ancient sources wanted to impress their audiences that Moses was ignorant of the answer. He was unaware of the entity's name.

Inside the original ancient setting there would be no other reason to include this rather awkward piece of evidence. That scriptural editors did so anyway lends enormous credibility to the tradition. Again, the lawgiver Moses actually did not know the deity's name. Such a name, if name ever existed, was **never** disclosed. At least not within Mosaic tradition.

So we need to get technical. In the Revised Standard Version (RSV) of the Bible (utilized by nearly all biblical scholars), above the Exodus 3.13 citation is the header: "The Divine Name Revealed." But in the description below it the "Divine Name" was in fact left *unrevealed*. "God said to Moses, 'I am who I am' [or I am what I am or I will be what I will be]. And he said, 'Say this to the people of Israel, 'I am has sent me to you'" (Ex 3.14, RSV). Does any reader, casual or otherwise, recognize a name? If so, what is that name? I AM? I WILL BE WHAT I WILL BE?

Respectfully, asking tolerance in advance to all literal-minded Christians and Jews, "I AM" (or any derivative) is **not** representative of an actual name. But a categorical *refusal* to offer a name. Again, nowhere in the scriptural texts focused on the Mosaic stories was a NAME actually endorsed. We should repeat (with emphasis): "I AM" is not a name … .

Just below the RSV citation are the following literary comments:

"God also said to Moses, 'Say this to the people of Israel, 'The Lord [literally "YHWH" or "YHVH" connected with the verb "*hayah*" probably meaning "TO BE"], the God of your fathers, the God of Abraham, the God of Isaac, and the God of Jacob, has sent me to you': this is my name for ever, and thus I am to be remembered throughout all generations'" (Ex 3.15, RSV).

So in all of this explanation where is the actual name? In fact, a deific name *never* appeared. In the RSV, below this citation are the rather cryptic editorial comments: "I appeared to Abraham, to Isaac, and to Jacob, as God Almighty [Heb. "El Shaddai"], but by my name the Lord [again, "TO BE"] I did not make myself known to them" (Ex 6.3, RSV).

With all of those comments, none of the denotations just cited refers to a *name*. Excepting the earlier pre-mosaic "El Shaddai," they are merely brief descriptive references. Noticeably, the ancient Israelites apparently kept their divinity's actual name close to the vest. Or otherwise. Again, the great lawgiver himself was admittedly ignorant of any formal name.

Perhaps by now readers have caught on. But for *El Shaddai*, in these examples, an actual NAME for G-d was never revealed. The Israelites (as well as the gentile Na'aman) simply used the expression *calling upon a divinity's name*. Similarly, in direct contact with the deity, Moses was left with

"I will be what I will be ... ." These intertwining memories suggestively preserve an *extremely* cogent point.

In the Christian Testament, Jesus never attached a name to G-d either. Most often he simply denoted the (or my) "Father."

Critically, this analysis pinpoints a unity in outlooks between Jesus and his Israelite brethren. In public, *Yeshu ha-Notzri* referred to the divine presence as the "Father." Not with any meaningful appellation or title. Simply *Father*. The canonical gospels were uniform on this detail.

> "In the same way, let your light shine before others, that they may see your good deeds and glorify your Father in heaven" (Mt 5.16, RSV).

> "In the same way your Father in heaven is not willing that any of these little ones should perish" (Mt 18.14, RSV).

> And when you stand praying, if you hold anything against anyone, forgive them, so that your Father in heaven may forgive you your sins" (Mk 11.25, RSV).

> "But about that day or hour no one knows, not even the angels in heaven, nor the Son, but only the Father" (Mk 13.32, RSV).

> "Be merciful, just as your Father is merciful" (Lk 6.36, RSV).

> At that time Jesus, full of joy through the Holy Spirit, said, "I praise you, Father, Lord of heaven and earth, because you have hidden these things from the wise and learned, and revealed them to little children. Yes, Father, for this is what you were pleased to do" (Lk 10.21, RSV).

> Jesus said to them, "If God were your Father, you would love me, for I proceeded and came forth from God; I came not of my own accord, but he sent me" (Jn 8.42, RSV).

> "I came from the Father and have come into the world; again, I am leaving the world and going to the Father" (Jn 16.28, RSV).

Coincidentally (and rather mysteriously), beyond the canonical traditions, this expression ("the Father") was adapted in every one of Paul's existent letters (whether authenticated or not). There were **no** exceptions. Not in one individual piece of correspondence was the term "Father" in reference to the Godhead lacking.

Such a consistent, uninterrupted trend is *extremely* rare in the hellenistic Pauline literature. Examples follow (with emphasis):

We were buried therefore with him by baptism into death, so that as Christ was raised from the dead by the glory of the *Father*, we too might walk in newness of life (Rom 6.4, RSV).

[Y]et for us there is one God, the *Father*, from whom are all things and for whom we exist, and one Lord, Jesus Christ, through whom are all things and through whom we exist (1 Cor 8.6, RSV).

The God and *Father* of the Lord Jesus, he who is blessed forever, knows that I do not lie (2 Cor 11.31, RSV).

Grace to you and peace from God the *Father* and our Lord Jesus Christ, who gave himself for our sins to deliver us from the present evil age, according to the will of our God and Father (Gal 1.3-4, RSV).

For this reason I bow my knees before the *Father* ... (Eph 3.14, RSV).

Therefore God has highly exalted him and bestowed on him the name which is above every name, that at the name of Jesus every knee should bow, in heaven and on earth and under the earth, and every tongue confess that Jesus Christ is Lord, to the glory of God the *Father* (Phil 2.9-11, RSV).

And whatever you do, in word or deed, do everything in the name of the Lord Jesus, giving thanks to God the *Father* through him (Col 3.17, RSV).

Now may our God and *Father* himself, and our Lord Jesus, direct our way to you (1 Thess 3.11, RSV).

Now may our Lord Jesus Christ himself, and God our *Father*, who loved us and gave us eternal comfort and good hope through grace, comfort your hearts and establish them in every good work and word (2 Thess 2.16-17, RSV).

To Timothy, my true child in the faith: Grace, mercy, and peace from God the *Father* and Christ Jesus our Lord (1 Tim 1.2, RSV).

To Timothy, my beloved child: Grace, mercy, and peace from God the *Father* and Christ Jesus our Lord (2 Tim 1.2, RSV).

To Titus, my true child in a common faith: Grace and peace from God the *Father* and Christ Jesus our Savior (Tit 1.4, RSV).

Grace to you and peace from God our *Father* and the Lord Jesus Christ (Phile 1.3, RSV).

Besides this, we have had earthly fathers to discipline us and we respected them. Shall we not much more be subject to the *Father* of spirits and live? (Heb 12.9, RSV).

Thus, when either Jesus or Paul referred to the "Father," the *precise* context of usage was the nameless divinity of the Hebrew people. The Father (capitalized) of Jesus and Paul was the same "I am who I am" addressed by the ancient prophets. To bring the idea full circle, this divinity was the same eternal presence invoked by Moses upon the sacred mountain somewhere in the ancient Sinai millennia or so before Jesus.

As mentioned, there are numerous citations (mentioning "Father") in the canonical gospels. *The Gospel of John*, however, laps the field. *John's* direct references to "Father" are nearly double the entire synoptic tradition (i.e. three gospels) *combined*.[2]

There is literally no other reasonable explanation but that Jesus taught his earliest followers to consider the divinity as "the" or "my" Father (capitalized). Thus, entirely consistent with ancient tribal Judaism (and true to his heritage), rabbi Jesus avoided even *indirect* naming references to the altogether **unnamable**.

We are not talking in abstractions now. In fact, there is a historical context to this whole discussion. In former days, commonly felt in many cultures, the ancients believed that grasping onto a simple name could be a skeleton key to the stars.

Along the Mediterranean and across the Near East, various peoples contemplated the proper way to approach the sublime. However, many cultures agreed on one central point. In pursuit of an elusive deity, there was no option but to somehow acquire that entity's proper name.[3]

Long before Jesus there was the famous tale of the Egyptian creator-god Ra. By the time of this tale Ra was portrayed as very old and nearing the end. The way the story goes, the goddess Isis was close by, smelling a plan. And in due course, ultimate power.

With little to lose, she implored the greatest of the dynastic divinities to reveal his *true name*. Among ancient peoples, to some extent one's true *name* was the key to unlocking their identity. Accordingly, when disclosed, it was believed this knowledge enabled the beneficiary to exert control over them.[4]

Apparently, after some cajoling, the mighty Ra gave in. So from Egyptian mythology the ancients inherited the tradition that Isis gained power over the great Ra.[5] She somehow acquired the deity's true or secret name.

In various ways experts tell us that peoples in the ancient past linked the dual ideas – name and identity – into some form of common denominator. According to prevailing belief, one was wise not to go about imploring the gods unless one had credible knowledge of the divinity's secret name.[6]

We have to understand all of this talk of names isn't pie-in-the-sky. Archaeology inevitably adds a much appreciated historical twist. In the ancient city of Thebes (the modern Egyptian "Luxor") at the temple of Amen-Rā (or Amun-Ra) the written words of an ancient scribe have been recovered.

The words depicted that the deity's name was invoked to over-throw a ruler by the name of Apepi, a historical Hyksos ruler in the north. Apparently Apepi had insulted the pharaoh Seqenenre Ta'O – "the great" or "the brave" – of Thebes in 1560 BCE.[7]

According to this thinking, worshippers in contact with a deity's true (or secret) name were known to have entitlement. Experts are fairly sure about this widespread practice. Within the ancient setting, knowledge of a secret name enabled the individual to come in direct contact with a higher power. Not only that but to some extent control the divinity's purpose.[8]

Christian readers today might pause to consider that this shouldn't sound so out of line. Noted above, beyond Palestine the Jesus movement had been known to invoke the formal name of their Christian Savior. And even other cultic powers (like angels or saints). A majority of the time they did this to gain authority over demons, physical ailments, or untoward circumstances.[9]

Unless informed by the occult, this probably sounds peculiar today. But it is quite accurate as a testament to residual, Pauline-Christian reli-gious practices.

A late story from the *Gospel of Mark* comes to mind. The Galilean healer was portrayed directly brushing against themes framing this prac-tice: "And Jesus asked him [i.e. the demon], 'What is your name?' He replied, 'My name is Legion; for we are many'" (Mk 5.9, RSV).

The account was clearly an apocryphal thread. Self-conscious links to the overthrow of Roman power (i.e. "Legion"[10]) were thrown in. Nevertheless, the post-Palestine Markan tradition spoke directly to the idea of gaining dominion over otherworldly forces. By acquiring a secret name. Sound familiar?

Now the focus abruptly switches gears. Interestingly, and rarely touched upon in modern studies, one line of thinking speaks to Jesus and other first-century Jews as advocates for an essentially *unnamed* G-d. The term "Father" would simply have comprised everyday usage.

Again, the same deific entity was reportedly encountered by Moses on Mount Sinai (also called "Mount Horeb"[11]).

> Then Moses said to God, "If I come to the people of Israel and say to them, 'The God of your fathers has sent me to you,' and they ask me, 'What is his name?' what shall I say to them?" God said to Moses, "I am who I am." And he said, "Say this to the people of Israel, 'I am has sent me to you'" (Ex 3.13-14, RSV).

"I am who I am." Some scholars insist that the thrust of the conversation focused on the divinity's *nameless essence*. Within this understanding, the Judeo-Christian god was conveying that He had no true or secret name.[12] For convenience sake, He simply came to be known as I AM.

This form of reply represented quite an effective antidote for anyone's attempt to gain control over the indefinable deity. A nameless identity provided the ultimate defense.

Based on considerable literary evidence, chances are this reasonably explains why the Israelites left their divinity entirely unnamed. Of course, that doesn't leave out practical considerations. In conversation their god was referred to as the widely held Tetragrammaton – four consonantal "semi-vowels" with a root probably best described as "to be."[13]

But (again) "TO BE" or anything even remotely related didn't encapsulate a *name*. Amazing how many people past and present avoid the simple logic. This characterization was only a practical way of referring to the nameless, transcendent, eternal One. As an aside, for purposes of discussion, the dilemma remains unresolved in modern studies.[14]

Of higher importance, the focus of the Mosaic "I AM" was to depict the divinity's active presence among His people. According to early tradition, such an accord (Ex 33.14) was guaranteed in a formal covenantal union between the *Most High* and the *Children of Israel* (Ex 19.1-7; Deut 11.13-21, RSV). We call this mutual promise the "Mosaic" or "Sinaitic" covenant.[15]

Major story themes in the Hebrew Testament reinforced this idea of G-d's active presence among His people ...

Worship at Mount Sinai (Ex 3.12)

Cloud and fire (Ex 13.21)

The portable tabernacle (Ex 25.8-9)

The ark of the covenant (Ex 25.10-11)

The stone tablets of the covenant (Ex 24.12-13)

The Hebrew temple on Mount Moriah (2 Chr 3.1)

There is no easier way of making G-d's presence known than in the simple self-declarative: "I AM." For Judaists, to this day, the very idea revisits the trek of Moses leading his "Chosen People" to the land of *milk and honey* promised by the supreme divinity (Ex 3.8, 17, RSV).

In a liturgical sense, if worshippers have the ability to detect a purpose in these two words, then they have an ability to feel G-d's presence: "I will be with you." The Moses character representationally drilled down the most complex concept in human experience – the presence of G-d – to its most unassuming, basic evaluation: "I AM."

Even today, from memories of the original encounter on Sinai, what believers experience becomes a moment of self-revelation. Any pretentious, highbrow status ultimately resolves into the simplest verbal delineation available in any language: "I AM."

As to the original scriptural memory, there are two further considerations. In the context of Mosaic experience: 1) whether this brief enunciation actually enlisted an inward revelation at a quiet time of contemplation;

or 2) whether the experience was originally cast as an authentic other-worldly visitation at a supernaturally induced, "burning bush."

In a sectarian sense, however, they are really two sides of the same coin. Does it really matter to observant Y-H-V-H believers? The moral of the story rings true: The divine presence is perpetually active in the lives of His Chosen People – for "I AM" or "I exist in the here-and-now." In other words, I possess thought processes that transcend human forms of under-standing. I am the undefinable life force that watches over a unique people. I hold all power in My hand. On and on the narrative threads configure.

That is what the ancient storytellers really remembered. And attempted to convey. To them an unnamed divine presence was real. So real that from the date of covenantal union this entity was invoked in every conceivable real-life scenario. From calls of righteous indignation. To the birth of a child. From declarations of war. To observing shooting stars.

In ancient times a covenantal agreement had been formed between a loose confederation of nomadic tribes and an invisible, eternal presence. The terms of this agreement had been hammered out somewhere beyond memory in a forgotten desert wilderness. Only the sun and stars and desert sands had witnessed the momentous event. It would forever after guide even the minutest nuances of an entire religious culture.

So in modern times many of us have perhaps overlooked a critical factor. Moses finding his destiny through an encounter with the famous "I AM" was not in any way related to name recognition. In plain language, those four consonantal semi-vowels, the *Tetragrammaton*, had zip to do with name or ultimate identity.

Today, they seem to address us at another level. Perhaps, as men-tioned, mildly suggesting *refusal* to offer a name.[16] Then the circumspect rejoinder: "I AM has sent me to you." Not Yohanan ben Zakkai. Or Akiva ben Yosef. But I AM – beyond any possible confusion: **nameless**.

The Tetragrammaton was simply a means of representing the piously most sacred. A deific presence announcing its sovereignty over the realm of fire and air and water. Most times, without fanfare or trumpet blasts. A metaphysical self-revealing. Simply: "I AM." Or, perhaps, more provocatively: "I AM ALL … ."

Attaching a name, in the Hebraic sense, was a contradiction. Their divinity was identified with an otherworldly entity that could never be form-fitted inside the limited lens of human reality. Judaists had been visited by an eternal "presence" that was entirely impervious to any *human* sense of existence.[17] Their unnamed divinity transcended our way of thinking: "I will be what I will be."

The ancient storytellers, however, were committed to staging the famous Mosaic dialogue as a tangible form of remembered tradition. And this conversation had to make sense to their early nomadic audiences. Depicting the sublime, they chose the simple self-declarative: "I AM." Entirely without name. Entirely bereft of even the vaguest glimpse of material existence.

By the time of Moses, in their interactions with the world around them, the Hebrew tribes refused to intermingle their G-d with contemporary pagan idols.[18] Even the thought was anathema. Interestingly, such a practice, if accurately recalled, with but few scattered exceptions,[19] was entirely set apart from the known world. The combined ancient Mediterranean/Near Eastern setting held few, if any, even loose parallels.

Modern Hebrew scholars sometimes declare that this rather involved, esoteric concept in its proper light was not easy to grasp. Perhaps not even for the character of Moses.[20] Nevertheless, positioning their divinity within the spatial dimensions of our atomized world was utterly taboo.[21] Thus, for all intents and purposes, the Hebraic divinity was invisible to the naked eye.

There is a certain seamless rationale to this aspect of the discussion. In just a few words a clearly articulated, otherworldly understanding has been firmly established. The Hebraic divinity was nameless. And beyond material representation. Utterly unseen.

Readers have been indirectly invited either to accept or deny its validity. But now this point needs to be *overturned*. Completely. Now is time for a proper timeout. Yes, now is time for a substantial rebuttal entirely in keeping with scriptural tradition.

Despite all that has been said so far, in the Hebrew Testament Y-H-V-H was indeed at times portrayed as a *physical entity*. Some ancient storytellers wanted us to know this beyond any reasonable doubt. For, apparently, under certain circumstances, the divine presence arrived on the human scene in some kind of physically recognizable form.

In scriptures the list of examples is quite extensive. Here are several widely cited instances:

The Lord had appeared to Abram (Gen 17.1, RSV).

Jacob named the location of Peniel because he had seen God face to face (Gen 32:27–30, RSV).

God spoke to Moses "as a man speaks to his friend" (Ex 33.11, RSV).

As a group Moses, Aaron, Nadab, and Abi'hu as well as seventy elders of Israel "saw the God of Israel" (Ex 24.9-10, RSV).

The prophet Amos claimed to have seen the Lord "standing upon the altar" [i.e. probably located in David's tent temporarily acting as the cultic temple] (Amos 9.1, 11, RSV).

Isaiah saw "the Lord seated upon a throne, high and lifted up" (Is 6.1, RSV).

"[T]he Lord revealed himself to Samuel at Shiloh" (1 Sam 3.21, RSV).

As stated, these are only examples. Within this broad, established theme many other citations follow. They may be intended as symbolic expressions. Or some form of emblematic representation beyond our knowledge. But maybe not. We know from the Hebrew Bible that this same unnamed presence was also familiar to the likes of Elijah, Ezekiel, Micah, and others.[22] Now as this discussion pertains to the figure of Jesus.

No known gospel tradition suggested that the Father appeared to Jesus. There is the Johannine statement: "Not that anyone has seen the Father except him who is from God; he has seen the Father" (Jn 6.46, RSV).

In this context, "seen" was not intended as *visual*. But an inner awareness or recognition. Even including Paul's ecstatic visions, definitively, no early reliable Christian source ever claimed that Y-H-V-H, the Judeo-Christian "Father," appeared in the material world. In any form.

This whole discussion may sound rather technical, but it is absolutely critical to understanding key religious concepts related to our most familiar biblical figures. For Moses, Jesus, Paul and many of the prophets, the divine presence was entirely NAMELESS and (more times than naught) featureless. This divine existence was considered too sacred to attach even synthetic identifiers. Exceptions have been touched upon above.

The point is that Y-H-V-H worship identified with an entirely different reality than Greco-Roman idols venerated across the ancient Near East. Cultic activities revolving around the numerous pagan divinities dominated Mediterranean and Near Eastern antiquity. Jewish Palestine and its Diaspora were essentially alone in solemn observance of their peerless deity too circumspect even to carry a name.

Beyond a few experts in elite academic institutions, nowadays this topic has been generally ignored. But glimpsing the basic concept is crucial to gaining a proper understanding of the historical Jesus.

At least at an intellectual level, we must find a way to envision the God Jesus worshipped. From the Nazarene's perspective, the very meaning of his existence. Or we are denied access to the earliest footprint.

In Christian tradition the dual themes of Jesus the Nazarene and the identity of the invisible Judaic divinity are somewhat intertwined.

Clearly, in history Yeshu's ultimate aim was to please this mysterious entity. Apparently, above all other priorities in life. No exceptions.

If we are in any way pointed at an early dialogue, this critical starting point at least needs mentioning. Within a reasonable historical context. And for good reason.

The rather neutral designation of "Father" can only be understood in light of the Nazarene's authentic Judaic cultic roots. Religious threads that are far removed from most Christianized points of view. Which includes expert analysis subject to a decidedly Pauline interpretation of scriptural tradition.

In scholarly studies one won't very often find the Nazarene's usage of *Father* linked to a Judaist milieu. But that is the direct historical context of this ancient appellation. Jesus was a devout Jew. When identifying the cultic divinity, the literary evidence overwhelmingly claims that he preferred "Father." Many other Judaists preferred the "Holy One" or the "Lord" or the "God of Israel" or the "God of Zion" or the "God of Heaven" (in later antiquity).

Essentially, representations like "Father" were right in line with the beliefs of everyday Jews. This usage avoided even vague reference to a "secret" name.[23] So in this instance we are plausibly in line with a historically based sensitivity.

Because "Father" was so universally applied throughout canonical tradition we are able to fairly conclude that the term represents a root memory inside originating Jesus tradition preserved even past migration to foreign lands. As stated, even Paul from Tarsus often made use of this informal appellative.

FINAL THOUGHTS

Yeshu ha Notzri was born and raised in a cultural environment devoted to the late second-temple cultic setting. So a central pillar in any historical study is Yeshu's utter devotion to the Jerusalem temple and its Mosaic code.

For at least a century New Testament scholars have focused almost complete attention on the *synoptic* stories as the historical basis upon which to build a realistic profile. Hopefully, by now at least some have realized that this strategy is clearly unsustainable. On many fronts post-Palestine synoptic editors avoided the human figure. The historical figure. After all, they were seeking to build religious faith.

Planted squarely in Israelite society, Jesus was not focused on creating a new religion. He was not witnessed as a supernatural figure. He did not direct itinerants to convert the Palestinian countrysides. A main focus of the synoptic stories, Jesus did not practice exorcism. In the early part of the first century, demon possession was unrecognized in Israelite culture. We will explore that aspect in this two volume set. However, in a historical light, this list goes on and on.

As the study progresses, we will investigate more historically plausible scenarios. In the canonical texts, such scenarios are often supported by thin fragments of tradition mostly distributed in *John's Gospel*. We might call these fragments "source traditions."

As a historical backdrop, in the early part of the first century Israelite teachers were beginning to be recognized through the public appellation "rabbi."

Miraculous deeds were at times compared to Moses and his sojourn towards the Promised Land. Such deeds were from time to time recognized as Mosaic "signs."

Across the late second-temple setting, devotion to the periodic seasonal festivals continued to be enormously popular. The Jewish feasts and their related cultic activities were apparently central to Judaic life.

Within the first-century Hebraic dialogue, some individuals were compared to heroic figures from Israel's past. A few were even identified as "prophets."

As surprising as it might seem, readers should understand that the synoptic stories categorically rejected ALL of this historically laden subject matter. Many synoptic related threads simply arose too late to appreciate an organically *Judaic* ambiance.

In other areas Pauline Christianity was determined to replace the early Jesus movement's legitimate Hebraic foundations with more contemporary, hellenized conceptions.

The post-Palestinian synoptic editors avoided the expression "rabbi." In fact, inside the only Synoptic Gospel where the term was actually set forth, the usage was decidedly *negative*: "They [scribes and Pharisees] do all their deeds to be seen by men; for they make their phylacteries broad and their fringes long, and they love the place of honor at feasts and the best seats in the synagogues, and salutations in the market places, and being called rabbi by men. But you are not to be called rabbi, for you have one teacher, and you are all brethren" (Mt 23.5-8, RSV). A shocking usage of the word originally signifying dignity and respect, to say the least.

As to *signs*, Markan editors put forth: "Why does this generation seek a sign? Truly, I say to you, no sign shall be given to this generation" (Mk 8.12, RSV). Clearly, *Mark's* post-Palestine dogmatic sources were unfamiliar with the – in some ways – desperate plight of the Jewish people in the homeland. *Signs* represented a first-century rallying cry to remember Y-H-V-H's covenantal promise to *preserve* His Chosen People. Mosaic signs represented hope to the Judaic population.

Astonishingly, across his ministry the synoptic Jesus attended only **one** Jerusalem feast – the final Passover in common gospel tradition. Inside this segment of the literature, no other Jewish festival was even mentioned. This, more than any other thematic factor, should inform attuned scholars of the lack of relevant historical connections inside the combined synoptic voice. The numerous periodic festivals were considered pivotal to the everyday lives of worshipping Jews. Including Jesus.

The synoptic editors avoided identifying Jesus as a Judaic "prophet." Within the late post-Palestine cultural environment, the title of choice among synoptic editorial interests was the supernatural Pauline "Christos." Amazingly, Paul himself never cited the popular Judaic cultic term "prophet" in reference to Jesus. Not once in all of his extensive correspondence. In the Pauline literate world a supernaturally induced descriptor always shone through. Keywords like Lord, Kyrios, Christos, image of the invisible God, firstborn of all creation, Son of God, the form of God, the fullness of God, etc. dominated the Pauline thought-world.

When this study claims that the synoptic stories did not support a characterization of Jesus as a "human" figure utterly devoted to Judaism, the literature we have access to today overwhelmingly promotes this claim. Readers will rarely hear this easily defendable observation from New Testament scholars. But the fact remains.

Coincidentally, a Johannine early layer of tradition (sometimes referred to as "source tradition"):

repeatedly referred to Jesus as "rabbi";

across the entire Gospel witnessed *Yeshu ha-Notzri* performing Mosaic signs;

built much of its original narrative structure around Jesus attending the Jerusalem festivals;

referred repeatedly and explicitly to Jesus as a Judaic "prophet"("Sir, I perceive that you are a prophet" – 4.19, RSV // "This is indeed the prophet who is to come into the world!" – 6.14, RSV // "This is really the prophet" – 7.40,

RSV // So they again said to the blind man, "What do you say about him, since he has opened your eyes?" He said, "He is a prophet" – 9.17, RSV);

never once referred to exorcism or demon possession; *John's Gospel* contained no such fictionalized episodes.

Finally, we must recognize common, early themes preserved in all four canonical tracks. The synoptic editors didn't get everything wrong. They didn't build at least some of their characterizations out of whole cloth. Nor did later traditions added to *John's* original story define the entire Gospel. Many aspects preserved in his story are decidedly *late*. The various contradictions to some extent will be investigated as the series moves on.

Ultimately, we will even investigate a more realistic explanation for the Resurrection pericope at least partially reconstructed from the memory of a probable eyewitness. If in search of history, this study contends that readers will find these two books worth their while. What are we saying? Readers will in fact uncover a highly plausible explanation for what this series refers to as "the earliest footprint of Jesus." A "footprint" presumably observed in *history*.

CHAPTER TWO
References

Baker, Mona, ed. *Routledge Encyclopedia of Translation Studies* (New York, NY: Routledge, 1998). (Abbr. "Routledge Encyclopedia Translation Studies")

Barrick, William D. "The Mosaic Covenant," *The Masters Seminary Journal* 10/2 (Fall 1999), 213-232. (Abbr. "The Mosaic Covenant")

Bikerman, E. "Anonymous Gods," *Journal of the Warburg Institute*, Vol. 1, No. 3 (Jan., 1938), pp. 187-196. (Abbr. "Anonymous Gods")

Burge, Gary M., et al. *The New Testament in Antiquity: A Survey of the New Testament within Its Cultural Context* (Grand Rapids, MI: Zondervan, 2009). (Abbr. "New Testament in Antiquity")

Davis, Carl Judson. *The Name and Way of the Lord: Old Testament Themes, New Testament Christology* (Sheffield, England: Sheffield Academic Press Ltd, 1996). (Abbr. "Name of the Lord")

Dempster, Stephen G. Micah (Grand Rapids, MI: William B. Eerdmans Publishing Company, 2017). (Abbr. "Micah")

Irwin, William H. "The Course of the Dialogue between Moses and Yhwh in Exodus 33:12-17," *The Catholic Biblical Quarterly*, Vol. 59, No. 4 (October 1997), pp. 629-636. (Abbr. "Course of the Dialogue")

Johnson, Aubrey Rodway. *The Cultic Prophet in Ancient Israel* (Cardiff, Wales: University of Wales Press, 1962). (Abbr. "Cultic Prophet")

Kimondo, Stephen Simon. The Gospel of Mark and the Roman-Jewish War of 66-70 CE: Jesus' Story as a Contrast to the Events of the War (Eugene, OR: Pickwick Publications, 2018). (Abbr. "Mark and Roman-Jewish War")

Kirsch, Jonathan. *Moses: A Life* (New York, NY: The Ballantine Publishing Group, 1998). (Abbr. "Moses a Life")

Leach, Ted. *Companion to the Old Testament: For the Interpreter Within Each of Us* (Bloomington, IN: WestBow Press, 2013). (Abbr. "Companion to Old Testament")

Linville, James R. *Amos and the Cosmic Imagination* (Burlington, VT: Ashgate Publishing Company, 2008). (Abbr. "Amos and Cosmic Imagination")

McCabe, Elizabeth A. *An Examination of the Isis Cult with Preliminary Exploration into New Testament Studies* (Lanham, MD: University Press of America, Inc., 2008). (Abbr. "Examination of Isis Cult")

McDonough, Sean M. *YHWH at Patmos: Rev. 1:4 in Its Hellenistic and Early Jewish Setting* (Eugene, OR: Wipf and Stock Publishers, 1999). (Abbr. "YHWH at Patmos")

Mitchell, Lucy Myers Wright. *A History of Ancient Sculpture* (New York, NY: Dodd, Mead, and Company, 1905). (Abbr. "History of Ancient Sculpture")

Mojsov, Bojana. *Osiris: Death and Afterlife of a God* (Malden, MA: Blackwell Publishing, 2005). (Abbr. "Osiris – Death and Afterlife")

Satcher, Mikel E. *For The Sake Of My Holy Name: The Divine Reputation In Ezekiel As A Literary Phenomenon* (Bloomington, IN: Xlibris Corporation, 2012). (Abbr. "My Holy Name")

Schreiber, Mordecai, et al., eds. *The Shengold Jewish Encyclopedia*, Third Edition (Rockville, MD: Schreiber Publishing, 2003). (Abbr. "Shengold Jewish Encyclopedia")

Sicker, Martin. *Aspects of Jewish Metarational Thought* (Lincoln, NE: iUniverse, Inc., 2005). (Abbr. "Jewish Metarational Thought")

Society of Antiquaries in London. *Archaeologia: Or, Miscellaneous Tracts Relating to Antiquity*, Volume 52 (London, England: Nichols and Sons, 1890). (Abbr. "Miscellaneous Tracts")

Soulen, R. Kendall. "Jesus and the Divine Name," *Union Seminary Quarterly Review*, September 16, 2015, pp. 47-58. (Abbr. "Jesus and Divine Name")

Takács, Sarolta A. "Divine and Human Feet: Records of Pilgrims Honoring Isis," in *Pilgrimage in Graeco-Roman and Early Christian Antiquity: Seeing the Gods*, Elsner, Jaś and Rutherford, Ian, eds. (Oxford, UK: Oxford University Press, 2005), pp. 353-372. (Abbr. "Honoring Isis")

Wilkinson, Robert J. Tetragrammaton: Western Christians and the Hebrew Name of God: From the Beginnings to the Seventeenth Century (Leiden, The Netherlands: Brill, 2015). (Abbr. "Tetragrammaton")

CHAPTER TWO
Endnotes

1 Davis 1996, Name of the Lord, 128.

2 Matthew (39); Mark (4); Luke (11); John (92).

3 Bikerman 1938, Anonymous Gods, 187.

4 Mojsov 2005, Osiris – Death and Afterlife, 31; Leach 2013, Companion to Old Testament, 67, note 70.

5 Takács 2005, Honoring Isis, 355; McCabe 2008, Examination of Isis Cult, 102.

6 Bikerman 1938, Anonymous Gods, 187.

7 Society of Antiquaries in London 1890, Miscellaneous Tracts, 443.

8 Takács, 2005, 353-372.

9 Burge, et al. 2009, New Testament in Antiquity, 240.

10 See Kimondo 2018, Mark and Roman-Jewish War, 158.

11 Number of mentions in the Hebrew Bible – Mount Sinai: 35 times; Mount Horeb: 17 times. Clearly, both terms were common to the ancient Jews.

12 Leach 2013, Companion to Old Testament, 67, note 70. Livy among the ancient Romans apparently confirmed this practice (McDonough 1999, YHWH at Patmos, 87).

13 See Wilkinson 2015, Tetragrammaton.

14 Baker, ed. 1998, Routledge Encyclopedia Translation Studies, 272.

15 For background, see Barrick 1999, The Mosaic Covenant, 213-232.

16 Kirsch 1998, Moses a Life, 115.

17 Schreiber et al., eds. 2003, Shengold Jewish Encyclopedia, 93.

18 Bikerman 1938, Anonymous Gods, 195.

19 For example, "The Pelasgians [forerunners of the ancient Greeks], according to tradition, worshipped at Dodona one highest god, Zeus, but without images. Moreover, they brought offerings and prayed to many 'nameless gods'" (Mitchell 1905, History of Ancient Sculpture, 139).

20 For example, Irwin 1997, Course of the Dialogue, 629-636.

21 Sicker 2005, Jewish Metarational Thought, 2.

22 For Elijah, see Johnson 1962, Cultic Prophet. For Amos, see Linville 2008, Amos and Cosmic Imagination. For Ezekiel, see Satcher 2012, My Holy Name. For Micah, see Dempster 2017, Micah.

23 Soulen 2015, Jesus and Divine Name, 49.

3

Historical Backdrop

By the time of our story those the Nazarene had trusted were most likely gone. Lost to the depths of Sheol. Lost forever. A distant, haunting, half-forgotten memory at some point perhaps whispered in his ear ...

> And as he [Moses] finished speaking all these words, the ground under them split asunder; and the earth opened its mouth and swallowed them up, with their households and all the men that belonged to Korah and all their goods. So they and all that belonged to them went down alive into Sheol; and the earth closed over them, and they perished from the midst of the assembly. And all Israel that were round about them fled at their cry; for they said, "Lest the earth swallow us up!" And fire came forth from the Lord, and consumed the two hundred and fifty men offering the incense (Num 16.31-35).

The current crop of followers would eventually forsake *Yeshu ha-Notzri*. We know them as *the disciples*. They had sought a war leader. Killer. *King*. "Perceiving then that they were about to come and take him by force to make him king, Jesus withdrew again to the mountain by himself" (Jn 6.15, RSV). Readers might wish to underline "by himself."

So where were his *faithful* knights? Not so faithful anymore. Rejecting coronation, he had found himself alone. *By himself*. Against the world.

Most scholars interpret these Johannine lines differently. But in a genuine *historical* reading the implications are obvious. The memories, as they exist today, probably lead back to older, originating sources ultimately discarded by religious editors translating familiar oral stories into written forms.

Peculiarly and quite conspicuously, the written gospels never mentioned Galilee's two major population centers: Sepphoris and Tibe'ri-as.[1] Wisely, throughout his career the Nazarene most likely kept out of sight. The historical ministry was limited to villages and small towns.[2] Evidence shows that *Yeshu ha-Notzri* avoided prying eyes. Unwanted attention. In the end, all for naught.

By the time of his infamous trial, informers had evidently apprised Rome of disturbing seditious behavior in rural zones ...

Pilate entered the praetorium again and called Jesus, and said to him, "Are you the King of the Jews?" (Jn 18.33, RSV).

But you [Pilate addressing Judaic officials] have a custom that I should release one man for you at the Passover; will you have me release for you the King of the Jews? (Jn 18.39, RSV).

[T]hey [i.e. Roman soldiers] came up to him, saying, "Hail, King of the Jews!" and struck him with their hands (Jn 19.3, RSV).

Now it was the day of Preparation of the Passover; it was about the sixth hour. He [Pilate] said to the Jews [i.e. Judaic authorities], "Behold your King!" (Jn 19.14, RSV).

Pilate also wrote a title and put it on the cross; it read, "Jesus of Nazareth, the King of the Jews" (Jn 19.19, RSV).

The chief priests of the Jews then said to Pilate, "Do not write, 'The King of the Jews,' but, 'This man said, I am King of the Jews'" (Jn 19.21, RSV).

How did Pilate acquire his information? We usually assume that Jerusalem elites were responsible. But is this assumption correct?

To help us archaeology has uncovered residual evidence of early Roman occupation. "[N]otable for rural inhabitants were minor forts, watchtowers, and road stations disbursed along the road system."[3] So in the trial scene Pilate's repeated probes could have legitimately mirrored some form of secret communiques distributed amongst the Romans.

However, within the historical setting, the likelihood is that instead of royal dispensations, across his ministry, those Jesus encountered found healing. Hope. Renewal. That is, before final passover eve when Rome and Jerusalem had by then joined forces (Jn 18.2-3, 12-13).

In hindsight, among his own followers, another plausible scenario exists. It is quite feasible that, minimally, a second turncoat (besides Judas) had betrayed our protagonist. Throughout the story, amongst the disciples the quality in shortest supply seemed to be *loyalty*.

Who had supplied the Roman prefect with such intimate details of Yeshu's ministry? Roman spies? Disloyal disciples? More dependable details (especially) enunciated in the Johannine tale demand readers' attention. By the time of the infamous trial scene Judas was out of the picture. And Pilate was definitely on cue. Who had apprised the Roman prefect of the Nazarene's activities?

Strangely, throughout the historical ministry, Jesus the Nazarene seemed at times to be provocatively decked. According to the original pre-Johannine storytellers, someone or some group had visited upon his reputation a "royal" theme.

Rumors persisted. Presumably, at a fairly early stage someone either in or out of his immediate group had attempted to designate *Yeshu ha-Notzri* as the long-awaited "King of the Jews."

Nathan'a-el answered him, "Rabbi, you are the Son of God! You are the King of Israel!" (Jn 1.49, RSV).

Perceiving then that they were about to come and take him by force to make him king, Jesus withdrew again to the mountain by himself (Jn 6.15, RSV).

So they took branches of palm trees and went out to meet him, crying, "Hosanna! Blessed is he who comes in the name of the Lord, even the King of Israel!" (Jn 12.13, RSV).

"Fear not, daughter of Zion; behold, your king is coming, sitting on an ass's colt!" (Jn 12.15, RSV).

Pilate also wrote a title and put it on the cross; it read, "Jesus of Nazareth, the King of the Jews" (Jn 19.19, RSV).

Nicode'mus also, who had at first come to him by night, came bringing a mixture of myrrh and aloes, about a hundred pounds' weight. They took the body of Jesus, and bound it in linen cloths with the spices, as is the burial custom of the Jews (Jn 19.39-40, RSV).

The narrative evidence is consistent. And fairly explicit. The last description, with its vast supply of spices, would have met the requirements of a state funeral conducted for a reigning antiquarian monarch. Not a lowly village rabbi.

In the early stages of the Johannine story, it is hard pinning an oath breaker claim on Judas. Apparently, he had been entrusted with keeping track of the group's coinage. The *Fourth Gospel* tells us: "Some thought that, because Judas had the money box, Jesus was telling him, 'Buy what we need for the feast'; or, that he should give something to the poor" (Jn 13.29, RSV).

For disadvantaged near-indigents, money would have been in very short supply. In the historical setting Judas must have exhibited some reliable quality to promote such trust. From the stories, Jesus clearly grasped the inner workings of human nature. For most of the ministry Judas had been counted upon as a trusted disciple.

During the Roman era, within Judaic culture such a phenomenon as crowning "kings" was rather commonplace. For the benefit of readers, memories of this theme were *historically* invoked. Flavius Josephus had later noted: "At this time there were great disturbances in the country, and that in many places; and the opportunity that now offered itself induced a great many to set up for kings" (Josephus, *War* 2.4.1).

Remembered by Josephus, three figures from diverse geographical regions serve as useful examples: 1) Judas, son of Ezekias (Galilee – *War* 2.4.1; *Ant* 17.5.5); 2) Simon (Perea – *War* 2.4.2; *Ant* 17.10.6); 3) Athronges and his brothers (Judea – *War* 2.4.2; *Ant* 17.10.6).

The following details list some key elements these individuals and their movements shared with historical impressions of Jesus and his early followers:

> These individuals and their supporters rose from the common people.
>
> The image their movements conveyed did not coincide with thematic development found in Pharisaic and Essene literature.
>
> In each case the movements themselves were focused on both foreign and domestic oppression perpetrated by elites.
>
> They were not backed by foreign powers but emerged from local, groundswell support.
>
> Each of the movements had originated in rural settings beyond the cities.
>
> . Each of the movements claimed to be led by a "king."
>
> Critically, for our examination, the various groups were largely comprised of *dubious and violent characters*.[4]

For us, the last point – the "dubious and violent" aspect – is particularly notable. This theme mirrors so closely to a drilldown of character studies on the Nazarene's original disciples. As with certain profiles amongst Jesus's immediate followers, one cannot miss a legitimate and conspicuous related finding. According to Josephus …

JUDAS, SON OF EZEKIAS:

There was also Judas, the son of that Ezekias who had been head of the robbers; which Ezekias was a very strong man, and had with great difficulty been caught by Herod. This Judas, having gotten together a multitude of men of a profligate [alternate translation: "desperate"] character about Sepphoris in Galilee, made an assault upon the palace (Josephus, *Ant* 17.10.5).

SIMON FROM PEREA:

[F]or Gratus, when he had joined himself to some Roman soldiers, took the forces he had with him, and met Simon, and after a great and a long fight, no small part of those that came from Perea, who were a disordered body of men, and fought rather in a bold than in a skillful manner, were destroyed (Josephus, *Ant* 17.10.6).

ATHRONGES AND HIS FOUR BROTHERS:

But in process of time they grew more cruel to all sorts of men, nor could anyone escape from one or other of these seditions, since they slew some out of the hopes of gain, and others from a mere custom of slaying men (Josephus, *Ant* 17.10.7).

Various individuals in these different movements were consistently portrayed by Josephus as "desperate men."[5]

After the reign of Herod from Idumea, plus the Roman invasion, the masses were in urgent need of a divinely appointed cultic figure to alter the balance. They were looking to form messianic movements around symbolic acts that invoked crowning an Israelite "king."[6] In each instance King David from Judaic history seemed to serve as their model.[7]

To complement this observation, in gospel tradition we find not only Mosaic but *Davidic* influences. They are virtually everywhere filtering across and through the shared canonical story. Thus, such attestations are "early and widespread."[8]

In the most reliable memory stream depicting *Yeshu ha-Notzri*, no viable socioeconomic demographic seemed to endorse his efforts. That is, but one: the destitute; the poor; the disadvantaged. They were his people. They, more than any other character profile, sought his prayers. Undeniably, if they could, they would crown a king.[9]

Or could the "royal" influence in gospel development have been orchestrated by romanticized impressions of the *disciples* balancing their own itinerary? Rumors that would eventually manage to get *Yeshu ha-Notzri* killed …

When Jesus had spoken these words, he went forth with his disciples across the Kidron valley, where there was a garden, which he and his disciples entered. Now Judas, who betrayed him, also knew the place; for Jesus often met there with his disciples. So Judas, procuring a band of soldiers and some officers from the chief priests and the Pharisees, went there with lanterns and torches and weapons (Jn 18.1-3, RSV).

In the end, the whole lot of them (aka "original supporters") would flee the cross. Like rats from the proverbial burning ship. The four canonical accounts consistently memorialized that no disciple had lingered to witness the Nazarene's violent death (Mt 27.55-56; Mk 15.40; Lk 23.49; Jn 19.25). Not one. Why is that?

Very suspiciously, at the arrest scene neither Rome nor Jerusalem appeared to be after any of these, arguably, marginal characters. At the garden site no one but Jesus was apprehended by a massive force of arms.

This reliable snapshot represents a somewhat strange coincidence since in the gospels these individuals had lingered in plain sight at the scene of the crime. The Nazarene's captors had amassed in overwhelming numbers. According to a reliable shared thread, the old olive grove, presumably dubbed "Gethsem'ane" by later Christian pilgrims, had managed to preserve numerous authentic impressions.

As far as disregarded disciples, our knowledge of the eventual outcome forces further deliberation: Why did they abandon their leader? Why hadn't they at least been picked up for questioning? Had any among them colluded with Judas? Was some reason other than cowardice behind abandoning Yeshu at the cross?

Drilldown on just a few of the disciple profiles places further suspicion around the whole "loyalty" scenario. Between the lines some of these individuals hinted at anything but straight shooters. Faithful devotees. Starry-eyed seekers beholden to their mystic sage. In reality, legitimate impressions do suggest that some were far closer to social pariahs. Marginal players at times nursing extreme grudges worthy of vicious criminals.

In the ancient past how individuals were identified in the social mix often portrayed symbolic meanings. People's assigned names regularly indicated the character behind the persona. So etymologies often traced how individuals were seen by others within society.[10] This key observation seriously plays into the oldest memory threads surrounding *Yeshu ha-Notzri's* early supporters.

In the synoptic stories, early on the co-called *Bo-aner'ges brothers* (Mk 3.17) had entered the picture. Their profiles were right in line with the scriptural "Sons of Thunder" the *Bo-aner'ges* name invoked.[11] Images of bloodshed and carnage clouded their path.[12]

Half-hidden in sacramentally textured prose lies a far more critical, intemperate gaze. In one scene a Samaritan hamlet impeded their way. "Lord, do you want us to bid fire come down from heaven and consume them?" [the brothers asked] (Lk 9.54, RSV).

In isolation these words evoke harsh, brutal images no objective reader could miss. What may surprise us: the sons of Zeb'edee (again, see Mk 3.17) were not alone.

In this collage of violent characters, even more stark than the *Bo-aner'ges brothers*, a genuine *cutthroat* had somehow joined the band. Simon "the Zealot" (Lk 6.15, Acts 1.13) was portrayed as an original disciple.

Who was this Jesus the Nazarene that recruited stone-cold killers? If historical, Simon had emerged from the most radicalized political faction in Roman Palestine. The most active organized group resisting occupation.[13] But that is only half the story.

During the Nazarene's lifetime, so-called "Zealots" were more likely common "brigands" or "bandits."[14] The Zealot nomenclature became commonplace only decades later. During or after the first Roman War. When the synoptic texts were presumably formulated.

In Scriptures the term lacked historical ties "as evidence for a pre-war Zealot party."[15] Portrayed in the gospel story, Simon was merely a brigand or bandit. Nevertheless, through the later designation, most likely a disaffected, looming figure most people would take necessary steps to avoid.

The original Greek name "Philip" also preserved violent undertones. Interestingly, in the Johannine Gospel Philip was one of a handful of original disciples. We cite here an early 20th century expert commentary:

> *Philip* is Greek: … *a lover of horses*, meaning a knight, *warlike*. For Philip was as a warhorse of Christ against the Jews and infidels. Concerning this, see the Apoc. (vi. 2), "and behold a white horse, and he that sat upon him had a bow, and a crown was given unto him, and he went forth conquering and to conquer."[16]

Flashbacked to a reconstructed historical setting and the connotations were obvious. The name "Philip" implied *warlike* or extremely "aggressive."

In synoptic tradition the disciple Philip was always mentioned alongside the disciple "Bartholomew" (Mt 10.3; Mk 3.18; Lk 6.14). In *John's Gospel*

Philip appeared beside Nathan'a-el (Jn 1.45, 48). From that basis scholarship has concluded that the disciples "Nathan'a-el" and "Bartholomew" probably represented the same individual.[17]

Within this logic, interestingly, the Greek name for Bartholomew is "Ptolemaios" (or Ptolemy).[18] Hellenistic kings out of Egypt went by this name. So during antiquity such a given name was popular among the common people. Should we be surprised that "Ptolemy" also meant *warlike* in its original form?[19]

Next was *Simon Peter.* Or Simon "Bar-Jona." Leave off the hyphen and the name translated to "bariona." Or *Simon Bariona.* We must point in that direction because discerning experts have revealed that the more familiar "Simon, son of Jonah" contains stylistic peculiarities. In fact, "without any parallels in biblical, or talmudic literature."[20] Ultimately, consistent with this study's focus, the *Simon, son of Jonah,* naming was extremely doubtful in history.

So now we are properly situated to encounter a more dependable theme: "Bariona" in the original Aramaic meant "fugitive from justice, or outlaw."[21] A rendering that would presumably strike **h-o-r-r-o-r** in the hearts of later canonical religious editors shaping oral memories into written forms.

Related, "Simon means 'Hot-tempered, Volatile, and Violent.'"[22] A twofold rendering that would, coincidentally, fit neatly with the Sons of Thunder, Simon the Zealot, and the two "warlike" characters.

Hopefully, readers are now beginning to get a clearer picture of an original thematic *context* behind the Nazarene's (so-called) closest followers. And plausible thematic strings behind his betrayal.

Historically infused snapshots decisively inform us that an authentic backdrop to the Nazarene's story was not built upon first-century "flower children" or harmless hellenistic "cynics" miraculously transmutated from the Athenian Agora.

The fact is initial threads (still preserved in the stories) impressed upon their audiences that numerous first disciples were hardened, angry men. Dangerous men.

However, we should also bear in mind that direct access to some form of early resurrection account dramatically impacted at least some within the group. This astonishing narrative stream would have altered the lives of most anyone who had directly known *Yeshu ha-Notzri*. And previously witnessed his miraculous *signs*.

Quite expectedly, after the Nazarene's passing, at least several first disciples devoted their remaining days to memorializing his words and deeds. Their lives had been irrevocably altered by the teacher's shocking reappearance. A recipient of Yahweh's ultimate power and beneficence. Inexplicably portrayed in a land dominated by pagan intervention, autocratic betrayal, random suffering, and early death.

Given this social backdrop, to properly frame a historical core, at all cost we should avoid romanticized themes. We should remind ourselves that Simon Bariona was remembered in *John's Gospel* as having cut off the ear of the high priest's servant, Malchus: "Then Simon Peter, having a sword, drew it and struck the high priest's slave and cut off his right ear. The slave's name was Malchus" (Jn 18.10, RSV).

This brief recollection is entirely consistent with the thumbnail sketch drawn herein. We should probably remind ourselves that Peter was the only disciple in the New Testament who was witnessed performing an overtly *violent* act.[23]

In a similar way, the surname in "Judas Iscariot" is informative. This family name derived from the Latin/Semitic transcription *sicarius* or "assassin." Some scholars faithfully track this reading.[24] That would be in opposition to a Judean town or village called *Kerioth*. For reference, see: "Now the name of Hebron formerly was Kiríath-arba" (Josh 14.15, RSV).

An interesting memory was preserved in *Matthew's Gospel*:

And as he sat at table in the house, behold, many tax collectors and sinners came and sat down with Jesus and his disciples. And when the Pharisees saw this, they said to his disciples, "Why does your teacher eat with tax collectors and sinners?" But when he heard it, he said, "Those who are well have no need of a physician, but those who are sick. Go and learn what this means, 'I desire mercy, and not sacrifice.' For I came not to call the righteous, but sinners" (Mt 9.13, RSV).

Remarkable thematic consistency in the naming of numerous *original* disciples lent a direct focus on which category of "sinners" the ministry of Jesus seemed to attract. Answer: the violent kind. Yes, the *category* in question would consistently translate to men of undiluted *violence*. Individuals living on the fringes of society. Those who would be most prone to forming into *revolutionary* groups. In this context, should we be so surprised if the disciples had harbored a hidden agenda: to crown an Israelite king?

We read more than once in New Testament studies that the Nazarene's early disciples came from "the poor people in the towns and villages of Galilee."[25] In the case of his immediate followers predominantly *violent* poor people may aptly be added.

Hopefully, readers are beginning to get a taste for more historically reliable themes. Earlier in the original oral tradition, half-obscured memories were intended to draw certain impressions. Again, *historical realities* suggest to us that in many ways the real story of Jesus radically parted company with later popular appraisals slanted by post-Palestine, hellenized, religious editors.

What are we really saying? The original story was not filled with lost lambs and smiling children. In fact, the most primitive strands of tradition in some ways radically bucked romanticized imagery evoked by traditional Pauline-Christian ecclesiology.

At some meaningful level, the original story represented an aggressive bugle call for native Israelite *renewal*. Ultimate salvation from Roman and Jerusalem elite tyranny. A very real, cultically accessible, response to the historical setting of first-century Palestine.

When focusing the lens on historical probabilities, one gets the sense that *Yeshu ha-Notzri* would take any necessary measure to preserve his sacred *Promised Land*. Was violent resistance possible? Maybe. Maybe not.

We know one thing for sure: Jesus the Nazarene was crucified at "Gol'gotha (which means the place of a skull)" (Mt 27.33; Mk 15.22; Jn 19.17, RSV). "No amount of intra-Jewish religious quarreling, which provides the bulk of the gospels' contents, can explain Jesus' very political, very Roman execution."[26] Through Roman eyes, the Nazarene's "sin" was *politically*, not *religiously*, invoked.

We don't have to go far to cogently articulate this highly suggestive snapshot. Overwhelmingly, impartial narrative evidence suggests *Yeshu ha-Notzri* was surrounded by very dubious characters. Extremely violent men. A reality that lends penetrating historical insight to his most cruel demise. That he was *crucified* is an established fact.[27] And may hold a breadcrumb of historical irony.

In the pursuit of authentic memories we cannot ignore the cross. Yeshu hung between two so-called "robbers" (Mt 27.38; Mk 15.27, RSV). Given the social backdrop probably more accurately depicted as vessels of Judaic resistance. They had just happened to be in the wrong place at the wrong time.[28] Count that three out of three.

For most people today, on top of these rather unorthodox ideas, in the previous century Rome had conquered the whole Palestinian region. In the Nazarene's day, an overriding impression is that the foreign, pagan occupiers were *hated* by most local Judaic populations.[29] Would the historical Jesus and his early followers be included in this demographic mix? Very, very hard to say *no*. His historical ministry notoriously avoided pagans (Mt 10.5-6; 15.24; Mk 7.27; Jn 4.22) and urban zones where such population groups more often situated.[30]

From the first page, this entire narrative stream begs for additional evidence. Probably for most readers the logic behind some ideas, at least, seems so extreme as to exist beyond the scope of reality. Further, most modern scholars often avoid related areas of investigation. Determined drilldown is often necessary to even *approach* expert findings. In this study, not "all for naught," however.

So what of the time and place setting? What about physical artifacts? Can we paint a sympathetic picture that reasonably tracks the historical figure to at least some of the intersecting data points suggested above?

This study is not devoted to vaguely recalled conspiracies and "fringe theories" regarding the life of a legitimate historical figure. Nevertheless, archaeology definitely has something important to say about life in first-century Palestine. Let us turn the page to physical remains.

CHAPTER THREE
References

Adams, *Samuel L. Social and Economic Life in Second Temple Judea* (Louisville, KY: Westminster John Knox Press, 2014). (Abbr. "Social-Economic Life")

Aune, David E. *Jesus, Gospel Tradition and Paul in the Context of Jewish and Greco-Roman Antiquity: Collected Essays II* (Tübingen, Germany: Mohr Siebeck, 2013). (Abbr. "Gospel Tradition and Paul")

Barker, Margaret. *Revelation of Jesus Christ: Which God Gave to Him to Show to His Servants What Must Soon Take Place* (Revelation 1.1) (Edinburgh, Scotland: T&T Clark Ltd, 2000). (Abbr. "Revelation of Jesus Christ")

Bermejo-Rubio, Fernando and Zeichmann, Christopher B. "Where Were the Romans and What Did They Know? Military and Intelligence Networks as a Probable Factor in Jesus of Nazareth's Fate," *Scripta Classica Israelica* (2019), pp. 83-116. (Abbr. "Where Were the Romans")

Bird, Michael F. *Jesus and the Origins of the Gentile Mission* (New York, NY: T&T Clark International, 2006). (Abbr. "Jesus and Origins")

Brandon, S. G. F. *Jesus and the Zealots: A Study of the Political Factor in Primitive Christianity* (New York, NY: Charles Scribner's Sons, 1967). (Abbr. "Jesus and Zealots")

Buchanan, George Wesley. *The Consequences of the Covenant* (Leiden, The Netherlands: Brill, 1970). (Abbr. "Consequences of the Covenant")

Charlesworth, James H. *The Historical Jesus: An Essential Guide* (Nashville, TN: Abingdon Press, 2008). (Abbr. "Historical Jesus Essential Guide")

Cresswell, Peter. *Jesus the Terrorist* (Hants, UK: O Books, 2010). (Abbr. "Jesus the Terrorist")

Cullmann, Oscar. *The State in the New Testament* (New York, NY: Charles Scribner's Sons, 1956). (Abbr. "State in New Testament")

Culpepper, R. Alan. *John, the Son of Zebedee: The Life of a Legend* (Columbia, SC: University of South Carolina Press, 1994). (Abbr. "John, Son of Zebedee")

Donaldson, T. L. "Rural Bandits, City Mobs, and the Zealots," *Journal for the Study of Judaism in the Persian, Hellenistic, and Roman Period*, Vol. 21, No. 1 (JUNE 1990), pp. 19-40. (Abbr. "City Mobs and Zealots")

Duling, Dennis C. "The Jesus Movement and Network Analysis," in *The Social Setting of Jesus and the Gospels*, Stegemann, Wolfgang, et. al., eds. (Minneapolis, MN: Fortress Press, 2002). (Abbr. "Network Analysis")

Eisler, Robert. *The Enigma of the Fourth Gospel, Its Author and Its Writer* (London, England: Methuen & Co. Ltd., 1938). (Abbr. "Enigma Fourth Gospel")

Evans, Craig A. *Jesus and His Contemporaries: Comparative Studies* (Leiden, The Netherlands, Brill Academic Publishers, Inc., 2001). (Abbr. "Jesus and His Contemporaries")

Ferguson, John. *Jesus in the Tide of Time: An Historical Study* (London, UK: Routledge & Kegan Paul, 1980). (Abbr. "Jesus Tide of Time")

Fiensy, David A. *Christian Origins and the Ancient Economy* (Eugene, OR: Cascade Books, 2014). (Abbr. "Christian Origins")

Fredriksen, Paula. "Arms and The Man: A Response to Dale Martin's 'Jesus in Jerusalem: Armed and Not Dangerous'," *Journal for the Study of the New Testament*, Volume 37, Issue 3 (2015), pp. 312-325. (Abbr. "Arms and the Man")

Free, Michael L. *CBT and Christianity: Strategies and Resources for Reconciling Faith in Therapy* (West Sussex, UK: John Wiley & Sons, Ltd., 2015). (Abbr. "CBT and Christianity")

Goodman, Martin. *The Ruling Class of Judaea: The Origins of the Jewish Revolt Against Rome A.D. 66 – 70* (New York, NY: Cambridge University Press, 1987). (Abbr. "Ruling Class")

Green, Joel B., et al., eds. *Dictionary of Jesus and the Gospels: A Compendium of Contemporary Biblical Scholarship* (Downers Grove, IL: InterVarsity Press, 1992). (Abbr. "Compendium Contemporary Biblical Scholarship")

Hirschberg, Harris. "Simon Bariona and the Ebionites," *Journal of Biblical Literature*, Vol. 61, No. 3 (Sep., 1942), pp. 171-191. (Abbr. "Simon Bariona")

Horsley, Richard A. "Popular Messianic Movements around the Time of Jesus," *The Catholic Biblical Quarterly*, Vol. 46, No. 3 (July, 1984), pp. 471-495. (Abbr. "Popular Messianic Movements")

Horsley, Richard A. "The Zealots. Their Origin, Relationships and Importance in the Jewish Revolt," *Novum Testamentum*, Vol. 28, Fasc. 2 (Apr., 1986), pp. 159-192. (Abbr. "Zealots: Origin, Relationships")

Horsley, Richard A. "Unearthing a People's History," in *Christian Origins*, Horsley, Richard A., ed. (Minneapolis, MN: Augsburg Fortress, 2010), pp. 1-22. (Abbr. "People's History")

Keene, Michael. *St. Mark's Gospel and the Christian Faith* (Cheltenham, UK: Stanley Thomes Publishers Ltd., 2002). (Abbr. "St. Mark's Gospel").

Lapide, Cornelius à. *The Great Commentary of Cornelius à Lapide: S. Matthew's Gospel – Chapters X-XXI*, Mossman, Thomas W., trans. (Edinburgh, Scotland: John Grant, 1908). (Abbr. "The Great Commentary")

Lee, G. Avery. *The Glorious Company* (Nashville, TN: Broadman Press, 1986). (Abbr. "The Glorious Company")

Luff, Rosemary Margaret. *The Impact of Jesus in First-Century Palestine: Textual and Archaeological Evidence for Long-standing Discontent* (New York, NY: Cambridge University Press, 2019). (Abbr. "Impact of Jesus")

McDowell, Sean. *The Fate of the Apostles: Examining the Martyrdom Accounts of the Closest Followers of Jesus* (New York, NY: Routledge, 2016). (Abbr. "Fate of the Apostles")

McIver, Robert K. "The Archaeology of Galilee and Palestine from the Maccabees to the Jewish Second Jewish Revolt (167 BC-AD 135)," in *The Content and the Setting of the Gospel Tradition*, Harding, Mark and Nobbs, Alanna, eds. (Grand Rapids, MI: William B. Eerdmans Publishing Company, 2010), 1-27. (Abbr. "Archaeology, Galilee, and Palestine")

Meier, John P. *A Marginal Jew: The Roots of the Problem and the Person − Volume 1* (New York, NY: Doubleday, 1991). (Abbr. "Roots of the Problem")

Nomenology Project. *The Hidden Truth of Your Name: A Complete Guide to First Names and What They Say About the Real You* (New York, NY: The Random House Publishing Group, 1999). (Abbr. "Guide to First Names")

Root, Bradley W. *First Century Galilee: A Fresh Examination of the Sources* (Tübingen, Germany: Mohr Siebeck, 2014). (Abbr. "First Century Galilee")

Schnabel, Eckhard J. *Mark* (Downers Grove, IL: Intervarsity Press, 2017). (Abbr. "Mark")

Schröter, Jens. "Jesus of Galilee: The Role of Location in Understanding Jesus," in *Jesus Research: An International Perspective: − The Proceedings of the Biennial Princeton-Prague Symposium on the Current State of Studies on the Historical Jesus*, Charlesworth, J. H. and Pokorný, Petr, eds. (Grand Rapids, MI: William B. Eerdmans Publishing Company, 2009), pp. 36-55. (Abbr. "Jesus of Galilee")

Thomas Nelson, *The King James Study Bible* (Nashville, TN: Thomas Nelson Publishing Company, 1988). (Abbr. "King James Study Bible")

Watt, Jan van der and Kok, Jacobus. "Violence in a Gospel of Love," in *Coping with Violence in the New Testament*, Villiers, Pieter G. R. de and

Henten, Jan Willem van, eds. (Leiden, The Netherlands: Brill, 2012), pp. 151-184. (Abbr. "Violence Gospel of Love")

Wilson, A. N. *Jesus: A Life* (New York, NY: W. W. Norton & Company, 2004). (Abbr. "Jesus: A Life")

CHAPTER THREE
Endnotes

1 Schröter 2009, Jesus of Galilee, 46; Fiensy 2014, Christian Origins, 32; Root 2014; First Century Galilee, 61.

2 McIver 2010, Archaeology, Galilee, and Palestine, 25.

3 Bermejo-Rubio and Zeichmann 2019, Where Were the Romans, 86.

4 For this study, this whole line of thinking was originally inspired by Richard Horsley's influential early 80s article: "Popular Messianic Movements around the Time of Jesus," The Catholic Biblical Quarterly, Vol. 46, No. 3 (July, 1984), pp. 471-495.

5 Horsley 1984, Popular Messianic Movements, 485.

6 Evans 2001, Jesus and His Contemporaries, 53-82.

7 Horsley 1984, Popular Messianic Movements, 475.

8 Meier 1991, Roots of the Problem, 219.

9 Brandon 1967, Jesus and Zealots, 16-18.

10 Nomenology Project 1999, Guide to First Names, 4.

11 Culpepper 1994, John, the Son of Zebedee, 39-40.

12 Keene 2002, St. Mark's Gospel, 81.

13 Wilson 2004, Jesus: A Life, 128.

14 Horsley 1986, Zealots: Origin, Relationships, 190.

15 Donaldson 1990, City Mobs and Zealots, 23.

16 Lapide 1908, The Great Commentary, 7.

17 Lee 1986, The Glorious Company, 62; Green et al., eds. 1992, Compendium Contemporary Biblical Scholarship, 10; McDowell 2016, Fate

of the Apostles, 27.

18 Schnabel 2017, Mark, 88.

19 S. L. Adams 2014, Social-Economic Life, 146.

20 For a full discussion, see Hirschberg 1942, Simon Bariona, 171-191.

21 Eisler 1938, Enigma Fourth Gospel, 71; Hirschberg 1942, Simon Bariona, 172; Cullmann 1956, State in New Testament, 16-17; Buchanan 1970, Consequences of the Covenant, 39; Ferguson 1980, Jesus Tide of Time, 41; Barker 2000, Revelation of Jesus Christ, 55.

22 Thomas Nelson, King James Study Bible, 1607.

23 Watt and Kok 2012, Violence Gospel of Love, 168-169.

24 An interesting and comprehensive interpretation is found here: Cresswell 2010, Jesus the Terrorist, 287-331.

25 Free 2015, CBT and Christianity, 42.

26 Fredriksen 2015, Arms and the Man, 312.

27 No qualified scholar questions this conclusion. References here are entirely redundant.

28 Brandon 1967, Jesus and Zealots, xiv.

29 Across the first-century era Palestinian populations somehow had to manage existence skirting "the oppressive Roman legions and a Roman governor" (Charlesworth 2008, Historical Jesus Essential Guide, 47). Also, see Goodman 1987, Ruling Class, 9-11; Horsley 2010, People's History, 8.

30 Duling 2002, Network Analysis, 325; Bird 2006, Jesus and Origins, 103; Aune 2012, Gospel Tradition and Paul, 217; Luff 2019, Impact of Jesus, 192.

4

Physical Evidence

For Palestinian archaeology 1968 proved to be a memorable year. First, largescale excavations got underway in Jerusalem at a site near the Temple Mount. The unearthings would last a full 10 years.[1] In the same year, three years beyond archaeological digs at Masada, remains of the 28 last defenders were reburied.[2]

In May of that year, *The Biblical Archaeologist* published astonishing findings on the oldest dwellings yet uncovered in Palestine (9000 years removed).[3] The remains had been excavated at the Neolithic site of *Beidha* ("Little Petra") near Petra, Jordan.

In 1968, too, around the midway point, just north of Jerusalem, archaeologists uncovered limestone ossuaries. This was near Mount Scopus. Four ancient cave-tombs were discovered. This site properly frames the life and times. Our determined focus.

Adding traction to our study, a quarter of the recovered skeletons (nine individuals out of thirty-five) had met *extreme* circumstances around the time of death:

Three children (determined from eight months to eight years) had died from starvation.

An arrow had penetrated the skull of a fourth child who had apparently experienced prolonged suffering prior to death.

A young woman (probably in her early twenties) had perished in flames.

A young man around the age of the young woman had also died in a fire. But evidence produced by bone charring suggested that the man was intentionally flayed on a rack or some related instrument of torture.

Another young man in his mid-twenties had been crucified. A nail was still wedged in his ankle along with a preserved piece of olive wood.

A woman who was probably in her early thirties had died in childbirth. The unborn fetus was still lodged in her pelvis.

An elderly woman had died instantly from a blow to the head. We have to assume that this was accomplished by a mace-like weapon.[4]

The other bones were from individuals who presumably died by illness or accident. Many experts agree that the historical trend was poor health, early mortality, and violent times.[5] These bones, matching wildly divergent demographics, suggest as much.

Let's take a closer look. Most of us have watched enough television to surf past fire, torture, crucifixion, maces to the head. What jumps out is three *starving* children aged eight months to eight years. Starving children? How did little kids living near the Holy City die from starvation around the time of Jesus? Wouldn't someone have discovered them and offered help?

Experts look at the 1968 dig as too small for designating societal trends. But we have to think: was this report anomalous? Was starvation widespread in first-century Palestine?

We must view the world around us. Not our world. The ancient world. To form credible snapshots we have nowhere to turn but to modern day experts.

In 1973 and 1976 a team of archaeologists conducted an extensive field survey. The team explored 20 first-century sites in territorial Galilee. Both Upper and Lower regions. As well as the Golan. In the Galilee at Meiron (formerly "Merom"), pathological data produced significant numbers of *child mortality*.

Experts concluded that the data suggested a high incidence of "protein and iron deficiencies ... caused either by disease or 'socioeconomic' conditions."[6] In other words, high rates of poverty.

Key to understanding the results was the presence in Galilee of unusually small agricultural plot sizes.[7] And the entire region overwhelmingly identified itself as an agrarian society.[8] Thus, archaeology team leaders concluded that in first-century Galilee many farming families lived "on the subsistence margin."[9] They simply didn't have enough to eat.

In plain language farming sites lacked proper spatial dimensions. Tilled fields could not possibly produce economic returns necessary to minimally sustain the nutritional needs of whole families.[10]

Even in this abbreviated investigation we might be inclined to wonder. Why on earth did rural Galilean homesteads lack the nominal acreage necessary to produce minimal economic yields? Harvests that adequately met basic needs. Many farming plots were just too small. But why?

The disadvantaged, who earned their living off the sweat of their brow, would have known this fact instinctively. They would not have needed modern-day specialists to tell them. If so, then what happened? Why did Galilean families go hungry? Why did they settle on undersized farming plots?

Important for us, we need to understand that these comments are not blind speculation. They are based on competent archaeological surveys. And conclusions drawn by legitimate experts.

These modern specialists are fairly clear that evidence exists defending the argument of smaller land divisions being absorbed into larger estates.[11] If our scholars are correct, then entire villages at times had been transformed into holdings owned by a single elite interest.[12] In their turn, many local farmers and their families were subjugated to becoming mere "dayworkers." Maybe that is one legitimate explanation.

Simply put, ancestral farms of rustic folk were giving way to larger holdings. Such estates were controlled by socio-political-economic elites. These elites almost always lived in urban zones.[13]

In an agricultural dominated economy, farm produce translated to wealth. Entire farming communities were being absorbed into vast agricultural estates. The few aristocrats that owned such holdings possessed influence and power that dominated the inner world of first-century Palestine.

However, that still does not answer the basic question – why? Why would small farmers voluntarily relinquish the means to their survival as freemen? Why would the common people downsize to land holdings that inadequately met their primary needs? Why would local farmers voluntarily drive their own families into economic ruin as day laborers (or worse)?

If archaeology and accounts in the Hebrew Mishnah are to some extent accurate, attention must focus on the subjects of political and economic power. That is, power to incur long-term debt. Power to subjugate entire rural communities when the debt instruments were left unfulfilled. Such a unique profile must relate either to invasion by outsiders. Or internal elite persecution on a macro scale that over time bled the people dry.

Within this devastating socioeconomic model sons and daughters of tenant farmers were defenseless against debt slavery. Such a catastrophic outcome would occur when the father either lost his land, suffered serious illness, or was substantially upside down to lenders.[14]

Such elite disdain and blind disregard of peasant populations was not unique to Palestine. Regardless of ethnic affiliations, across the Mediterranean the wealthy dominated ancient society.[15]

In the Land of Israel, what was in fact *unique* in the activities of the elite class was their open, unselfconscious disregard of ancient Mosaic law. In Hebrew Scriptures, torah-based cautionary prescriptions against exploiting the poor were too numerous to count. A few examples are mentioned below:

If you lend money to any of my people with you who is poor, you shall not be to him as a creditor, and you shall not exact interest from him. If ever you take your neighbor's garment in pledge, you shall restore it to him before the sun goes down; for that is his only covering, it is his mantle for his body; in what else shall he sleep? And if he cries to me, I will hear, for I am compassionate (Ex 22:25-27, RSV).

Take no interest from him or increase, but fear your God; that your brother may live beside you (Lev 25:36, RSV).

To a foreigner you may lend upon interest, but to your brother you shall not lend upon interest; that the Lord your God may bless you in all that you undertake in the land which you are entering to take possession of it (Deut 23:20, RSV).

At the end of every seven years you shall grant a release. And this is the manner of the release: every creditor shall release what he has lent to his neighbor; he shall not exact it of his neighbor, his brother, because the Lord's release has been proclaimed (Deut 15:1-2, RSV).

As a practical matter, in the spirit of Torah and righteous conduct, even Flavius Josephus the wealthy Roman sympathizer offered ethical guidance to his Palestinian countrymen:

Let no one lend to any one of the Hebrews upon usury, neither usury of what is eaten or what is drunken, for it is not just to make advantage of the misfortunes of one of thy own countrymen; but when thou hast been assistant to his necessities, think it thy gain if thou obtainest their gratitude to thee; and withal that reward which will come to thee from God, for thy humanity towards him (Josephus, *Ant* 4.8.25, RSV).

It is important to recognize the role of longstanding scriptural admonitions supporting the disadvantaged. Prevailing tradition in fact attempted to protect the rights of those less fortunate. Today's scholars generally agree.[16]

However, throughout ancient Palestine, day-to-day living was far more divisive and unquestionably divided along class lines of demarcation. It all came down to this single point: during the first century the priorities and expectations of many elites were fulfilled through direct exploitation of the agricultural economy of the poor. Among many well-to-do this seems to have become a general rule.

This "general rule" would have unselfconsciously seeped into the daily lives of most rural folk living in Galilee and other parts. For all but the filthy rich daily life was reduced to a mean struggle just to survive.[17] This era witnessed a steady stream of poor who lost their lands to aristocrats. The Palestinian socioeconomic mix was far more similar to the Roman model than ever before.[18]

To some extent, the gospel stories reflected this rather cruel paradigm.[19] But at times underemphasized and half-hidden in innuendo.

A few years beyond the 1973 and 1976 digs, in the 1980s the Sackler School of Medicine in Tel Aviv excavated an archaeological site in Nazareth (Galilee). Most readers will recognize this location as the traditional ancestral home of Jesus. Their findings were illuminating and in some ways supplemented the conclusions of the '73 and '76 surveys.

The final report spoke of "Harris lines" and a profound lack of bone growth. Bottom line: findings revealed that half of all children born in or near Nazareth "never reached the age of five."[20]

A running hypothesis suggested a rather sweeping and depressing trend. Over a defined historical range, many people in rural Galilee lacked basic nutrition to sustain what we would consider a "normal lifespan."

Related, we can't let the following go unmentioned: by far, experts looking at ancient times to present-day saw parts of the Galilean region as the most nutrition-rich agricultural environment in all of Palestine.[21]

We know now that lack of proper nourishment weakens resistance to all the biological entities that thrive within population groups. There is no way getting around this basic fact. Obviously, ancient populations would have been enormously impacted by poor diets.

In all fairness we should probably consider that the initial 1968 Jerusalem dig does not seem so "out of left field" after all. During the Jesus era, children living near Jerusalem could conceivably have died of complications linked to exceedingly poor health brought on by dietary and related complaints. Undeniable evidence of such a phenomenon was archaeologically supported in the Galilean region.

Drilling down further on this general topic, the statistical results of numerous first-century mortality studies across a wide geographical range flirt on the *unfathomable*. Qualified experts would tell us the story of Jesus emerged in a culture regulated by a median mortality rate somewhere in the *early to mid-twenties*.[22]

Supporting this overall conclusion, based on studies in Egypt,[23] other experts inform us that life expectancy throughout the Roman Empire was 25 to 30 years of age.

Further, for more specific results, at the ancient Roman port of Ostia, modern archeologist digs revealed that about 80 percent of those buried had died before 30 years old.[24] Again, 80 percent! These two rather largescale studies have left many modern day specialists thinking that illness and related complaints dominated the lives of most ancient populations.[25]

One final comment takes a look at the ancient Judaic privileged or aristocratic sector in Jerusalem. Conspicuously, in Yeshu's day the rich would have constituted a small fraction of the overall population. Nevertheless, the following account adds an interesting footnote to the overall discussion.

In November 1990, while excavating south of the Old City's Temple Mount for a proposed waterpark (in Jerusalem's *Peace Forest*), a bulldozer penetrated the roof of a first-century burial cave. Amongst other discoveries, the cave revealed an "extravagantly ornate" ossuary that faced the former Jewish Temple.[26] The ossuary was situated in a large cemetery with rock-cut burial chambers. According to experts, the cemetery dated somewhere between the first century BCE and the first century CE.

From the uncovered tomb the remains stood out as incredibly ornate.[27] Experts concluded that this was the resting place of an individual of immense wealth.[28] On its side, crudely carved (probably with an iron nail) was the name *Yehosef bar Qafa* (Joseph, son of Ca'iaphas).[29] Curiously, for those who are unaware, the hereditary name of "Ca'iaphas" was rare in Jewish antiquity.[30]

In scriptural history Joseph Ca'iaphas (alternate: *Yosef Bar Kayafa*) held the post of high priest in Jerusalem from 26 CE to 37 CE. Then procurator of the Palestinian territories of Judea and Samaria, Valerius Gratus, under the Roman emperor Tiberius, had appointed him.[31] Ca'iaphas had presided as president of the Jewish Council (*Sanhedrin*, a "sitting together" or "council").

High Priest Ca'iaphas is mentioned in three Christian Testament Gospels (Mt 26.3, 57; Lk 3.2; Jn 11.49; 18.13, 14, 24, 28), as well as in the *Book of Acts* (4.6). He is also mentioned in the writings of the ancient historian Flavius Josephus (*Ant* 18.2.2; 18.4.3). Incidentally, some scholars believe Ca'iaphas – not Judas, the Sanhedrin, or Pilate – bore ultimate responsibility for the crucifixion of Jesus (see Mk 14.61-64; Jn 11.49-50; 18.24, 28, 30, 35).[32]

The Ca'iaphas ossuary (not at all surprising in New Testament scholarship – some experts disputed the finding[33]) was not the only news that November day in 1990. Inside the burial chamber 63 additional skeletons were unearthed.

Forensic analysis disclosed that several of the skeletons had suffered from parasites. Others showed signs of "degenerative disease."[34] 40 percent of those individuals had died *before five years old*. More than 6 Judeans out of 10 in the Ca'iaphas family tomb *had never reached puberty*.[35]

When one is reminded that most (if not all) of these individuals represented socioeconomic elites, such statistical data translates to *inconceivable*.

Actually – more than that. The individuals buried in the Ca'iaphas family tomb – for the times – were not just rich people. They were *filthy* rich people!

The Ca'iaphas clan would have occupied extremely lavish accommodations. They would have been privy to the meat provided by sacrifices from Judaic believers at the Jerusalem temple.[36]

In addition, we know for certain that this particular family would have had access to flowing water and underground plumbing.[37] Such luxuries would have been regarded as unthinkable to the common population.

Undoubtedly, within the ancient setting, Joseph Ca'iaphas and his kin, with probably no exceptions, would have defined "the one-tenth of one percent"[38] so often bandied about today. Across Palestine social-political-economic elites were almost an imperceptible quantitative fraction of the population. Such a relatively thin slice from the aggregate Jewish-Palestinian mainstream was vastly far from representative of all Israelites.[39]

In terms of health and welfare, the remains discovered in Jerusalem's *Peace Forest* indisputably represented the very *crème de la crème* of first-century Palestinian society. Yet the study's underlying results strongly suggested that *all* Palestinian social strata – not just the disadvantaged – experienced degrees of what we today would consider *extreme circumstances* that most often translated to early death.

To reinforce this whole thematic flow, reliable sources report a live birthrate in the ancient territorial setting of *forty per thousand*.[40] That translates to a shocking *forty live babies delivered out of every one thousand pregnancies!* Today, most of us would probably ask: is that really feasible? These are appalling figures. Truly unbelievable.

Taking this all in, what are we getting at? The probable answer is life for nearly all Israelites was filled with dramatic and often profound setbacks. Illness and suffering dominated the era. Already mentioned, most individuals in first-century Palestine died long before the age of 30. Statistically, much closer to the age of 20. Male and female. From the Ca'iaphas discovery we can almost definitively add: rich and poor.

How does this statistical survey impact our impressions of the earliest footprint of Jesus? Clearly, during the first century death was a constant companion. That a primitive oral tradition arose around the figure of a village *healer* is probably not so out of whack. The archaeological record certainly does not eliminate this view.

Ancient Israel was a patently *religious* culture. During the late second-temple period, people would have been desperate to glimpse cultically-inspired answers to the catastrophic mortality rate. So why we *really* remember the historical Jesus probably needs reassessing in the wake of archeology and a more focused understanding of the time and place setting.

We are reminded of Joseph the reputed father figure in the canonical accounts. Maybe some readers might have noticed his absence in most of the gospel stories. The traditional family patriarch was barely mentioned in these tales. The narrative testimony strongly suggests that if Joseph was historically recalled, then probably he wasn't alive far into Yeshu's childhood.[41]

Patriarchal figures played a central role in Judaic society. We need to recognize that the findings of numerous archaeological excavations and consistent mortality statistics uncritically endorse the muted gospel depictions of Joseph from Nazareth.

The socioeconomic picture really does factor into any legitimate understanding of the historical Jesus. In Palestinian zones the era was very much defined by related themes we commonly associate with the poor: inadequate housing, social unrest, poor health and sanitation, and the rest.[42]

The indebtedness of small farmers was an obvious factor. Experts sometimes use colorful language referring to this trend as "a regular process of pauperization."[43] Such imagery depicting a "process of pauperization" in so many words nowadays seems to comprise a quite popular topic in New Testament studies.[44]

This whole discussion of poverty and poor health measures up to a rather discouraging final assessment. Over the decades of the first century, in the Land of Israel – by any fair measure – things were not getting better. But progressively worse.[45]

The Greek term *ptōchoi* not only refers to the poor but can also describe the *destitute* among the poor – equivalent in modern parlance to "beggars."[46] This very real ancient subclass was assiduously represented in all four New Testament Gospels (Mt 19.21, 26.9, 11; Mk 10.21, 14.5, 7; Lk 7.36-50, 18.22, 19.8; Jn 12.1-8, 13.29).

Further drilldown reveals to scholars that the hypothetical Q tradition seems to associate Jesus with "the begging poor (*ptōchos*)."[47] Supporting this argument, they link discussion to the *Gospel of Luke*: "And Jesus said to him, 'Foxes have holes, and birds of the air have nests; but the Son of man has nowhere to lay his head'" (Lk 9.58, RSV).

Finally, the following probably puts this phase of the discussion to rest. As shocking as it might sound to us, according to a mid-first-century church father:

> We know that many among us gave themselves up unto bonds, that they might deliver others. Many have given themselves up unto slavery, and, having received their own price, have therewith fed others (Clement of Rome, *First Epistle*, 55.2).

Clement represented a legitimate (and reliable) first-century historical source. While written from Rome, not within territorial Palestine, unlike nearly all writings of the Apostolic Fathers, *I Clement* is sometimes considered roughly contemporary to the production of the written gospel texts.[48]

At the heart of this brief historical fragment, without enough food to eat, apparently early Christians in Rome were selling themselves into slavery to save the lives of fellow believers. *They were starving*!

Inside the Land of Israel, across the decades of the first century, life at times among the poor probably wasn't much better. For us today, there is no missing the fact that a slow-burning momentum towards upheaval and the breakdown of longstanding social structures reinforced essential themes underlying the early Christian commentator just cited above.

For during this same century, the century of John the Baptizer and Jesus the Nazarene, a catastrophic impetus for foreign intervention, unchecked greed, and uncontrolled lust for power had taken hold of the Judaic aristocracy. Ultimately, this terrifying social-cultural breakdown would assure Roman domination and the utter destruction of the Jewish state.

CHAPTER FOUR
References

Adams, Samuel L. Social and Economic Life in Second Temple Judea (Louisville, KY: Westminster John Knox Press, 2014). (Abbr. "Social-Economic Life")

Agosto, Efrain. Servant Leadership: Jesus and Paul (St. Louis, MO: Chalice Press, 2005). (Abbr. "Servant Leadership")

Atkinson, Kenneth. Queen Salome: Jerusalem's Warrior Monarch of the First Century B.C.E. (Jefferson, NC: McFarland and Company, Inc., Publishers, 2003). (Abbr. "Salome")

Beard, Mary. SPQR: A History of Ancient Rome (New York: NY: Liveright Publishing Corporation, 2015). (Abbr. "SPQR")

Beebe, H. Keith. "Ancient Palestinian Dwellings," The Biblical Archaeologist, Vol. 31, No. 2 (May, 1968), pp. 37-58. (Abbr. "Ancient Palestinian Dwellings")

Bock, Darrell L. with Simpson, Benjamin I. Jesus according to Scripture: Restoring the Portrait from the Gospels (Grand Rapids, MI: Baker Academic, 2017). (Abbr. "Restoring Portrait")

Bodley, John H. Anthropology and Contemporary Human Problems, Sixth Edition (Lanham, MD: Altamira Press, 2012). (Abbr. "Bodley, Contemporary Human Problems")

Bolt, Peter G. Jesus' Defeat of Death: Persuading Mark's Early Readers (New York, NY: Cambridge University Press, 2003). (Abbr. "Jesus' Defeat of Death")

Bond, Helen K. The Historical Jesus: A Guide for the Perplexed (New York, NY: T&T Clark International, 2012). (Abbr. "Guide for the Perplexed")

Bond, Helen Katharine. Caiaphas: Friend of Rome and Judge of Jesus? (Louisville, KY: Westminster John Knox Press, 2004). (Abbr. "Caiaphas")

Borg, Marcus J. Conflict, Holiness, and Politics in the Teachings of Jesus (New York, NY: Continuum International Publishing Group, 1998). (Abbr. "Conflict, Holiness, Politics")

Botha, Pieter J. J. Orality and Literacy in Early Christianity (Eugene, OR: Cascade Books, 2012). (Abbr. "Orality and Literacy")

Bruner, Frederick Dale. Matthew – A Commentary: Volume 1: The Christbook, Matthew 1-12. Revised & Expanded Edition (Grand Rapids, MI: William B. Eerdmans Publishing Company, 2004). (Abbr. "Christbook")

Byrne, Ryan and McNary-Zak, Bernadette, eds. Resurrecting the Brother of Jesus: The James Ossuary Controversy and the Quest for Religious Relics (Chapel Hill, NC: The University of North Carolina Press, 2009). (Abbr. "James Ossuary Controversy")

Capps, Donald. Jesus: A Psychological Biography (Eugene, OR: Wipf and Stock Publishers, 2000). (Abbr. "Psychological Biography")

Carson, D. A. The Gospel According to John (Grand Rapids, MI: William B. Eerdmans Publishing Company, 1991). (Abbr. "Gospel John")

Carter, Warren. John: Storyteller, Interpreter, Evangelist (Grand Rapids, MI: Baker Academic, 2006). (Abbr. "Storyteller, Interpreter, Evangelist")

Charlesworth, J. H. "Jesus and Jehohanan: An Archaeological Note on Crucifixion," The Expository Times, February 1, 1973, pp. 147-150. (Abbr. "Jesus and Jehohanan")

Chilton, Bruce. Rabbi Jesus: An Intimate Biography (New York, NY: Doubleday, 2000). (Abbr. "Rabbi Jesus")

Cohn, Haim. The Trial and Death of Jesus (Philadelphia, PA: Westminster Press, 1963). (Abbr. "Trial, Death, Jesus")

Crosby, Stephen R. Healing: Hope Or Hype? Why Genuine Healings are Rare in Local Churches and What We Can Do About It (Durham, CT: Strategic Book Group, 2008). (Abbr. "Healing: Hope or Hype")

Evans, Craig A. Jesus and the Ossuaries (Waco, TX: Baylor University Press, 2003). (Abbr. "Ossuaries")

Evans, Craig A., ed. The Routledge Encyclopedia of the Historical Jesus (New York, NY: Routledge, 2008). (Abbr. "Routledge Encyclopedia Historical Jesus")

Faulkner, Neil. Apocalypse: The Great Jewish Revolt Against Rome AD 66-73 (Glouchestershire, United Kingdom: Amberly Publishing, 2011). (Abbr. "Apocalypse")

Fiensy, David A. Christian Origins and the Ancient Economy (Eugene, OR: Cascade Books, 2014). (Abbr. "Christian Origins")

Freyne, Sean. "The Revolt From a Regional Perspective," in The First Jewish Revolt: Archaeology, History, and Ideology, Berlin, Andrea M. and Overman, J Andrew, eds. (New York, NY: Routledge, 2002), pp. 43 56. (Abbr. "Revolt From Regional Perspective")

Geis, Robert. Life of Christ (Lanham, MD: University Press of America, Inc., 2013). (Abbr. "Life")

Goodman, Martin. The Ruling Class of Judaea: The Origins of the Jewish Revolt Against Rome A.D. 66 – 70 (New York, NY: Cambridge University Press, 1987). (Abbr. "Ruling Class")

Gori, Maja. "The Stones of Contention: The Role of Archaeological Heritage In Israeli-Palestinian Conflict," Archaeologies: Journal of the World Archaeological Congress, Volume 9, Number 1 (April 2013), pp. 213-229. (Abbr. "The Stones of Contention")

Greenberg, Raphael and Keinan, Adi. Israeli Archaeological Activity in the Westbank 1967-2007: A Sourcebook (Jerusalem, Israel: The

Westbank and East Jerusalem Archaeological Database Project, 2009). (Abbr. "Israeli Archaeological Activity 1967-2007")

Hendricks, Jr., Obery M. The Politics of Jesus: Rediscovering the True Revolutionary Nature of Jesus' Teachings and How They Have Been Corrupted (New York, NY: Three Leaves Press, 2006). (Abbr. "Politics of Jesus")

Jeffers, James S. The Greco-Roman World of the New Testament: Exploring the Background of Early Christianity (Downers Grove, IL: InterVarsity Press, 1999). (Abbr. "Background Early Christianity")

King, Gordon W. Seed Falling on Good Soil: Rooting Our Lives in the Parables of Jesus (Eugene, OR: Cascade Books, 2016). (Abbr. "Seed Falling Good Soil")

Kloppenborg, John S. Excavating Q: The History and Setting of the Sayings Gospel (Minneapolis, MN: Fortress Press, 2000). (Abbr. "Excavating Q")

Laes, Christian. Children in the Roman Empire: Outsiders Within (New York, NY: Cambridge University Press, 2011). (Abbr. "Outsiders Within")

Leyerle, Blake. "Pilgrims to the Land: Early Christian Perceptions of the Galilee," in Galilee Through the Centuries: Confluence of Cultures, Meyers, Eric M., ed. (Winona Lake, IN: Eisenbrauns, 1999). (Abbr. "Early Christian Perceptions")

Malina, Bruce J. and Rohrbaugh, Richard L. Social-Science Commentary Gospel of John (Minneapolis, MN: Fortress Press, 1998). (Abbr. "Social-Science Commentary John")

Maynard-Reed, Pedrito U. Poverty and Wealth in James (Eugene, OR: Wipf and Stock Publishers, 2004). (Abbr. "Poverty and Wealth")

McIver, Robert K. "The Archaeology of Galilee and Palestine from the Maccabees to the Jewish Second Jewish Revolt (167 BC-AD 135)," in The Content and the Setting of the Gospel Tradition, Harding, Mark and Nobbs, Alanna, eds. (Grand Rapids, MI: William B.

Eerdmans Publishing Company, 2010), 1-27. (Abbr. "Archaeology, Galilee, and Palestine")

Moore, Nicholas Carl. The Belligerent Christ (VisionQuest, LLC, 2012). (Abbr. "Belligerent Christ")

Oakman, Douglas E. "Execrating? Or Execrable Peasants!", in The Galilean Economy in the Time of Jesus, Fiensy, David A. and Hawkins, Ralph K., eds. (Atlanta, GA: Society of Biblical Literature, 2013), pp. 139-164. (Abbr. "Excrable Peasants")

Oakman, Douglas E. "Late Second Temple Galilee: Socio-Archaeology and Dimensions of Exploitation in First-Century Palestine," in Galilee in the Late Second Temple and Mishnaic Periods: Life, Culture, and Society, Fiensy, David A. and Strange, James Riley, eds. (Minneapolis, MN: Fortress Press, 2014), pp. 346-356. (Abbr. "Galilee Exploitation")

Orlin, Eric, et al., ed., Routledge Encyclopedia of Ancient Mediterranean Religions (New York NY: Routledge, 2016). (Abbr. "Ancient Mediterranean Religions")

Pilch, John J. The Cultural Dictionary of the Bible (Collegeville, MN: The Liturgical Press, 1999). (Abbr. "Cultural Dictionary")

Poling, James Newton. Render Unto God: Economic Vulnerability, Family Violence, and Pastoral Theology (Eugene, OR: Wipf and Stock Publishers, 2012). (Abbr. "Render Unto God")

Reed, Jonathan L. Archaeology and the Galilean Jesus: A Re-examination of the Evidence (Harrisburg, PA: Trinity Press International, 2001). (Abbr. "Re-Examination")

Reed, Jonathan L. The HarperCollins Visual Guide to the New Testament: What Archaeology Reveals About the First Christians (New York, NY: HarperOne, 2007). (Abbr. "What Archaeology Reveals")

Rock, Ian E. Paul's Letter to the Romans and Roman Imperialism: An Ideological Analysis of the Exordium (Romans 1:1-17) (Eugene, OR: Pickwick Publications, 2012). (Abbr. "Paul's Letter")

Rohrbaugh, Richard L. "The Jesus Tradition: The Gospel Writers' Strategies of Persuasion," in The Early Christian World, Volume 1, Esler, Philip Francis, ed. (New York, NY: Routledge, 2000), pp. 198-230. (Abbr. "Strategies of Persuasion")

Skinner, Andrew C. "A Historical Sketch of Galilee," Brigham Young University Studies, Vol. 36, No. 3, Masada and the World of the New Testament (1996-97), pp. 113-125. (Abbr. "Historical Sketch")

Stegemann, Ekkehard W. and Stegemann, Wolfgang. The Jesus Movement: A Social History of Its First Century. Dean, Jr., O. C., trans. (Minneapolis, MN, Fortress Press, 1999). (Abbr. "Jesus Movement")

Struckmeyer, Kurt. A Conspiracy of Love: Following Jesus in a Postmodern World (Eugene, OR: Resource Publications, 2016). (Abbr. "Conspiracy of Love")

Talbott, Rick F. Jesus, Paul, and Power: Rhetoric, Ritual, and Metaphor in Ancient Mediterranean Christianity (Eugene, OR: Cascade Books, 2010). (Abbr. "Rhetoric, Ritual")

Tzaferis, Vassilios. "Crucifixion – The Archaeological Evidence," Biblical Archaeology Review 11: 1, January/February 1985, pp. 44-53. (Abbr. "Crucifixion")

Walvoord, John F. and Zuck, Roy B., eds. Bible Knowledge Commentary: An Exposition of the Scriptures by Dallas Seminary Faculty, New Testament edition (Colorado Springs, CO: David C. Cook, 1983). (Abbr. "Bible Knowledge Commentary")

Webb, Robert L. John the Baptizer and Prophet: A Socio-historical Study (Eugene, OR: Wipf and Stock Publishers, 2006). (Abbr. "Socio-historical Study")

Weiss, Zeev. "Houses of the Wealthy in Roman Galilee," in The Roman Villa in the Mediterranean Basin: Late Republic to Late Antiquity, Marzano, Annalisa and Métraux, Guy P. R., eds. (New York, NY: Cambridge Universisy Press, 2018), pp. 317-327. (Abbr. "Houses of the Wealthy")

Wilkerson, Robert. Characters of the Crucifixion (Enumclaw, WA: WinePress Publishing, 2011). (Abbr. "Crucifixion")

Wilson, Samantha. Israel, Second Edition (The Vale Chalfont St Peter, Bucks, England: Bradt, 2011). (Abbr. "Israel")

Young, Stephen E. Jesus Tradition in the Apostolic Fathers: Their Explicit Appeals to the Words of Jesus in Light of Orality Studies (Tübingen, Germany:Mohr Siebeck, 2011). (Abbr. "Apostolic Fathers")

CHAPTER FOUR

Endnotes

1 Greenberg and Keinan 2009, Israeli Archaeological Activity 1967-2007, 8.

2 Gori 2013, The Stones of Contention, 220.

3 Beebe 1968, Ancient Palestinian Dwellings, 39.

4 See Charlesworth 1973, Jesus and Jehohanan, 147-150; Tzaferis 1985, Crucifixion, 44-53; McIver 2010, Archaeology Galilee and Palestine, 20-21.

5 McIver 2010, Archaeology Galilee and Palestine, 20.

6 Fiensy 2014, Christian Origins, 139.

7 Stegemann and Stegemann 1999, Jesus Movement, 51; Oakman 2013, Execrable Peasants, 148.

8 Bond 2012, Guide for the Perplexed, 77.

9 Oakman 2013, Execrable Peasants, 148.

10 Stegemann and Stegemann 1999, Jesus Movement, 51; Oakman 2013, Execrable Peasants, 148.

11 Goodman 1987, Ruling Class, 61.

12 Skinner 1996-97, Historical Sketch, 121.

13 Fiensy 2014, Christian Origins, 14-16; Oakman 2014, Galilee Exploitation, 351-354; King 2016, Seed Falling Good Soil, 22; Weiss 2018, Houses of the Wealthy, 317.

14 Adams 2014, Social-Economic Life, 78-79.

15 See Beard 2015, SPQR, 436.

16 Orlin, et al., eds. 2016, Ancient Mediterranean Religions, 36.

17 Hendricks, Jr. 2006, Politics of Jesus, 82-83.

18 Rock 2012, Paul's Letter, 222.

19 Reed 2001, Re-examination, 97.

20 Moore 2012, Belligerent Christ, 14. NOTE TO READERS: The author has not been able to corroborate the findings of this study from any other secondary bound or electronic source. The Sackler School of Medicine has not replied to electronically generated requests. Nevertheless, the author has used this reference on the notion that the data matches a consistent pattern in the archaeological record.

21 Leyerle 1999, Early Christian Perceptions, 353; Kloppenborg 2000, Excavating Q, 215; Wilson 2011, Israel, 179.

22 Jeffers 1999; Background Early Christianity, 44; Laes 2011, Outsiders Within, 26; Botha 2012, Orality and Literacy, 150.

23 Laes 2011, Outsiders Within, 26.

24 Jeffers 1999, Background Early Christianity, 44.

25 Bolt 2003, Jesus' Defeat of Death, 27-28.

26 Evans, ed. 2008, Routledge Encyclopedia Historical Jesus, 33.

27 Byrne and McNary-Zak, eds. 2009, James Ossuary Controversy, 324.

28 Bond 2004, Caiaphas, 7.

29 Reed 2007, What Archaeology Reveals, 10; Evans, ed. 2008, Routledge Encyclopedia Historical Jesus, 33.

30 Reed 2007, What Archaeology Reveals, 10.

31 "According to Josephus then, by inference Tiberius appointed Gratus very soon after becoming emperor (17 September, 14 AD)" (Geis 2013, Life, 366).

32 See Carson 1991, Gospel John, 601-602; Bock with Simpson, Restoring Portrait, 662; Wilkerson 2011, Crucifixion, 1-6.

33 In this study's view, Helen Bond's fair, professional treatment mentions that all of the onsite "archaeologists and other epigraphical experts" who performed the actual excavation were in agreement that the ossuary contained the remains of Joseph Caíaphas. See Bond 2004, Caiaphas, 1-8. For arguments defending the rejection of the biblical Caíaphas, see Evans 2003, Ossuaries, 107-112.

34 Evans 2003, Ossuaries, 23.

35 Atkinson 2003, Salome, 65.

36 Chilton 2000, Rabbi Jesus, 218.

37 Reed 2007, What Archaeology Reveals, 10.

38 This is not simply a neat slogan. Together this tiny, fractional population sector as individuals owns approximately "27 percent of the global stock market" (Bodley 2012, Contemporary Human Problems, 21-22). A truly unimaginable representation of material wealth. Since 2012 (year of publication), that percentage ratio has probably significantly increased.

39 Fiensy 2014, Christian Origins, 23.

40 Crosby 2008, Healing: Hope Or Hype, 274.

41 Capps 2000, Psychological Biography, 135-136.

42 Rohrbaugh 2000, Strategies of Persuasion, 208.

43 Stegemann and Stegemann 1999, Jesus Movement, 112.

44 Cohn 1963, Trial, Death, Jesus, 5-6; Walvoord and Zuck, eds. 1983, Bible Knowledge Commentary, 160; Tzaferis 1985, Crucifixion; Goodman 1987, Ruling Class, 58-60; Skinner 1996-1997, Historical Sketch, 121; Malina and Rohrbaugh 1998, Social-Science Commentary John, 349; Borg 1998, Conflict, Holiness, Politics, 100; Stegemann and Stegemann 1999, Jesus Movement, 112, 134, 136; Pilch 1999, Cultural Dictionary, 25; Rohrbaugh 2000, Strategies of Persuasion, 208; Reed 2001, Re-Examination, 97; Freyne 2002, Revolt From Regional Perspective, 51; Bolt 2003, Jesus' Defeat of Death, 27-28; Maynard-Reed 2004, Poverty and Wealth, 238; Agosto 2005, Servant Leadership, 17; Webb 2006,

Socio-historical Study, 356-357; Carter 2006, Storyteller, Interpreter, 33; McIver 2010, Archaeology Galilee and Palestine, 20; Faulkner 2011, Apocalypse, 62; Rock 2012, Paul's Letter, 222; Poling 2012, Render Unto God, 171; Botha 2012, Orality and Literacy, 150; Fiensy 2014, Christian Origins, 139; Struckmeyer 2016, Conspiracy of Love, 76-77.

45 Webb 2006, Socio-historical Study, 356-357.

46 Bruner 2004, Christbook, 160.

47 Talbott 2010, Rhetoric, Ritual, 58.

48 Young 2011, Apostolic Fathers, 112.

5

Fractured Picture

Historical realities produced the first heartbeat – the first rumor.[1] Historical realities gave rise to the earliest thread. Broken fragments glimpsing a local hero.[2] Faith healer.[3] Village rabbi.[4] Stories shared amongst the disadvantaged. Stories re-enacted amongst the poor.[5]

Looking back, the view is rather frightening. Horrific images haunt our dreams. Deep canyons of fear and despair. Had they got it right? Could whole populations check out before 30? That is what they say. The experts. Some conclude mortality rates at 20 to 25 years old.[6] Is that picture even possible? Archaeology seems to thinks so.

The name "Yeshu ha-Notzri"[7] probably depicts the most accurate historical designation of the remembered figure. The epithet is cited in *Talmud b.Sanhedrin.43a.* from older oral tradition (see epigraph to this work).[8] The nomenclature was codified sometime around 188-217 CE. The referenced Talmudic account revolved around memories recounting a series of sequenced events we call *The Passion*.

Today, sole surviving backup for the "Yeshu" description is found in an ancient document called the "Munich Talmud."[9] Other preserved Talmud copies do not feature this jargon. But the words, while very faint, are still readable.[10] Again, history backs this appellative as a more forthright approach to the Nazarene's true identity.[11]

Picking up the pieces around the time of his baptism, Jesus is already old.[12] The village gaffer. In the rural setting, as a senior figure *Yeshu ha-Notzri* represents the lone voice of discretion. A source of wisdom and compassion to the disadvantaged poor.

The reference to "old" is trustworthy. If the 20 to 25 mortality figure holds water and the Nazarene passed in his early 30s then the "gaffer" label realistically sticks. During the first century, Jesus the Nazarene was alive past his time. All of his contemporaries would have concluded thus. They just had to look around them.

Within this general discussion, subsistence living dominated the masses.[13] Most often associated with the Nazarene's hypothesized demographic, *laborers* and *artisans* inhabited rock bottom on the socioeconomic scale.

"Artisans were usually disdained by the Greeks and Romans."[14] To be fair, Jesus would probably be characterized as "near or borderline" indigent.[15] One or two notches above displaced persons on the run. Nevertheless, in the early part of the first century "craftsmen were often itinerant, especially those living in villages or small towns."[16]

These comments are not attacks on believers. A preserved record of the Nazarene's Judaic "dedication" whilst a babe helps tell the story. *The Gospel of Luke* portrayed his parents observing Hebrew tradition inside the Jerusalem temple:

> And when the time came for their purification according to the law of Moses, they brought him up to Jerusalem to present him to the Lord (as it is written in the law of the Lord, "Every male that opens the womb shall be called holy to the Lord") and to offer a sacrifice according to what is said in the law of the Lord, "a pair of turtledoves, or two young pigeons" (Lk 2.22-24, RSV).

The source behind this memory had attempted to reproduce longstanding Judaic protocol. After 40 days, even the *poor* and/or *indigent* were permitted to participate in purification offerings. The Hebrew Testament offered guidance:

And if she cannot afford a lamb, then she shall take two turtle-doves or two young pigeons, one for a burnt offering and the other for a sin offering; and the priest shall make atonement for her, and she shall be clean (Lev 12.8, RSV).

Both passages are so specific there is hardly room for disagreement. We can call them what we like. In this instance post-Palestine religious editors did not misrepresent the historical milieu. With no risk to their divine "Christos" ideology, Lukan sources managed to uphold longstanding, pre-diasporan tradition. A historically reliable memory that Joseph and Mary were originally portrayed as *dirt poor*.

We need to take in a picture of Yeshu's parents being "so poor that they could not give the normal sacrifice for purification."[17] These are the best impressions available to us. They accurately reproduce what the original tradition intended.

As far as the view today being somewhat "frightening" (mentioned at the top), the evidence is solid. From a postmodern point of view, people died young. Very young. At least from a statistical standpoint.

Why was the mortality rate so high? Why were lives cut so short? Can experts help us? A proper response would definitely offer insight on the era.

As most experts know, archaeology has a way of *contextualizing* time and place.[18] In crucial instances archaeologists have delivered key evidence to redirect *misguided* impressions. All historical scholars know this to be true.

Our aim in this study is to track those voices who legitimately witnessed Jesus. Those who originally framed his activities. In our day, archaeologists, classical historians, and social experts give us reasonably accurate glimpses of life around him. They help us to stay clear of objectionable deviations. Certain reasoning that would ultimately cloud our way.

In this instance formal deliberations by highly qualified experts offer rather extreme sketches. They depict the life and times. But in vivid, stark colors. They present images like *desperation, exploitation, poverty, early mortality*.[19] Peruse the substantial literature and one realizes that numerous specialists tend to paint harsh and graphic pictures.

Inside the Galilee (Yeshu's home territory), one dependable argument suggests the era witnessed a measurable population segment in freefall. Experts tell us that many from the common people digressed from independent, free farmers, to leaseholders, to day laborers, then to beggars.[20]

From this rather morose, though apparently trustworthy, synthesis by the time of Yeshu's public ministry in his early 30s (beyond statistical life expectancy), what would a reasonably accurate physical portrait offer?

For one, the Nazarene's teeth would probably be falling out. No dental checkups or even basic hygiene to rely upon.

Not to mention a declining hairline. Perhaps more. From multiple ancient Judean archaeological sites head lice have been identified on personal combs in remains.[21] These microscopic critters can potentially cause serious illness including "epidemic typhus, trench fever, and relapsing fever."[22]

As an alleged artisan performing heavy manual labor (i.e. lifting rocks and/or bricks) over a significant timeframe, by his early thirties Jesus may have walked bent over. Or even with a limp.

It is difficult even to write but presumably his ribs would be showing. Archaeology through bone growth studies has definitively established that many Galilean poor did not eat properly.[23]

And as we can expect an older person like Jesus may have had a hard time hearing.[24]

So straightaway we need to adopt a proper, visual profile. Our initial knowledge regarding *Yeshu ha-Notzri* emerged from certain reliable memory threads preserved amongst the underclasses of lower Galilee. In the original time and place setting, such images were not painted on a romanticized canvas.

Unless we want to see Jesus the Nazarene as a hellenized Pauline godman floating above the general population, later in life the Nazarene's physical appearance would have to some extent deteriorated. This development would have reflected a rather common demographic profile. A real-life profile. The profile of the disadvantaged.

Nowadays for readers such an assessment would be considered extreme. Our sensitivities to life around us are so dominated by physical impressions. And the more trivial aspects of day-to-day living. However, in a real-world review, those initial glimpses of our protagonist represent fair and impartial readings of the archaeological record. And historical knowledge of the milieu.

In so many words, we need to consider a realistic take on hygiene, diet, and basic healthcare to advancing years. We need to digest that here in these pages Jesus the Nazarene is looked upon as a real, breathing *human being*.

The stories tell us that he sang songs (Mt 26.30; Mk 14.26), drank wine (Mt 15.10-11; Lk 7.33-35), and celebrated cyclical feast days (Jn 2.13; 5.1; 7.10; 10.22-23; 12.12-13) like other rural Jews. He did not wear an aureole over his head. He was not above angry retorts to – what he perceived as – hypocrites (see Mt 6.2, 5, 16; 7.5; 15.7; 22.18; 23. 13, 15, 23, 25, 27-28; Mk 7.6; 12.15; Lk 6.42; 12.1, 56; 13.15).

Jesus most certainly did not challenge His Satanic Majesty out in some desert place (Mt 4.1-11, Mk 1.12-13, Lk 4.1-13) companioned by wild beasts and ministering angels (Mk 4.13). These popular snapshots represented later hellenized, religious imagery produced beyond the Land of Israel. Decades past the original stories. The synoptic tales were filled with such late, mythologized details. Many aspects of these accounts categorically rejected original historical threads.

To enlist a well-placed critical eye we are forced to be hypersensitive to a more accurate reading. True-to-life depictions. We have to believe that in many ways *Yeshu ha-Notzri* was just like other poor people of the era. More often than naught struggling just to survive.

Archaeology offers strong impressions. The physical profile above, while unorthodox, ultimately paints a fair and reasonably accurate picture. This sketch would have closely followed the particulars of many disadvantaged during the late second-temple era. Why not Jesus?

With that said, there is another aspect to consider. We also need to factor inherent Judaic reverence for the elderly. This social attitude would have definitely impacted many people's impressions of the aging village healer. "You shall rise up before the hoary head, and honor the face of an old man, and you shall fear your God: I am the Lord" (Lev 19.32, RSV). At least to some extent, adopting this attitude was a mainstay in ancient Judaic society.

Historical circumstances dictated that Rome had at some point regarded *Yeshu ha-Notzri* as *politically dangerous*.[25] In this instance, following the Johannine track, we are probably not so far off course. In fact, *John's Gospel* produced a rather uncluttered, historically evocative, impression.

> So the chief priests and the Pharisees gathered the council, and said, "What are we to do? For this man performs many signs. If we let him go on thus, everyone will believe in him, and the Romans will come and destroy both our holy place and our nation." But one of them, Ca'iaphas, who was high priest that year, said to them, "You know nothing at all; you do not understand that it is expedient for you that one man should die for the people, and that the whole nation should not perish" (Jn 11.47-50).

In the canonical literature, according to this distinctively illuminated thread, the Nazarene's popularity was becoming an issue for the Jerusalem ruling hierarchy. Apparently, he had performed various miracles that reconnected the populace on a gut level with ancient Mosaic tradition (i.e.

vis-à-vis miraculous "signs"). From the vantage point of authorities, *Yeshu ha-Notzri* was *stirring up* the populace.

Across antiquity *signs* symbology had enjoined Judaic believers to the heartbeat of traditional Israelite cultic life. During the mythic Exodus, the Hebrew people were sustained by miraculous *signs*. In desperate straits, time and again their revered lawgiver managed to successfully impel the divine presence to act. So in the early part of the first century *Mosaic signs* performed by *Yeshu ha-Notzri* reconnected the common people to their originating cultic myth.

With the Roman occupation, when inspired by the Nazarene's miraculous deeds, we have to assume that first-century Jews would often revisit this vivid, dramatic, cultic rallying cry. Such portrayals understandably infused echoes of Judaic *renewal* into the hearts of the faithful.

That this theme was being revisited in the first century through the ministering acts of a near-destitute village rabbi would have gathered electric energy from the common people. One of their own, through answered prayers, was standing up against the yoke of Roman power. Not only Roman power but rampant corruption from their own governing officials.

Incidentally, as far as we know, none of the first-century Israelite figures attracting movements around themselves were put on trial by the Sanhedrin for *blasphemy*. Not one. All were stamped out by Roman hands under the guise of ridding local populations of "political revolutionaries."[26] Ringleaders were rounded up and killed for *seditious* behavior. In the end, "seditious" to the Roman state.

Why would treatment of a Galilean peasant healer be any different? That his message happened to be nonviolent would not in the least quell elite concerns. Across history, revolutions did not always erupt with spontaneous mob violence. They were often momentum building. One rather innocuous incident after another.

The movements themselves were often paved by inspirational figures who did not always endorse violence. At least on the surface. During the first century, both Rome and Jerusalem would have been hypersensitive to inspirational characters that stirred the populace. No doubt remains that *Yeshu ha-Notzri* met that criteria.

We should probably recognize in this distinctive Johannine thread "a tradition concerning Jesus that must be primitive and authentic."[27] Suggested above, the citation itself resonates at some measurable level in aspects of the actual historical record.

With that said, we should clarify by stating that "in the earliest stratum [of Johannine tradition], there is no indication that the 'Jesus movement' had any political or military aims."[28] This scholarly comment is crucially important for reconstructing an accurate picture. From all available evidence, Jesus himself was not a violent provocateur.

The only recorded act of aggression in all of canonical tradition was Peter's attack on the high priest's servant in the unnamed garden: "Then Simon Peter, having a sword, drew it and struck the high priest's slave and cut off his right ear. The slave's name was Malchus" (Jn 18.10, RSV). As stated, there were no other remembered incidents underlining violent intent.

If the Nazarene's activities truly drew large crowds, then we must bear in mind that in the ancient world to some extent "crowds shaped Roman policy."[29] This expert insight is enormously illuminating. So, in any historical sense, readers are encouraged to see that the reactions of the "chief priests and Pharisees" in *John's* cited memory (Jn 11.47-50 noted above) would have been spot-on and running parallel to *history*.

Crucial to the framing of this study's overall thesis is the idea that elites (both Judaic and Roman) would have panicked at Yeshu's wide popular appeal. If he turned the common people, Sanhedrin officials were concerned Rome would take action against all of Israel. In history such a reaction represented a fully credible, entirely consistent response.

At least in this scene the political circumstances depicted in *John's* final draft rejected religious imagery of one kind or another. In other words, any form of Christological take focused on the Johannine catechism was absent from this profile. Instead, we fully observe a real-life snapshot depicting a *political* matter ultimately directed on preserving peaceful governance. And the elite status quo.

The overriding point: in any accurate reading, all concerned would have taken Yeshu's threat of potential unrest *very seriously*.[30] No doubt exists that a sizable following of common people were smitten by this rural rabbi. A miracle worker who so credibly reinstated the image and (to some extent) legacy of their faithful lawgiver.

Eventually, we know that *Yeshu ha-Notzri* was crucified by Roman power for the crime of *sedition*. Many reputable experts mistakenly point at overturning moneylender tables (Mt 21.12-17; Mk 11.15-19; Lk 19.45-48; Jn 2.13-16) as an explanation for the downward spiral.[31]

The logic, though, is difficult to follow. There is nothing in the literature (or plain common sense) to support such thinking. In other words:

Moneylenders–to–Arrest–to–Trial–to–Scourging–to–
Crucifixion

… resists a credible reply. History demands a radically altered scenario than the moneylenders-to-crucifixion track.

Beyond religiously invoked messaging, understanding the historical character of Jesus and the distinctive time-and-place Judaic ambience is crucial. In a temple fray he may have been pointed out by local authorities. Not as subversive. But for being "touched." Haywire. Temporarily out of his wits. This should probably be explained. The truth isn't what some readers might think.

The ancient Hebrew prophets, in particular, were viewed this way.[32] At times a bit "off" so to speak. In various scenes the gospels offered a vision of an ancient seer in the tradition of Jeremiah. Or Eli'jah.

Now when Jesus came into the district of Caesare'a Philippi, he asked his disciples, "Who do men say that the Son of man is?" And they said, "Some say John the Baptist, others say

Eli'jah, and others Jeremiah or one of the prophets" (Mt 16.13-14; also, Mk 8.27-28; Lk 9.18-19, RSV).

Over the course of their spiritual quests many Judaic seers were known to display emotional tantrums.[33] Just mentioned, Jesus in public forums had more than once been placed alongside prophets of yore.[34]

In religious circles such behavior was probably not even frowned upon. Certainly not during the Jewish Passover season when sometimes wild outbursts prone to severe righteous indignation (and occasional violence) took hold of more fervid worshippers.[35]

In a quest for deeper understanding, only the *Gospel of John* recorded true-to-life snapshots of the numerous periodic Jewish feasts. Authentic testimony depicting a cultic environment dominated by agriculture and "the changing seasons."[36]

This is a reminder that no matter what scholars want to tell us about late Johannine origins, we must vehemently reject such distressingly unjustified proposals. Our grounded defense is not mere speculation but heavily weighted evidence embedded in the text itself.[37] Unique to canonical tradition, the pre-Johannine source (i.e. an originating layer of tradition behind *John's* story) is virtually inundated by a coherent Judaic festival theme.

During the periodic Jewish festivals Jerusalem temple police regularly kept watch over hundreds of thousands of, at times, raucous celebrants. Quite naturally, like law enforcement across every era, they had met all types. The plain truth: mentioned already, at thirty-something *Yeshu ha-Notzri* would have been regarded as an elderly figure. A respected rural rabbi honored in village culture.

So set inside the sometimes volatile first-century cultic setting, we must adhere to historical probabilities. We must deduct a highly plausible outcome. We must view a potential "table-turning" scene in the heat of a typical Judaic passover season.

We must come to realize that an exasperated elderly rabbi screaming at moneylenders would not have even raised eyebrows. Considering his age, status, and overburdened emotions absorbed in the pageantry of the cultic celebration, *Yeshu ha-Notzri* would have simply been ushered away. Then calmed down and released to friends.[38]

Postmodern readers must come to understand that "the Jews" were not out to get Jesus. Maybe governing officials. Not the populace. He healed their wounds. By his humble origins and inspirational example assuaged their woes. Offered a vision in familiar Mosaic metaphors that intimated hope and light to the disadvantaged. Why would they possibly hate him? We must come to see that a negative tilt is not supported in history. Jesus was a Jew.

This highly credible picture was the cultural and social reality that first-century Judaic worshippers knew. The truth is: set inside the moneychanger story, no one would have been embarrassed or threatened by Yeshu's overt and demonstrative protest. He was a village rabbi who honored the old ways. And wished them to be preserved. No devotional Jew would have remonstrated his attitude.

At his age, that *Yeshu ha-Notzri* would have been otherwise engaged in any form of intense physical exertion isn't feasible. Such strength limitations would have obviously included physically (not symbolically) overturning moneychanger tables (Mt 21.12; Mk 11.15; Lk 19.45; Jn 2.15). Moral outrage: yes. Feats of brute strength: no. Not a chance.

In a real-life setting, considering his widely reported service to the lowly, it is probable that many Jews had as much compassion for *Yeshu ha-Notzri* as he had for them. By his thirties, at times just getting around would have required concentrated energies.

If Yeshu was truly undernourished like most in his demographic, then there is really no doubt as to predictive streams of behavior. Long term undernourishment took its toll on the physiques of everyone. Even saints.

As far as modern studies, experts have crafted various approaches to answering the high percentile mortality rate. The bottom line is that across the ancient era, whether rich or poor, our metabolic resistance to biological breakdown was found wanting. On a massive scale. Crucial historical testimony defends this extreme limitation placed upon all human beings living inside the ancient setting.

Whether in Rome, Damascus, Alexandria, or Galilee, whether rich or poor, in ancient times populations lacked basic hygienic understanding or practice.[39] A long laundry list of researched evidence defends this conclusion. Here are brief highlights:

> More times than naught people were in want of protection against infection and biological invaders (i.e. "infectious disease"[40]). The most prominent – varieties of plague, as well as malaria and tuberculosis (the last two often associated with close proximity to domesticated animals[41]).

> Waterborne pathogens were common and probably contributed considerably to early mortality (not to mention intestinal pathogens from improper waste management).[42]

> Vitamin and mineral deficiencies were presumably widespread.[43]

> Most women remained pregnant across their shortened lifespans.[44]

> Not to mention high concentrations of disadvantaged challenged by the systemic impact of long term malnutrition.[45]

We shouldn't kid ourselves into accepting sympathetic "big-screen" portrayals. As juveniles today we are so concerned about pimples. As adults we watch our weight. In the declining years we form close relationships with medical advisers. But for almost all ancient humans health management was really a mess. To somehow account for the incredibly high mortality rate, there is really no other reasonable logic. Or reliable outcome.

Thus, antiquity was not for moaners or faint of heart. As a local village healer, readers can rest assured that *Yeshu ha-Notzri* nursed a long waiting line of abandoned and suffering almost anywhere he traveled.

One specific observation needs emphasis. Seen thru a historical lens, mortality numbers would have even been *higher* around the Galilean lake, the stalking grounds of Jesus and his early mates. We should remind ourselves that seasonal malaria would have often decimated village communities. On a regional basis, the shores around Lake Kinneret comprised a central breeding ground for invasive and fatal disease carriers.[46]

This reminder represents a topographical actuality often ignored in historical studies. When considering the day-to-day activities of a village healer, basic geography at times formed crucial patterns. During this historical era, virtually from every corner, Jesus the Nazarene would have been overwhelmed by pleas for help.

In fact, directly linked to our historical impressions, the most discernible aspect of any authentic sketch is emphasis on miraculous healing.[47] Experts' true-to-life findings emphasize such appeals.

So we should not be surprised that from everything we know, by the time *Yeshu ha-Notzri* gained widespread public acclaim, his reputation was already synonymous with helping others. The ancient narratives are pivotal in this regard.

> And Jesus answered them, "Go and tell John what you hear and see: the blind receive their sight and the lame walk, lepers are cleansed and the deaf hear, and the dead are raised up, and the poor have good news preached to them (Mt 11.4-5; Lk 7.22, RSV).

Inside the Nazarene's historical ministry, apart from anything else, it was the subject of *healing* that drew popular acclaim.[48] Further, such remarkable demonstrations of religious continuity would have impressed passionate social activists like John the Baptizer.[49] Healings would have gained attention from the more well-intentioned among the Jerusalem council.[50] And healings would have earned enormous respect from local village elders.[51]

We need to bear in mind that during this era the vast majority of Judaic faithful accepted that the divine hand healed the sick.[52] Israelites firmly believed that Y-H-V-H (not Y-H-W-H – see Appendix 'A' in back) answered petitions from consecrated worshippers.

Within the cultic setting, religious devotion drove the maintenance of physical health as it did spiritual health. On an individual basis, faith in the divinity overwhelmingly dominated healthcare. "[In the end] the healing process was based on the elementary notion that faith alone could cure illness (Avalos 1999:75)."[53]

One practical reason for this understanding, in many instances there were no viable alternatives. In Judea, but for the sole exception of the Essene religious order, for all intents and purposes healthcare for the masses did not exist.[54]

So in the ancient setting, the Nazarene's portrait as village healer succinctly matched a quite dependable social picture. It is reinforced today by professional appraisals like "the evidence for Jesus as a wonderworker is overwhelming in the relevant sources."[55] There are many related quotables in modern studies.

A reliable memory preserved by late first-century historian Flavius Josephus minced no words. In an entirely uncluttered style, Josephus referred to Jesus as a "doer of wonderful works" (Josephus *Ant* 18.3.3). Within the ancient setting, this comment, of course, directly elicited images of religiously invoked healing.

Important for us, the Josephus comment was conceived independently of mid-first-century Pauline ecclesiology. For even the most pessimistic today this solidly historical observation strongly implies that the Nazarene's prayers legitimately offered hope to sufferers.

The modern argument that through reciting Judaically inspired proverbs and sayings and overturning moneychanger tables the Nazarene somehow transformed himself into a candidate for Roman crucifixion utterly rejects historical realities. There is no plausible defense for such naive thinking.

Across Palestine the Jews were already well supported by a rather dense, existent, cultic mythology. Jesus and his direct supporters were all devoted to torah principles and Mosaic iconography.

On the other hand, modern archaeology maintains that a large segment among local populations was perpetually in need of relief. Not for inspirational ditties. But physical recovery.

Again, most of us today have not sufficiently registered that during the late second-temple period the mortality rate was so high that no one in our era but specialized, archaeologically-attuned, medical experts would seriously consider such numbers.[56]

Nevertheless, on top of this extremely reliable professional finding postmodern scholarship stresses a litany of political, social, economic, and other societal red flags that would have significantly hindered the underclasses.[57]

Again, as to authentic memory streams surrounding Jesus, we should not be surprised that initial glimpses preserved fleeting impressions of *miraculous healing*. Moving in any alternate direction would virtually reject history. *Yeshu ha-Notzri* gained his reputation by helping the poor.

This more plausible, historically charged, explanation has been ignored time and again in New Testament studies. The importance of *healing* and its impact on local populations constitutes the single essential reason why no scholar to date has even come close to uncovering "the earliest footprint of Jesus." Nor even couched this Mosaically promoted theme in its proper historical light. But for a mere handful of scholarly exceptions, crucial related narrative development is almost always lacking.

Nearly all scholars have failed to grasp the deep implications of *authentic* healing on accurate impressions of the historical figure. A remembered outcome that would have drawn profound responses from the original socio-cultural setting. Such an explanation legitimizes the theme of shared oral memories. Cherished reminiscences of a rural village healer.

Let us not forget: it was the exasperated chief priests and Pharisees, not the common people, who were remembered for seamlessly framing quite plausible notions: "What are we to do? For this man performs many signs[!]" (Jn 11.47, RSV).

In expert discussions today this claim is obviously unprovable. But aspects of archaeology point at very high probabilities. When focusing the lens with dexterity, we observe that, according to the stories, healing the lowly was central to the life of the village rabbi.

A memorialized healing ministry in tandem with some realistic glimpse of "Passion" and "Resurrection" thematic development constitutes the foremost reason(s) why he is still recalled today. Scholars often miss the fact that when properly framing our best impressions of history such ideas are nearest proximity to the Nazarene's authentic "digital map."

Albeit the alternate "sage-teacher" profile dispensing proverbs and sayings fits neatly into postmodern university halls. However, not often contemplated is the fact that bestowing wisdom among large numbers who were too weak even to tend their fields blindly ignores the archaeological record. And historical realities. In real life the common people would have been far more focused on survival than inspirational verse.

Yeshu ha-Notzri prayed for his countrymen who were, more times than naught, unwell. The disadvantaged. The poor. The humble in heart. Considering this more *realistic* model – realistic for the times, realistic for the characters our sketches trace, realistic for the archaeology we have unearthed – historical probabilities offer us no other viable choice.

Attuned to a much more realistic narration, we might wish to consider that Yeshu would have been last among his inner circle to proclaim a "divine nexus" (i.e. self-deification). In short, comparisons to otherworldly entities. Though rarely taken up in scholarly circles, there is perhaps a solid reason why.

The day-in and day-out psychological and emotional grind, as well as gradual physical breakdown, would have over time taken their toll. Even on successful faith healers. Further, older narrative streams suggest that the Nazarene's secret thoughts utterly lacked a sense of self-prescience for celestial arenas.

> Then Jesus said to him, "Begone, Satan! for it is written, 'You shall worship the Lord your God and him only shall you serve'" (Mt 4.10, Lk 4.8, RSV).

> And Jesus said to him, "Why do you call me good? No one is good but God alone (Mk 10.18, Lk 18.19, RSV).

Yeshu ha-Notzri seemed to be more at home with simple reverence for a mysterious, archaic, tribal icon he called "Father." An invisible presence. Unnamed. Primeval in origin. Elusive and indefinable.

At times Jesus was known to have left his village for a quiet place all night to pray (Lk 6.12). Such openly sincere behavior seems to naturally reject supernatural impressions of the occult.

In the synoptics we encounter Jesus in abbreviated snapshots among his students. As well as inside local populations. And from time to time helping the needy. Not in the least gravitating towards self-glorification. But in humble service to the poor.

Despite imposing challenges, the stories suggest that Jesus the Nazarene rallied on. Apparently, with some success. Indeed, we need go no further than the following scriptural extract to sense that a legitimate, historical strand survived a violent era of exploitation and intense human suffering. It is quite simple in its proclamation and promise. But opens up a brief, unapologetic glimpse on a genuine window from the past:

> And a multitude followed him,
>
> because they saw the signs which he did
>
> on those who were diseased (Jn 6.2, RSV).

In more authentically memorialized scenes Mosaically inspired "signs" were never far from the ancient dialogue.[58]

Thus, again, the most credible topic that preserves a historical basis is answered prayers. Yes, *miracles*! From what we learn, even municipal authorities were hearing word of inexplicable "signs" performed by a village teacher.

As far as pre-Christian stirrings, talk of miracle signs apparently first emerged among rural groups of Israelites telling stories about Jesus. It is virtually impossible to accept that the *signs* theme originated beyond Palestine. Thus, for lack of a better term (and in harmony with modern research), we might wish to call these first miracle stories "source traditions."[59]

Accompanied by prevailing trends of inadequate harvests,[60] poor health,[61] pressing taxation,[62] debt slavery,[63] land loss,[64] and limited personal safety,[65] in village gatherings set aside for inspiration and cultic renewal, shared consciousness would have focused on the *miraculous*. Not jingoistic morality lessons most, of which, were already well-familiar inside the late second-temple religious apparatus.

In fact, if the Lukan fragment cited below can be counted upon, even the ruthless governing tetrarch, Herod Antipas, had heard rumors of the Nazarene's spectacular deeds.

> When [the Roman Prefect, *Marcus Pontius Pilatus*, aka] Pilate heard this, he asked whether the man [Jesus] was a Galilean. And when he learned that he [Jesus] belonged to Herod's jurisdiction, he [Pilate] sent him over to Herod, who was himself in Jerusalem at that time. When Herod saw Jesus, he was very glad, for he had long desired to see him, because he [Herod Antipas] had heard about him [Jesus], and he was hoping to see some *sign* [emphasis added] done by him (Lk 23.6-8, RSV).

Given our knowledge of the historical era, we cannot escape the fact that inside rural villages healing stories would have occupied the hearts and minds of many struggling to go on. In witness to a legitimate and quite plausible historical track, this point cannot be overemphasized.

CHAPTER FIVE
References

Abel, Ernest L. "The Psychology of Memory and Rumor Transmission and Their Bearing on Theories of Oral Transmission in Early Christianity," *The Journal of Religion*, Vol. 51, No. 4 (Oct., 1971), pp. 270-281. (Abbr. "Memory and Rumor Transmission")

Adams, Samuel L. *Social and Economic Life in Second Temple Judea* (Louisville, KY: Westminster John Knox Press, 2014). (Abbr. "Social-Economic Life")

Allison Jr., Dale C. *The Historical Christ and the Theological Jesus* (Grand Rapids, MI: William B. Eerdmans Publishing Company, 2009). (Abbr. "Historical Christ Theological Jesus")

Andrade, Nathanael. "Ambiguity, Violence, and Community in the Cities of Judaea and Syria," *Historia: Zeitschrift für Alte Geschichte*, Bd. 59, H. 3 (2010), pp. 342-370. (Abbr. "Ambiguity, Violence, Community")

Arbel, Yoav. *Ultimate Devotion: The Historical Impact and Archaeological Expression of Intense Religious Movements* (New York, NY: Routledge, 2014). (Abbr. "Ultimate Devotion")

Audlin, James David. *The Gospel of John: The Original Version Restored and Translated with Commentaries – Volume Two: Commentaries on the Text* (Chiriquí, Panamá: Volcán Barú, 2017). (Abbr. "Original Version")

Aune, David E. *Jesus, Gospel Tradition and Paul in the Context of Jewish and Greco-Roman Antiquity: Collected Essays II* (Tübingen, Germany: Mohr Siebeck, 2013). (Abbr. "Gospel Tradition and Paul");

Bammel, Ernst. "The Poor and the Zealots," in *Jesus and the Politics of His Day*, Bammel, Ernst and Moule, C.F.D., eds. (New York, NY:

Cambridge University Press, 1984), pp. 109-128. (Abbr. "Poor and Zealots")

Becker, Heinz. *Die Reden des Johannesevangeliums und der Stil der gnostischen Offenbarungsrede* (Göttingen, Germany: Vandenhoeck und Ruprecht, 1956). (Abbr. "Gnostischen Offenbarungsrede")

Becker, Jürgen. "Wunder und Christologie," *New Testament Studies* 16 (1969–70), pp. 130–48. (Abbr. "Wunder und Christologie")

Berlin, Andrea M. "Jewish Life Before the Revolt: The Archaeological Evidence," *Journal for the Study of Judaism in the Persian, Hellenistic, and Roman Period*, Vol. 36, No. 4 (2005), pp. 417-470. (Abbr. "Jewish Life Before Revolt")

Bird, Michael F. and Crossley, James G. *How Did Christianity Begin?: A Believer and Non-Believer Examine the Evidence* (Peabody, MA: Hendrickson Publishers, Inc., 2008). (Abbr. "Believer and Non-Believer")

Block, Daniel I. *The Book of Ezekiel: Chapters 1-24* (Grand Rapids, MI: William B. Eerdmans Publishing Company, 1997). (Abbr. "Book of Ezekiel")

Blumell, Lincoln. "Social Banditry? Galilean Banditry from Herod until the Outbreak of the First Jewish Revolt," *Scripta Classica Israelica* 27 (2008): 35 – 53. (Abbr. "Social Banditry")

Bock, Darrell L. *Studying the Historical Jesus: A Guide to Sources and Methods* (Grand Rapids, MI: Baker Academic, 2002). (Abbr. "Studying the Historical Jesus")

Boer, Roland and Petterson, Christina. *Time of Troubles: A New Economic Framework for Early Christianity* (Minneapolis, MN: Fortress Press, 2017). (Abbr. "Times of Trouble")

Boismard, M. E. "L'évolution du theme eschatologique dans les traditions johanniques", *Revue Biblique*, 68 (1961), pp. 507-525. (Abbr. "évolution eschatologique johanniques")

Bolt, Peter G. *Jesus' Defeat of Death: Persuading Mark's Early Readers* (New York, NY: Cambridge University Press, 2003). (Abbr. "Jesus' Defeat of Death")

Botha, P. J. J. "The Social Dynamics of the Early Transmission of the Jesus Tradition," *Neotestamentica*, Vol. 27, No. 2 (1993), pp. 205-231. (Abbr. "Social Dynamics")

Botha, Pieter J. J. "Houses in the World of Jesus," *Neotestamentica*, Vol. 32, No. 1 (1998), pp. 37-74. (Abbr. "Houses in World Jesus")

Botha, Pieter J. J. *Orality and Literacy in Early Christianity* (Eugene, OR: Cascade Books, 2012). (Abbr. "Orality and Literacy")

Brandon, S. G. F. *Jesus and the Zealots: A Study of the Political Factor in Primitive Christianity* (New York, NY: Charles Scribner's Sons, 1967). (Abbr. "Jesus and Zealots")

Brookins, Timothy A. *Corinthian Wisdom, Stoic Philosophy, and the Ancient Economy* (New York, NY: Cambridge University Press, 2014). (Abbr. "Corinthian Wisdom")

Broome, Jr., Edwin C. "The Sources of the Fourth Gospel," *Journal of Biblical Literature*, 63 (1944), pp. 107-121. (Abbr. "Sources Fourth Gospel")

Brown, Raymond E. *An Introduction to the Gospel of John*, Moloney, Francis J., ed. (New Haven, CT: Yale University Press, 2010). (Abbr. "Introduction Gospel of John")

Brown, Raymond E. *The Gospel According to John I-XII: Introduction, Translation, and Notes* (Garden City, NY: Doubleday & Company, Inc., 1966). (Abbr. "John i-xii")

Brown, Raymond E. *The Gospel According to John XIII-XXI: Introduction, Translation, and Notes* (New York, NY: Doubleday, 1970). (Abbr. "John xiii-xxi")

Bultmann, Rudolf. *The Gospel of John: A Commentary*, Beaseley-Murray, G. R. trans. Hoare, R. W. N. and Riches, J. K., eds. (Philadelphia, PA: Westminster Press, 1971). (Abbr. "Gospel John Commentary")

Burkill, T. A. "The Trial of Jesus," *Vigiliae Christianae*, Vol. 12, No. 1 (May, 1958), pp. 1-18. (Abbr. "The Trial of Jesus")

Capper, Brian J. "Essene Community Houses and Jesus' Early Community," in *Jesus and Archaeology*, Charlesworth, James H., ed. (Grand Rapids, MI: William B. Eerdmans Publishing Company, 2006), pp. 472-502. (Abbr. "Essene Community Houses")

Capper, Brian. J. "The Essene Religious Order of Ancient Judaea and the Origins of Johannine Christianity," *The Qumran Chronicle*, Vol. 22, No. 1-4 (December 2014), pp. 39-71. (Abbr. "The Essene Religious Order")

Capps, Donald. *Jesus: A Psychological Biography* (Eugene, OR: Wipf and Stock Publishers, 2000). (Abbr. "Psychological Biography")

Carter, Warren. "Matthew's People," in *Christian Origins: A People's History of Christianity, Volume 1*, Horsley, Richard A., ed. (Minneapolis, MN: Fortress Press, 2010), pp. 138-161. (Abbr. "Matthew's People")

Casey, Maurice. *Jesus of Nazareth: An Independent Historian's Account of his Life and Teaching* (New York, NY: T&T Clark International, 2010). (Abbr. "Independent Historian Account")Chapman and Schnabel, Trial and Crucifixion, 137, note 499).

Chapman, David Wallace and Schnabel, Eckhard J. *The Trial and Crucifixion of Jesus: Texts and Commentary* (Tübingen, Germany: Mohr Siebeck, 2015). (Abbr. "Trial and Crucifixion")

Charlesworth, James H. The Historical Jesus: An Essential Guide (Nashville, TN: Abingdon Press, 2008). (Abbr. "Historical Jesus Essential Guide")

Charlesworth, James Hamilton. "The Temple, Purity, and the Background to Jesus' Death," *Revista Catalana de Teologia, [en línia]*, 2008, Vol. 33, Núm. 2, p. 395-42. (Abbr. "Temple, Purity, Jesus' Death")

Cook, Christopher, C. H. *Hearing Voices, Demonic and Divine: Scientific and Theological Perspectives* (New York, NY: Routledge, 2019). (Abbr. "Hearing Voices, Demonic, Divine")

Cope, Lamar. "The Earliest Gospel Was the 'Signs Gospel,'" in *Jesus, the Gospels, and the Church: Essays in Honor of William R. Farmer*, Sanders, E. P., ed. (Macon, GA: Mercer University Press, 1987), pp. 17-24. (Abbr. "Signs Earliest Gospel")

Crook, Zeba. "Honor, Shame, and Social Status Revisited," *Journal of Biblical Literature*, Vol. 128, No. 3 (Fall, 2009), pp. 591-611. (Abbr. "Social Status")

Crosby, Stephen R. *Healing: Hope Or Hype? Why Genuine Healings are Rare in Local Churches and What We Can Do About It* (Durham, CT: Strategic Book Group, 2008). (Abbr. "Healing: Hope or Hype")

Deines, Roland. "Galilee and the Historical Jesus in Recent Research," in *Galilee in Late Second Temple and Mishnaic Periods: Volume 1, Life, Culture, and Society*, Fiensy, David A. and Strange, James Riley, eds. (Minneapolis, MN: Fortress Press, 2014), pp. 11-50. (Abbr. "Jesus Recent Research")

Diakonoff, I. M. "General Outline of the First Period of the History of the Ancient World and the Problem of the Ways of Development," in *Early Antiquity*, Diakonoff, I. M., ed. (Chicago, IL: The University of Chicago Press, 1991), pp. 27-66. (Abbr. "First Period of History")

Dodd, C. H. *Historical Tradition in the Fourth Gospel* (New York, NY: Cambridge University Press, 1963). (Abbr. "Historical Tradition Fourth Gospel")

Dodd, C. H. *The Fourth Gospel* (New York, NY: Cambridge University Press, 1954). (Abbr. "The Fourth Gospel")

Dodd, Sarah Drakopoulou and Gotsis, George N. "Some Economic Implications of Synoptic Gospel Theology: A Short Review," *History of Economic Ideas*, Vol. 8, No. 2 (2000), pp. 7-34. (Abbr. " Economic Implications Synoptic Theology")

Downs, David J. "Economics, Taxes, and Tithes," in *The World of the New Testament: Cultural, Social, and Historical Contexts*, Green, Joel B. and McDonald, Lee Martin, eds. (Grand Rapids, MI: Baker Academic, 2013), pp. 156-168. (Abbr. "Economics, Taxes, Tithes")

Drali, Rezak. "Human Lice in Palaeoentomology and Paleomicrobiology," in *Paleomicrobiology of Humans*, Drancourt, Michel and Raoult, Didier, eds. (Washington DC: ASM Press, 2017), pp. 181-190. (Abbr. "Human Lice in Palaeoentomology").

Drazin, Israel. *A Rational Approach to Judaism and Torah Commentary* (Jerusalem: Israel, Urim Publications, 2006). (Abbr. "Rational Approach to Judaism")

Dunn, James D. G. *Christianity in the Making: Beginning From Jerusalem, Volume 2* (Grand Rapids, MI: William B. Eerdmans Publishing Company, 2009). (Abbr. "Beginning From Jerusalem")

Dunn, James D. G. *Jesus Remembered: Christianity in the Making, Volume 1* (Grand Rapids, MI: William B. Eerdmans Publishing Company, 2003). (Abbr. "Jesus Remembered")

Eck, Ernest van. *The Parables of Jesus the Galilean: Stories of a Social Prophet* (Eugene, OR: Cascade Books, 2016). (Abbr. "Parables of Jesus")

Edwards, Douglas R. "The Social, Religious, and Political Aspects of Costume in Josephus," in *The World of Roman Costume*, Sebesta, Judith Lynn and Bonfante, Larissa, eds. (Madison, WI: The University of Wisconsin Press, 2001), pp. 153-162. (Abbr. "Social, Religious, Political")

Esler, Philip F. "Jesus and the Reduction of Intergroup Conflict," in *The Social Setting of Jesus and the Gospels*, Stegemann, Wolfgang, et al., eds. (Minneapolis, MN: Fortress Press, 2002), pp. 185-206. (Abbr. "Jesus Intergroup Conflict")

Evans, Craig. A. "Authenticating the Activities of Jesus," in *Authenticating the Activities of Jesus*, Chilton, Bruce D. and Evans, Craig A., eds. (Boston, MA: Brill Academic Publishers, Inc., 2002), pp. 3-30. (Abbr. "Authenticating Jesus Activities")

Fiensy, David A. *Christian Origins and the Ancient Economy* (Eugene, OR: Cascade Books, 2014). (Abbr. "Christian Origins")

Fiensy, David A. *Insights From Archaeology* (Minneapolis, MN: Fortress Press, 2017). (Abbr. "Insights From Archaeology")

Fortna, Robert T. "Jesus Tradition in the Signs Gospel," in *Jesus in Johannine Tradition*, Fortna, Robert T. and Thatcher, Tom, eds. (Louisville, KY: Westminister John Knox Press, 2001), pp. 199-208. (Abbr. "Signs Gospel")

Fortna, Robert T. "Source and Redaction in the Fourth Gospel's Portrayal of Jesus' Signs," *Journal of Biblical Literature*, Vol. 89, No. 2 (Jun., 1970), pp. 151-166. (Abbr. "Portrayal of Jesus' Signs")

Fortna, Robert Tomson. *The Fourth Gospel and Its Predecessor: From Narrative to Present Gospel* (Minneapolis, MN: Fortress Press, 2007). (Abbr. "Fourth Gospel and Predecessor")

Fortna, Robert T. *The Gospel of Signs: A Reconstruction of the Narrative Source Underlying the Fourth Gospel* (New York, NY: Cambridge University Press, 1970). (Abbr. "Signs Reconstruction")

Freed, Edwin D. and Hunt, Russell B. "Fortna's Signs-Source in John," *Journal of Biblical Literature*, Vol. 94, No. 4 (Dec., 1975), pp. 563-579. (Abbr. "Signs-Source John")

Freehof, Solomon Bennett. *Book of Jeremiah: A Commentary* (New York, NY: Union of American Hebrew Congregations, 1977). (Abbr. "Book of Jeremiah")

Freyne, Sean. "A Galilean Messiah?", *Studia Theologica – Nordic Journal of Theology*, Volume 55, Issue 2 (2001), pp. 198-218. (Abbr. "A Galilean Messiah")

Freyne, Sean. "Bandits in Galilee: A Contribution to the Study of Social Conditions in First-Century Palestine," in *The Social World of Formative Christianity and Judaism. Essays in Tribute to Howard Clark Kee*, Neusner, Jacob, et al., eds. (Philadelphia, PA: Fortress Press, 1988), pp. 50-68. (Abbr. "Bandits in Galilee")

Gardner, Gregg E. "Support for the Poor in Early Rabbinic Judaism," *Hebrew Union College Annual*, Vol. 86 (2015), pp. 37-62. (Abbr. "Support for Poor")

Geering, Lloyd. *The World to Come: From Christian Past to Global Future* (Santa Rosa, CA: Polebridge Press, 1999). (Abbr. "Christian Past")

Gotsis, George N. and Drakopoulou-Dodd, Sarah. "Economic Ideas in the Epistle of James," *History of Economic Ideas*, Vol. 12, No. 1 (2004), pp. 7-35. (Abbr. "Economic Ideas in James")

Green, Gene L. "Macedonia," in *The World of the New Testament: Cultural, Social, and Historical Contexts*, Green, Joel B. and McDonald, Lee Martin, eds. (Grand Rapids, MI: Baker Academic, 2013), pp. 532-543. (Abbr. "Macedonia")

Greene, John T. "Prolegomana," in *The Fruits of Madness: Perspectives on the Prophetic Movements in Three Traditions*, Greene, John Tracy, ed. (Newcastle upon Tyne, UK: Cambridge Scholars Publishing, 2016), xi-xxvii. (Abbr. "Prolegomana")

Guijarro, Santiago. "The Family in First-Century Galilee," in *Constructing Early Christian Families: Family as Social Reality and Metaphor*, Moxnes, Halvor, ed. (New York, NY: Routledge, 1997), pp. 42-65. (Abbr. "Family Galilee")

Guthrie, Donald. "The Importance of Signs in the Fourth Gospel," *Vox Evangelica* 5 (1967), pp. 72 – 83. (Abbr. "Importance of Signs")

Häkkinen, Sakari. "Poverty in the first-century Galilee," *HTS Teologiese Studies*, Vol 72, No 4 (2016), pp. 1-9. (Abbr. "Poverty in First-century Galilee")

Hallevy, Gabriel. "The Shadows of Normality: Legal Insanity under Modern Criminal Law," in *The Insanity Defense: Multidisciplinary Views on its History, Trends, and Controversies*, White, Mark D., ed. (Santa Barbara, CA: ABC-CLIO, 2017), pp. 97-132. (Abbr. "The Shadows of Normality")

Hanson, Kenneth C. and Oakman, Douglas E. *Palestine in the Time of Jesus: Social Structures and Social Conflicts*, Second Edition (Minneapolis, MN: Fortress Press, 2008). (Abbr. "Social Structures, Social Conflicts")

Harland, Philip A. "The Economy of First Century Palestine: State of the Scholarly Discussion," in *Handbook of Early Christianity: Social Science Approaches*, Blasi, Anthony J., et al., eds. (Walnut Creek, CA: AltaMira Press, 2002), pp. 511-527. (Abbr. "Economy Palestine")

Hartke, Wilhelm. *Vier urchristliche Parteien und ihre Vereinigung zur apostolischen Kirche*, 2 vols. (Berlin, Germany: Deutsche Akademie-Verlag, 1961). (Abbr. "Vier urchristliche Parteien")

Havukainen, Tuomas. "Birger Gerhardsson on the Transmission of Jesus Traditions – How Did the Rabbinic Model Advance a Scholarly Discourse?", *IESUS ABOENSIS: Åbo Akademi Journal for Historical Jesus Research*, Vol 1, No 1 (2015), pp. 49-63. (Abbr. "Transmission of Jesus Traditions")

Hearon, Holly. "The Story of 'the Woman Who Anointed Jesus' as Social Memory: A Methodological Proposal for the Study of Tradition as Memory," in *Memory, Tradition, And Text: Uses of the Past in Early Christianity* (Atlanta, GA: Society of Biblical Literature, 2005). pp. 99-118. (Abbr. "Woman Who Anointed Jesus")

Hedrick, Charles W. *The Wisdom of Jesus: Between the Sages of Israel and the Apostles of the Church* (Cambridge, UK: James Clarke & Co., 2017). (Abbr. "The Wisdom of Jesus")

Hendricks, Jr., Obery M. *The Politics of Jesus: Rediscovering the True Revolutionary Nature of Jesus' Teachings and How They Have Been Corrupted* (New York, NY: Three Leaves Press, 2006). (Abbr. "Politics of Jesus")

Henriksen, Jan-Olav and Sandnes, Karl Olav. *Jesus as Healer: A Gospel for the Body* (Grand Rapids, MI: William B. Eerdmans Publishing Company, 2016). (Abbr. "Jesus as Healer")

Horbury, William. "Christ as Brigand in Ancient Anti-Christian Polemic," in *Jesus and the Politics of His Day*, Bammel, Ernst and Moule, C.F.D., eds. (New York, NY: Cambridge University Press, 1984), pp. 183-196. (Abbr. "Christ as Brigand")

Horsley, Richard A. "Josephus and the Bandits," *Journal for the Study of Judaism*, Volume 10, Issue 1 (Jan 1979), pp. 37-63. (Abbr. "Josephus and Bandits")

Horsley, Richard A. "Popular Prophetic Movements at the Time of Jesus: Their Principal Features and Social Origins," in *New Testament Backgrounds: A Sheffield Reader*, Evans, Craig A. and Porter, Stanley E., eds. (Sheffield, England: Sheffield Academic Press Ltd, 1997), pp. 124-148. (Abbr. "Popular Prophetic Movements")

Horsley, Richard A. "Power Vacuum and Power Struggle in 66-7 C.E.," in *The First Jewish Revolt: Archaeology, History and Ideology*, Berlin, Andrea M. and Overman, J. Andrew, eds. (New York, NY: Routledge, 2002), pp. 87-109. (Abbr. "Power Vacuum")

Horsley, Richard A. "The Language(s) of the Kingdom: From Aramaic to Greek, Galilee to Syria, Oral to Oral-Written," in *A Wandering Galilean: Essays in Honour of Seán Freyne*, Rodgers, Zuleika Rogers, et al., eds. (Leiden, The Netherlands: Brill, 2009), pp. 401-426. (Abbr. "Oral to Oral-Written")

Houtart, Francois. "Palestine in Jesus' Time," *Social Scientist*, Vol. 4, No. 6 (Jan., 1976), pp. 14-24. (Abbr. "Palestine in Jesus' Time")

Instone-Brewer, David. "Jesus of Nazareth's Trial in the Uncensored Talmud," *Tyndale Bulletin* 62.2 (2011), pp. 269-294. (Abbr. "Uncensored Talmud")

Jeffers, James S. *The Greco-Roman World of the New Testament: Exploring the Background of Early Christianity* (Downers Grove, IL: InterVarsity Press, 1999). (Abbr. "Background Early Christianity")

Johns, Loren L. and Miller, Douglas B. "The Signs as Witnesses in the Fourth Gospel: Reexamining the Evidence," *The Catholic Biblical Quarterly*, Vol. 56, No. 3 (July, 1994), pp. 519-535. (Abbr. "Signs as Witnesses")

Keener, Craig S. *The Gospel of John: A Commentary, Volume Two* (Grand Rapids, MI: Baker Academic, 2003). (Abbr. John, Commentary, ii. (Abbr. "Gospel of John, ii")

Keener, Craig S. *The Historical Jesus of the Gospels* (Grand Rapids, MI: William B. Eerdmans Publishing Company, 2009). (Abbr. "Historical Jesus Gospels")

Kelber, Werner H. "Orality and Literacy in Early Christianity," *Biblical Theology Bulletin: Journal of Bible and Culture*, Vol 44, Iss 3 (2014), pp. 144-155. (Abbr. "Orality and Literacy")

King, Helen. "Introduction: What is Health?", in *Health in Antiquity*, King, Helen, ed. (New York, NY: Routledge, 2005), 1-11. (Abbr. "What is Health")

Klinghoffer, David. *Why the Jews Rejected Jesus: The Turning Point in Western History* (New York, NY: Doubleday, 2006). (Abbr. "Why Jews Rejected Jesus")

Kloppenborg, John S. "Unsocial Bandits," in *A Wandering Galilean: Essays in Honour of Seán Freyne*, Rodgers, Zuleika, et al., eds. (Leiden, The Netherlands: Brill, 2009), pp. 451-484. (Abbr. "Unsocial Bandits")

Köstenberger, Andreas J. "Jesus as Rabbi in the Fourth Gospel," *Bulletin for Biblical Research* 8 (1998): 97-128. (Abbr. "Jesus as Rabbi")

Laes, Christian. *Children in the Roman Empire: Outsiders Within* (New York, NY: Cambridge University Press, 2011). (Abbr. "Outsiders Within")

Lang, Graeme. "Oppression and Revolt in Ancient Palestine: The Evidence in Jewish Literature from the Prophets to Josephus," *Sociological Analysis*, Vol. 49, No. 4 (Winter, 1989), pp. 325-342. (Abbr. "Oppression and Revolt")

Lenski, Gerhard, Lenski, et al. *Human Societies: An Introduction to Macrosociology*, 6th Edition (New York, NY: McGraw-Hill, 1991). (Abbr. "Human Societies")

Loader, William. "What Happened to 'Good News for the Poor' in the Johannine Tradition?" in *John, Jesus, and History, Volume 3: Glimpses of*

Jesus Through the Johannine Lens, Anderson, Paul N., et al., eds. (Atlanta, GA: SBL Press, 2016), pp. 469-480. (Abbr. "What Happened Good News")

Longenecker, Bruce W. *Remember the Poor: Paul, Poverty and the Greco-Roman World* (Grand Rapids, MI: William B. Eerdmans Publishing Company, 2010). (Abbr. "Remember the Poor")

Magness, Jodi. *Stone and Dung, Oil and Spit: Jewish Daily Life in the Time of Jesus* (Grand Rapids, MI: William B. Erdmans Publishing Company, 2011). (Abbr. "Stone, Dung, Oil, Spit")

Malina, Bruce J. "Social Scientific Methods in Jesus Research," in *The Social Setting of Jesus and the Gospels*, Stegemann, Wolfgang, et al., eds. (Minneapolis, MN: Fortress Press, 2002), pp. 3-26. (Abbr. "Social-Scientific Jesus Research")

Malina, Bruce J. and Rohrbaugh, Richard L. *Social-Science Commentary on the Synoptic Gospels* (Minneapolis, MN: Fortress Press, 2003). (Abbr. "Social-Science Commentary Synoptics")

Mare, W. Harold. "Teacher and Rabbi in the New Testament Period," *Grace Theological Journal* 11.3 (1970), pp. 11-21. (Abbr. "Teacher and Rabbi")

Martyn, J. Louis. *History and Theology in the Fourth Gospel*, Third Edition (Louisville, KY: Westminster John Knox Press, 2003). (Abbr. "History, Theology, Fourth Gospel")

Maynard-Reed, Pedrito U. *Poverty and Wealth in James* (Eugene, OR: Wipf and Stock Publishers, 2004). (Abbr. "Poverty and Wealth")

McIver, Robert K. "The Archaeology of Galilee and Palestine from the Maccabees to the Jewish Second Jewish Revolt (167 BC-AD 135)," in *The Content and the Setting of the Gospel Tradition*, Harding, Mark and Nobbs, Alanna, eds. (Grand Rapids, MI: William B. Eerdmans Publishing Company, 2010), 1-27. (Abbr. "Archaeology, Galilee, and Palestine")

Meier, John P. *A Marginal Jew: Rethinking the Historical Jesus – Volume 2, Mentor, Message, and Miracles* (New York, NY: Doubleday, 1994). (Abbr. "Mentor, Message, Miracles")

Meier, John P. *A Marginal Jew: The Roots of the Problem and the Person – Volume 1* (New York, NY: Doubleday, 1991). (Abbr. "Roots of the Problem")

Merlier, Octave. *Le quatrieme Evangile: La question Johannique XI. etudes Neo-Testamentaires*, 2. (Paris, France: Presses Universitaires de France, 1961). (Abbr. "La question Johannique XI")

Moore, Daniel F. "Jesus, An Emerging Jewish Mosaic," in *Jesus Research – New Methodologies and Perceptions: The Second Princeton-Prague Symposium on Jesus Research*, Charlesworth, James H., ed. With Rhea, Brian and Pokorny, Petr (Grand Rapids, MI: William B. Erdmans Publishing Company, 2014), pp. 58-81. (Abbr. "Jewish Mosaic")

Mumcuoglu, Kosta Y. and Hadas, Gideon. "Head Louse (Pediculus humanus capitis) Remains in a Louse Comb from the Roman Period Excavated in the Dead Sea Region," *Israel Exploration Journal*, Volume 61, Number 2 (2011), pp. 223-229. (Abbr. "Louse Dead Sea Region")

Mumcuoglu, Yani K. and Zias, Joseph. "Head Lice, Pediculus humanus capitis (Anoplura: Pediculidae) from Hair Combs Excavated in Israel and Dated from the First Century B.C. to the Eighth Century A.D.," *Journal of Medical Entomology*, Volume 25, Issue 6 (1988), pp. 545-547. (Abbr. "Head Lice, Pediculus Humanus")

Mumcuoglu, Yani Kosta Y., et al. "Body Louse Remains Found in Textiles Excavated at Masada, Israel," *Journal of Medical Entomology*, Volume 40, Issue 4 (2003), pp. 585-587. (Abbr. "Body Louse at Masada")

Nel, Marius J. "The Forgiveness of Debt in Matthew 6:12, 14-15," *Neotestamentica*, Vol. 47, No. 1 (2013), pp. 87-106. (Abbr. "Forgiveness of Debt")

Neyrey, Jerome H. *Honor and Shame in the Gospel of Matthew* (Louisville, KY: Westminster John Knox Press, 1998). (Abbr. "Honor and Shame")

Nicol, Willem. *The Sēmia in the Fourth Gospel: Tradition and Redaction* (Leiden, Netherlands: Brill, 1972). (Abbr. (Abbr. "Sēmia Fourth Gospel")

Nussbaum, Kurt. "Abnormal Mental Phenomena in the Prophets," *Journal of Religion and Health*, Vol. 13, No. 3 (Jul., 1974), pp. 194-200. (Abbr. "Abnormal Mental Phenomena Prophets")

Oakman, Douglas E. "Execrating? Or Execrable Peasants!", in *The Galilean Economy in the Time of Jesus*, Fiensy, David A. and Hawkins, Ralph K., eds. (Atlanta, GA: Society of Biblical Literature, 2013), pp. 139-164. (Abbr. "Excrable Peasants")

Oakman, Douglas E. "Jesus and Agrarian Palestine: The Factor of Debt," in *The Social World of the New Testament*, Neyrey, Jerome H. and Stewart, Eric C., eds. (Peabody, MA: Hendrickson Publishers, Inc., 2008), pp. 63-82. (Abbr. "Jesus and Agrarian Palestine")

Oakman, Douglas E. *Jesus, Debt, and the Lord's Prayer: First-Century Debt and Jesus' Intentions* (Cambridge, UK: James Clarke & Co, 2014). (Abbr. "Jesus, Debt, Lord's Prayer")

Oakman, Douglas E. "Late Second Temple Galilee: Socio-Archaeology and Dimensions of Exploitation in First-Century Palestine," in *Galilee in the Late Second Temple and Mishnaic Periods: Life, Culture, and Society*, Fiensy, David A. and Strange, James Riley, eds. (Minneapolis, MN: Fortress Press, 2014), pp. 346-356. (Abbr. "Galilee Exploitation")

Oakman, Douglas E. "Was Jesus a Peasant?: Implications for Reading the Samaritan Story," *Biblical Theology Bulletin: Journal of Bible and Culture*, Volume 22, Issue 3 (1992), pp. 117-125. (Abbr. "Was Jesus a Peasant")

Orlin, Eric, et al., ed., *Routledge Encyclopedia of Ancient Mediterranean Religions* (New York NY: Routledge, 2016). (Abbr. "Ancient Mediterranean Religions")

Overman, J. Andrew. "Late Second Temple Galilee: A Picture of Relative Economic Health," in *Galilee in the Late Second Temple and Mishnaic Periods: Life, Culture, and Society*, Fiensy, David A. and Strange, James

Riley, eds. (Minneapolis, MN: Fortress Press, 2014), pp. 357-365. (Abbr. "Galilee Relative Economic Health")

Reed, Jonathan L. *Archaeology and the Galilean Jesus: A Re-examination of the Evidence* (Harrisburg, PA: Trinity Press International, 2001). (Abbr. "Re-Examination")

Reed, Jonathan L. "Instability in Jesus' Galilee: A Demographic Perspective," *Journal of Biblical Literature*, Vol. 129, No. 2 (SUMMER 2010), pp. 343-365. (Abbr. "Instability Jesus' Galilee")

Reed, Jonathan L. "Mortality, Morbidity, and Economics in Jesus' Galilee," in *Galilee in the Late Second Temple and Mishnaic Periods, Volume I: Life, Culture, and Society*. Fiensy, David A. and Strange, James Riley, eds. (Minneapolis, MN: Fortress Press, 2014), pp. 242-252. (Abbr. Mortality, Morbidity, Economics Galilee")

Reed, Jonathan L. *The HarperCollins Visual Guide to the New Testament: What Archaeology Reveals About the First Christians* (New York, NY: HarperOne, 2007). (Abbr. "What Archaeology Reveals")

Reim, Günter. *Studien Zum Alttestamentlichen Hintergrund Des Johannesevangeliums* (Cambridge, UK: Cambridge University Press, 1974). (Abbr. "Hintergrund Johannesevangeliums")

Retief, Francis P. and Cilliers, Louise. "The Influence of Christianity on Graeco-Roman Medicine Up to the Renaissance," *Acta Theologica Supplementum* 7 (2005), pp. 259-277. (Abbr. "Influence Christianity Medicine")

Reyes, E. Christopher. *In His Name* (Bloomington, IN: AuthorHouse, 2010). (Abbr. "In His Name")

Richardson, Peter and Edwards, Douglas. "Jesus and Palestinian Social Protest," in *Handbook of Early Christianity: Social Science Approaches*, Blasi, Anthony J, et al., eds. (New York, NY: Altamira Press, 2002), pp. 247-266. (Abbr. "Jesus, Palestinian Social Protest")

Rocca, Samuel. *Herod's Judaea: A Mediterranean State in the Classical World* (Tübingen, Germany: Mohr Siebeck, 2008). (Abbr. Herod's Judaea")

Rock, Ian E. *Paul's Letter to the Romans and Roman Imperialism: An Ideological Analysis of the Exordium (Romans 1:1-17)* (Eugene, OR: Pickwick Publications, 2012). (Abbr. "Paul's Letter")

Rohrbaugh, Richard L. "Introduction," in *The Social Sciences and New Testament Interpretation* (Grand Rapids, MI: Baker Academic, 1996). (Abbr. "The Social Sciences")

Rohrbaugh, Richard L. *The New Testament in Cross-Cultural Perspective* (Eugene, OR: Cascade Books, 2006). (Abbr. "NT Cross-Cultural Perspective")

Rosenfeld, Ben-Zion. "Innkeeping in Jewish Society in Roman Palestine," *Journal of the Economic and Social History of the Orient*, Vol. 41, No. 2 (1998), pp. 133-158. (Abbr. "Innkeeping Jewish Society)

Rosenfeld, Ben-Zion and Menirav, Joseph. "Fraud: From the Biblical Basis to General Commercial Law in Roman Palestine," *Journal for the Study of Judaism in the Persian, Hellenistic, and Roman Period*, Vol. 37, No. 4 (2006), pp. 594-627. (Abbr. "Fraud Biblical Basis")

Rosenfeld, Ben-Zion and Perlmutter, Haim. "The Poor as a Stratum of Jewish Society in Roman Palestine 70-250 CE: An Analysis," *Historia: Zeitschrift für Alte Geschichte*, Bd. 60, H. 3 (2011), pp. 273-300. (Abbr. "Poor Stratum Jewish Society")

Salier, Willis Hedley. *The Rhetorical Impact of the Sēmeia in the Gospel of John* (Tübingen, Germany: Mohr Siebeck, 2004). (Abbr. "Rhetorical Impact Sēmeia")

Sallares, Robert. Malaria and Rome: *A History of Malaria in Ancient Italy* (New York, NY: Oxford University Press, 2002). (Abbr. "Malaria and Rome")

Sanders, E. P. *Jesus and Judaism* (Philadelphia, PA: Fortress Press, 1985). (Abbr. "Jesus and Judaism")

Sanders, E. P. *The Historical Figure of Jesus* (New York, NY: Penguin Books, 1995). (Abbr. "Historical Figure of Jesus") (Abbr. "Historical Figure of Jesus")

Schäfer, Peter. *The History of the Jews in the Greco-Roman World: The Jews of Palestine from Alexander the Great to the Arab Conquest*, 2nd Edition (New York, NY: Routledge, 2003). (Abbr. "History Jews Palestine")

Schnackenburg, Rudolf. *The Gospel According to St John, Volume One* (New York, NY: The Crossroad Publishing Company, 1982). (Abbr. "St John, i")

Schnackenburg, Rudolf. *The Gospel According to St. John, Volume Two: Commentary on Chapters 5-12*, Hastings, Cecily, et al., trans. (New York, NY: Seabury Press, 1980). (Abbr. "St John, ii")

Schulz, Siegfried. *Komposition und Herkunft der Johanneischen Beitrage zur Wissenschaft vom Alten und Neuen Testament* (Stuttgart, Germany: Kohlhammer, 1960). (Abbr. "Herkunft der Johanneischen")

Skinner, Andrew C. "A Historical Sketch of Galilee," *Brigham Young University Studies*, Vol. 36, No. 3, Masada and the World of the New Testament (1996-97), pp. 113-125. (Abbr. "Historical Sketch")

Smith, D. Moody. "The Setting and Shape of a Johannine Narrative Source," *Journal of Biblical Literature*, Vol. 95, No. 2 (Jun., 1976), pp. 231-241. (Abbr. "Setting and Shape Johannine")

Stark, Rodney. "Antioch as the Social Situation for Matthew's Gospel," in *Social History of the Matthean Community: Cross-Disciplinary Approaches*, Balch, David L., ed. (Minneapolis, MN: Fortress Press, 1991), pp. 189-210. (Abbr. "Antioch as Social Situation")

Stegemann, Ekkehard W. and Stegemann, Wolfgang. *The Jesus Movement: A Social History of Its First Century*, Dean, Jr., O. C., trans. (Minneapolis, MN, Fortress Press, 1999). (Abbr. "Jesus Movement")

Stein, Robert H. *Jesus the Messiah: A Survey of the Life of Christ* (Downers Grove, IL: InterVarsity Press, 1996). (Abbr. "Jesus the Messiah")

Taylor, N. H. "Popular Opposition to Caligula in Jewish Palestine," *Journal for the Study of Judaism in the Persian, Hellenistic, and Roman Period*, Vol. 32, No. 1 (2001), pp. 54-70. (Abbr. "Opposition Caligula Jewish Palestine")

Tenney, Merrill C. "Topics From the Gospel of John Part II: The Meaning of the Signs," *Bibliotheca Sacra* 132 (April 1975), pp. 145-160. (Abbr. "Meaning of the Signs")

Theissen, Gerd. "Jesus as an Itinerant Teacher: Reflections from Social History on Jesus' Roles," in *Jesus Research: An International Perspective: – The Proceedings of the Biennial Princeton-Prague Symposium on the Current State of Studies on the Historical Jesus,* Charlesworth, J. H. and Pokorný, Petr, eds. (Grand Rapids, MI: William B. Eerdmans Publishing Company, 2009), pp. 98-122. (Abbr. "Social History Jesus")

Thompson, Marianne Meye. "Signs and Faith in the Fourth Gospel," *Bulletin for Biblical Research* 1 (1991), 89-108. (Abbr. "Signs and Faith")

Toit, Andrie B. du. "'God's beloved in Rome' (Rm 1:7). The Genesis and Socio-Economic Situation of the First Generation Christian Community in Rome," *Neotestamentica*, Vol. 32, No. 2, The church, one yet multifarious — a study from many perspectives: essays in honour of John H Roberts (1998), pp. 367-388. (Abbr. "Socio-Economic Christian Community Rome")

Udoh, Fabian. "Taxation and Other Sources of Government Income in the Galilee of Herod and Antipas," in *Galilee in the Late Second Temple and Mishnaic Periods: Life, Culture, and Society*, Fiensy, David A. and Strange, James Riley, eds. (Minneapolis, MN: Fortress Press, 2014), pp. 357-365. (Abbr. "Taxation, Herod, Antipas")

Ukpong, Justin. "The Parable of the Talents (Matt 23:14-30): Commendation or Critique of Exploitation?: A Socio-Historical and Theological Reading," *Neotestamentica*, Vol. 46, No. 1 (2012), pp. 190-207. (Abbr. "Parable of Talents – Exploitation")

Vena, Osvaldo D. *Jesus, Disciple of the Kingdom: Mark's Christology for a Community in Crisis* (Eugene, OR: Pickwick Publications, 2014). (Abbr. "Disciple of the Kingdom")

Vourinen, Heikki S. "Water and Health in Antiquity: Europe's Legacy," in *Environmental History of Water: Global Views on Community Water*

Supply and Sanitation, Juuti, Petri S., et al., eds. (London, UK: IWA Publishing, 2007), pp. 45-68. (Abbr. "Water and Health Antiquity")

Wahlde, Urban C. von. *Gnosticism, Docetism, and the Judaisms of the First Century: The Search for the Wider Context of the Johannine Literature and Why It Matters* (New York, NY: Bloomsbury T&T Clark, 2015). (Abbr. "Gnosticism, Docetism")

Wahlde, Urban C. von. *The Earliest Version of John's Gospel: Recovering the Gospel of Signs* (Wilmington, DE: Michael Glazier, Inc, 1989). (Abbr "Earliest Version")

Wahlde, Urban C. von. "The First Edition of John's Gospel in Light of Archaeology and Contemporary Literature," in *The Gospel of John in Historical Research*, Charlesworth, James H. and Pruszinski, Jolyon G. R., eds. (New York, NY: T&T Clark, 2019), pp. 99-141. (Abbr. "First Edition John's Gospel")

Wahlde, Urban C. von. *The Gospel and Letters of John, Volume 1: Introduction, Analysis, and Reference* (Grand Rapids, MI: William B. Eerdmans Publishing Company, 2010). (Abbr. "Gospel and Letters, i")

Wallis, Ian G. *The Galilean Wonderworker: Reassessing Jesus' Reputation for Healing and Exorcism* (Eugene, OR: Cascade Books, 2020). (Abbr. "Galilean Wonderworker")

Walter, Nikolaus. "Die Auslegung überlieferter Wundererzählungen im Johannes-Evangelium," in *Theologische Versuche* 2 (Berlin: Germany: Evangelische Verlagsanstalt, 1970), pp. 93-107. (Abbr. "Auslegung überlieferter Wundererzählungen")

Webb, Robert L. *John the Baptizer and Prophet: A Socio-historical Study* (Eugene, OR: Wipf and Stock Publishers, 2006). (Abbr. "Socio-historical Study")

Weitzman, Steven. "From Feasts into Mourning: The Violence of Early Jewish Festivals," *The Journal of Religion*, Vol. 79, No. 4 (Oct., 1999), pp. 545-565. (Abbr. "From Feasts into Mourning")

Welch, John W. "Legal and Social Perspectives on Robbers in First-Century Judea," *BYU Studies Quarterly*, Vol. 36, No. 3 (1996), pp. 141-153. (Abbr. "Legal, Social Perspectives Robbers")

Wilkens, Wilhelm. *Die Entstehungsgeschichte des vierten Evangeliums* (Zollikon: Evangelischer Verlag, 1958). (Abbr. "Entstehungsgeschichte Evangeliums")Zias 1991, Death and Disease, 149. Wilkens, Wilhelm. *Die Entstehungsgeschichte des vierten Evangeliums* (Zollikon: Evangelischer Verlag, 1958). (Abbr. "Entstehungsgeschichte Evangeliums")

Zias, Joseph. "Current Archaeological Research in Israel: Death and Disease in Ancient Israel," *The Biblical Archaeologist*, Vol. 54, No. 3 (Sep., 1991), pp. 146-159. (Abbr. "Death and Disease")

CHAPTER FIVE
Endnotes

1 See Abel 1971, Memory and Rumor Transmission, 270-281; Hearon 2005, Woman Who Anointed Jesus, 102, note 3; Botha 1993, Social Dynamics, 205-231; Aune 2013, Gospel Tradition and Paul, 172-175; Kelber 2014, Orality and Literacy, 144-155.

2 As to "fragments," see Meir 1991, Roots of the Problem, 25, 31.

3 Sanders 1985, Jesus and Judaism, 11; Meir 1994, Mentor, Message, and Miracles, 630; Evans 2002, Authenticating Jesus Activities, 12; Bird and Crossley 2008, Believer and Non-Believer, 22; Charlesworth 2008, Historical Jesus Essential Guide, 81; Allison, Jr., 2009, Historical Christ Theological Jesus, 77; Keener 2009, Historical Jesus Gospels, 242.

4 Mare 1970, Teacher and Rabbi, 16; Köstenberger 1998, Jesus as Rabbi, 106-107; Havukainen 2015, Transmission of Jesus Traditions, 58-59.

5 We have to take into account that Palestine was an agrarian dominated society. Most villagers who worked with their hands would have "lived close to the subsistence level, struggling to maintain a state of 'wantless-ness'" (Magness 2011, Stone, Dung, Oil, Spit, 14). For deeper drilldown, see Oakman's realistic, thumbnail-sketch depicting a rather burgeoning rural class of indebted "poor" (Oakman 2008, Jesus and Agrarian Palestine, 68-75).

6 See Stark 1991, Antioch as Social Situation, 195; Lenski and Nolan 1991, Human Societies, 173; Botha 1993, Social Dynamics, 217-218; Rohrbaugh 1996, The Social Sciences, 5; Sallares 2002, Malaria and Rome, 277-278; Bolt 2003, Jesus' Defeat of Death, 28-30; Reed 2010, Instability Jesus' Galilee, 353-355; Fiensy 2017, Insights From Archaeology, 114-115.

7 Klinghoffer 2006, Why Jews Rejected Jesus, 73.

8 See Reyes 2010, Name, 349.

9 The Munich Talmud is "the earliest full manuscript of the Talmud" (Chapman and Schnabel 2015, Trial and Crucifixion, 137, note 499).

10 Instone-Brewer 2011, Uncensored Talmud, 272.

11 Reyes 2010, Name, 349.

12 Crosby 2008, Healing: Hope or Hype, 274; Wallis 2020, Galilean Wonderworker, 38.

13 The latest (hypothetical) socio-economic models posited by experts represent 80-90% of first century CE Palestinians at, near, or under the "subsistence" level. Numerous resources offer valuable insights. Among them: Longenecker 2010, Remember the Poor, 44-53; Brookins 2014, Corinthian Wisdom, 119-122; Häkkinen 2016, Poverty in First-century Galilee, 1-9. For background: Houtart 1976, Palestine in Jesus' Time, 14-24; Horsley 1979, Josephus and Bandits, 37-63; Bammel 1984, Poor and Zealots, 109-128; Horbury 1984, Christ as Brigand, 183-196; Freyne 1988, Bandits in Galilee, 50-68; Lang 1989, Oppression and Revolt, 325-342; Welch 1996, Legal, Social Perspectives Robbers, 141-153; Guijarro 1997, Family Galilee, 42-65; Horsley 1997, Popular Prophetic Movements, 124-148; Rosenfeld 1998, Innkeeping Jewish Society, 133-158; Botha 1998, Houses in World Jesus, 37-74; Toit 1998, Socio-Economic Christian Community Rome, 367-388; Neyrey 1998, Loss of Wealth, 139-158; Dodd and Gotsis, Economic Implications Synoptic Theology, 7-34; Edwards 2001, Social, Religious, Political, 153-162; Taylor 2001, Opposition Caligula Jewish Palestine, 54-70; Harland 2002, Economy Palestine, 511-527; Esler 2002, Jesus Intergroup Conflict, 185-206; Malina 2002 Social-Scientific Jesus Research, 3-26; Horsley 2002, Power Vacuum, 87-109; Richardson and Edwards 2002, Jesus, Palestinian Social Justice, 247-266; Schäfer 2003, History Jews Palestine, 89-134; Rosenfeld and Menirav 2006, Fraud Biblical Basis, 594-627; Blumell 2008, Social Banditry, 35-53; Rocca 2008, Herod's Judea, 197-239; Crook

2009, Social Status, 591-611; Horsley 2009, Roman Rule, 335-360; Theissen 2009, Social History Jesus, 98-122; Kloppenborg 2009, Unsocial Bandits, 451-484; Reed 2010, Instability Jesus' Galilee, 343-365; Andrade 2010, Ambiguity, Violence, Community, 342-370; Rosenfeld and Perlmutter 2011, Poor Stratum Jewish Society, 273-300; Ukpong 2012, Parable of Talents – Exploitation, 190-207; Nel 2013, Forgiveness of Debt, 87-106; Green 2013, Macedonia, 532-543; Downs 2013, Economics, Taxes, Tithes, 156-168; Reed 2014, Mortality, Morbidity, Economics Galilee, 242-252; Oakman 2014, Galilee Exploitation, 346-356; Overman 2014, Galilee Relative Economic Health, 357-365; Udoh 2014, Taxation, Herod, Antipas, 357-365; Gardner 2015, Support for Poor, 37-62.

14 Fiensy 2014, Christian Origins, 33.

15 Such characterizations are often sidestepped in New Testament studies. The following scholars make clear statements from a realistically recalled socioeconomic scenario: Oakman 1992, Was Jesus a Peasant, 117-125; Bock 2002, Studying the Historical Jesus, 120; Capper 2006, Essene Community Houses, 472-502; Carter 2010, Matthew's People, 145; Magness 2011, Stone, Dung, Oil, Spit, 14; Vena 2014, Disciple of the Kingdom, 185; Hedrick 2017, Wisdom of Jesus, 186.

16 Malina and Rohrbaugh 2003, Social-Science Commentary Synoptics, 169.

17 Stein 1996, Jesus the Messiah, 53.

18 See Berlin 2005, Jewish Life Before Revolt, 418-420.

19 Skinner 1996-97, Historical Sketch, 121; Jeffers 1999, Background Early Christianity, 44; Stegemann and Stegemann 1999, Jesus Movement, 112, 134, 136; Capps 2000, Psychological Biography, 135-136; Reed 2001, Re-examination, 97; Bolt 2003, Jesus' Defeat of Death, 27-28; Gotsis and Drakopoulou-Dodd 2004, Economic Ideas in James, 10; Maynard-Reed 2004, Poverty and Wealth, 87; Hendricks, Jr. 2006, Politics of Jesus, 82-83; Rohrbaugh 2006, NT Cross-Cultural Perspec-

tive, 28; Webb 2006, Socio-historical Study, 356-357; Reed 2007, What Archaeology Reveals, 50-51; Hanson and Oakman 2008, Social Structures, Social Conflicts, 111; Dunn 2009, Beginning from Jerusalem, 13; McIver 2010, Archaeology Galilee and Palestine, 20; Laes 2011, Outsiders Within, 26; Botha 2012, Orality and Literacy, 150; Moore 2012, Belligerent Christ, 14; Rock 2012, Paul's Letter, 222; Oakman 2013, Execrable Peasants, 148, 151; Deines 2014, Jesus Recent Research, 29; Fiensy 2014, Christian Origins, 139; Oakman 2014, Jesus, Debt, Lord's Prayer, 3; Eck 2016, Parables of Jesus, 238; Loader 2016, What Happened Good News, 469-472; Orlin, et al., eds. 2016, Ancient Mediterranean Religions, 36-38.

20 Stegemann and Stegemann 1999, Jesus Movement, 112; Freyne 2001, A Galilean Messiah, 204.

21 Mumcuoglu and Zias 1988, Head Lice, Pediculus Humanus, 545-547; Mumcuoglu, et al. 2003, Body Louse at Masada, 585-587; Mumcuoglu and Hadas 2008, Louse Dead Sea Region, 223-229.

22 Drali, et al., Human Lice in Palaeoentomology, 184.

23 Moore 2012, Belligerent Christ, 14.

24 For select background on all of these items, see Zias 1991, Disease and Death, 146-159; Rohrbaugh 1996, The Social Sciences, 5; Jeffers 1999, Background Early Christianity, 44; Bolt 2003, Jesus' Defeat of Death, 27-28; Hendricks, Jr. 2006, Politics of Jesus, 82-83; McIver 2010, Archaeology, Galilee, and Palestine, 20; Botha 2012, Orality and Literacy, 150; Fiensy 2014, Christian Origins, 139.

25 Brandon 1967, Jesus and Zealots, 16-17.

26 Burkill 1958, The Trial of Jesus, 9.

27 Brandon 1967, Jesus and Zealots, 16. Also, Dodd 1954, The Fourth Gospel, 444-453; Dodd 1963, Historical Tradition Fourth Gospel, 24, 97-98, 120; Brown 1966, John i-xii, 441-442; Keener 2003, Gospel of John ii, 852.

28 Von Wahlde 2019, First Edition John's Gospel, 140.

29 Charlesworth 2008, Temple, Purity, Jesus' Death, 430.

30 Von Wahlde 2019, First Edition John's Gospel, 140.

31 For example, Sanders 1995, Historical Figure of Jesus, 13; Dunn 2003, Jesus Remembered, 769-770.

32 Nussbaum 1974, Abnormal Mental Phenomena Prophets, 194-200; Greene 2016, Prolegomena, xxvii, note 1; Hallevy 2017, The Shadows of Normality, 108-109; Cook 2019, Hearing Voices, Demonic, Divine.

33 Examples: (Jeremiah) Freehof 1977, Book of Jeremiah, 131; (Ezekiel) Block 1997, Book of Ezekiel, 338; (Elijah) Drazin 2006, Rational Approach to Judaism, 188.

34 See Jn 4.19; 6.14; 7.40; 9.17.

35 Weitzman 1999, From Feasts into Mourning, 545-565.

36 Geering 1999, Christian Past, 130.

37 While the author is not a scholar, aspects of the research behind this study is quite thorough. In the next volume, the chapter titled "Markan Mythos" features an endnote citing numerous scholars defending John's early origins. The list moves from the year 1922 onward.

38 For in-depth background, see Charlesworth 2008, Temple, Purity, Jesus' Death, 433-435.

39 Diakonoff, First Period of History, 52.

40 Zias 1991, Death and Disease, 149.

41 King 2005, What is Health, 8.

42 Vuorinen 2007, Water and Health Antiquity, 61.

43 Fiensy 2014, Christian Origins 139.

44 Fiensy 2017, Insights From Archaeology, 71.

45 Botha 2012, Orality and Literacy, 150.

46 Boer and Petterson, Times of Trouble, 54, note 20.

47 Meir 1994, Mentor, Message, and Miracles, 630; Evans 2002, Authenticating Jesus Activities, 12; Keener 2009, Historical Jesus Gospels, 242.

48 See Sanders 1995, Historical Figure of Jesus, 145.

49 "Now when John heard in prison about the deeds of the Christ, he sent word by his disciples and said to him, 'Are you he who is to come, or shall we look for another?' And Jesus answered them, 'Go and tell John what you hear and see: the blind receive their sight and the lame walk, lepers are cleansed and the deaf hear, and the dead are raised up, and the poor have good news preached to them. And blessed is he who takes no offense at me'" (Mt 11.2-6; also, Lk 7.18-23, RSV).

50 "So the chief priests and the Pharisees gathered the council, and said, 'What are we to do? For this man performs many signs'" (Jn 11.47, RSV).

51 "Yet many of the people believed in him; they said, 'When the Christ appears, will he do more signs than this man has done?'" (Jn 7.31, RSV).

52 Casey 2010, Independent Historian's Account, 239.

53 Retief and Cilliers 2005, Influence Christianity Medicine, 264.

54 Capper 2006, Essene Community Houses, 472-502; Capper 2014, The Essene Religious Order, 57-60; 62, 64, 66-67, 70.

55 Henriksen and Sandnes 2016, Jesus as Healer, 10.

56 Reed 2014, Mortality, Morbidity, Economics Galilee, 242-243.

57 Arbel 2014, Ultimate Devotion, 83.

58 For a diversity of scholarly insights: Broome, Jr. 1944, Sources Fourth Gospel, 107-121; Heinz Becker 1956, Gnostischen Offenbarungsrede; Wilkens 1958, Entstehungsgeschichte Evangeliums; Schulz 1960, Herkunft der Johanneischen; Boismard 1961, évolution eschatologique johanniques; Hartke 1961, Vier urchristliche Pareien; Merlier 1961, La question Johannique XI; Dodd 1963, Historical Tradition Fourth Gospel, 174-232; Brown 1966, John i-xii, cxxxviii-cxliv; Guthrie 1967, Importance of Signs, 73-78; Jürgen Becker 1969–70, Wunder und Christologie, 130–48; Fortna 1970, Portrayal of Jesus' Signs. 151-166; Walter

1970, Auslegung überlieferter Wundererzählungen, 93-107; Fortna 1970, Signs Reconstruction, 29-98; Nicol 1972, Sēmia Fourth Gospel, 53-62; Reim 1974, Hintergrund Johannesevangeliums; Freed and Hunt 1975, Signs-Source John, 563-579; Tenney 1975, Meaning of the Signs, 145-160; D. M. Smith 1976, Setting and Shape Johannine, 231-241; Cope 1987, Signs Earliest Gospel, 17-24; Von Wahlde 1989, Earliest Version, 66-155; Thompson, Signs and Faith, 89-108; Johns and Miller 1994, Signs as Witnesses, 519-535; Martyn 2003, History, Theology, Fourth Gospel, 92-94; Salier 2004, Rhetorical Impact Sēmeia, 146-173; Fortna 2007, Fourth Gospel and Predecessor, 15-117; Von Wahlde 2010, Gospel and Letters, i, 58-62; Von Wahlde 2015, Gnosticism, Docetism, 2-7; Audlin 2017, Original Version, 612-722, 736-731,782-790,797-815, 818-823; Von Wahlde 2019, First Edition John's Gospel, 99-141.

59 Brown (1966, 1970, 2010), Bultmann (1971), Fortna (1970, 2001, 2007), Martyn (2003), Schnackenburg (1980, 1982), and von Wahlde (1989, 2010, 2019) are among other high-profile scholars who at some point in their professional work defend the Johannine "source tradition" proposal. On multiple levels, the author's own conclusions are entirely sympathetic to von Wahlde's unique, provocative thesis. After all, the book is dedicated to his immensely original research. This study is convinced that von Wahlde's thesis is ultimately the most likely path that confidently intersects with history.

60 Häkkinen 2016. Poverty in First-century Galilee, 3, 7.

61 McIver 2010, Archaeology, Galilee, and Palestine, 20; Botha 2012, Orality and Literacy, 150.

62 Stegemann and Stegemann 1999, Jesus Movement, 134; Deines 2014, Jesus Recent Research, 29.

63 S. L. Adams 2014, Social-Economic Life, 78-79.

64 Loader 2016, What Happened Good News, 469.

65 Botha 1993, Social Dynamics, 218-219.

6

Literacy

We need to recognize that the final canonical texts often inaccurately portrayed *original* remembered details. In tandem with this understanding is a companion aspect. We should acknowledge that **oral** sources would have been far closer to the earliest time and place setting. Far closer than (1) post-Palestine, (2) gentile-based, (3) dogmatically-edited, (4) written stories. In short, hellenized religious tracts finalized in pagan lands.

Which, in the search for the earliest footprint, brings us to the enormously important subject of *orality*. How extensively this archaic communication form dominated the ancient world. How the earliest footprint of Jesus was deeply influenced by an exclusively *oral* venue.

This topic will be explored in the next segment. An introduction is provided here.

We should open by emphatically stressing a more plausible view that history utterly rejects the posture of modern fabricated profiles. Studies that cast Jesus as a purely *mythical* character reminiscent of half-feathered creatures watching over the pyramids.[1] Or Roman Flavian promotional ploys.[2] Or cynic philosophers transmigrated from the Athenian *agora* ("marketplace").[3]

For this study, such highly imaginative creations are wholly out of whack with the historical era. Like proselytizing disciples, virgin births, and demon stories, a postmodern academic class is in want of a sustaining message that accurately tracks a regular heartbeat. A heartbeat that at one point was situated in the *real world*. A heartbeat native to the Land of Israel. Appallingly, the great majority of these modern creations ignore even a modicum of rational thought.

This study insists that the earliest footprint is buried beneath the rubble of a colossal religious monument, a surviving archaeological remnant inside David's City. Only random impressions and giant stone foundations remain.

Such a footprint is situated in archaic architectural grids of family homesteads peppering the Galilean countryside. In virtually every case the remains reflect modest habitations and population groups in close social contact.

Further, the earliest footprint is encountered somewhere in a riverbed near the eastern shore of the River Jordan. Two social reformers once sought spiritual renewal in submersion baptism and visual imagery depicting the Mosaic mythos.

What we articulate here (hopefully) with some degree of accuracy is the fact that within distant, antiquated, geographical settings righteous indignation seethed in the throes of pagan rule and aristocratic corruption. Filled with pain and loss, a whole population, dominated by disadvantaged social groups, cried out for radical reform. A historical setting tailormade for demographic profiles matching the likes of courageous social aspirants such as John and Jesus.

Inside these pages we examine residual evidence of a well-documented historical figure. We reaffirm a human drama that caught wind of an extraordinary village healer. We monitor the activities of a rural rabbi who witnessed impoverished population groups and impossible mortality rates. We assess a human life that by virtue of moral transcendence alone threatened the very core of autocratic rule.

In putting forth a determined effort, however, the postmodern era claims a formidable barrier blocks our path. From legal experts. To child psychologists. From scientific authorities. To lead detectives. From highly trained health professionals. To congressional oversight committees. Each of these categories credibly argues that human memory *cannot* be trusted. And a dense set of researched findings boldly argues the case.

According to highly qualified technical experts, *how* we remember is selective. Very often creative. At times unintentionally filled with gaps. Or at other times *unknowingly* false. That is what our specialists profess. That is what the overwhelming majority claims.

Subject matter can range from "suggestibility" to "bias" to "absent-mindedness."[4] There is false memory in "witness interviews."[5] As well as the "reconstructive" aspects of remembering.[6] Even adding creative "details" when memories are incomplete.[7] Or, on a more personal note, "false memory syndrome." Especially relevant in cases of reported sexual abuse.[8]

These details could all be true. However, within the framework of identifying a proper methodology for tapping the *earliest footprint* there really and truly is *a lot more to say*. A lot more that seems to slip through the cracks. A lot more that moves well past the often highly technical musings of today's cutting-edge authorities.

Readers should know straight-up that in this phase of the discussion we are not referring to issues of faith. Like it or not, such thinking is beyond the scope of this study. No, we are pointing at historical *probabilities*. High probabilities. Whether or not they hold religious value.

Most modern day historical scholars like to apply their theories quoting reputable sources. In academic circles this approach establishes credibility. Having learned enough to know that the story of Jesus grew from oral – not written – origins, as would be typically expected, more recently they pattern their "historical" findings off the kinds of expert types mentioned above.

With enormous confidence, Western experts break the news. Carefully assessed results of formal memory research insist that most set-in-stone impressions of the historical figure cannot be trusted. The figure of Jesus, that is.

We, an ignorant public, must understand that many decades separated original events (in the early 30s CE) from conversion to written forms (60s to 90s CE). The long duration plainly forbad any degree of accuracy in final tabulations. Lack of written instruments in between confidently detailed this objective reality.

Way too long to remember. Way too long to keep it straight. It's as simple as that. Our current picture of Jesus leans toward "legendary" at best. So say postmodern experts propped up by reams of precious, highly technical, analytical data.

They insist that, in any general sense, over time our memory banks are incapable of maintaining accuracy. Then or now. This reality is quite damming to measuring a trustworthy synthesis. But nothing can really be done. Facts are facts. The human mind has its limits. On and on the experts go so pleased with their studied deductions.

However, implied above, there is another approach that is characteristically overlooked. An approach far more relevant within the bounds of *history*. An approach that ultimately lays waste to postmodern expert proposals.

Truth be told, their energetically and thoroughly documented remarks, (one can imagine) quite popular in the current scholarly environment, prove at best to be *convoluted*. At worst, *nonsensical*. And virtually no one across the broad Western academic spectrum seems aware of the driving need for **context**.

First, for casual readers, we need to properly set the stage. We need to properly introduce an evaluation of the ancient past that probably few of us really know. Or even guess. An evaluation that is systematically ignored by most New Testament scholars. And trifled at by niche professionals. A most crucial evaluation that literally *dominated* real life settings in virtually every historical era across the world.

A socioeconomic birds eye view of first-century Judaic culture could not have missed the fact that most people were *illiterate*. One hesitates to promote such generalities. But it is unavoidable today not to observe that this view has been commonly held among many well-established experts for at least several decades.[9] Based on the evidence, such a conclusion is quite reliable.

Readers need to understand that during this period (nearly) all communication among the common people was oral. In other words in some form of conversation. Entirely independent of reading and writing.

Excluding Jerusalem temple operatives, urban officials, and scattered village scribes, almost all of Palestine could not read or write. Thus, nearly everyone was illiterate. The only exceptions would perhaps have constituted some merchants, traders, political, and religious figures (mostly) embedded in the upper classes.

Almost impossible for our day to grasp, in the context of Jesus and his era, as a rule only people who lived above the masses could read. Fewer could write. Fewer still lived in rural villages.[10] Nearly all situated in the "literate zone" were city-dwellers.[11]

As a summary statement, outside the urban centers of Palestine peasant populations were almost entirely illiterate.[12] We are further convinced when learning that archaeology tends to support this valuation.[13]

As a practical matter this means we face the inevitable conclusion that with very high likelihood neither Jesus nor his early disciples could either read or write.[14] That is very hard for many religious people in the modern West to accept. But the Nazarene's social demographic occupied an entirely redefined cultural synthesis than what most people today usually evaluate.

We need to remember that *Yeshu ha-Notzri's* first followers were simple fishermen, farmers, laborers, and (possibly) artisans from rural locales.[15] Within the ongoing social drama of "haves" versus "have nots," these individuals were not cast from the mold of Paul from Tarsus. To say the least.

Paul hailed from one of the largest and most influential academic centers in the combined Mediterranean and Near Eastern world. In Paul's time, for knowledge and philosophical debate, Tarsus was right up there with Alexandria and Athens.[16]

For us today, when evaluating the life of Paul against the life of Jesus, this aspect is really important. This aspect begins to sketch a more probable outline leaving dogmatic appeals to supplementary discussions.

Paul from Tarsus was educated and thrived in a Hellenistic world. Jesus the Nazarene was not and did not. Based on the evidence, we are led to believe they represented, demographically, close to polar opposites. Paul grew up a city dweller. Jesus grew up in the countryside.

For those who are unaware, numerous contrasts filled out the character sketches. Such contrasts would have overwhelmed their common Judaic heritage. Though even shared religious observance would have been tinged by "Palestine" versus "Diaspora" upbringing.

As for literacy, we know for certain that agrarian population settlements throughout the Land of Israel were filled by the lower classes (however one wishes to define them). In addition, across the region (even more so in rural Galilee) the availability of literate village scribes would often have been extremely limited (to non-existent).[17]

Under the rare exceptions in remote rural settings when village scribes *were* present, some scholars believe their function was *not* to teach literacy. But scriptural traditions and various aspects of torah.[18]

Other experts have concluded these scribes were tasked to teach the so-called "wisdom literature" to peasant audiences.[19] In either case this hardly suggests the laborious and time-consuming effort (many years) required to instill full-blown literacy skills.

The view that Jesus and his first followers were illiterate is partially supported in Scriptures (though the meaning is at times hotly debated on both sides).

Now when they saw the boldness of Peter and John, and perceived that they were uneducated, common men, they wondered; and they recognized that they had been with Jesus (Acts 4.13, RSV).

Impartial observers today have to admit that the *Acts* citation, if trustworthy, seems to be pretty decisive.

Considering the dearth of ancient documentary sources in general, support for the "illiteracy" of Yeshu's earliest followers in strong testimony beyond Christian scriptures is evocative. In fact, we do have ancient sources testifying to the disciples' pointblank *unread* status.

One early source, the Pseudo-Clementine "Recognitions," has been acknowledged as one of the clearest examples of original Palestinian "Jewish-Christian" thinking available to us.[20] And happens to explicitly mention the subject of *literacy*.

> Therefore Caiaphas, again looking at me [i.e. Simon Peter], and sometimes in the way of warning and sometimes in that of accusation, said that I ought for the future to refrain from preaching Christ Jesus, lest I should do it to my own destruction, and lest, being deceived myself, I should also deceive others. Then, moreover, he charged me with presumption, because, *though I was unlearned, a fisherman, and a rustic* [emphasis added], I dared to assume the office of a teacher. As he spoke these things, and many more of like kind, I said in reply, that I incurred less danger, if, as he said, this Jesus were not the Christ, because I received Him as a teacher of the law; but that he was in terrible danger if this be the very Christ, as assuredly He is: for I believe in Him who has appeared; but for whom else, who has never appeared, does he reserve his faith? *But if I, an unlearned and uneducated man, as you say, a fisherman and a rustic* [emphasis added], have more understanding than wise elders, this, said I, ought the more to strike terror into you. For if I disputed with any learning, and won over you wise and learned men, it would appear that I had acquired this power by long learning, and not by the grace of divine power; but now, when, as I have said, we *unskilled men* [emphasis added] convince and overcome you wise men, who that has any sense

does not perceive that this is not a work of human subtlety, but of divine will and gift?" (Clement, *Recognitions*, 1.62).

Interestingly, this memory preserved in *Recognitions* mirrored basic details from the episode in the *Book of Acts* (chapter 4) just mentioned.

Origen, the early church father, was just as outspoken:

Now, who is there on seeing fishermen and tax-gatherers, who had not acquired even the merest elements of learning (as the Gospel relates of them, and in respect to which Celsus believes that they speak the truth, inasmuch as it is their own ignorance which they record) [emphasis added], discoursing boldly not only among the Jews of faith in Jesus, but also preaching Him with success among other nations, would not inquire whence they derived this power of persuasion, as theirs was certainly not the common method [emphasis added] followed by the multitude? (Origen, Contra Celsum 1.62).

The earliest followers *illiteracy* argument is typically supported by a measurable number of reliable experts in New Testament studies.[21] This idea does not represent a circumstantial oddity promoted by "way out there" sycophants.

In the postmodern era a radically altered first-century world is re-sculpted for discerning eyes focused on *history*. Not till transmigration from rural districts to urban settings (probably to locales beyond the Land of Israel) would accounts of Jesus have had any hope of inscription to writing.

The near-unanimous *illiteracy* in these ancient rural zones severely discourages the idea of, not only written Gospels, but written sayings and parables as well. We must remember that the stalking grounds of Jesus and his early followers were entirely *rural* in makeup and composition.

Over the years, in line with biblical tracts, sectarian interests have aggressively defended Jesus the Nazarene's literacy. One method is the definition itself. Some have considered literacy per se as the ability to *sign one's name.*

Such a defense, however, is easily refuted. One scholarly source points out that a signature can be equated to drawing a picture.[22] In possession of only this isolated ability, however, limited to the equivalent of "artistic" skills, such proposals do not hold water.

Others have defended Jesus's literacy simply on the basis of modern doctrinal models: he was a religious teacher so he must have been able to read Scriptures. However, ancient manuscripts were extremely difficult to master. They required an enormous secondary knowledge related to deciphering grammer and phrasing. The composition of these documents featured no breaks in letters. Words were formulated from long strings of unbroken text. Everything was strewn together.[23]

We need to see that the first stories about *Yeshu-ha-Notzri* were formed deep inside rural Palestinian village communities. And not by scribal editors. During the early period these stories were not intended to be written down. Set inside this socio-cultural microcosm, they were clearly intended to be *remembered.*

In the case of later written texts performed live, memorization was still a required skill. Reading from the ancient narratives required a substantial specialized skillset. Individuals were forced to straightaway process the various markings into meaningful, understandable sentence structures.

Such unique in-depth training represented an advanced aptitude that went far beyond writing one's name or methodically deciphering isolated phrases.[24]

Raised in a rural village setting, who would have been available and qualified to devote *literally years* to teaching a youthful *Yeshu-ha-Notzri* to read Hebrew. Not just Hebrew but some Galilean variation of Aramaic, the language of the common people?[25] The answer, unfortunately, is no one.

Furthermore, most scholars would probably agree that whilst the Jewish historian Josephus claimed widespread education in Palestine, the reality was closer to mirroring education for children of elites, the political and social class of which Flavius Josephus was surely a member.[26] Few modern experts would agree with the Josephus prognosis.

As far as results from Galilean dig sites, the home region of Jesus and his first disciples, the physical testimony supports our "illiteracy" argument to a tee. Across the region very few written inscriptions from that era have been identified.[27]

Interestingly, the most controversial canonical evidence defending the relative *literacy or illiteracy* of Jesus is probably found in the *Gospel of John*. During a Jerusalem festival when Yeshu was teaching within the temple precincts the narrative account depicted Judaic scribes muttering: "How is it that this man has learning [or this man knows his letters], when he has never studied?" (Jn 7.15, RSV).

The testimony suggests that if Jesus were not literate then his extraordinary mastery of traditional religious imagery was suggestive of what people today would describe as *photographic recall*. Far from a "supernatural" facility, Jesus didn't need to read because he probably remembered with extreme precision. A well-documented advance skill especially familiar within culturally based social settings.[28]

Whether he could read or write, no qualified scholar would deny that Jesus possessed an innate aptitude to disseminate spiritual absolutes in provocatively visual imagery. Descriptive images that plain folk could easily absorb. He interpreted the traditional sacred writings with such original insight as to inspire other Israelites (even perceived enemies) in ways the postmodern era probably cannot fully appreciate.

CHAPTER SIX
References

Adams, Sean A. "The Tradition of Peter's Literacy: Acts, 1 Peter, and Petrine Literature," in *Peter in Early Christianity*, Bond, Helen K. and Hurtado, Larry W., eds. (Grand Rapids, MI: William B. Eerdmans Publishing Company, 2015), pp. 130-145. (Abbr. "Peter's Literacy")

Atwill, Joseph. *Caesar's Messiah: The Roman Conspiracy to Invent Jesus: Flavian Signature Edition* (North Charleston, SC: CreateSpace, 2011). (Abbr. "Caesar's Messiah")

Balch, David L. "The Suffering of Isis/Io and Paul's Portrait of Christ Crucified (Gal. 3:1): Frescoes in Pompeian and Roman Houses and in the Temple of Isis in Pompeii," *The Journal of Religion*, Vol. 83, No. 1 (Jan., 2003), pp. 24-55. (Abbr. "Suffering of Isis")

Bar-Ilan, Meir. "Illiteracy in the Land of Israel in the First Centuries C.E.," in *Essays in the Social Scientific Study of Judaim and Jewish Society*, Fishbane, Simcha, et al., eds. (New York, NY: KTAV Publishing House, Inc., 1992), pp. 46-61. (Abbr. "Illiteracy in Israel")

Bauer, Bruno. *Christ and the Caesars – The Origin of the Christians: From the Mythology of Rome*, Second Printing (Berlin, Germany: Eugen Grosser, 1879). (Abbr. "Christ and Caesars")

Betz, Hans Dieter. "Jesus and the Cynics: Survey and Analysis of a Hypothesis," *The Journal of Religion*, Vol. 74, No. 4 (Oct., 1994), pp. 453-475. (Abbr. "Jesus and Cynics")

Boas, George. *Essays on Primitivism and Related Ideas in the Middle Ages* (Baltimore, MD: John Hopkins University Press, 1948). (Abbr. "Essays on Primitivism")

Borg, Marcus. *Jesus in Contemporary Scholarship* (Harrisburg, PA: Trinity Press International, 1994). (Abbr. "Jesus in Contemporary Scholarship")

Botha, Pieter J. J. *Orality and Literacy in Early Christianity* (Eugene, OR: Cascade Books, 2012). (Abbr. "Orality and Literacy")

Boyd, Gregory A. *Cynic Sage or Son of God?: Recovering the Real Jesus in an Age of Revisionist Replies* (Eugene, OR: Wipf and Stock Publishers, 2010). (Abbr. "Cynic Sage")

Brainerd, C. J. and Reyna, V. F. "False Memory in Criminal Investigation: 1 – Adult Interviewing and Eyewitness Identification," in *The Science of False Memory* (New York, NY: Oxford University Press, 2005), pp. 219-289. (Abbr. "False Memory Criminal Investigation")

Byrskog, Samuel. Story as History – History as Story: The Gospel Tradition in the Context of Ancient Oral History (Tübingen, Germany: Mohr Siebeck, 2000). (Abbr. "Story as History")

Cameron, Ron. "What Have You Come Out To See?': Characterizations of John and Jesus in the Gospels," *Semeia* 49 (1990), pp. 35–69. (Abbr. "Come Out")

Charles, J. Daryl. *The Unformed Conscience of Evangelicalism: Recovering the Church's Moral Vision* (Downers Grove, IL: InterVarsity Press, 2002). (Abbr. "Unformed Conscience of Evangelicalism")

Cooper, William Ricketts. *The Horus Myth in Its Relation to Christianity* (London, England: Hardwicke & Bogue, 1877). (Abbr. "Horus Myth")

Craffert, Pieter F. and Botha, Pieter J.J. "Why Jesus Could Walk on the Sea But He Could Not Read and Write," *Neotestamentica*, Vol. 39, No. 1 (2005), pp. 5-38. (Abbr. "Read and Write")

Crenshaw, James L. *Education in Ancient Israel: Across the Deadening Silence* (New York, NY: Doubleday, 1998). (Abbr. "Education in Ancient Israel")

Crossan, John Dominic. *Jesus: A Revolutionary Biography* (San Francisco, CA: Harper Collins Publishers, 1994). (Abbr. "Revolutionary Biography")

Davidson, Ivor J. *The Birth of the Church: From Jesus to Constantine, A.D. 30-312*, Woodbridge, John D. and Wright, David F., Consulting eds. (Oxford, England: Monarch Books, 2005). (Abbr. "Birth of the Church")

Dewey, Joanna. *The Oral Ethos of the Early Church: Speaking, Writing, and the Gospel of Mark* (Eugene, OR: Cascade Books, 2013). (Abbr. "Speaking, Writing, Mark")

Downing, F. Gerald. "Deeper Reflections on the Jewish Cynic Jesus," *Journal of Biblical Literature*, Vol. 117, No. 1 (Spring, 1998), pp. 97-104. (Abbr. "Jewish Cynic")

Dudley, Donald R. *A History of Cynicism: From Diogenes to the 6ᵗʰ Century A.D.* (London, England: Methuen & Co. Ltd., 1937). (Abbr. "History of Cynicism")

Dunn, James D. G. *The Oral Gospel Tradition* (Grand Rapids, MI: William B. Erdmans Publishing Company, 2013). (Abbr. "Oral Gospel Tradition")

Dutch, Robert. The Educated Elite in 1 Corinthians: Education and Community Conflict in Graeco-Roman Context (New York, NY: T&T Clark International, 2005). (Abbr. "Educated Elite")

Eddy, Paul Rhodes. "Jesus as Diogenes? Reflections on the Cynic Jesus Thesis," *Journal of Biblical Literature*, Vol. 115, No. 3 (Autumn, 1996), pp. 449-469. (Abbr. "Jesus as Diogenes")

Fideler, David. *Jesus Christ – Sun of God: Ancient Cosmology and Early Christian Symbolism* (Wheaton, IL: Quest Books Theosophical Publishing House, 1993).

Finegan, Jack. *Light from the Ancient Past: The Archaeological Background of the Hebrew-Christian Religion, Volume 1* (Princeton, NJ: Princeton University Press, 2015). (Abbr. "Archaeological Background, i")

Gadalla, Moustafa. *Ancient Egyptian Roots of Christianity*, Expanded 2nd Edition (Greensboro, NC: Tehuti Research Foundation, 2018). (Abbr. "Egyptian Roots")

Gzella, Holger. *A Cultural History of Aramaic: From the Beginnings to the Advent of Islam* (Leiden: The Netherlands, Bill, 2015). (Abbr. "Cultural History of Aramaic")

Halliday, W. R. *The Pagan Background of Early Christianity* (London, England: The University Press of Liverpool Ltd., 1925). (Abbr. "Pagan Background")

Harpur, Tom. *The Pagan Christ: Recovering the Lost Light* (New York, NY: Walker Publishing Company Inc., 2004). (Abbr. "Pagan Christ")

Harris, William V. *Ancient Literacy* (Cambridge, MA: Harvard University Press, 1991). (Abbr. "Ancient Literacy")

Hatch, Edwin. *The Influence of Greek Ideas on Christianity* (New York, NY: Harper & Row, 1966). (Abbr. "Greek Ideas")

Hearon, Holly E. "The Implications of Orality for Studies of the Biblical Text," in *Performing the Gospel: Orality, Memory, and Mark: Essays Dedicated to Werner Kelber*, Horsley, Richard A., et al., eds. (Minneapolis, MN: Fortress Press, 2006), pp. 3-20. (Abbr. "Implications of Orality")

Hendricks, Jr., Obery M. The Politics of Jesus: Rediscovering the True Revolutionary Nature of Jesus' Teachings and How They Have Been Corrupted (New York, NY: Three Leaves Press, 2006). (Abbr. "Politics of Jesus")

Hezser, Catherine. *Jewish Literacy in Roman Palestine* (Tübingen, Germany: Mohr Siebeck, 2001). (Abbr. "Jewish Literacy Roman Palestine")

Höistad, Ragnar. *Cynic Hero and Cynic King: Studies in the Cynic Conception of Man* (Uppsala, Sweden: University of Uppsala, 1948). (Abbr. "Cynic Hero")

Horsley, Richard A. *Archaeology, History, and Society in Galilee* (Harrisburg, PA: Trinity Press International, 1996). (Abbr. "Archaeology, History in Galilee")

Horsley, Richard A. *Jesus in Context: Performance, Power, and People* (Minneapolis, MN: Fortress Press, 2008). (Abbr. "Jesus in Context")

Hull, Michael F. *Baptism on Account of the Dead (1 Cor 15:29): An Act of Faith in the Resurrection* (Leiden, The Netherlands: Brill, 2005). (Abbr. "Baptism Account of Dead")

Huller, Stephan. *The Real Messiah: The Throne of St. Mark and the True Origins of Christianity* (London, UK: Watkins Publishing, 2009). (Abbr. "Real Messiah")

Keith, Chris. *Jesus Against the Scribal Elite: The Origins of the Conflict* (Grand Rapids, MI: Baker Academic, 2014). (Abbr. "Scribal Elite")

Keith, Chris. *Jesus' Literacy: Scribal Culture and the Teacher from Galilee* (New York, NY: Bloomsbury T&T Clark, 2011). (Abbr. "Jesus' Literacy")

Kelley, Nicole. *Knowledge and Religious Authority in the Pseudo-Clementines* (Tübingen, Germany: Mohr Siebeck, 2006). (Abbr. "Pseudo-Clementines")

Kelly, Lynne. The Memory Code: The Secrets of Stonehenge, Easter Island and Other Ancient Monuments (New York, NY: Pegasus Books Ltd, 2017). (Abbr. "The Memory Code")

Kuhn, Alvin Boyd. *Who Is This King of Glory? A Critical Study of the Christos-Messiah Tradition* (Elizabeth, NJ: Academy Press, 1944). (Abbr. "King of Glory")

Lang, Bernhard, ed. *International Review of Biblical Studies, Volume 48 (2001-2002)* (Boston, MA: Brill, 2003). (Abbr. "International Review Biblical Studies")

Mack, Burton L. *A Myth of Innocence: Mark and Christian Origins* (Minneapolis, MN: Fortress Press, 2006). (Abbr. "Myth of Innocence")

Massey, Gerald. Ancient Egypt: The Light of the World – A Work of Reclamation and Restitution in Twelve Books (London, England: T. Fisher Unwin, 1907). (Abbr. "Ancient Egypt")

Mournet, Terence C. "The Jesus Tradition as Oral Tradition," in *Jesus in Memory: Traditions in Oral and Scribal Perspectives* (Waco, TX: Baylor University Press, 2009), pp. 39-61. (Abbr. "Jesus Oral Tradition")

Nadel, Lynn and Sinnott-Armstrong, Walter P. "Introduction: Memory in the Legal Context," in *Memory and Law*, Nadel, Lynn and Sinnot-Armstrong, Walter P., eds. (New York, NY: Oxford University Press, 2012), pp. 3-6. (Abbr. "Memory in Legal Context")

Poirier, John C. "Education/Literacy in Jewish Galilee: Was There Any and at What Level?" in *Galilee in the Late Second Temple and Mishnaic Periods – Volume 1: Life, Culture, and Society*, Fiensy, David A. and Strange, James Riley, eds. (Minneapolis, MN: Fortress, 2014), pp. 253-260. (Abbr. "Education-Literacy Jewish Galilee")

Reuchlin, Abelard and Reek, Hevel V. *The True Authorship of the New Testament* (Kent, WA: Abelard Reuchlin Foundation, 1979). (Abbr. "True Authorship")

Rhoads, David. "Performance Events in Early Christianity: New Testament Writings in an Oral Context," in *The Interface of Orality and Writing: Speaking, Seeing, Writing in the Shaping of New Genres*, Weissenrieder, Annette and Coote, Robert B., eds. (Eugene, OR: Cascade Books, 2015), pp. 166-193. (Abbr. "Performance Events")

Rix, Rebecca A., ed. *Sexual Abuse Litigation: A Practical Resource for Attorneys, Clinicians, and Advocates* (New York, NY: Routledge, 2011). (Abbr., "Sexual Abuse Litigation")

Schacter, Daniel L. *The Seven Sins of Memory: How the Mind Forgets and Remembers* (New York, NY: Houghton Miflin Company, 2001), (Abbr. "Seven Sins of Memory")

Schams, Christine. *Jewish Scribes in the Second-Temple Period* (Sheffield, England: Sheffield Academic Press, 1998). (Abbr. "Jewish Scribes Second Temple")

Schneider, Carl. *Geistesgeschichte des antiken Christentums*, 2 vols. (Munich, Germany: Beck, 1954). (Abbr. "Antiken Christentums")

Shiner, Whitney. *Proclaiming the Gospel: First-Century Performance of Mark* (Harrisburg, PA: Trinity Press International, 2003). (Abbr. "Proclaiming the Gospel")

Spencer, Aída Besançon and Spencer, William David. *2 Corinthians* (Grand Rapids, MI: Lamplighter Books, 1989). (Abbr. "2 Corinthians")

Tavris, Carol and Aronson, Elliot. "Memory, the Self-Justifying Historian," in *Mistakes Were Made (But Not by Me): Why We Justify Foolish Beliefs, Bad Decisions Hurtful Acts* (New York, NY: Mariner Books, 2015), pp. 88-121. (Abbr. "Memory, Self-Justifying Historian")

Thatcher, Tom, et al., eds., *The Dictionary of the Bible and Ancient Media* (New York, NY: Bloomsbury, 2017). (Abbr. "Ancient Media")

Tuckett, C. M. "A Cynic Q?" *Biblica*, Vol. 70, No. 3 (1989), pp. 349-376. (Abbr. "Cynic Q")

Vaage, Leif. "Q: The Ethos and Ethics of an Itinerant Intelligence" (Ph.D. dissertation, Claremont Graduate School, 1987). (Abbr. "Ethos and Ethics")

Valliant, James S. and Fahy, C. W. *Creating Christ: How Roman Emperors Invented Christianity* (Hertford, NC: Crossroad Press, 2016). (Abbr. "Creating Christ")

Wechsler, Eduard. *Hellas im Evangelium* (Berlin, Germany: Metzner, 1936). (Abbr. "Hellas Evangelium")

Young, Stephen E. Jesus Tradition in the Apostolic Fathers: Their Explicit Appeals to the Words of Jesus in Light of Orality Studies (Tübingen, Germany: Mohr Siebeck, 2011). (Abbr. "Apostolic Fathers")

CHAPTER SIX

Endnotes

1 Cooper 1877, Horus Myth; Massey 1907, Ancient Egypt; Kuhn 1944, King of Glory; Fideler 1993, Sun of God; Balch 2003, Suffering of Isis, 24-55; Harpur 2004, Pagan Christ; Murdock 2011, Who Was Jesus; Gadalla 2018, Egyptian Roots.

2 Bauer 1879, Christ and Caesars; Reuchlin and Reek 1979, True Authorship; Atwill 2011, Caesar's Messiah; Valliant and Fahy 2016, Creating Christ. A relative of this theory is Huller 2009, Real Messiah that argues Jesus acted as a herald on behalf of the "true" Messiah, Marcus Julius Agrippa (Herod Agrippa II), the last Herodian ruler in Palestine.

3 Halliday 1925, Pagan Background, 126, 169-171, 201-202; Wechsler 1936, Hellas Evangelium, 242-266; Dudley 1937, History of Cynicism, 173-175, 204-207; Höistad 1948, Cynic Hero, 199, 221; Boas 1948, Essays on Primitivism, 87-128; Schneider 1954, Antiken Christentums, i, 1.31-45; Hatch 1966, Greek Ideas, 138-170; Vaage 1987, Ethos and Ethics; Tucket 1989, Cynic Q, 349-376; Cameron 1990, Come Out, 35-69; Betz 1994, Jesus and Cynics, 453-475; Crossan 1994, Revolutionary Biography; Eddy 1996, Jesus as Diogenes, 449-469; Downing 1998, Jewish Cynic, 97-104; Mack 2006, Myth of Innocence; Boyd 2010, Cynic Sage.

4 Schacter 2001, Seven Sins of Memory, 4.

5 Brainerd and Reyna 2005, False Memory Criminal Investigation, 219-289.

6 Tavris and Aronson 2015, Memory, Self-Justifying Historian, 88-121.

7 Nadel and Sinnott-Armstrong, Memory in Legal Context, 4.

8 Rix 2011, ed., Sexual Abuse Litigation, 32.

9 Harris 1991, Ancient Literacy; Bar-Ilan 1992, Illiteracy in Israel, 46-61; Byrskog 2000, Story as History, 9-10, 16, 23, 34, 46, 61, 93-94, 107-144, 300-301; Hezser 2001, Jewish Literacy Roman Palestine, 496-504; Shiner 2003, Proclaiming the Gospel, 11-13; Hearon 2006, Implications of Orality, 102-104; Dewey 2008, Speaking, Writing, Mark, 11; Horsley 2008, Jesus in Context, 4-5, 28-29, 57-59, 89-90, 111, 129, 148; Mournet 2009, Jesus Oral Tradition, 51; Keith 2011, Jesus' Literacy, 71-123; Botha 2012, Orality and Literacy, 39-61; Dunn 2013, Oral Gospel Tradition, 5, 51, 74, 94, 220, 277, 290.

10 Borg 1994, Jesus in Contemporary Scholarship, 101; Dutch 2005, Educated Elite, 183.

11 Hezser 2001, Jewish Literacy Roman Palestine, 496.

12 See Rhoads 2015, Performance Events, 167, note 4.

13 Horsley 2008, Jesus in Context, 89.

14 See a very detailed and fairhanded discussion in Keith 2011, Jesus' Literacy.

15 Davidson 2005, Birth of the Church, 14.

16 Spencer and Spencer 1989, 2 Corinthians, 19; Charles 2002, Unformed Conscience of Evangelicalism, 147; Hull 2005, Baptism Account of Dead, 125. Hendricks, Jr. 2006, Politics of Jesus, 81; Finegan 2015, Archaeological Background, i, 255.

17 Horsley 2008, Jesus in Context, 58.

18 Schams 1998, Jewish Scribes Second-Temple, 20.

19 Lang, ed. 2003, International Review Biblical Studies, 375-376.

20 Kelley 2006, Pseudo-Clementines, vii.

21 Keith 2011, Jesus' Literacy, 165-188; Craffert and Botha 2005, Read and Write, 26; Mournet 2009, Jesus Oral Tradition, 50-51; Adams 2015, Peter's Literacy, 130-145.

22 Young 2011, Apostolic Fathers, 76.

23 Horsley 1996, Archaeology, History, in Galilee, 156.

24 See Thatcher, et al., eds. 2017, Ancient Media, 4; Crenshaw 1998, Education in Ancient Israel, 43.

25 See Gzella 2015, Cultural History of Aramaic, 306.

26 See Keith 2014, Scribal Elite, 23.

27 Poirier 2014, "Education/Literacy Jewish Galilee, 255.

28 Kelly 2017, The Memory Code, 1-33.

7

Oral Formula

Thankfully, at least some scholars agree that even before the Nazarene's passing Galilean villagers began to tell stories. This charismatic Israelite and the healings he inspired could not be ignored.

Such stories began, quite sensibly, with *rumors*. Everyday Galileans in urban zones as well as in more isolated, rural areas in conversations amongst each other exchanged mental snapshots of the Nazarene's remarkable activities.[1] Thus, scholarship has properly assessed that "[r]umors are said to have played an important role in spreading knowledge about him and his healing faculties."[2]

As readers can expect, such "rumors" were entirely *oral* in composition. Again, they were initially passed along during Yeshu's lifetime. These first rough sketches eventually matured into oral stories celebrated in rural village assemblies.

Three independent structural elements would have strongly influenced oral formulations. Such historically reliable aspects were absolutely necessary to preserving original memories associated with Jesus. These individuals could not rely upon the written word. They were illiterate.

Fortunately, these three facets quite effectively breached the gap. They strongly influenced why we today still have relatively clear impressions of the historical figure. They defiantly reject most postmodern expert evaluations based on research entirely *irrelevant* to the ancient stage.

Implied, academic elites have categorically *ignored* very reliable historical influences surrounding initial orientations. Unfortunately, experts are still, for the most part, focused on probing for theologically leaning insights. A somewhat "ahistorical" approach from the get-go. An approach that often somehow winds up mimicking *historical* commentary. But in the end misses its ultimate target: accurate and authentic appraisals of the early first-century milieu.

Within the ancient setting, the three underlying elements just mentioned melded into a rough "memory system" of sorts. A calculated strategy to preserve maximum *accuracy* in oral recall. They explain why we can be confident that, minimally, a brief, somewhat untarnished, glimpse of the real-life figure was originally encoded into shared remembrance.

This quite effective thematic synthesis helps explain why a preponderance of postmodern experts happens to be definitively *wrong* about at least one aspect of the ancient setting. That is, the surprising ability of *illiterate poor* to preserve relatively accurate streams of oral tradition. Most experts today would deny this fact. It is *categorically* true.

Yes, across at least several generations of historical time social collectives of rural peasantry we might call "Jesus groups" remembered quite distinctly. Quite accurately.

Long enough to pull together at least some crucial details.

Long enough to transform core memory threads into shared awareness.

Long enough to transcribe oral accounts to written forms.

In very generic language, those "three independent structural elements" translate to the following brief descriptions:

Depictions of the recollected Jesus were initially recalled in organized *group* social settings.

Inside the originating cultural milieu, such narrative streams were structurally organized within the medium of traditional oral *storytelling*.

Early recitals were monitored by authority figures customarily identified as village *elders*.

Again, why we can feel confident that antiquity preserved a somewhat *accurate* silhouette relates *directly* to these three essential aspects. Inside original village environs, such discrete, *networked* elements blended to form a most powerful encoding instrument.

So what are we saying? It is this: illiterate, disadvantaged village groups managed to preserve plausible memories of an extraordinarily gifted local healer. Those still frames were ultimately organized in the form of a hologram of "living tradition."[3]

What most of us haven't learned (probably even most scholars) is that the historical roots behind this applied *modus operandi* stretched far back into the dim mists of prehistory.

Initially, many centuries before writing, this highly structured social form was probably focused on some type of "simple chant, set to the rhythm of some tribal occupation."[4] Yes, long before the time of Jesus. Long before the Land of Israel.

In fact, at some measurable level of awareness, such a concrete aptitude, repeatedly demonstrated in shared consciousness, "is likely linked to aspects inherent in our human physiology."[5]

There is an enormously important sociological aspect to this claim. At its most fundamental level, such a commonly shared behavioral characteristic comprises one of those unique traits that helps define our own humanity. Given illiteracy and tribal (or village) oriented populations, with minimal variations, the fusion of these individual characteristics seems to be native to the human condition.

Suggestively, in direct historical context, we are invited in what follows below to observe snapshots of *living memory* from various time settings and cultural environments all around the world. We are able to observe recognizable common links in all of them. A brief, representational review helps highlight this crucial assessment:

> Such a multitiered orality formula patterned into precisely
> applied human ingenuity helps explain why the Australian

Bibulmun Aboriginal tribe claimed that elders or "old ones" through oral tradition passed along to younger generations lifesaving wisdom from the distant past.[6]

Why the Klamath people in south-central Oregon still remember a time before Crater Lake more than 7,600 years ago. Not only before the lake but specific details of the lake's formation including the self-destruction of the volcano known as Mount Mazama.[7]

Why Native American Navajo Elders distributed to modern-day American zoologists the names, sounds, behaviors, and habitats of 700 insect species.[8]

Why archaeology has confirmed the burial site of Chief Roymata (dated to around 1200 CE) on Retoka Island off Efate (renamed "Sandwich Island" by Captain James Cook) in Vanuatu (in the South Pacific) matching "precisely the oral traditions."[9]

Why the Tareumiut and Nunamiut Eskimos in Northwest Alaska recorded oral histories that would assist them in long term survival when tribal crises arose due to food shortages from caribou populations or whaling activities failing to mirror normal patterns.[10]

Why in West African societies the elderly were honored as resources for history and knowledge.[11]

Why oral memories preserved by local elders in central Guatemala remembering the activities of Pedro de Alvarado (conquering their lands) happened to be more historically accurate than official written records.[12]

Why by means of "an old Ethiopian chronicle" we are able to verify oral tradition concerning "a Hadiya leader" across 500 years.[13]

Why even today eight artic indigenous people groups – "the Inuit, Sami, Aleut, Gwich'in, other Dene/Athahabaskan groups and indigenous nations of Northern Russia"[14] – as well as tropical island groups across the globe are consulted by UNFCCC (United Nations Framework Convention on Climate Change). In every individual case their historical knowledge base is *vast* and far more comprehensive than scientific studies.

Why during the Middle Ages Hungarians maintained an origins memory that they arrived in the West from the Russian steppes during the 890s. But some among their lineage remained in the original homeland. A Dominican friar from Hungary during the 1230s visited the foothills of the Ural mountains. "The folk memory was accurate: a people who spoke a version of Finno-Ugrian lived in the foothills of the Urals."[15]

Why early biblical tradition preserved at least some historical memories across a minimum of 500 years. In the *Book of Amos* (9.7) Y-H-V-H was said to have led the Philistines from Caphtor (Crete and the Aegean region). In the same way He led Arameans (i.e. "Syrians") from Qir. "Archaeological and textual evidence shows that for the Philistines this historical memory is accurate. In the early twelfth century B.C.E., the Philistines did arrive from the Aegean region."[16]

Why in the original Mong society of present-day Laos the thirteen respectful Elders used the oral tradition to preserve cultural memories of the past. They specifically recalled the chants of Shamans that included "some Mandarin Chinese words in them, because long ago [beginning at least 6,000 years ago in the Yellow River basin[17]] the Mandarin Chinese and the Mong were brotherhoods [*kwvtij*]. They lived together in China and their religious rituals influenced one another."[18]

Why, for untold millenia, in Central Australia local tribesmen replicated various animal behaviors orally. Details included minute physical descriptions, as well as quite effective butchering techniques.[19]

Why Yup'ik Elders living on the west central coast of Alaska and along nearby rivers inland baffle scientists today. With centuries of indigenous wisdom to rely upon, their wealth of knowledge defies modern understandings. By noting weather patterns, precipitation, and vegetation growth they are able to predict the timing of salmon runs with uncanny precision.[20]

Finally, why a research professor of Middle Eastern New Testament Studies based in Jerusalem for decades witnessed storytellers across the region reciting historical knowledge in community gatherings within a discipline characterized as "informal controlled oral tradition."[21] The format for such recitals explicitly included community gatherings, common memories, and oral storytelling – all conscientiously monitored by village elders.[22]

These details drive home an important, germane theme. As one expert puts it: "The claim of some biblical scholars that oral tradition cannot retain historical memories for more than 150 years is simply untenable."[23]

Today, we are overwhelmed by reliable historical remnants of the ancient past. Peoples and cultural milieus across the globe preserved untarnished snapshots of former times.[24] In some cases for exceedingly long periods of historical time. Far longer than what we can expect of original oral memories of Jesus. This conclusion constitutes a simple, undiluted, undeniable fact. In many cases, the three crucial elements mentioned above consistently highlighted the efforts of these widely disbursed people groups.

In fact, across millennia these three aspects seemed to distinguish the social behaviors and oral processes of multitudes of ancient tribal societies. Thus, chances are that in the early part of the first century, prior to written instruments, rural Galilean villagers still managed to retain authentic snapshots of a former local rabbi. That accomplished entirely independent of conclusions drawn in postmodern expert thinking.

In all fairness, within the historical milieu, we have to believe that some individuals who helped formulate the original stories had even known this inspirational figure *by name*. A remarkable healer. A charismatic leader. A measureless resource for wisdom and spiritual insight. A beloved martyr-figure to Galilean rural poor. While hypothetical, any other conclusion would ultimately besmirch this study's goal of absolute impartiality promoting accuracy and honest results.

Even without writing, three historically identified features (when witnessed together) tell us with some degree of certainty that *original* memories of Jesus were dependably encoded. And survived a violent, uncertain era among scattered groups of near-destitute rural poor. Following is brief, related discussion on each of the three characteristics:

GROUP DYNAMIC

In ancient times, one of the keys for preserving *accurate* memories related to how most people were organized. Almost universally they formed into "social groups." Usually by blood relations. As far as we know, within these people groups, no matter where we turn in the ancient era we see that such social groups exchanged oral stories within varying forms of community gatherings.

Crucially, the likelihood is that most who participated were afforded an opportunity to verify accuracy.[25] Or at least offer insights. The point is: not just community leaders were entitled. All were vested to preserve the accuracy of shared tradition.

This immensely important observation is *crucial* to understanding why we actually have in hand a fairly accurate sketch. The origins of Yeshu's story derived from *group* settings. All who participated were on the hook to get it right. To preserve an authentic framing.

So from a historical standpoint, we need to understand that in preserving the *earliest traditions* "quite strong group processes were involved."[26] The indefatigable *group* setting wants to assure us of its *historical* value.[27]

In Western society today what largely separates the modern social model from ancient times is the role of the *individual*. This comment does not need a defense. Those of us who live in the postmodern West all recognize its validity without requiring experts to confirm.

We conduct the public moments of our lives as socially independent units. We are free to move in or out of virtually any collective social setting at will. Or go it alone. Under numerous scenarios, matching this cultural model would have had grave consequences in the ancient Land of Israel.

Prior to written stories, in Galilean villages it was the *group* scenario that mattered. Not the individual.[28] True, each member was held responsible for their actions. But together they were strong. Need it be said that uncertain times required that they stand together?

Ancient Israelite culture was overshadowed by a longstanding cultic mythos. This society, like many rural societies, practiced a *collectivist* attitude.[29] This way of thinking dominated values, worldviews, and expectations. People lived and breathed and viewed the world around them through collectivist eyes. Social experts have come to understand that the *shared* mindset tended to harbor "in-group" versus "out-group" attitudes.[30]

In the next chapter we will discuss that villagers in the Land of Israel were not generally open to strangers. They were rather standoffish.[31] Thus, this very realistic assessment proffered authentic glimpses of a true-to-life social complex. A societal view from the original pre-Hellenistic social setting that categorically rejected later redactional claims of the synoptic proselytizing stories.

The truth is, Palestinian rural inhabitants would have considered wandering itinerants with extreme suspicion. In light of their social pedigree, such village groups would hardly be receptive to (what they considered) atypical religious rhetoric carried by unknown strangers into their villages. Rhetoric that aggressively challenged the shared myth of their beloved "Promised Land." Within the historical social milieu, wherever they traveled in Israel, indigent disciples would definitely be cast as the *out-group.*

Again, this attitude was commemorated in ancient texts. The Roman historian Tacitus (*Histories* 5.5.1) claimed, "[T]he Jews feel only hatred and enmity toward every other people (*adversus omnes alios hostile odium*)."[32]

So first take away the obvious bias. What is left? Answer, when categorizing the various players and associated behaviors, the substance of the Roman historian's remarks identically matched certain particulars described above. First-century Israelites would not be receptive to wandering disciples. For impartial readers, even disciples of Jesus.

Consequently, the synoptic proselytizing stories we read are definitively disconnected from the original historical setting. Understandably, a defensive posture tended to dominate Palestinian villagers' reactions to strangers. But it was more than just the Romans. Readers may wish to evaluate a far more convoluted sociopolitical environment accurately depicting the times. During the first century, Israelites were pressured on every side:

There were Herod's pagan communities scattered across the land.[33]

There was aggressive taxation from governing authorities.[34]

And mounting personal debt.[35]

There was the threat of losing one's land in the event of sudden illness or accident.[36]

Cited in this study, archaeology informs us of the everpresent hazard of malnutrition among family members.[37]

There was imminent violence in many villages.[38]

On the road there was the lurking danger of highway robbery.[39]

And of course (already suggested) there was the vile Roman presence. For many Israelites a plague upon their sacred "Promised Land."[40]

For these reasons (and probably more), generally speaking, during the first century populations living in the Land of Israel experienced greater anxiety confronting strangers than peoples living in more urbanized, cosmopolitan, hellenistic settings.[41]

For Israel, dominated by rather small rural villages across the geographical landscape, attention and priorities were more fixed on immediate living groups. In other words, family and community. There is really very little question that everyone knew everyone else in these geographically close-knit rural settings.

Observed within a strict *social* context, the final outcome is members within these communities knew each other rather intimately. In any perceived threat to fellow villagers, most would have had each other's backs. Survival depended upon staying together. Plainly, a *collective* reality. First-century Israelites did not tolerate threats against this concrete social dynamic.

Thus, with some degree of confidence we can draw a general conclusion that these disadvantaged population groups weren't enthusiastic about exchanging ideas with people they didn't personally know. Or at least recognize.

The collectivist mindset tended to "generalize" about *out-groups*.[42] In the *Acts of the Apostles*, Stephen, recognized by many as the first Christian martyr, complained of the Jews: "You stiff-necked people, uncircumcised in heart and ears, you always resist the Holy Spirit. As your fathers did, so do you" (Acts 7.51, RSV).

In this scene the Stephen character represented himself as a member of the *in-group*, Hellenistic Jesus believers. He was portrayed putting forth a *generalization* against the *out-group*. They were represented by the Judaic high priest supported by the Jerusalem Council.

An interesting corollary has been observed by experts today. In Pauline Christian tradition, believers shied away from using "kinship terms when addressing non-Christian gentiles."[43] In other words, early Christians (i.e. the *in-group*) avoided phrasings like "the lord Jesus" or "the Lord" when speaking to non-Christians (i.e. the *out-group*).

In an uncertain world, for most ancient peoples the idea of separation from the "village" or *in-group* meant loss of hope. You were quite literally on your own. With nowhere to hide. Strength in numbers counted. The group dynamic was critically important placed inside the ancient, often destabilized, social world of first-century Palestine.

Suggestively, a more reliable silhouette of *Yeshu ha-Notzri* does not reimagine a rural village rabbi creating new religious doctrine. Quite the opposite. Within a historical framework, in many platitudes he was revisiting the *very origins of Mosaic thought*. During the era, memories of Moses constituted "common 'knowledge' in the social memory (e.g. Sir 46:1; Wis 11:1; Tg. Ps. 90:1)."[44]

For example, at the heart of the Nazarene's message was to love unselfishly. To methodically shirk the baggage of an *independent* self. To quite literally love one's neighbor as oneself.

In this familiar social blend we revisit the everpresent "group" dynamic on proverbial *steroids*. We need to get this: the real gospel of Jesus emphasized and re-emphasized *inclusion*. Prioritization of the *group* or community (versus the individual).

Historically, we know this original, Mosaically inspired, core message was eventually expanded to become nearly universal in early Christian thought:

And behold, one came up to him, saying, "Teacher, what good deed must I do, to have eternal life?" And he said to him, "Why do you ask me about what is good? One there is who is good. If you would enter life, keep the commandments." He said to him, "Which?" And Jesus said, "You shall not kill, You shall not commit adultery, You shall not steal, You shall not bear false witness, Honor your father and mother, and, You shall love your neighbor as yourself" (Mt 19.16-19, RSV).

And the scribe said to him, "You are right, Teacher; you have truly said that he is one, and there is no other but he; and to love him with all the heart, and with all the understanding, and with all the strength, and to love one's neighbor as oneself, is much more than all whole burnt offerings and sacrifices." And when Jesus saw that he answered wisely, he said to him, "You are not far from the kingdom of God." (Mk 12.32-34, RSV).

And he answered, "You shall love the Lord your God with all your heart, and with all your soul, and with all your strength, and with all your mind; and your neighbor as yourself" (Lk 10.27, RSV).

A new commandment I give to you, that you love one another; even as I have loved you, that you also love one another. By this all men will know that you are my disciples, if you have love for one another (Jn 13.34-35, RSV).

[L]ove one another with brotherly affection; outdo one another in showing honor (Rom 12.10, RSV).

The commandments, "You shall not commit adultery, You shall not kill, You shall not steal, You shall not covet," and any other commandment, are summed up in this sentence, "You shall love your neighbor as yourself" (Rom 13.9, RSV).

For the whole law is fulfilled in one word, "You shall love your neighbor as yourself" (Gal 5.14, RSV).

If you really fulfil the royal law, according to the scripture, "You shall love your neighbor as yourself," you do well (Jas 2.8, RSV).

He who loves his brother abides in the light, and in it there is no cause for stumbling (1 Jn 2.10, RSV).

By this it may be seen who are the children of God, and who are the children of the devil: whoever does not do right is not of God, nor he who does not love his brother (1 Jn 3.10, RSV).

And this commandment we have from him, that he who loves God should love his brother also (1 Jn 4.21, RSV).

Within the ancient setting, hovering over the social reality of "village" society, we observe a "group-think" attitude spread out across the entire mental and visual network. This familiar social microcosm was dominated by *collectivist* worldviews and expectations.[45] People in first-century Palestine very much viewed daily life from a *group* perspective.

Jesus emphasized the status of his "brother" so often in the literature that sometimes we tend to misplace the *extreme* emphasis. Not only in his adherence to torah dictates. But due to the fact that *Yeshu ha-Notzri* **literally** derived from a *village* social setting.

Besides direct relations, his neighbors in village life truly constituted his *brothers*. He was part of a thick, thriving, intertwined, social network of rural villagers sharing common priorities, goals, concerns, and views of life around them. In Yeshu's day this inner fusion was not a matter for deep intellectual discussion. It was a cultural and social *reality* that helped define the very fabric of day-to-day living.

To stress the "social network" theme, from a purely attitudinal standpoint, in village settlements sprinkled across the Galilean countryside,

traditional Mediterranean *honor* and *shame* values were constantly emphasized. Honor to one's extended family. Honor to the village.[46]

Archaeology informs us that inside the physical geography various
family units shared ovens and millstones.[47] They utilized common cisterns
or reservoirs.[48] They built both individual and community ritual pools
or (pl.) *mikva'ot* for cultic purification.[49] They worshiped together at local
synagogues, either in homes or in some cases common structures they
themselves had built and maintained.[50] In such humble village settlements
archaeology emphasizes that housing was reflected in closely situated
building floorplans.[51] Life itself was continuously expressed, mentally and
physically, within a communal or "in-group" mindset.

Thus, the people around *Yeshu ha-Notzri* literally lived and worked side
by side as "brothers." Just as he preached. They were literally immersed in
a shared communal reality. Such a commonly interpreted day-to-day existence revolved around a networked consciousness depicting their shared
cultural mythos, social attitudes, and nearly identical perceptions of the
world around them. Again, in a postmodern sense these rural, clustered,
community groups were seen as *collectivists*.[52] Keeping to our overall focus,
how did this communal blend preserve shared memories?

In the original settings, "people were with other people virtually all
the time, and what one person knew everyone knew."[53] That is as plain
and simple as we can get. Categorically, this was not true of Paul's later
urbanized social formula.

After group prayers and recitals, inside Paul's hellenized urban settings people went along their way. In such cluttered municipal settings,
even the most dedicated to a relationship with the Pauline Christos maintained their own lives. A shared frame of reference flowed from Hellenistic
pagan culture.

But, articulated above, the lifestyle in rural Galilee was entirely
reversed. The beginning and end of human existence centered on
Jerusalem and the temple religious apparatus. Y-H-V-H worship was

virtually unknown to the gentile world. Thus, the extreme suspicion among foreign societal elites who often questioned what the Jews were up to.

Beyond the basic cultic framework, those villagers who first recalled memories of rabbi Jesus were linked to a shared awareness of their home village and rural life around them. In large part this flowed from coming and going seasons of the year, a preset behavioral structure, and rather intimate and well-familiar kinship diversification. This type of social network defined the very fabric of their lives.

These kinds of observations in modern formal studies comprise a *crucial* defining factor explaining why original memories of *Yeshu ha-Notzri* did not just flitter away with his passing. In clustered social groups too many people in close contact retained vivid recollections of the same individual and his activities.

The life of Jesus spelled hope to so many desperate families living within the original rural setting. And hope across the first century was in *very* short supply.

Such easy, deliberate logic goes a long way toward explaining just why we can trust certain primitive aspects of Yeshu's common tradition. Contrary to modern claims, inside the original Palestinian social setting, core memories were not at any point displaced by *mythology*.

In the initial stages of development, too many people in close contact were privy to the Nazarene's authentic, originating memory stream. Mythologizing did occur. But later. Within post-Palestine, hellenized geographies. The first common story was formed by rural, devotional Jews.

When village groups initially formalized memories of rabbi Jesus (and there had to be "initial" impressions), they would have formatted their thoughts *corporately*. Together as a collective social unit. From what archaeology, ancient texts, and modern social science tells us, beyond any reasonable doubt this underlying assumption is rooted in history.

Pauline religious editors responsible for the final written stories would not have found a place at the table (so to speak). Palestinian rural villagers in group settings initially witnessed the delivery of oral stories about an extraordinary local healer. Hellenistic *redactive* voices were never consciously considered.

Nor in Palestine did village criers *read* tales of Jesus the Nazarene to rural audiences. Explained above, such scenes would not be possible. For all intents and purposes, no one within these rural social groups knew how to read.

In the end, whatever methods were actually utilized by originating Galilean poor, a common concern dominated awareness. Far beyond any modern "burden of proof," from village to village their commitment to preserving *accuracy* was shockingly consistent. How can we be sure?

Even today, we have irrefutable proof that an early common tradition had been maintained in all **four** canonical accounts. We are saying that whichever Gospel one chooses to open common themes witnessed in the other three helped define crucial early story development. A first primitive layer of tradition.

So beyond Palestine, in compiling their written stories some very basic oral memories were not substantially altered. Even after migration to foreign lands. This tells us that a common memory stream from village to village had been initially preserved inside the original Galilean network. A common memory stream that eventually migrated beyond the Land of Israel. A common memory stream that was, nevertheless, still protected in the final tally.

Thus, we are suggesting that many shared oral threads *universally* impressed post-Palestine, pre-Christian devotional communities. Regardless of geographical location. Or differing social influences. Or unique cultural perspectives. Or founding figures. Such core themes were not substantially altered by later editorial interests. All four canonical stories testify to this simple, easily detected conclusion. In Israel a common story was first preserved. And distributed among early village groups.

The world of nonsectarian scholars today is a world of *prioritization*. Which Gospel takes precedent over the others. Experts build their intellectual theses off such underlying assumptions. But history doesn't appear to coincide with such thinking.

Nearly all scholars today claim that *Mark* was first. *Matthew* and *Luke* simply nicked a large swatch of original Markan tradition. And made it their own. Thus writing *Mark's* recollections into their scripts. But in impartial analysis real residual *evidence* still available to us defies such interpretations.

This assurance has a lot to do with the fourth canonical tale. Most scholars recognize *John's Gospel* as *independent* tradition. *John* within this common dialogue largely **replicates** the three synoptic texts. This factor is vital to truly resolving the issue. Many of *John's* original recollections were mirrored inside the synoptic stories. And vice versa. It is impossible to ignore the fact that a core tradition of shared memories is at the heart of each canonical track.

As expected, there are also *late* memories identifiable in the individual stories. For example, by "late" we are talking about hellenistic "godmen" challenged by evil demons.[54] Angels cruising the night skies (Lk 2.13-14). Hundreds of Roman soldiers in full armor cowed by elderly village rabbis with a scattering of near-indigent hotheads to defend him (Jn 18.6). These ideas all comprise late, post-Palestine redacted allusions. Arguably, *hellenistic* allusions.

The proof is seen in a close reading of the surviving texts. Common source memories originally shared among all four traditions are an inevitable consequence of such thinking. That one or another tradition was set to writing early or late, in a search for the earliest footprint, is ultimately *irrelevant*.

When past Palestine the sophisticated Hellenistic thought world of Paul from Tarsus ultimately seeped into the various canonical accounts. In all four canonical stories later editorial interests engaged religious outlooks and perspectives virtually unknown in the Land of Israel.

Regardless, that does not in any way discount those original, common threads. Concrete memories still preserved in all four traditions even when transferred to writing. Very early shared memories celebrating an extraordinary inspirational life. Again, memories still identifiable (in fragmented form) within the final texts today.

Following is a glimpse of the original common story. With some later adapted scenes. Nevertheless, a story first preserved in remote Galilean agronomic settings. Group settings that honored an authentic local hero. A teacher. Healer. Inspirational leader. Perhaps more accurately designated – a rural village rabbi.

DATABASE OF SHARED CANONICAL MEMORIES (I.E. MOSTLY EARLY STREAMS COMMON TO ALL FOUR GOSPELS)

BAPTISM

Jesus a figure in history (Mt 1.1; 2.1; Mk 1.1-11; Lk 2.1-7; Jn 1.29-34)

Yeshu is baptized (Mt 3.1-17; Mk 1.1-11; Lk 3.1-22; Jn 1.15-34)

The character of John the Baptist (Mt 3.1-6; Mk 1.2-6; Lk 3.1-6; Jn 1.19-23)

"Whose sandals I am unworthy to tie" (Mt 3.11-12; Mk 1.7-8; Lk 3.15-18; Jn 1.24-28)

EARLY MINISTRY

Early Galilean ministry (Mt 4.12-17; Mk 1.14-15; Lk 4.14-15; Jn 2.1-12)

FACES OF JESUS

Jesus the Judaic teacher or "rabbi" (Mt 8.19; 9.11; 12.38; 17.24; 19.16; 22.16, 24, 36; 26.18; Mk 4.38; 5.35; 9.17, 38; 10.17, 20, 35; 12.14, 19, 32; 13.1; 14.14; Lk 7.40; 8.49; 9.38; 10.25; 11.45; 12.13; 18.18; 19.39; 20.21, 28, 39; 21.7; 22.11; Jn 1.38, 49; 3.2, 26; 4.31; 6.25; 8.4; 9.2; 11.8, 28; 13.13; 20.16)

Jesus the Judaic prophet (Mt 21.11; Mk 6.14-15; 8.28; Lk 7.16-17; Jn 4.19, 6.14; 7.40; 9.17)

"A prophet has no honor in his own country" (Mt 13.57; Mk 6.4; Lk 4.24; Jn 4.44)

Jesus the Judaic Messiah (or Christ) (Mt 1.16, 18; 11.2; 16.20; 23.10; Mk 1.1; 8.29; Lk 2.11; 4.41; 9.20; Jn 1.17, 41; 4.25-26; 7.26-31; 11.27; 17.3; 20.31)

Yeshu publicly refers to G-d as "Father" (Mt 5.16; 18.14; Mk 11.25; 13.32; Lk 6.36; 10.21; Jn 8.42; 16.28)

CALLS DISCIPLES

Jesus returns to Galilee and preaches (Mt 4.12, 17; Mk 1.14-15; Lk 4.14-15; Jn 4.43-45)

Call of first followers (Mt 4.18-22; Mk 3.14-20; Lk 5.1-11; Jn 1.35-51)

Twelve named disciples (Mt 10.1-2; Mk 3.14; Lk 6.13; Jn 6.67-71)

Peter's confession (Mt 16.13-20; Mk 8.27-30; Lk 9.18-21; Jn 6.66-69)

"If any man would come after me" (Mt 16.24-28; Mk 8.34-9.1; Lk 9.23-27; Jn 12.24-25)

MINISTERS TO THE POOR

Yeshu cares for the poor (Mt 19.21, 26.9, 11; Mk 10.21, 14.5, 7; Lk 7.36-50, 18.22, 19.8; Jn 12.1-8, 13.29)

MIRACLE WORKER

Jesus heals the paralytic (Mt 9.1-8; Mk 2.1-12; Lk 5.17-26; Jn 5.1-18)

He heals the blind (Mt 9.27-31; 12.22; 20.29-34; Mk 8.22-26; 10.46-52; Lk 18.35-43; Jn 9.1-41)

He raises the dead (Mt 9.18-19, 23-26; Mk 5.21-43; Lk 7.11-15; 8.40-42, 49-56; Jn 11.1-44)

They return to the Sea of Galilee (Mt 14.13; Mk 6.30-32; Lk 9.10; Jn 6.1)

Yeshu's prayer feeds the five thousand men (Mt 14.13-21; Mk 6.30-44; Lk 9.10-17; Jn 6.1-14)

He calms the storm (Mt 8.23-27; Mk 4.35-41; Lk 8.22-25; Jn 6.16-21)

PRE-PASSION

Bethany anointing (Mt 26.6-13; Mk 14.3-9; Lk 7.36-50; Jn 12.1-8)

Triumphal Jerusalem entry (Mt 21.1-17; Mk 11.1-11; Lk 19.29-40; Jn 12.12-19)

He cleanses the temple (Mt 21.12-13; Mk 11.15-17; Lk 19.45-46; Jn 2.13-22)

PASSION OPENING

The last supper (Mt 26.17-29; Mk 14.12-25; Lk 22.7-23; Jn 13.1-35)

Jesus discloses betrayer (Judas) (Mt 26.21-25; Mk 14.18-21; Lk 22.21-23; Jn 13.21-30)

Judas betrayal (Mt 26.14-16; 47-50; Mk 14.10-11; 14.43-46; Lk 22.3-6; 47-48; Jn 18.1-8)

ARREST

Gethsem'ane arrest (Mt 26.36-56; Mk 14.32-52; Lk 22.39-53; Jn 18.1-12)

DENIAL

Peter's denial predicted (Mt 26.30-35; Mk 14.26-31; Lk 22.31-34; Jn 13.36-38)

Peter's denial (Mt 26.69-75; Mk 14.66-72; Lk 22.54-62; Jn 18.15-18; 25-27)

TRIAL

Hearing before chief priests (Mt 26.57-68; Mk 14.53-65; Lk 22.54; Jn 18.13-16, 19-24)

Jesus is delivered to Pilate (Mt 27.1-2; Mk 15.1; Lk 23.1; Jn 18.28-30)

Trial before Pilate (Mt 27.11-14; Mk 15.2-5; Lk 23.2-5; Jn 18.29-38)

Chief priests implicated in Yeshu's death (Mt 27.11-13; Mk 15.3-4; Lk 23.1-5; Jn 19.12-16)

Barabbas released (Mt 27.15-23, 26; Mk 15.6-15; Lk 23.17-25; Jn 18.39-40)

Pilate delivers Jesus to be crucified (Mt 27.24-26; Mk 15.15; Lk 23.24-25; Jn 19.13-16)

He is scourged by Roman military (Mt 27.26-31; Mk 15.16-20; Lk 22.63-65; Jn 19.1-3)

CRUCIFIXION

Road to Gol'gotha (Mt 27.31-34; Mk 15.20-23; Lk 23.26-33; Jn 19.17)

Crucifixion at Gol'gotha (Mt 27.32-56; Mk 15.21-41; Lk 23.26-49; Jn 19.17-37)

Eyewitnesses to crucifixion (Mt 27.55-56; Mk 15.40-41; Lk 23.49; Jn 19.25-27)

"King of the Jews" titulus (Mt 27.37; Mk 15.26; Lk 23.38; Jn 19.19)

On cross Jesus utters last words (Mt 27.46; Mk 15.34; Lk 23.34, 43, 44; Jn 19.26-30)

Jesus dies (Mt 27.45-54; Mk 15.33-39; Lk 23.44-48; Jn 19.28-30)

Soldiers cast lots for Yeshu's clothes (Mt 27.35; Mk 15.24; Lk 23.34; Jn 19.23-24)

BURIAL

Jesus is buried in a new tomb (Mt 27.57-61; Mk 15.42-47; Lk 23.50-56; Jn 19.38-42)

RESURRECTION

He is raised to life on the "third" day (Mt 27.1, 2, 9; 28.1-10; Mk 16.1, 2, 9; Lk 24.1-3, 13-15; Jn 20.1)

Female returned-from-death witness named Mary Mag'dalene (Mt 27.56, 61; 28.1; Mk 15.40, 47; 16.1, 9; Lk 24.10; Jn 20.1-18)

Female(s) at open tomb (Mt 28.1-3; Mk 16.1-4; Lk 24.1-2; Jn 20.1)

Angels announce Resurrection (Mt 28.1-8; Mk 16.1-8; Lk 24.1-8, 12; Jn 20.11-13)

Woman/women find apostles (Mt 28.1, 8; Mk 16.1-4, 8; Lk 9.1-2, 9-11; Jn 20.1-2, 18)

Post-Resurrection appearance(s) (Mt 28.9-10, 16-20; Mk 16.9-18; Lk 24.13-49; Jn 20.11-29)

A rather detailed common story shared among all four canonical Gospels cannot be credibly denied. Specific intersecting data points are shown above. They are indisputable.

Early Galilean village groups promoted an original oral story that was not entirely lost in the final redacted texts. Such testimony is effectively displayed in the aforementioned citational listings. As stated, such an observed common narrative appears to be *incontrovertible*.

Again, the finding should prove beyond a reasonable doubt that early village groups preserved an original story depicting the life of a rural rabbi. And somehow managed to reproduce this core tradition decades later. Even in written form. Even in social environments radically altered from the originating cultural setting.

The earliest tradition may not have been articulated by individuals named Matthew, Mark, Luke, or John. But the anonymous Galilean rural enclaves that first celebrated a near identical database of original images and outlooks – like it or not – represented the original "group" purveyors of Jesus tradition. They defined the initial communal settings that first lit the torch of shared understanding.

In spite of many decades, territorial boundaries, and diverse cultures in between, rural Galilean poor in the end managed to have their way. Lest we forget, the whole developmental process had originally commenced in archaic *village group settings*.

STORYTELLING

Peoples of the Near East and roundabout used memory and oral performance to enunciate the "customs, values, history, and beliefs"[55] of their common cultural heritage. Recognizing the historical connections of this early widespread social phenomenon reinforces the idea that why we remember Jesus at all is directly attributable to *storytelling* in discrete village settings across rural Palestine.[56]

From the outset readers should understand an important point that has been nearly *universally* misrepresented in modern New Testament studies: "There is ample evidence that indigenous people distinguish imaginary folklore from reality within myth."[57]

The modern theory that ancient peoples could not distinguish fact from fiction represents a rather bizarre fabrication by (mostly Western) academics. A disgustingly *inaccurate* and degrading response from intellectual elites.

Tapping into the historical aspects of weaving the ancient tapestry implies that somewhere behind the written biblical traditions were fragments of primitive stories, some collected very early-on, that remembered a real-life figure named *Yeshu ha-Notzri* from a rural village in lower Galilee.[58]

Even in the scientific-materialist, postmodern era we cannot ignore the fact that beyond any doubt there was a critical *historical* basis upon which Jesus stories *first* evolved. There were remembered accounts behind the details from people who witnessed real-time events. This was an epoch in human history built and sustained by memory and storytelling.

In modern times some experts have recognized storytelling as "the oldest form of communication."[59] They tell us that storytelling in ancient cultures constituted "the foundation of tribal life."[60] Within this social synthesis, it should be no surprise that memory functioned as "the lifeblood of oral/aural cultures."[61]

Within the language of such an original and authentic social platform, storytelling implies preserved memories among ancient people groups sharing a common identity.[62] Experts tell us that these social units established "an accepted version of the past, a sort of genealogy of identity."[63]

In the historical settings of antiquity, from Athens to Rome, from Alexandria to Jerusalem, from Carthage to Londinium, ancient peoples were storytellers. During the Nazarene's era, this communication form thrived within a vibrant, multicultural, (mostly) non-literate setting.[64]

Stories about Jesus emerged because real people witnessed real events they could not soon forget.[65] Moreover, related expert testimony tells us that the closer to original events the more accurate the reports.

Contrary to quite embarrassing miscalculations today, at the outset of source tradition "it is most difficult for legendary accretions to develop."[66] This comment comes from a bonafide classical *historian*. Not a "historical" scholar whose profile dominates the field of New Testament studies.

"The worth and workings of memory are crucial, for without some scheme – some memory device – there is no survival of the meaning."[67] Ancient social groups were looking for meaning. For continuity. For preservation of shared consciousness. For confirmation of their networked reality. They found all of these dynamics in storytelling performed in group settings.

Storytelling provided "a natural way to order and connect events and explain them in a meaningful way."[68] Such a shared social venue provided a reasonable means to protect the self-identified social unit from lurking danger. Life and death scenarios often dictated that retaining accuracy in telling stories was absolutely essential. This crucial *survival* theme is *conveniently forgotten today* by the very experts who should know better.

Illustrating the "accuracy" dynamic is not a difficult matter. For example, not remembering across generations that one located water source was good to drink and another was contaminated would have had considerable impact on long-term survival. Or that a certain snake with distinct coloring was highly poisonous compared to another species similar in appearance though with slightly offset coloring.[69] Practical examples go on and on and on. With absolute certainty, this entire calculous would have been preserved in *group storytelling*.

Within the original oral paradigm, considering our instinct for survival, and taking into account a myriad of life-and-death scenarios in the everyday lives of our progenitors, lacking a capacity for retaining reasonably accurate, shared consciousness across multiple generations seems *highly unlikely.* Almost *impossible.* This hardcore conclusion is often dismissed today. Academics love their theories. But we can't get past the inevitability of simple logic.

To supplement this hypothesis, there is one thing we know for sure: we belong to a breed of primates (some 200 species) that across the ages distinguished itself from all others. Narrowed further, among *Homo habilis, Homo erectus, Homo neanderthalensis, Denisovans, Homo floresiensis, Homo naledi, and Homo sapiens* we happen to be the "last man standing" (so to speak). We should not be surprised by the fact that *Homo sapiens* has been character-ized, scientifically, as "wise man."

Thus, the way our survival mechanism seems to operate it is rather doubtful that mother nature would have neglected to sharpen our mental capacity for accurately retaining and transmitting received tradition. Or with high probability (regardless of modern prognostications to the con-trary[70]) *Homo sapiens* would not have endured the inevitable catastrophic consequences of spotty recall. Across millenia upon millenia, it was a com-petitive "jungle" out there. In the end, we finished on top. Not for lack of *remembering*.

Across the world ancient man eventually chiseled out an audio-vi-sual formula for preserving crucial information. Within conscious aware-ness various forms of storytelling seemed to reinforce memorization. In storytelling we were better adapted to reload accurate visualizations stored in our brains.

Perhaps readers can understand now why the tradition of storytell-ing is claimed to be the oldest known method for preserving reasonably accurate snapshots of the past. And why the veracity of those memories was so important to isolated as well as integrated social groups.

Probably unbeknownst to nearly all readers, as far as can be judged the art of storytelling dates back to some historical epoch near the dawn of man.[71] The earliest form of preserved storytelling is perhaps best demon-strated in surviving Paleolithic cave art.

In 1994 three spelunkers made the discovery of a lifetime in *Vallon-Pont-d'Arc*, France. Their discovery occurred at a location now known as the Chauvet Cave site.[72]

This remarkable find constitutes a vast, hidden (by landslides) sub-terranean network. What eventually made the site world famous relates to artwork. On rock surfaces inside the cave environment we are able to observe mating rituals, lurking beasts preying upon underground inhabi-tants, and varieties of other wild species in diverse action poses.[73]

Numerous etchings still grace Chauvet's rock expanses. These walls in some cases are constituted of enormous extended faces. Within the various chambers, at multiple junctures, ancient artists captured a superior elegance and artistic grace that is deemed – even in a postmodern world – quite rare.

Assorted action-sequenced poses framed each rendering. These action poses told stories.[74] Perhaps some of the oldest ever recorded.[75] Inside the enclosed Chauvet cave system early man had attempted to emulate aspects of the natural world around him.

With incremental archeological finds, the famous *Chauvet* cave site has lit up our anthropological understanding of ancient life. Today, this spot is a designated "World Heritage" location. It is claimed to be one of the oldest destination points on Earth where evidence of "storytelling" in visual articulation was fastidiously preserved.[76] Even for our more sophisticated expectations today plentiful, elaborate rock art still manages to evoke a vivid, ancient past.

Admiring these artistic treasures, irrespective of the dramatic changes in scenery, cultural identities, and social attitudes, we quite naturally pause to consider some inescapable common threads. Like us, Chauvet unapologetically asserts that prehistoric man was *consumed* by an innately "human" need *to tell stories*. To connect in shared consciousness with others. Today, our alarming addiction to social media bears credible witness of this inner aspect in human consciousness.

Quite understandably, some specialists nowadays think that telling stories is almost synonymous with being human.[77] We should not be surprised that in the ancient past indigenous peoples learned to "construct ... patterns by telling stories."[78] Notably (and unsurprisingly), evidence of storytelling has graced the stages of every human era. And every major population group around the globe.[79] Civilizations without storytellers did not exist.

Storytelling was the necessary substitute during a vast historical era when writing had not yet been contemplated.[80] And even for many millennia after. Available to us are actual fragments of oral stories eventually written down. The sources are as diverse as Babylon, Canaan, Sumer, Anatolia (i.e. Hittites), Egypt, China, and India (i.e. Sanskrit).[81]

From a historical standpoint, in Judeo-Christian tradition the *group* pattern – in this case, "tribal" – storytelling was originally evident in preservation of the Israelite *exodus* tales.[82] Especially in recorded memories of main supporting characters. Again, as far as we know, from the start of Mosaic tradition the ancient Israelites were formed into diverse *tribal* units.

An early biblical point of contact immediately recalls the memory stream of the prophetess Miriam, sister to Aaron and Moses. A prophetess named Miriam who "took a tambourine, and all the women followed her with drums and dancing."[83] For casual readers, this is one of the most celebrated accounts in the entire scriptural cycle.

Within the shared Israelite myth, the Miriam character is quite a remarkable figure. For us today her story seems to emote a timeless quality. Her memory thread is sometimes recognized as one of the oldest and most beautifully rendered soliloquies in all of Judeo-Christian tradition.[84]

Centuries after her, Micah, the Judaic prophet, was probably a historical figure. If so he lived sometime between 742 and 686 BCE.[85] From the title in his name ("Micah of Mo'resheth"[86]), we are on safe ground considering Mo'resheth, some 23 miles southwest of Jerusalem,[87] as his ancestral home.

The literary construction of dramatic sequences in Micah's book[88] strongly suggest *live performance*.[89] We have to believe that Israelites originally shared Micah's tradition in *group* settings.

In the Micah litany a curious verse was once codified:

> For I brought you up from the land of Egypt,
>
> and redeemed you from the house of bondage;
>
> and I sent before you Moses,
>
> Aaron, and *Miriam* (Mic 6.4, RSV).

Readers who study the Hebrew Bible are well-familiar with Miriam, traditional sister to Moses and Aaron. In the ancient accounts (even beyond scriptures) references to Miriam are quite extensive.[90] The Micah source is an effective cross-reference to the preservation of her memory within the shared Israelite cultural narrative.

A point of fact, the Hebrew Testament time and again confirmed the role of "prophetess" in Israelite culture.[91] That Micah second evaluational layer is extremely important as a useful resource to the cultic status of the original character.

So what we learn: the Micah depiction of Miriam alongside her famous brothers is clearly plausible as a piece of historically-inspired narrative tradition.

Israelites were still glimpsing the figure of Miriam well beyond Micah's time. In fact, even at Qumran (the historical location of the Dead Sea Scrolls) many centuries after Micah. And more than glimpsing. 4Q365[92] contains a *full-scale* song attributed to Miriam.[93] Fragments remain.[94]

Beyond her title as prophetess, some aspects of Miriam's original memory are entirely credible. For one, in ancient Israel females traditionally sang victory songs.[95] This characterization is entirely consistent with Miriam's reconstructed profile.

However, right now the historical aspects of Miriam's account are not what we are after. We are demonstrating the uninterrupted preservation of ancient memories within a preserved *oral* milieu. For many centuries, the Israelite tribes glimpsed a probable historical figure. They persistently lifted her memory in reverence and celebration.

As breathtaking as it sounds for us today, even after a *thousand years* Israelites refused to let go. Miriam the prophetess was deeply important among the Hebrew tribes. She was not considered mythological, typecast to perform miraculous deeds. Certain fragments of tradition surrounding her memory are plausibly *historical*.

This celebrated figure was portrayed as a courageous female supporter who, like her peers, ventured in Y-H-V-H's shadow with one set goal – to gain the *milk and honey* of the Hebraic "Promised Land." One individual from a collection of loosely linked, semitic-speaking tribes of Near Eastern origin. Who witnessed the impossible. And lived to tell the story. In memorable song and dance.

What brought these tribes together was a uniquely shared cultic identity. A common heritage that reveled in the covenantal fidelity of a "divine presence" (they believed to be) active in everyday lives.

They never forgot Miriam at the Reed Sea. In fact, confirmed at Qumran, apparently in the interim centuries the old stories underwent a period of not so surprising *expansion*. By the time of Jesus the figure of Miriam had emerged as an authentic heroic character of the Israelite people.

The Miriam episode clearly added a sense of "cultural relativism"[96] to the remembered time and place setting. Their dramatic escape from Egyptian domination at the legendary Sea of Reeds is widely accepted as a key steppingstone in Hebraic cultic mythmaking.[97]

Yet originally celebrated not by kings or prophets. But by a *sister* to the higher profile Moses and Aaron. And the prophetess Miriam declared to the assembled: "Sing to the Lord, for he has triumphed gloriously; the horse and his rider he has thrown into the sea" (Ex 15.21, RSV).

Today, nearly all New Testament experts are wholly in the dark on the real influence of social memories and storytelling on preserving original glimpses of the historical Jesus. Fewer still have any real concept of their practical consideration in greater Christian history.

Scholars' continued dependence on "classical form criticism"[98] and faulty logic will forever block the way to enlightened understanding. We will not get into that rather controversial subject here. But some knowledgeable experts will perhaps appreciate the relevance.

In remote times stories helped to explain the unknown as well as the movements of local deities impacting the lives of the people. These stories came to reflect the values espoused by the various cultures.[99] In any historical context, storytelling truly dominated the lives of ancient humans.[100]

When we talk about ancient storytelling, the images we manage to collect refer to people formed into *groups*. Not individuals. For earlier man in most cases "tribal" and then later "village" groups. Storytelling helped define and substantiate their way of life.[101]

VILLAGE ELDERS

Within Judeo-Christian tradition the idea of "Elders" represents an archaic concept to the extreme. This thematic model derives from a completely *original* focus. In the sacred, foundational exodus stories the "elders of Israel" often played a crucial role. For example:

> So Moses cried to the Lord, "What shall I do with this people? They are almost ready to stone me." And the Lord said to Moses, "Pass on before the people, taking with you some of the elders of Israel; and take in your hand the rod with which you struck the Nile, and go. Behold, I will stand before you there on the rock at Horeb; and you shall strike the rock, and water shall come out of it, that the people may drink." And Moses did so, in the sight of the elders of Israel. And he called the name of the place Massah and Mer'ibah, because of the faultfinding of the children of Israel, and because they put the Lord to the proof by saying, "Is the Lord among us or not?" (Ex 17.4-7).

Many centuries past the first Judaic stories, in Asia Minor the *Elders* title was once again popular. This appellation frequently attached itself to those individuals who served as community leaders. We observe this phenomenon consistently mirrored in both small and large population groups.[102]

So across the Greco-Roman world, and in the Land of Israel, the term "Elders" was associated with assuming "the role of local leadership."[103] During the first century, we can fairly conclude that such a designation was commonly witnessed in villages across territorial Galilee.

This view is supported by the historian Josephus who claimed that "seven elders" formed a lower court in Israelite "towns and villages."[104] In Judaic society such a social arrangement reflected the "persistence of old tribal structures, practices, and beliefs."[105] As suggested, within Judeo-Christian tradition the underlying idea of *elders* reliably filtered back to the originating Exodus stories and wandering tribes led by Moses.

In local Galilean populations visited by *Yeshu ha-Notzri*, we are certain that village elders would have presided in some form of public setting. One proposal in archaeology is that during the late second-temple period towns and villages scattered across the lower Galilean hills featured multipurpose buildings that "functioned as house of assembly for the elders, court of justice, and synagogue."[106] In other words, multipurpose physical structures focused on community social gatherings.

From a practical standpoint, this proposal only makes sense. Though based on their plotted physical dimensions, inside such structures largescale meetings for any reason would have been fairly cramped.

The term "Elders" and its usage is consistently endorsed in the New Testament. Representative examples follow:

And when he entered the temple, the chief priests and the elders of the people came up to him as he was teaching, and said, "By what authority are you doing these things, and who gave you this authority?" (Mt 21.23, RSV).

And they came again to Jerusalem. And as he was walking in the temple, the chief priests and the scribes and the elders came to him (Mk 11.27, RSV).

Now a centurion had a slave who was dear to him, who was sick and at the point of death. When he heard of Jesus, he sent to him elders of the Jews, asking him to come and heal his slave (Lk 7.2-3, RSV).

When they [i.e. Barnabas and Paul] had preached the gospel to that city and had made many disciples, they returned to Lystra and to Ico'nium and to Antioch, strengthening the souls of the disciples, exhorting them to continue in the faith, and saying that through many tribulations we must enter the kingdom of God. And when they had appointed elders for them in every church, with prayer and fasting, they committed them to the Lord in whom they believed (Acts 14.21-23, RSV).

Let the elders who rule well be considered worthy of double honor, especially those who labor in preaching and teaching … . Never admit any charge against an elder except on the evidence of two or three witnesses (1 Tim 5.17, 19, RSV).

Is any among you sick? Let him call for the elders of the church, and let them pray over him, anointing him with oil in the name of the Lord (Js 5.14, RSV).

So I exhort the elders among you, as a fellow elder and a witness of the sufferings of Christ as well as a partaker in the glory that is to be revealed (1 Pet 5.1, RSV).

Round the throne were twenty-four thrones, and seated on the thrones were twenty-four elders, clad in white garments, with golden crowns upon their heads (Rev 4.4, RSV).

The list above is by no means comprehensive. The notion of connecting local elders (or wise ones) with traditional storytelling has been consistently conveyed across virtually all eras and geographical settings of man. In other words, this basic idealization was expressed around the world. Across all cultures, societies, and historical eras, the concept of "elders" linked to "storytelling" was deeply embedded in the collective human consciousness.

In some settings elders actually *performed* as storytellers. Such individuals often exhibited substantial "oratorical skills."[107] In other environments they served as official monitors verifying the accuracy of presentations. Notably, in many instances they were in possession of "secret knowledge." This would have afforded them the opportunity to correct erroneous claims.

Regardless, the elders role was crucial to the conveyance and maintenance of information essential to local populations. Even today, inside indigenous cultures, officially designated "Elders are recognized for their wisdom and integrity, their knowledge of traditional values and practices, and their deep spiritual connections to all of creation."[108] Early Christianity articulated the basic idea thus:

> So I exhort the elders among you, as a fellow elder and a witness of the sufferings of Christ as well as a partaker in the glory that is to be revealed. Tend the flock of God that is your charge, not by constraint but willingly, not for shameful gain but eagerly, not as domineering over those in your charge but being examples to the flock (1 Pet 5.1-3, RSV).

During the life of Jesus, village leaders in Galilee monitored orally disclosed information for accurate recall. Again, without writing, group settings required *accuracy* in the important function of *remembering*. Such leaders were consistently identified as "elders."[109]

The group setting not only enabled designated elders to scrutinize oral accounts. But we have to assume that *everyone* present was afforded an opportunity to confirm that shared information was accurate.

Across the world, often such designated elders were able to synthesize and recite preserved cultural memories with amazing accuracy.[110] It is surely possible that at a real-time level such conditions were mirrored in the historical settings surrounding early accounts of Jesus.

We must take into consideration an added factor that some first-century village audiences actually included *eyewitnesses* who were heard and influenced group discussions. Not to do so would be unpardonably biased on our part.[111]

Realistically, there were, in fact, *eyewitnesses* to the deeds of *Yeshu ha-Notzri* who would have vividly recalled his activities. When we make the effort to admit this very high probability, it is impossible concluding they just kept their mouths shut. And went along their merry way. Such an attitude would have been entirely outside the ancient social spectrum. Or expected human behavior.

Within a strong "kinship" social dynamic,[112] with several extended families in rural parts constituting individual villages, eyewitnesses would have naturally shared their experiences among family members.

Would anyone in their right mind keep eyewitness accounts of the Nazarene's marvelous deeds to themselves? We have to re-emphasize that ancient Israel was, what we today would consider, a *collectivist-dominated* society. Such a scenario of individual eyewitnesses blocking out family members from their direct experiences of the "good news" isn't a feasible option.

To preserve order, by common consent village "elders" held sway. They were often the oldest. The experienced. The levelheaded.

We note that the canonical Gospels had somehow managed to preserve an authentically remembered term in "elders."

"Why do your disciples transgress the tradition of the elders? For they do not wash their hands when they eat" (Mt 15.2).

(For the Pharisees, and all the Jews, do not eat unless they wash their hands, observing the tradition of the elders) (Mk 7.3).

In the ancient setting, rural villagers lifted up "the tradition of the elders." The synoptic stories referred to the social structures of their day using this metaphor. In that same spirit, Josephus called the phenomenon the "tradition of our forefathers."

What I would now explain is this, that the Pharisees have delivered to the people a great many observances by succession from their fathers, which are not written in the laws of Moses; and for that reason it is that the Sadducees reject them, and say that we are to esteem those observances to be obligatory which are in the written word, but are not to observe what are derived from the tradition of our forefathers (Josephus, *Ant* 13.10.6).

In direct contrast, we look upon today's world. In mostly urban settings, we see that the oldest, wisest members are put away. Discarded. Forgotten. They are feeble. Helpless. A detriment to progress. A burden on society.

Despite our present social predicament, we should come to understand that the threefold orality formula – group settings, storytelling, village elders – was more crucial and more dependable to invoking original memories of Jesus than any written Gospel preserved decades after the Nazarene's time. In this category are the canonical stories as well as *Q*, *Hebrews*, *Peter*, and *Thomas*.

Further, as far as "earliest" is concerned, the original oral formula outweighed any Pauline letter, the Didache, the letter of James, or preserved writings from early church fathers including Clement, Polycarp, and Origen. Oral storytelling was first. And has *real* priority over all other (so-called) source traditions.

We need to recognize that, with slight variations, this unique three-fold oral methodology stands out in history as the primary means for encoding original information across the ages of man. This accomplished regardless of race, culture, geography, or era. In short, without literacy, such practice was as close to "foolproof" as ever witnessed for retaining accurate snapshots of the past.

In light of our pursuit of Jesus, to rephrase: in a non-urban rural world dominated by *orality* we are talking about original memories shared by eyewitnesses in group settings monitored by village elders. Regardless of subject matter or precise methodologies, in a word we are referring to a form of traditional "storytelling."

Quite important for us, there is no evidence whatsoever that after the Nazarene's passing the disciples formed oral traditions among groups of early followers. For one, they certainly were not made up of "kinship" groups. Most likely, such individuals possessed no distinct knowledge of sharing common memories in group settings.[113] Or how such groups could be organized to execute such narrowly based parameters.

The first permanent memories of *Yeshu ha-Notzri* were formed in anonymous rural communities among those who had witnessed Jesus. Possibly the disciples would have been seen among these early groups. Perhaps have even helped develop some of the first tales inside initial gatherings.

Experts often refer to "kinship groups" in terms of "extended families" or "clans." A lineage referred to the oldest member and all of his or her descendants. Within the village environment, any line could number up to several hundred individuals. As senior members, *elders* naturally emerged in leadership roles.[114]

As far as preserving stories, we must once again remind ourselves that these extended groups lived together, worked together, participated in cultic activities together, socialized together, and told stories together.[115]

Within any authentic framing, successfully preserving common memories of Jesus should not sound so out of line. Even without writing.

We should not forget that various timelines were reflected in canonical narrative development. We have to understand that these gospel traditions evolved orally across decades and in diverse cultural, social, and spiritual settings.

Following is one exception to the early "rule." An example of late thematic development in the three synoptic stories:

> And every one who has left houses or brothers or sisters or father or mother or children or lands, for my name's sake, will receive a hundredfold, and inherit eternal life (Mt 19.29, RSV).

> Jesus said, "Truly, I say to you, there is no one who has left house or brothers or sisters or mother or father or children or lands, for my sake and for the gospel" (Mk 10.29, RSV).

> And he said to them, "Truly, I say to you, there is no man who has left house or wife or brothers or parents or children, for the sake of the kingdom of God" (Lk 18.29, RSV).

As a recognized rabbi from a rural village in Galilee, the above approach allegedly prescribed by Jesus was not possible. At least in *history* it was not. Not in the Land of Israel.

Casual readers really need to understand this point. The Nazarene's alleged behaviors portrayed above were entirely out of joint with the initial historical model. They reflect more closely the later *hellenized world* of Paul from Tarsus.

Interestingly, despite late messaging, the gospels somehow still managed to preserve a far older, more credible thread. An earlier, unfailingly *Israelite* viewpoint. Far more in line with native Judaic values and behaviors, the following is a direct contradiction of what we just reviewed:

For God commanded, 'Honor your father and your mother,' and, 'He who speaks evil of father or mother, let him surely die' (Mt 15.4 – also, 19.19; Mk 7.10; 10.19; Lk 18.20).

Very, very strong words uttered similarly in all three synoptic texts. In real life, *Yeshu ha-Notzri* would never dishonor essential elements of Torah (i.e. "for my name's sake"). Given the demographic profile of a publicly acknowledged "rabbi," it just wouldn't happen. This last citation is more reflective of *earlier* thematic development.

The oral formula dominates our ability to preserve an original glimpse of a unique figure. Without it, posterity would have never retained a thin fragment of tradition that echoed authentic, historical events.

Jesus the Nazarene is recalled not because of the disciples. At critical junctures, they *literally* ran away. We remember an authentic synthesis because near-destitute rural kinship units did not. They are the real heroes in the celebration of real memories surrounding an extraordinary village healer. At a crucial stage of story development they kept the flame alive.

CHAPTER SEVEN
References

Ackerman, Susan. "Why Is Miriam Also among the Prophets? (And Is Zipporah among the Priests?)," *Journal of Biblical Literature*, Vol. 121, No. 1 (Spring, 2002), pp. 47-80. (Abbr. "Miriam Among Prophets")

Allison Jr., Dale C. *Constructing Jesus: Memory, Imagination, and History* (Grand Rapids, MI: Baker Academic, 2010). (Abbr. "Constructing Memory")

Anderson, Bernard W. and Bishop, Steven. Out of the Depths: The Psalms Speak for Us Today, Third Edition (Louisville, KY: Westminster John Knox Press, 2000). (Abbr. "Out of the Depths")

Andrade, Nathanael. "Ambiguity, Violence, and Community in the Cities of Judaea and Syria," *Historia: Zeitschrift für Alte Geschichte*, Bd. 59, H. 3 (2010), pp. 342-370. (Abbr. "Ambiguity, Violence, Community")

Antor, Heinz. "The Ethics of a Critical Cosmopolitanism for the Twenty-First Century," in *Locating Transnational Ideals*, Goebel, Walter and Schabio, Saskia, eds. (New York, NY: Routledge, 2010). (Abbr. "Ethics of Critical Cosmopolitanism")

Asselbergs, Florine. "Rediscovering Forgotten Memories: Recollection and Emotion in Nahua Conquest Pictorials," in *Mesoamerican Memory: Enduring Systems of Remembrance, Wood*, Stephanie and Megged, Amos, eds. (Norman, OK: University of Oklahoma Press, 2012), pp. 33-50. (Abbr. "Rediscovering Forgotten Memories")

Avshalom-Gorni, Dina and Getzov, Nimrod. "Phoenicians and Jews: A Ceramic Case Study," in *The First Jewish Revolt: Archaeology, History and Ideology*, Berlin, Andrea M. and Overman, J. Andrew, eds. (New

York, NY: Routledge, 2002), pp. 74-84. (Abbr. "Phoenicians and Jews")

Bailey, Kenneth E. "Informal Controlled Oral Tradition and the Synoptic Gospels," *Themelios* 20.2 (January 1995): 4-11. (Abbr. "Informal Controlled Oral Tradition")

Bailey, Kenneth E. *Jesus Through Middle Eastern Eyes: Cultural Studies in the Gospels* (Downers Grove, IL: InterVarsity Press, 2008). (Abbr. "Middle Eastern Eyes")

Berlin, Andrea M. "Jewish Life Before the Revolt: The Archaeological Evidence," *Journal for the Study of Judaism in the Persian, Hellenistic, and Roman Period*, Vol. 36, No. 4 (2005), pp. 417-470. (Abbr. "Jewish Life Before Revolt")

Blumell, Lincoln. "Social Banditry? Galilean Banditry from Herod until the Outbreak of the First Jewish Revolt," *Scripta Classica Israelica* 27 (2008): 35 – 53. (Abbr. "Social Banditry")

Boer, Roland. *The Sacred Economy of Ancient Israel* (Louisville, KY: Westminster John Knox Press, 2015). (Abbr. Sacred Economy Ancient Israel")

Boesak, Allan Aubrey. Children of the Waters of Meribah: Black Liberation Theology, the Miriamic Tradition, and the Challenges of 21st Century Empire (Eugene, OR: Wipf and Stock Publishers, 2019). (Abbr. "Miriamic Tradition")

Bolt, Peter G. *Jesus' Defeat of Death: Persuading Mark's Early Readers* (New York, NY: Cambridge University Press, 2003). (Abbr. "Jesus' Defeat of Death")

Boomershine, Thomas E. "Jesus' Voice in John," *in Preaching John's Gospel: The World It Imagines*, Fleer, David and Bland, Dave, eds. (St. Louis, MO: Chalice Press, 2008). (Abbr. "Jesus' Voice in John")

Boomershine, Thomas E. "Peter's Denial as Polemic or Confession: The Implications of Media Criticism for Biblical Hermeneutics," *Semia* 39 (1987), pp. 47-68. (Abbr. "Peter's Denial Polemic-Confession")

Botha, P. J. J. "The Social Dynamics of the Early Transmission of the Jesus Tradition," *Neotestamentica*, Vol. 27, No. 2 (1993), pp. 205-231. (Abbr. "Social Dynamics")

Botha, Pieter J. J. "New Testament Texts in the Context of Reading Practices of the Roman Period: The Role of Memory and Performance," *Scriptura* 90 (2005), pp. 621-640. (Abbr. "Reading Practices")

Botha, Pieter J. J. "Oral and Literate Traditions," *Koers Journal*, Vol 57, No 3, Jan 1992, pp. 269-291. (Abbr. "Oral-Literate Traditions")

Botha, Pieter J. J. "Orality, Literacy and Worldview: Exploring the Interaction," *Communicatio*, Volume 17, Issue 2, 1991, pp. 2-15. (Abbr. "Orality, Literacy-Worldview")

Botha, Pieter J. J. "The Spelling Eye and the Listening Ear: Oral Poetics and New Testament Writings," *Scriptura* 117 (2018:1), pp. 1-18. (Abbr. "Oral Poetics")

Botha, Pieter J. J. and Kartzow, Marianne Bjelland, "Memory and Identity in Early Christianity," *Journal of Early Christian History*, Volume 1, Issue 2, Jan 2011, pp. 1-8. (Abbr. "Memory and Identity")

Botha, Pieter J. J. *Orality and Literacy in Early Christianity* (Eugene, OR: Cascade Books, 2012). (Abbr. "Orality and Literacy")

Boyd, Brian. "Tails Within Tales," in *Knowing Animals*, Simmons, Laurence and Armstrong, Philip, eds. (Leiden, The Netherlands: Brill, 2007), pp. 215-243. (Abbr. "Tails Within Tales")

Brundage, W. Fitzhugh. "Introduction: No Deed but Memory," in *Where These Memories Grow: History, Memory, and Southern Identity*, Brundage, W. Fitzhugh., ed. (Chapel Hill, NC: The University of North Carolina Press, 2000), pp. 1-28. (Abbr. "No Deed but Memory")

Byrskog, Samuel. "Introduction," in *Jesus in Memory: Traditions in Oral and Scribal Perspectives*, Kelber Werner H. and Byrskog, Samuel, eds. (Waco, TX: Baylor University Press, 2009), 1-20. (Abbr. "Intro Jesus in Memory")

Byrskog, Samuel. Story as History – History as Story: The Gospel Tradition in the Context of Ancient Oral History (Tübingen, Germany: Mohr Siebeck, 2000). (Abbr. "Story as History")

Capel, Evelyn Francis. The Timeless Storyteller: A Study of the Parables in the Gospels (London, UK: Temple Lodge Publishing, 1995). (Abbr. "Parables in the Gospels")

Cattell, Maria G. and Climo, Jacob J. "Introduction: Meaning in Social Memory and History: Anthropological Perspectives," in Social Memory and History: Anthropological Perspectives, Cattell, Maria G. and Climo, Jacob J., eds. (Oxford, UK: Altamira Press, 2002). (Abbr. "Meaning in Social Memory")

Chancey, Mark A. "The Ethnicities of Galileans," in Galilee in the Late Second Temple and Mishnaic Periods, Volume 1: Life, Culture, and Society, Fiensy, David A. and Strange, James Riley, eds. (Minneapolis, MN: Fortress Press, 2014), pp. 112-128. (Abbr. "Ethnicities of Galileans")

Charlesworth, James H. and Aviam, Mordechai. "Reconstructing First-Century Galilee: Reflections on Ten Major Problems," in Jesus Research – New Methodologies and Perceptions: The Second Princeton-Prague Symposium on Jesus Research, Charlesworth, James H., ed. With Rhea, Brian and Pokorny, Petr (Grand Rapids, MI: William B. Erdmans Publishing Company, 2014), pp. 103-137. (Abbr. "Reconstructing First-Century Galilee")

Coke, Marguerite M. and Twaite, James A. The Black Elderly: Satisfaction and Quality of Later Life (New York, NY: The Haworth Press, 1995). (Abbr. "The Black Elderly")

Coogan, Michael David ed. The Oxford History of the Biblical World (New York, NY: Oxford University Press, Inc., 2001). (Abbr. "Oxford History")

Crawford, Sidnie White, "Traditions about Miriam in the Qumran Scrolls" (2003), Faculty Publications, Classics and Religious Studies, University of Nebraska-Lincoln, pp. 33-44. (Abbr. "Traditions About Miriam")

Curtis, Gregory. *The Cave Painters: Probing the Mysteries of the World's First Artists* (New York, NY: Anchor Books, 2007). (Abbr. "The Cave Painters")

Deines, Roland. "Galilee and the Historical Jesus in Recent Research," in *Galilee in Late Second Temple and Mishnaic Periods: Volume 1, Life, Culture, and Society*, Fiensy, David A. and Strange, James Riley, eds. (Minneapolis, MN: Fortress Press, 2014), pp. 11-50. (Abbr. "Jesus Recent Research")

Dewey, Arthur J. "The Locus for Death: Social Memory and the Passion Narratives," in *Memory, Tradition, and Text: Uses of the Past in Early Christianity*, Kirk, Alan K. and Thatcher, Tom, eds. (Atlanta, GA: Society of Biblical Literature, 2005), pp. 119-128. (Abbr. "Social Memory Passion")

Dewey, Joanna. "Mark as Interwoven Tapestry: Forecasts and Echoes for a Listening Audience," *The Catholic Biblical Quarterly*, Vol. 53, No. 2 (April, 1991), pp. 221-236. (Abbr. "Mark Interwoven Tapestry")

Dewey, Joanna. "The Gospel of John in Its Oral-Written Media World," in *Jesus in Johannine Tradition*, Fortna, Robert T. and Thatcher, Tom, eds. (Louisville, KY: Westminster John Knox Press, 2001), pp. 239-252. (Abbr. "Oral-Written Media World")

Dewey, Joanna. "The Gospel of Mark as an Oral/Aural Narrative: Implications for Preaching," *Currents in Theology and Mission*, Vol 44, No 4 (2017), pp. 7-10. (Abbr. "Oral-Aural Narrative")

Dewey, Joanna. *The Oral Ethos of the Early Church: Speaking, Writing, and the Gospel of Mark* (Eugene, OR: Cascade Books, 2013). (Abbr. "Speaking, Writing, Mark")

Dragas, Areti. *The Return of the Storyteller in Contemporary Fiction* (New York, NY: Bloomsbury Academic, 2014). (Abbr. "Storyteller in Contemporary Fiction")

Dunn, James D. G. "John's Gospel and the Oral Gospel Tradition," in *The Fourth Gospel in First-Century Media Culture*, Donne, Anthony Le and Thatcher, Tom, eds. (New York, NY: T&T Clark International, 2011), 157-185. (Abbr. "John Oral Gospel")

Dunn, James D. G. *Jesus Remembered: Christianity in the Making, Volume 1* (Grand Rapids, MI: William B. Eerdmans Publishing Company, 2003). (Abbr. "Jesus Remembered")

Dunn, James D. G. *The Oral Gospel Tradition* (Grand Rapids, MI: William B. Erdmans Publishing Company, 2013). (Abbr. "Oral Gospel Tradition")

Eddy, Paul Rhodes and Boyd, Gregory A. *The Jesus Legend: A Case for the Historical Reliability of the Synoptic Jesus Tradition* (Grand Rapids, MI: Baker Academic, 2007). (Abbr. "The Jesus Legend")

Edelman, Diana V. "YHWH's Othering of Israel," in *Imagining the Other and Constructing Israelite Identity in the Early Second Temple Period*, Zvi, Ehud Ben and Edelman, Diana V., eds. (New York, NY: Bloomsbury T&T Clark, 2014), pp. 41-69. (Abbr. "YHWH's Othering of Israel")

Elliott, John H. "Elders as Leaders in 1 Peter and the Early Church," *HTS Theological Studies*, Vol 64, Num 2 (2008), pp. 681-695. (Abbr. "Elders as Leaders")

Eve, Eric. "Memory, Orality and the Synoptic Problem," *Early Christianity*, Volume 6, Issue 3 (2015), pp. 311-333. (Abbr. "Memory-Orality, Synoptic Problem")

Eve, Eric. "Orality is No Dead-End," *Journal for the Study of the Historical Jesus*, Volume 13, Issue 1 (2015), pp. 3-23. (Abbr. "Orality No Dead-End")

Eve, Eric. *Behind the Gospels: Understanding the Oral Tradition* (Minneapolis, MN: Fortress Press, 2013). (Abbr. "Understanding Oral Tradition")

Eve, Eric. *Writing the Gospels: Composition and Memory* (London, UK: SPCK Publishing, 2016). "Abbr. "Composition and Memory")

Feldman, Ariel. "The Song of Miriam (4Q365 6a ii + 6c 1-7) Revisited," *Journal of Biblical Literature*, Vol. 132, No. 4 (2013), pp. 905-911. (Abbr. "Song of Miriam")

Feldman, Louis H. *Jew and Gentile in the Ancient World: Attitudes and Interactions from Alexander to Justinian* (Princeton, NJ: Princeton University Press, 1993). (Abbr. "Jew and Gentile")

Fiensy, David A. "The Galilean Village in the Late Second Temple and Mishnaic Periods," in *Galilee in the Late Second Temple and Mishnaic Periods – Volume 1: Life, Culture, and Society*, Fiensy, David A. and Strange, James Riley, eds. (Minneapolis, MN: Fortress, 2014), pp. 177-207. (Abbr. "Galilean Village Second Temple")

Fiensy, David A. and Strange, James Riley. "Introduction to Galilee: Volumes 1 and 2," in *Galilee in the Late Second Temple and Mishnaic Periods – Volume 2: The Archaeological Record From Cities, Towns, and Villages*, Fiensy, David A. and Strange, James Riley, eds. (Minneapolis, MN: Fortress, 2015). (Abbr. "Introduction to Galilee")

Flexner, James, et al. "Beginning Historical Archaeology in Vanuatu: Recent Projects on the Archaeology of Spanish, French, and Anglophone Colonialism," in *Archaeologies of Early Modern Spanish Colonialism*, Montón-Subías, Sandra, et al., eds. (London, UK: Springer, 2016), pp. 205-228. (Abbr. "Historical Archaeology in Vanuatu")

Free, Michael L. *CBT and Christianity: Strategies and Resources for Reconciling Faith in Therapy* (West Sussex, UK: John Wiley & Sons, Ltd., 2015). (Abbr. "CBT and Christianity")

Geyer-Ryan, Helga. "Walter Benjamin's Philosophy of History," in *Visions and Blueprints: Avant-garde Culture and Radical Politics in Early Twentieth-Century Europe*, Timms, Edward and Collier, Peter, eds. (Manchester, UK: Manchester University Press, 1988), pp. 66-82. (Abbr. "Philosophy of History")

Goodman, Martin. *The Ruling Class of Judaea: The Origins of the Jewish Revolt Against Rome A.D. 66 – 70* (New York, NY: Cambridge University Press, 1987). (Abbr. "Ruling Class")

Greene, Ellin. *Storytelling: Art and Technique*, Third Edition (Westport, CT: Libraries Unlimited, 1996). (Abbr. "Storytelling")

Grey, Matthew J. and Spigel, Chad S. "Huqoq in the Late Hellenistic and Early Roman Periods," in *Galilee in the Late Second Temple and Mishnaic Periods — Volume 2: The Archaeological Record From Cities, Towns, and Villages*, Fiensy, David A. and Strange, James Riley, eds. (Minneapolis, MN: Fortress, 2015). (Abbr. "Huqoq Hellenistic, Roman Periods")

Guijarro, Santiago. "The First Disciples of Jesus in Galilee," *HTS Theological Studies*, Vol 63, No 3 (2007), pp. 885-908. (Abbr. "First Disciples of Jesus")

Häkkinen, Sakari. "Poverty in the first-century Galilee," *HTS Teologiese Studies*, Vol 72, No 4 (2016), pp. 1-9. (Abbr. "Poverty in First-century Galilee")

Hamilton, Bernard. "The Latin Empire and Western Contacts with Asia," in Contact and Conflict in Frankish Greece and the Aegean, 1204-1453: Crusade, Religion and Trade Between Latins, Greeks, and Turks, Chrissis, Nikolaos G. and Carr, Mike, eds. (New York, NY: Routledge, 2016), pp. 43-64. (Abbr. "Latin Empire")

Hay, Lewis S. "What Really Happened at the Sea of Reeds?," *Journal of Biblical Literature*, Vol. 83, No. 4 (Dec., 1964), pp. 397-403. (Abbr. "What Really Happened")

Hearon, Holly E. "A Social Semiotic Multi-modal Approach to Communication Practices in Early Christianity: Orality and Literacy in Early Christianity," *Journal of Early Christian History*, Volume 4, Issue 1, Jan 2014, pp. 44-67. (Abbr. "Communication Practices")

Hearon, Holly E. "Characters in Text and Performance: The Gospel of John," in *From Text to Performance*, Iverson, Kelly R., ed. (Eugene, OR: Wipf and Stock Publishers, Inc., 2014), pp. 53-79. (Abbr. "Text and Performance")

Hearon, Holly E. "From Narrative to Performance," in *Mark as Story: Retrospect and Prospect*, Iverson, Kelly R. and Skinner, Christopher W., eds. (Atlanta, GA: Society of Biblical Literature, 2011), pp. 211-232. (Abbr. "Narrative to Performance")

Hearon, Holly E. "Mapping Written and Spoken Word in the Gospel of Mark," in *The Interface of Orality and Writing: Seeing, Speaking, Writing in the Shaping of New Genres*, Weisenrieder, Annette and Coote, Robert, eds. (Tübingen, Germany: Mohr Siebeck, 2010), pp. 379-392. (Abbr. "Mapping Written-Spoken")

Hearon, Holly E. "Storytelling in Oral and Written Media Contexts of the Ancient Mediterranean World," in *Jesus, the Voice, and the Text*, Thatcher, Tom, ed. (Waco, TX: Baylor University Press, 2008), pp. 89-110. (Abbr. "Storytelling Oral-Written")

Hearon, Holly E. "The Construction of Social Memory in Biblical Interpretation," *Encounter* 6, No. 4 (2006), pp. 343-360. (Abbr. "Social Memory")

Hearon, Holly E. "The Implications of Orality for Studies of the Biblical Text," in *Performing the Gospel: Orality, Memory, and Mark: Essays Dedicated to Werner Kelber*, Horsley, Richard A., et al., eds. (Minneapolis, MN: Fortress Press, 2006), pp. 3-20. (Abbr. "Implications of Orality")

Hearon, Holly E. "The Interplay between Written and Spoken Word in the Second Testament as Background to the Emergence of Written Gospels," in *Oral-Scribal Dimensions of Scripture, Piety, and Practice: Judaism, Christianity, Islam*, Kelber, Werner H. and Saunders, Paul A., eds. (Eugene, OR: Cascade Books, 2016), pp. 67-88. (Abbr. "Interplay Written-Spoken")

Hearon, Holly E. "The Storytelling World of the First Century and the Gospels," in *The Bible in Ancient and Modern Media: Story and Performance*, Hearon, Holly E. and Ruge-Jones, Philip, eds. (Eugene, OR: Cascade Books, 2009), pp. 3-20. (Abbr. "Storytelling World")

Hearon, Holly E. "Uses of the 'Technical' Language of Tradition for Constructing Memory and Identity in Early Christian Communities," *Journal of Early Christian History* 1, No. 2 (2011), pp. 55-70. (Abbr. "Technical Language Tradition")

Hearon, Holly E. *The Mary Magdalene Tradition: Witness and Counter-Witness in Early Christian Communities* (Collegeville, MN: Liturgical Press, 2004). (Abbr. "Witness and Counter-Witness")

Hendel, Ronald. "The Exodus in Biblical Memory," *Journal of Biblical Literature*, Vol. 120, No. 4 (Winter, 2001), pp. 601-622. (Abbr. "Exodus in Biblical Memory")

Hendel, Ronald. *Remembering Abraham: Culture, Memory, and History in the Hebrew Bible* (New York, NY: Oxford University Press, 2005). (Abbr. "Remembering Abraham")

Hezser, Catherine. "Oral and Written Communication and Transmission of Knowledge in Ancient Judaism and Christianity," *Oral Tradition*, Volume 25, Number 1 (2010), pp. 75-92. (Abbr. "Oral and Written Communication")

Horsley, Richard A. "Oral and Written Aspects of the Emergence of the Gospel of Mark as Scripture," *Oral Tradition*, Volume 25, Number 1 (2010), pp. 93-114. (Abbr. "Oral and Written Aspects")

Horsley, Richard A. "The Gospel of Mark in the Interface of Orality and Writing" in *The Interface of Orality and Writing: Seeing, Speaking, Writing in the Shaping of New Genres*, Weisenrieder, Annette and Coote, Robert, eds. (Tübingen, Germany: Mohr Siebeck, 2010), pp. 144-165. (Abbr. "Interface Orality and Writing")

Horsley, Richard A. "The Language(s) of the Kingdom: From Aramaic to Greek, Galilee to Syria, Oral to Oral-Written," in *A Wandering Galilean: Essays in Honour of Seán Freyne*, Rodgers, Zuleika Rogers, et al., eds. (Leiden, The Netherlands: Brill, 2009), pp. 401-426. (Abbr. "Oral to Oral-Written")

Horsley, Richard A. *Archaeology, History, and Society in Galilee* (Harrisburg, PA: Trinity Press International, 1996). (Abbr. "Archaeology, History in Galilee")

Horsley, Richard A. *Text and Tradition in Performance and Writing* (Eugene, OR: Cascade Books, 2013). (Abbr. "Text and Tradition")

Howson, Alexandra. *Cultural Relativism* (Ipswich, MA: EBSCO Publishing Inc. 2009). (Abbr. "Cultural Relativism")

Hutchens, David. *Circle of the 9 Muses: A Storytelling Field Guide for Innovators and Meaning Makers* (Hoboken, NJ: John Wiley & Sons, Inc., 2015). (Abbr. "Circle of 9 Muses")

Keener, Craig S. "Weighing T.J. Weeden's Critique of Kenneth Bailey's Approach to Oral Tradition in the Gospels," *Journal of Greco-Roman Christianity and Judaism* 13 (2017), pp. 41-78. (Abbr. "Weeden's Critique of Bailey")

Keener, Craig S. *Christobiography: Memory, History, and the Reliability of the Gospels* (Grand Rapids, MI: William B. Eerdmans Publishing Company, 2019). (Abbr. "Memory, History, Reliability")

Kelber, Werner H. "The Authority of The Word in St. John's Gospel: Charismatic Speech, Narrative Text, Logocentric Metaphysics," *Oral Tradition*, 2/1 (1987): pp. 108-131. (Abbr. "Charismatic Speech")

Kelber, Werner H. "The Case of the Gospels: Memory's Desire and the Limits of Historical Criticism," *Oral Tradition Journal*, 17/1 (2002), pp. 55-87. (Abbr. "Memory's Desire")

Kelber, Werner H. The Oral and the Written Gospel: The Hermeneutics of Speaking and Writing in the Synoptic Tradition, Mark, Paul, and Q (Indianapolis, IN: Indiana University Press, 1997). (Abbr. "Hermeneutics Speaking, Writing")

Kelly, Lynne. The Memory Code: The Secrets of Stonehenge, Easter Island and Other Ancient Monuments (New York, NY: Pegasus Books Ltd, 2017). (Abbr. "The Memory Code")

Kessler, Rainer. *The Social History of Ancient Israel: An Introduction*, Maloney, Linda M., trans. (Minneapolis, MN: Fortress Press, 2008). (Appr. "Social History Ancient Israel")

Kim, Yung Suk. "Lex Talionis in Exod 21:22-25: Its Origin and Context," *Journal of Hebrew Scriptures*, Volume 6, Article 3 (2006), pp. 2-11. (Abbr. "Lex Talionis in Exod")

King, Philip J. and Stager, Lawrence E. *Life in Biblical Israel* (Louisville, KY: Westminster John Knox Press, 2001). (Abbr. "Life in Biblical Israel")

Kirk, Alan. "Social and Cultural Memory," in *Memory, Tradition, and Text: Uses of the Past in Early Christianity*, Kirk, Alan K. and Thatcher, Tom, eds. (Atlanta, GA: Society of Biblical Literature, 2005), pp. 1-24. (Abbr. "Social and Cultural Memory")

Levine, Lee I. "The Synagogues of Galilee," in *Galilee in the Late Second Temple and Mishnaic Periods – Volume 1: Life, Culture, and Society* (Minneapolis, MN: Fortress, 2014), pp. 129-150. (Abbr. "The Synagogues of Galilee")

Lewis, Bernard. *History Remembered, Recovered, Invented* (New York: Simon & Schuster, 1975). (Abbr. "History Remembered, Recovered, Invented")

Linn, Denise. Four Acts of Personal Power: How to Heal Your Past and Create a Positive Future (Carlsbad, CA: Hay House, Inc., 2007). (Abbr. "Personal Power")

MacDonald, Margaret Y. "Kinship and Family in the New Testament World," in *Understanding the Social World of the New Testament*, Neufeld, Dietmar and DeMaris, Richard, E., eds. (New York, NY: Routledge, 2010), pp. 29-43. (Abbr. "Kinship and Family")

Mackie, Diane M., et al. "Knowledge of the Advocated Position and the Processing of In-group and Out-group Persuasive Messages," *Personality and Social Psychology Bulletin*, Vol 18, Issue 2 (1992), pp. 148-151. (Abbr. "Processing In-Group and Out-Group")

Malina, Bruce J. "Collectivism in Mediterranean Culture," in *Understanding the Social World of the New Testament*, Neufeld, Deitmar and Demaris, Richard E., eds. (New York, NY: Routledge, 2015), pp. 17-28. (Abbr. "Collectivism in Mediterranean Culture")

Malina, Bruce J. *The New Testament World: Insights From Cultural Anthropology* (Louisville, KY: Westminster John Knox Press, 2001). (Abbr. "Insights Cultural Anthropology")

Malina, Bruce J. *Timothy: Paul's Closest Associate* (Collegeville, MN: Liturgical Press, 2008). (Abbr. "Timothy Paul's Closest Associate")

Malina, Bruce J. and Rohrbaugh, Richard L. *Social-Science Commentary Gospel of John* (Minneapolis, MN: Fortress Press, 1998). (Abbr. "Social-Science Commentary John")

Malina, Bruce J. and Rohrbaugh, Richard L. *Social-Science Commentary on the Synoptic Gospels* (Minneapolis, MN: Fortress Press, 2003). (Abbr. "Social-Science Commentary Synoptics")

Mars, Matthew M. "Bringing Objectivity to the Otherwise Abstract Nature of Cultural Innovation," in *A Cross-Disciplinary Primer on the Meaning of Principles of Innovation*, Mars, Matthew M. and Hoskinson, Sherry, eds. (Bingley, UK: Emerald Group Publishing Limited, 2013), pp. 13-34. (Abbr. "Bringing Objectivity to Nature")

Matilla, Sharon Lea. Inner Village Life in Galilee: A Diverse and Complex Phenomenon," in *Galilee in the Late Second Temple and Mishnaic Periods – Volume 1: Life, Culture, and Society*, Fiensy, David A. and Strange, James Riley, eds. (Minneapolis, MN: Fortress, 2014), pp. 312-345. (Abbr. "Inner Village Life Galilee")

McIver, Robert K. "Eyewitnesses as Guarantors of the Accuracy of the Gospel Traditions in the Light of Psychological Research," *Journal of Biblical Literature*, No. 3 (2012): pp. 529-546. (Abbr. "Eyewitnesses as Guarantors")

Merculieff, Ilarion (Larry) and Roderick, Libby. *Stop Talking: Indigenuous Ways of Teaching and Learning and Difficult Dialogues in Higher Education* (Anchorage, AK: University of Alaska Anchorage, 2013). (Abbr. "Stop Talking")

Morrill, Bruce T. *Divine Worship and Human Healing: Liturgical Theology at the Margins of Life and Death* (Collegeville, MN: Liturgical Press, 2009). (Abbr. "Divine Worship, Human Healing")

Mournet, Terence C. "The Jesus Tradition as Oral Tradition," in *Jesus in Memory: Traditions in Oral and Scribal Perspectives* (Waco, TX: Baylor University Press, 2009), pp. 39-61. (Abbr. "Jesus Oral Tradition")

Mournet, Terence C. Oral *Tradition and Literary Dependency: Variability and Stability in the Synoptic Tradition and Q* (Tübingen, Germany: Mohr Siebeck, 2005). (Abbr. "Oral-Literary Dependency")

Nakashima, Douglas, et al., "Indigenous Knowledge for Climate Change Assessment and Adaptation: Introduction," in *Indigenous Knowledge for Climate Change Assessment and Adaptation*, Nakashima, Douglas, et al., eds. (New York, NY: Cambridge University Press, 2018), pp. 1-22. (Abbr. "Indigenous Knowledge")

Neufeld, Dietmar and DeMaris, Richard, E. "Introduction," in *Understanding the Social World of the New Testament*, Neufeld, Dietmar and DeMaris, Richard, E., eds. (New York, NY: Routledge, 2010). (Abbr. "Introduction Social World")

Neyrey, Jerome H. *Honor and Shame in the Gospel of Matthew* (Louisville, KY: Westminster John Knox Press, 1998). (Abbr. "Honor and Shame")

Nunn, Patrick. *The Edge of Memory: Ancient Stories, Oral Tradition and the Post-Glacial World* (New York, NY: Bloomsbury Sigma, 2018). (Abbr. "The Edge of Memory")

Nyunt, Peter Thein. *Missions Amidst Pagodas: Contextual Communication of the Gospel in Burmese Buddhist Context* (Carlisle, Cumbria, UK: Langham Monographs, 2014). (Abbr. "Missions Amidst Pagodas")

Oakman, Douglas E. "The Countryside in Luke-Acts," in *The Social World of Luke–Acts: Models for Interpretation*, Neyrey, Jerome H., ed. (Peabody, MA: Hendrickson Publishers, Inc., 1991), pp. 151–80. (Abbr. "Countryside in Luke-Acts")

Pfoh, Emanuel. The Emergence of Israel in Ancient Palestine: Historical and Anthropological Perspectives (New York, NY: Routledge, 2014). (Abbr. "Emergence of Israel")

Rhoads, David and Dewey, Joanna. "Performance Criticism: A Paradigm Shift in New Testament Studies," in *From Text to Performance: Narrative and Performance Criticisms in Dialogue and Debate*, Iverson, Kelly R., ed. (Eugene, OR: Wipf and Stock Publishers, 2014), pp. 1-26. (Abbr. "Performance Criticism, Paradigm Shift")

Rhoads, David. "Biblical Performance Criticism: Performance as Research," *Oral Tradition: Oral Tradition in Judaism, Christianity, and Islam*, Volume 25, Number 1 (2010), pp. 157-198. (Abbr. "Performance as Research")

Rhoads, David. "Biblical Performance Criticism: Performance as Research," in *Oral-Scribal Dimensions of Scripture, Piety, and Practice: Judaism, Christianity, Islam*, Kelber, Werner H. and Sanders, Paula A., eds. (Eugene, OR: Cascade Books, 2016), pp. 188-239. (Abbr. "Biblical Performance Criticism")

Rhoads, David. "From Markan Narrative in Print to Markan Narrative in Performance," in *Anatomies of the Gospels and Beyond: Essays in Honor of R. Alan Culpepper* (Leiden, The Netherlands: Brill, 2018), pp. 156-173. (Abbr. "Narrative in Performance")

Rhoads, David. "Narrative Criticism and the Gospel of Mark," *Journal of the American Academy of Religion*, Vol. 50, No. 3 (Sep., 1982), pp. 411-434. (Abbr. "Narrative Criticism")

Rhoads, David. "Performance Events in Early Christianity: New Testament Writings in an Oral Context," in *The Interface of Orality and Writing: Speaking, Seeing, Writing in the Shaping of New Genres*, Weissenrieder, Annette and Coote, Robert B., eds. (Eugene, OR: Cascade Books, 2015), pp. 166-193. (Abbr. "Performance Events")

Richards, E. Randolph and James, Richard. *Misreading Scripture With Individualist Eyes* (Downers Grove, IL: InterVarsity Press, 2020). (Abbr. "Misreading Scripture Individualist Eyes")

Rocca, Samuel. "The Purposes and Functions of the Synagogue in Late Second Temple Period Judaea: Evidence from Josephus and

Archaeological Investigation," in *Flavius Josephus: Interpretation and History*, Mor, Menahem, et al., eds. (Leiden, The Netherlands: Brill, 2011), pp. 295-313. (Abbr. "Purposes, Functions of Synagogue")

Rohrbaugh, Richard L. "Introduction," in *The Social Sciences and New Testament Interpretation* (Grand Rapids, MI: Baker Academic, 1996). (Abbr. "The Social Sciences")

Rohrbaugh, Richard L. *The New Testament in Cross-Cultural Perspective* (Eugene, OR: Cascade Books, 2006). (Abbr. "NT Cross-Cultural Perspective")

Ross, Jennifer C. and Steadman, Sharon R. *Ancient Complex Societies* (New York, NY: Routledge, 2017). (Abbr. "Ancient Complex Societies")

Safrai, Ze'ev. *The Economy of Roman Palestine* (New York, NY: Routledge, 2014). (Abbr. "Economy of Roman Palestine")

Scharfstein, Sol. *Torah and Commentary: The Five Books of Moses – Translation, Rabbinic and Contemporary Commentary* (Jersey City, NJ: KTAV Publishing House, Inc., 2008). (Abbr. "Torah and Commentary")

Shea, Renee H., et al. *Advanced Language & Literature: For Honors and Pre-AP® English Courses* (New York, NY: BFW Publishers, 2016). (Abbr. "Advanced Language")

Smith, Mark D. The Final Days of Jesus: The Thrill of Defeat, The Agony of Victory – A Classical Historian Explores Jesus's Arrest, Trial and Execution (Cambridge, UK: The Lutterworth Press, 2018). (Abbr. "Final Days of Jesus")

Smith-Christopher, Daniel L. *Micah: A Commentary* (Louisville, KY: Westminster John Knox Press, 2015). (Abbr. "Micah: A Commentary")

Snyder, Julia A. Language and Identity in Ancient Narratives: The Relationship between Speech Patterns and Social Context in the *Acts of the Apostles, Acts of John*, and *Acts of Philip* (Tübingen, Germany: Mohr Siebeck, 2014).

Stegemann, Ekkehard W. and Stegemann, Wolfgang. *The Jesus Movement: A Social History of Its First Century*. Dean, Jr., O. C., trans. (Minneapolis, MN, Fortress Press, 1999). (Abbr. "Jesus Movement")

Stewart, Eric C. *Peter: First-Generation Member of the Jesus Movement* (Collegeville, MN: Liturgical Press, 2012). (Abbr. "Peter First Generation Member")

Sweeney, Marvin A. *The Prophetic Literature: Interpreting Biblical Texts Series* (Nashville, TN: Abingdon Press, 2005). (Abbr. "Prophetic Literature")

Tervanotko, Hanna K. *Denying Her Voice: The Figure of Miriam in Ancient Jewish Literature* (Göttingen, Germany: Vandenhoeck and Ruprecht GmbH and Co. KG, 2016). (Abbr. "Denying Her Voice")

Thao, Yer J. *The Mong Oral Tradition: Cultural Memory in the Absense of Written Language* (Jefferson, NC: McFarland & Company, Inc., 2006). (Abbr. "Mong Oral Tradition")

Thursby, Jacqueline S. *Story: A Handbook* (Westport, CT: Greenwood Press, 2006). (Abbr. "Story: A Handbook")

Tivel, David E. *Evolution: The Universe, Life, Cultures, Ethnicity, Religion, Science, and Technology* (Pittsburgh, PA: Dorrance Publishing Co., Inc., 2012). (Abbr. "Universe, Life, Cultures, Ethnicity")

Vansina, Jan. "Afterthoughts on the Historiography of Oral Tradition," in *African Historiographies: What History for Which Africa?*, Jewsiewicki, Bogumil and Newbury, David eds., (Newbury Park, CA: SAGE Publications, Inc., 1985). (Abbr. "Afterthoughts Histography Oral Tradition")

Volčič, Zala and Erjavec, Karmen. "'Media Memories' in Bosnia and Herzegovina," in *Public Memory, Public Media and the Politics of Justice*, Lee, Philip and Thomas, Pradip Ninan, eds. (Basingstoke, UK: Palgrave MacMillan, 2012), pp. 163-183. (Abbr. "Media Memories")

Waltke, Bruce K. *A Commentary on Micah* (Grand Rapids, MI: William B. Eerdmans Publishing Company, 2007). (Abbr. "Commentary on Micah")

Webb, Robert L. *John the Baptizer and Prophet: A Socio-historical Study* (Eugene, OR: Wipf and Stock Publishers, 2006). (Abbr. "Socio-historical Study")

Weiss, Zeev. "Houses of the Wealthy in Roman Galilee," in *The Roman Villa in the Mediterranean Basin: Late Republic to Late Antiquity*, Marzano, Annalisa and Métraux, Guy P. R., eds. (New York, NY: Cambridge Universisy Press, 2018), pp. 317-327. (Abbr. "Houses of the Wealthy")

West, Barbara A. *Encyclopedia of the Peoples of Asia and Oceania* (New York, NY: Facts on File, Inc., 2009). (Abbr. "Peoples of Asia")

Wilder, D. A. and Shapiro, P. N. "Roles of Out-group Cues in Determining Social Identity," *Journal of Personality and Social Psychology* 47 (1984), pp. 342-348. (Abbr. "Roles of Out-Group Cues")

Willis, Timothy. "Elders in the Old Testament Community," *Leaven*, Volume 2, Issue 1 , Article 4 (1992), pp. 8-12. (Abbr. "Elders Old Testament Community")

Wood, Joyce Rilett. "Speech and Action in Micah's Prophecy," *The Catholic Biblical Quarterly*, Vol. 62, No. 4 (October 2000), pp. 645-662. (Abbr. "Micah's Prophecy")

Zahn, Molly M. "The Problem of Characterizing the 4QReworked Pentateuch Manuscripts: Bible, Rewritten Bible, or None of the Above?," *Dead Sea Discoveries*, Vol. 15, No. 3 (2008), pp. 315-339. (Abbr. "Characterizing Pentateuch Manuscripts")

Zvi, Ehud Ben. "Exploring the Memory of Moses 'The Prophet' in Late Persian/Early Hellenistic Yehud/Judah," in *Remembering Biblical Figures in the Late Persian and Early Hellenistic: Social Memory and Imagination*, Edelman, Diana V. and Zvi, Ehud Ben, eds. (Oxford, UK: Oxford University Press, 2013). (Abbr. "Memory of Moses")

CHAPTER SEVEN
Endnotes

1 Botha 1993, Social Dynamics, 215-217.

2 Hezser 2010, Oral and Written Communication, 78.

3 See Mournet 2005, Oral-Literary Dependency, 91.

4 Greene 1996, Storytelling, 1.

5 Mournet 2009, Jesus Oral Tradition, 55.

6 Linn 2007, Personal Power, 5.

7 Nunn 2018, The Edge of Memory, 12-13.

8 Kelly 2017, The Memory Code, 16.

9 Flexner et al. 2016, Historical Archaeology in Vanuatu, 209.

10 Minc 1986, Scarcity and Survival, 79.

11 Coke and Twaite 1995, The Black Elderly, 27.

12 Asselbergs 2012, Rediscovering Forgotten Memories, 45.

13 Keener 2019, Memory, History, Reliability, 462.

14 Nakashima 2018, et al., Indigenous Knowledge, 2.

15 Hamilton 2016, Latin Empire, 47.

16 Hendel 2005, Remembering Abraham, 55.

17 West 2009, Peoples of Asia, 286.

18 Thao 2006, Mong Oral Tradition, 62.

19 Kelly 2017, The Memory Code, 16.

20 Merculieff and Roderick 2013, Stop Talking, 20-21.

21 Bailey, 1995, Informal Controlled Oral Tradition, 5.

22 Ibid., 4-11.

23 Hendel 2005, Remembering Abraham, 55.

24 Lewis 1975, History Remembered, Recovered, Invented, 43; Vansina 1985, Afterthoughts Historiography Oral Tradition, 12; Eddy and Boyd 2007, The Jesus Legend, 239-268 (esp. 252-59); Keener 2017, Weeden's Critique of Bailey, 49, note 38.

25 Dunn 2009, Jesus Remembered, 206.

26 McIver 2012, Eyewitnesses as Guarantors, 536.

27 Malina 2001, Insights Cultural Anthropology, 61-66; Guijarro, 2007, First Disciples of Jesus, 895-896; Morrill 2009, Divine Worship, Human Healing, 78; McIver 2012, Eyewitnesses as Guarantors, 536-537; Free 2015, CBT and Christianity, 42-43; Richards and James 2020, Misreading Scripture Individualist Eyes, 278.

28 Malina, 2001, Insights Cultural Anthropology, 58-76.

29 Malina 2001, Insights Cultural Anthropology, 62; Guijarro 2007, First Disciples of Jesus, 895; Morrill 2009, Divine Worship, Human Healing, 77; Stewart 2012, Peter First Generation Member, 41; Free 2015, CBT and Christianity, 42-43; Richards and James 2020, Misreading Scripture Individualist Eyes, 276.

30 Wilder and Shapiro 1984, Roles of Out-Group Cues, 342-348; Mackie, et al. 1992, Processing In-Group and Out-Group, 148-151; Malina and Rohrbaugh 2003, Social-Science Commentary Synoptics, 373-374; Malina 2008, Timothy Paul's Closest Associate, 13-16; Edelman 2014, YHWH's Othering of Israel, 42-43.

31 See Goodman 1987, Ruling Class, 97; Avshalom-Gorni and Getzov 2002, Phoenicians and Jews, 81; Edelman 2014, YHWH's Othering of Israel, 43.

32 Feldman, L. 1993, Jew and Gentile, 227.

33 Goodman 1987, Ruling Class, 13; Andrade 2010, Ambiguity, Violence, Community, 342-370.

34 Botha 1993, Social Dynamics, 219; Webb 2006, Socio-historical Study, 356-357; Blumell 2008, Social Banditry, 44-45; Deines 2014, Jesus Historical Research, 29; Häkkinen 2016, Poverty in First-century Galilee, 7-8.

35 Rohrbaugh 1996, The Social Sciences, 6; Stegemann and Stegemann 1999, Jesus Movement, 134.

36 Bolt 2003, Jesus' Defeat of Death, 27-28.

37 Rohrbaugh 1996, The Social Sciences, 5; Botha 2012, Orality and Literacy, 150.

38 Oakman 1996, Countryside in Luke-Acts, 168; Rohrbaugh 1996, The Social Sciences, 6; Rohrbaugh 2006, NT Cross-Cultural Perspective, 29.

39 Safrai 2014, Economy of Roman Palestine, 163.

40 Morrill 2009, Divine Worship, Human Healing, 78.

41 Edelman 2014, YHWH's Othering of Israel, 43.

42 Stewart 2012, Peter First Generation Member, 41.

43 Snyder 2014, Language and Identity, 80.

44 Zvi 2013, Memory of Moses, 337.

45 Malina and Rohrbaugh 1998, Social-Science Commentary John, 163-166; Rohrbaugh 2006, NT Cross-Cultural Perspective, 61-76; Morrill 2009, Divine Worship, Human Healing, 79; Stewart 2012, Peter First Generation Member, 41; Edelman 2014, YHWH's Othering of Israel, 42-43; Malina 2015, Collectivism in Mediterranean Culture, 17-28; Richards and James 2020, Misreading Scripture Individualist Eyes, 8.

46 Rohrbaugh 1996, The Social Sciences, 9; Malina 2001, Insights Cultural Anthropology, 27-53. Neyrey 2008, Honor and Shame Q, 85-102.

47 Horsley 1996, Archaeology, History, in Galilee, 89.

48 Fiensy 2014, Galilean Village Second Temple, 192.

49 Berlin 2005, Jewish Life Before Revolt, 428, 437, 451-453, 466, 469; Chancey 2014, Ethnicities of Galileans, 118-119; Deines 2014, Jesus

Recent Research, 32; Matilla 2014, Inner Village Life Galilee, 328; Fiensy and Strange 2015, Introduction to Galilee, 19; Grey and Spigel 2015, Huqoq Hellenistic, Roman Periods, 371-373.

50 Chancey 2014, Ethnicities of Galileans, 121-122; Eddy and Boyd 2007, The Jesus Legend, 122-123; Charlesworth and Aviam 2014, Reconstructing First-Century Galilee, 120-122; Levine 2014, The Synagogues of Galilee, 129-150; Weiss 2016, Josephus, Archaeology of Galilee, 187.

51 Fiensy 2014, Galilean Village Second Temple, 195.

52 See Malina 2001, Insights Cultural Anthropology, 61-66.

53 Rhoads 2010, Performance as Research, 158.

54 Touched upon in another area of this study, readers are aware that exorcism stories dominate the Synoptic Gospels.

55 Rhoads and Dewey 2014, Performance Criticism, Paradigm Shift, 13.

56 Rhoads 1982, Narrative Criticism; Kelber 1987, Charismatic Speech, 108-131; Dewey 1991, Mark Interwoven Tapestry, 221-236; Botha 1991, Orality, Literacy-Worldview, 2-15; Botha 1992, Oral-Literate Traditions, 269-291; Botha 1993, Social Dynamics, 205-231; Bailey 1995, Informal Controlled Oral, 4-11; Kelber 1997, Hermeneutics Speaking, Writing; Byrskog 2000, Story as History; Dewey 2001, Oral-Written Media World, 239-252; Cattell and Climo 2002, Meaning in Social Memory, 1-38; Kelber 2002, Memory's Desire, 55-87; Dunn 2003, Jesus Remembered, 173-254; Botha 2005, Reading Practices, 621-640; A. Dewey 2005, Social Memory Passion, 119-128; Mournet 2005, Oral-Literary Dependency; Hearon 2006, Social Memory, 343-360; Hearon 2006, Implications of Orality, 3-20; Bailey 2008, Middle Eastern Eyes; Hearon 2008, Storytelling Oral-Written, 89-110; Byrskog 2009, Intro Jesus in Memory; Horsley 2009, Oral to Oral-Written, 401-426; Hearon 2009, Storytelling World, 3-20; Mournet 2009, Jesus-Oral Tradition, 39-62; Horsley 2010, Interface Orality and Writing, 144-165; Hearon 2010, Mapping Written-Spoken, 379-392; Horsley 2010, Oral and Written

Aspects, 93-114; Dunn 2011, John Oral Gospel, 157-185; Hearon 2011, Technical Language Tradition, 55-70; Botha and Kartzow 2011, Memory and Identity, 1-8; Hearon 2011, Narrative to Performance, 211-232; Botha 2012, Orality and Literacy; Dunn 2013, Oral Gospel Tradition; Dewey 2013, Speaking, Writing, Mark; Eve 2013, Understanding Oral Tradition; Horsley 2013, Text and Tradition; Hearon 2014, Communication Practices, 44-67; Hearon 2014, Text and Performance, 53-79; Eve 2015, Memory-Orality, Synoptic Problem, 311-333; Rhoads 2015, Performance Events, 166-193; Eve 2015, Orality No Dead-End, 3-23; Rhoads 2016, Biblical Performance Criticism, 188-239; Eve 2016, Composition and Memory; Hearon 2016, Interplay Written-Spoken, 67-88; Dewey 2017, Oral-Aural Narrative, 7-10; Botha 2018, Oral Poetics, 1-18; Rhoads 2018, Narrative in Performance, 156-173.

57 Kelly 2017, The Memory Code, 21.

58 Coogan, ed. 2001, Oxford History, 70; Allison Jr. 2010, Constructing Memory, 25.

59 Geyer-Ryan 1988, Philosophy of History, 74.

60 Boomershine 2008, Jesus' Voice in John, 148.

61 Rhoads and Dewey 2014, Performance Criticism, Paradigm Shift, 14.

62 See Nyunt 2014, Missions Amidst Pagodas, 32.

63 Brundage 2000, No Deed but Memory, 4.

64 Rhoads and Dewey 2014, Performance Criticism, Paradigm Shift, 12.

65 Byrskog 2000, Story as History, 91.

66 M. D. Smith, Final Days of Jesus, 29.

67 A. Dewey 2005, Social Memory Passion, 121-122.

68 Eve 2013, Understanding Oral Tradition, 97.

69 For background on encyclopedic knowledge held by many indigenous peoples of their geographical surroundings and fauna see Kelly, Lynne. The Memory Code: The Secrets of Stonehenge, Easter Island and Oth-

er Ancient Monuments (New York, NY: Pegasus Books Ltd, 2017), pp. 1-17.

70 See Volčič and Erjavec 2012, Media Memories, 165.

71 See Boyd 2007, Tails Within Tales, 217; Mars 2013, Bringing Objectivity to Nature, 15.

72 Curtis 2007, The Cave Painters, 198.

73 Mars 2013, Bringing Objectivity to Nature, 15.

74 Boyd 2007, Tails Within Tales, 217; Mars 2013, Bringing Objectivity to Nature, 15; Shea et al. 2016, Advanced Language, 2.

75 Boyd 2007, Tails Within Tales, 217.

76 Hutchens 2015, Circle of 9 Muses, 4.

77 See Boyd 2007, Tails Within Tales, 217.

78 Antor 2010, Ethics of Critical Cosmopolitanism, 57.

79 Thursby 2006, Story: A Handbook, vii.

80 Capel 1995, Parables in the Gospels, 1.

81 Dragas 2014, Storyteller in Contemporary Fiction, 14.

82 Most of the Hebrew Bible in varying degrees celebrates aspects of the exodus story. See Hendel 2001, Exodus in Biblical Memory, 601.

83 Scharfstein 2008, Torah and Commentary, 198.

84 Hay 1964, What Really Happened, 401; Boesak 2019, Miriamic Tradition, 73.

85 Waltke 2007, Commentary on Micah, 3.

86 Mic 1.1; Jer 26.18.

87 Smith-Christopher 2015, Micah: A Commentary, 1.

88 Mic 1.1-16. 2.1-11; 3.1-12; 6.1-16; 7.1-9.

89 Wood 2000, Micah's Prophecy, 646.

90 Tervanotko 2016, Denying Her Voice, p. 19 mentions all known an-

cient references to the Miriam figure. Superb researched analysis.

91 Sweeney 2005, Prophetic Literature, 29.

92 "4Qreworked Pentateuch." For background, see Zahn 2008, Characterizing Pentateuch Manuscripts, 315-339.

93 Feldman, A. 2013, Song of Miriam, 905.

94 Crawford 2003, Traditions About Miriam, 36.

95 Ackerman 2002, Miriam Among Prophets, 48; King and Stager 2001, Life in Biblical Israel, 290.

96 This technical term describes the conscious attempt to view the core values, beliefs, and life practices of an outside culture from that culture's standpoint and not one's own. For a more detailed discussion, see Howson 2009, Cultural Relativism, 601-622.

97 See Anderson and Bishop 2000, Out of the Depths, 38.

98 Kirk 2005, Social and Cultural Memory, 1.

99 Tivel 2012, Universe, Life, Cultures, Ethnicity, 105.

100 Hearon 2009, Storytelling World, 24.

101 Boomershine 1987, Peter's Denial Polemic-Confession, 148.

102 Elliot 2008, Elders as Leaders, 686.

103 Ibid.

104 Rocca 2011, Purposes, Functions of Synagogue, 304.

105 Willis 1992, Elders Old Testament Community, 9.

106 Rocca 2011, Purposes, Functions of Synagogue, 310.

107 Willis, Elders Old Testament Community, 11.

108 Merculieff and Roderick 2013, Stop Talking, 20.

109 See Bailey 1995, Informal Controlled Oral Tradition, 4-11; Dunn 2009, Jesus Remembered, 206; Mournet 2009, Jesus Oral Tradition, 55.

110 Kelly 2017, The Memory Code, 34.

111 See Byrskog 2000, Story as History, 167.

112 Malina 2001, Insights Cultural Anthropology, 134-160; Kessler 2008, Social History Ancient Israel, 40-62; MacDonald 2010, Kinship and Family, 29-43; Neufeld and Demaris 2010, Introduction Social World, 6; Pfoh 2014, Emergence of Israel, 138-143; Boer 2015, Sacred Economy Ancient Israel, 82-109; Ross and Steadman 2017, Ancient Complex Societies, 18-19.

113 Byrskog 2000, Story as History, 70.

114 Willis 1992, Elders Old Testament Community, 10.

115 Kim 2006, Lex Talionis in Exod, 3.

8

Proselytizers

As we might expect, the original primitive threads celebrating the life of Jesus revisited foundational *Israelite* themes. In these accounts the portrayal of Jesus *the devout Jew* consistently eclipsed the stage.[1]

In the ancient era, we should not ignore the fact that a quite stable historical and literary trend complemented this view. Even as late as mid first-century the Roman empire still treated followers of *Yeshu ha-Notzri* as a "sect" within parent *Judaism*.[2] We are further convinced when the Apostle Paul himself periodically upheld this notion.

Achaía

But when Gallio was proconsul of Achaía, the Jews [i.e. local synagogue leaders] made a united attack upon Paul and brought him before the tribunal, saying, "This man is persuading men to worship God contrary to the law." But when Paul was about to open his mouth, Gallio said to the Jews, "If it were a matter of wrongdoing or vicious crime, I should have reason to bear with you, O Jews; but since it is a matter of questions about words and names and your own law, see to it yourselves; I refuse to be a judge of these things." And he drove them from the tribunal (Acts 18.12-16, RSV).

Caesareá

"Since through you we enjoy much peace, and since by your provision, most excellent Felix, reforms are introduced on behalf of this nation, in every way and everywhere we accept this with all gratitude. But, to detain you no further, I

[Tertullus the Jewish spokesman] beg you in your kindness to hear us briefly. For we have found this man a pestilent fellow, an agitator among all the Jews throughout the world, and a ringleader of the sect of the Nazarenes" (Acts 24.2-5, RSV).

"As you may ascertain, it is not more than twelve days since I [Paul] went up to worship at Jerusalem; and they did not find me disputing with any one or stirring up a crowd, either in the temple or in the synagogues, or in the city. Neither can they prove to you what they now bring up against me. But this I admit to you, that according to the Way, which they call a sect, I worship the God of our fathers, believing everything laid down by the law or written in the prophets." (Acts 24.11-14, RSV).

If Paul regularly attended synagogues and was even remembered visiting the Jerusalem temple, it is difficult imagining in his own mind that he rejected Judaism. At least within some basic level of understanding.[3]

Unlike the Pauline demographic profile touched upon in *Acts*, years before that the Nazarene's earliest followers had lived mostly beyond urban centers.[4] We would have viewed them occupying rural hamlets of a few hundred or so inhabitants in each location. Such village enclaves would have been scattered across the Galilean countryside.[5] Among these tiny communities lived the first recipients and the first to respond to Yeshu's outreach.

How did these rural hamlets first learn about a local village rabbi? Did Jesus visit them? Or did the disciples during their (alleged) missionary treks? This, in fact, opens a whole new area of investigation.

Most people today who reject Western religion probably look at the gospel stories as fairytales. Ancient books created out of whole cloth to promote certain religious attitudes.

On the other hand these same stories seen in the eyes of traditional advocates are often defended as historically inspired. They were written by religious groups who preserved sacred words and deeds performed by a teacher and healer that would otherwise be lost.

The likelihood is that most modern scholars line up on one side of the fence or the other. They spend their careers proving one or the other thesis. Their focus is not necessarily arriving at conclusions based on a preponderance of evidence. But rather to prove the validity of their personal beliefs.

This is obviously a controversial approach. But certain circumstantial evidence supports this view. Examples rather than discussion probably better serves us.

On the "fairytale" side, we see this basic stratagem applied in the 1990s and shortly thereafter. Ideas surrounding the Crucifixion were promoted by a group of scholars in widely publicized discussions. All popular media forms were in on the kill.

The "experts" gleefully sang a song of death. Death and shame. And churches across the Western world closed their doors.[6]

Jesus the Nazarene, these artful promoters claimed, had either been cast into a common grave reserved for criminals. Or left on a Roman cross to be picked apart by carrion. All the "history" pointed that way.

These so-called "impartial" scholars presented all sorts of damming "evidence" in defense of their theory. Cleverly exploiting banner headlines as visual aids, the well-organized propagandists resolutely prosecuted their case. To such an extent that many people today accept the myth.

Back then in the 90s, proponents who rejected Western religion lined up in droves to support this scholarly theory. The academic class had finally come to its senses. And hit upon a winning formula.

To further cast the net some scholars even (appallingly) portrayed themselves as "practicing Christians." But *new research* had proven beyond a reasonable doubt that Jesus the Nazarene had been laid to rest in a common pit. Or hung on a cross till his bones were picked dry.

In pursuit of the "facts," there was nothing anyone could do to soften the blow. *Yeshu ha-Notzri* had met a humiliating and tragic end.

Thus, the Christian "Resurrection" story merely proved that religious audiences were appallingly short of one vital dogmatic claim. Without a shadow of a doubt, the Nazarene's carcass had been devoured days before a miraculous "return" had supposedly graced the lives of certain rural poor.

Within the guild, however, a vocal opposition shouted, "Not so fast!" This expert minority insisted that the "fairytale" side was proving their case *out of context.* Those who defended "rebuttal" prosecuted their claim with evidence from Josephus and various other historical sources.[7] The first-century Hasmonaean historian was quite explicit ...

JOSEPHUS ...

Nay, they proceeded to that degree of impiety, as to cast away their dead bodies without burial, although the Jews used to take so much care of the burial of men, that they took down those that were condemned and crucified, and buried them before the going down of the sun (Josephus, *War* 4.5.2).

TORAH ...

And if a man has committed a crime punishable by death and he is put to death, and you hang him on a tree, his body shall not remain all night upon the tree, but you shall bury him the same day, for a hanged man is accursed by God; you shall not defile your land which the Lord your God gives you for an inheritance (Deut 21.22-23, RSV).

QUMRAN ...

> If a man is a traitor against his people and gives them up to a
> foreign nation, so doing evil to his people, you are to hang him
> on a tree until dead. On the testimony of two or three wit-
> nesses he will be put to death, and they themselves shall hang
> him on the tree. ... But you must not let their bodies remain
> on the tree overnight; you shall most certainly bury them that
> very day. Indeed, anyone hung on a tree is accursed of God
> and men, but you are not to defile the land that I am about to
> give you as an inheritance (*Temple Scroll*, 4Q524).

Key to this position was further evidence from Josephus...

> [W]hereas he [Apion] ought rather to have admired the mag-
> nanimity and modesty of the Romans, whereby they do not
> compel those that are subject to them to transgress the laws
> of their countries, but are willing to receive the honors due
> to them after such a manner as those who are to pay them
> esteem consistent with piety and with their own laws; for they
> do not thank people for conferring honors upon them, When
> they are compelled by violence so to do (*Contra Apionem* 2.6).

Thus, in peacetime Rome typically accommodated the customs of
conquered peoples. (Most historical scholars are well-familiar with this
incidental bit of datum.) Given the timing of the Nazarene's death (on the
eve of Jewish Passover), when hundreds of thousands of potentially fren-
zied Jews were in Jerusalem to celebrate their cultic heritage, it is almost
inconceivable that Pilate would have left the corpse of a former village
hero to the poor hanging to feed birds of prey. Or offended religious sensibilities by common burial thus, according to their customs, defiled the
purity of the Jews' venerated "Promised Land."[8]

During Passover (especially), on logistics alone Pilate's Roman guard would have been far-outnumbered in the hundreds, or possibly, *thousands to one*. Depending on the accuracy of the notoriously *inaccurate* Flavius Josephus.

Either way, the closest historical demographic example to Jesus the Nazarene was John the Baptizer. John had been executed at some point during the same generation that Yeshu lived. The sparse narrative evidence available to us nevertheless decisively concluded that John was buried.

> And immediately the king [Herod Antipas appointed by Rome] sent a soldier of the guard and gave orders to bring his [i.e. John's] head. He went and beheaded him in the prison, and brought his head on a platter, and gave it to the girl; and the girl gave it to her mother. When his disciples heard of it, they came and took his body, and laid it in a tomb (Mk 6.27-29, RSV).

Scholars favoring burial maintained that the rural rabbi certainly had died a *criminal's death*; but buried alone in a *tomb* set apart from others. This course was entirely in keeping with the cultic status quo. So as not to *defile the land*. Segregated from family relations. Death and burial certainly humiliating. But remembered within a plausible first-century historical track.

All things considered, this explanation (or something similar) almost certainly represents the truth behind the Nazarene's end. A former respected rabbi with direct connections to members of the Jerusalem council (see Mk 15.43; Jn 3.2) would not be thrown to the dogs. Quite literally. Especially at the time of the Jewish Passover. In history this line of reasoning seems the most probable.[9]

The "fairytalists," however, aren't the only guilty, creating exegetical analysis based on preconceived notions. It takes two to tango, so to speak. A more detailed example presented below takes on religious apologists in literal conformation with the synoptic texts.

This section examines a near-universal understanding within the guild of New Testament scholars that Jesus appointed his disciples to traverse the Palestinian countrysides. According to the gospels, armed to the teeth with faith and newfound religion, Yeshu's early followers were instructed to promote the Nazarene's teachings and perform good deeds on his behalf.

Nearly all scholars accept this familiar clarification to the budding movement's early growth. They consider this shared narrative theme (comporting within synoptic tradition) as highly likely.

Nevertheless, utilizing a more realistic *historical* model, we will demonstrate the extreme *unlikelihood* that such claims unfolded inside first-century, territorial Palestine.

This study suggests that because the synoptic gospels so stridently defended this evangelistic snapshot, with the religious Jesus even detailing specific operating instructions to the faithful, we today seem to let *historical* realities pass us by.

But if scholars are really in touch with history (as they so often claim), discussion below hopefully demonstrates that on occasion other objectives appear to get in the way. In fact, distinct aspects of this study's claim are probably fairly conclusive. And not in their favor.

Before we go on, this study wants to recognize that it walks a very thin line. The idea of an "earliest footprint" is intriguing. However, the "fairness" aspect presents enormous obstacles. In practice, as human beings evaluating the past, full "impartiality" is extremely challenging to pull off. Regardless, best efforts must be made to insure that historical *probabilities* are somehow enforced.

Entirely apart from pre-held religious convictions (or biases against), the playing field requires us to defend in certain instances gospel threads that legitimately derive from authentic tradition. That with high probability have at least some historical value.

On the other hand, the Bible's historicity cannot be defended *carte blanche*. For some who study the original time and place era, the Bible is not a history book. So stories influenced by cultural settings beyond the Land of Israel must be called out. These aspects in many cases likely did not reflect original memories.

In numerous canonical snapshots Jesus the Nazarene appeared to live as a fierce devotional advocate of late second-temple faith. In direct conflict, however, other canonical stories seemed to reflect post-Palestinian *reactionary attitudes* to explicitly *Judaic* cultic architectures.

Along these lines, one very valid response would have been *Yeshu ha-Notzri's* understanding of sacramental purity. That he would have broken purity strictures defined by Torah is extremely unlikely.[10] Purity was only one aspect, but crucial to proper religious observance in the ongoing Judaic, late second-temple, cultural drama.

For religious Jews, the first century was a time of nationalistic pride and hyper-cultic awareness. In history it is impossible imagining that a village rabbi, publicly recognized for his religious zeal, would have in any way defied social familiarity with sacramental themes surrounding ritual and moral purity.

Numerous synoptic stories did not see it that way, however. Notably, they were written decades past the time of Jesus and beyond the Land of Israel.

In context, in between this prominent traditional theme, we need to see that beyond the temple a popular grassroots attitude was directed at an additional layer of "purity" observance. Today, we call this additional set of behaviors "household purity." In fact, this category represents behaviors largely *unique* to the first century. Attitudes that drilled down even into intimate family settings.

The archaeology today is witnessed across the Palestinian region and happens to be utterly compelling.[11] So within the first-century historical track the trend among Judaic believers was not to reject purity forms but to utterly *embrace* them.

Related, many scholars are convinced that with high probability Jesus actively supported John the Baptizer in his popular water immersion ministry (see Jn 3.22-26). This aspect which is directly related to the purity element in Judaic faith happens to be, beyond doubt, historical.

John was engaged in a cultically inspired "renewal" of Israel.[12] Some of the stories in the old Hebrew Testament, from the Davidic view, offered important light *independent* of any ideological standpoint. One example is found in *First Chronicles*.

The Levitical tribe has a very long history. "Levi" was traditionally a son of Jacob (Gen 29.21-34). He was the great-grandfather of Aaron and Moses.[13] In the performance of cultic duties, Levites were considered the *most* trustworthy among Israelites. For the Levites belonged to G-d (Num 8.14).

Before building the temple, they bore the Tabernacle of the divine presence when it was transferrable from one location to the next.[14] No one else could assume that sacred role. Only direct members of the Levitic line.[15]

In *1ˢᵗ Chronicles* the narrator portrayed "times of renewal after unfaithfulness by the gathering of the Levites."[16] It was David himself who sought the cult's renewal with a gathering of Levitic officials.

> And David said to all the assembly of Israel, "If it seems good to you, and if it is the will of the Lord our God, let us send abroad to our brethren who remain in all the land of Israel, and with them to the priests and Levites in the cities that have pasture lands, that they may come together to us. Then let us bring again the ark of our God to us; for we neglected it in the days of Saul" (1 Chr 13.2-3).

David was forced to locate the Levitic officials that had been hitherto scattered during Saul's reign.[17] David's decision "to bring about renewal and restoration"[18] strongly suggests that the religious aspects of Judaic life had been hitherto neglected. Re-engaging the Levites added emphasis to the "renewal" theme.

1st Chronicles isn't an isolated example. In the *Book of Ezekiel*, we are reminded that chapters 40-48 established that the entire text "in its overall plan and shape [was] about renewal and hope."[19] Thus, for our purposes, both *1st Chronicles* and *Ezekiel* spoke directly and at length to the subject of Israelite *renewal*.

There is no doubt whatsoever that during *Yeshu ha-Notzri's* lifetime the common people would have been well-familiar with these collections of inherited stories. Considering hostile foreign occupation and opportunist Jerusalem elites, such themes fitted *directly* into the first-century historical drama. For the common people "renewal" was overdue.

In impartial analysis, available narrative evidence otherwise strongly suggests that for some measurable timeframe Jesus and his disciples actively supported John's cause.[20] Simply put, "[T]he goal was a renewal of Israel."[21] We have to understand that traditional Judaic "architectures" would have been entirely familiar and acceptable to Jesus and his early followers. As rural Judaists who avoided urban zones they would have most likely known no other alternative.

Exclusive to the original, pre-Johannine, oral tradition, such thematic development was representationally memorialized in Yeshu's and John's rather extensive baptizing activities. We have to remember that even Josephus, many decades after the fact, remembered John as a prophetic figure. A Moses-like character who "called the people into the wilderness in order to renew their identity as God's people there."[22]

Those surviving memory fragments surrounding the shared tradition of Jesus and John working in collaboration (confirmed in the final Johannine text) eventually whittled down to brief sketches of an otherwise complex cultic panorama (Jn 1.6-42; 3.22-30; 4.1; 5.30-38; 10.40-42). But against an authentic historical backdrop, these few lines meticulously rendered clear evidence of Yeshu's rather extensive involvement with John's ministry.

As far as *Yeshu ha-Notzri's* remembered story is concerned, much of post-Palestinian narrative development probably evolved to smooth the way for later gentile observance entirely opposed to certain Hebraic beliefs. And, by default, would have presented a stark contrast to the Judaic, rural villager demographic.

So the point here: while the following may be speculative, a catalogue of historical and literary evidence stands behind it. In real life, as a Galilean village rabbi, Jesus the Nazarene would have experienced enormous challenges negotiating the hellenized socio-cultural attitudes and backgrounds of post-Palestinian Christianity. As historical reflection, this seems to be a fairly reliable and uncontroversial working assumption.

Beyond this brief observation, we should probably move on and proceed to the first-century stage.

As an introduction to our subject, the synoptic gospels offered a unified picture of proselytizing itinerants moving across the Palestinian countryside. "The apostles returned to Jesus, and told him all that they had done and taught" (Mk 6.30; Lk 9.10, RSV).

Today, promoting this familiar ecumenical portrait is standard fare. *Yeshu ha-Notzri* dispatched his early followers to navigate the rural hillsides and evangelize local populations. The synoptic stories are rather explicit.

These twelve Jesus sent out, charging them, "Go nowhere among the Gentiles, and enter no town of the Samaritans, but go rather to the lost sheep of the house of Israel. And preach as you go, saying, 'The kingdom of heaven is at hand' (Mt 10.5-7, RSV).

Go therefore and make disciples of all nations, baptizing them in the name of the Father and of the Son and of the Holy Spirit (Mt 28.19, RSV).

And he appointed twelve, to be with him, and to be sent out to preach (Mk 3.14, RSV).

And he called to him the twelve, and began to send them out two by two, and gave them authority over the unclean spirits (Mk 6.7, RSV).

And he said to them, "Go into all the world and preach the gospel to the whole creation. He who believes and is baptized will be saved; but he who does not believe will be condemned" (Mk 16.15-16, RSV).

And he called the twelve together and gave them power and authority over all demons and to cure diseases, and he sent them out to preach the kingdom of God and to heal. And he said to them, "Take nothing for your journey, no staff, nor bag, nor bread, nor money; and do not have two tunics. And whatever house you enter, stay there, and from there depart. And wherever they do not receive you, when you leave that town shake off the dust from your feet as a testimony against them." And they departed and went through the villages, preaching the gospel and healing everywhere (Lk 9.1-6, RSV).

After this the Lord appointed seventy others, and sent them on ahead of him, two by two, into every town and place where he himself was about to come. And he said to them, "The harvest is plentiful, but the laborers are few; pray therefore the Lord of the harvest to send out laborers into his harvest (Lk 10.1-2, RSV).

What later religious editors behind these accounts wanted to impress upon their readers: The Nazarene's early lieutenants were crucial to an expanding ministry.[23] Twelve in number spread the good news.[24] They were armed with parables and sayings.[25] The original teachings were conveyed on this basis.[26]

All this Jesus said to the crowds in parables; indeed he said nothing to them without a parable (Mt 13.34, RSV).

[H]e did not speak to them without a parable, but privately
to his own disciples he explained everything (Mk 4.34, RSV).

Both sectarian and non-sectarian scholars routinely defend this literary
path as "authentic to Jesus."[27] In bullet point review, allegedly, a breakaway
Judaic teacher inaugurated a new religious faith in the following way ...

marshalling wandering disciples

armed with sayings and parables

preaching the "good news"

preserved as remembered teachings

adapted into written texts

witnessed as authentic tradition

Thus, to add more believers to the burgeoning assembly, Jesus was
portrayed commanding his early followers to spread out across the rural
hillsides. They were to preach the gospel, heal the sick, speak in new
tongues, cast out demons, pick up serpents, raise the dead, and so forth.[28]

According to the synoptic stories, early missionaries were further
instructed to follow specific operational guidelines:

Take no gold, nor silver, nor copper in your belts, no bag for
your journey, nor two tunics, nor sandals, nor a staff; for the
laborer deserves his food. And whatever town or village you
enter, find out who is worthy in it, and stay with him until you
depart (Mt 10.9-11, RSV).

He charged them to take nothing for their journey except a
staff; no bread, no bag, no money in their belts; but to wear
sandals and not put on two tunics. And he said to them,
"Where you enter a house, stay there until you leave the place.
And if any place will not receive you and they refuse to hear
you, when you leave, shake off the dust that is on your feet for
a testimony against them" (Mk 6.8-11, RSV).

"Take nothing for your journey, no staff, nor bag, nor bread, nor money; and do not have two tunics. And whatever house you enter, stay there, and from there depart. And wherever they do not receive you, when you leave that town shake off the dust from your feet as a testimony against them" (Lk 9.3-5, RSV).

Thus, many experts have reached a broad consensus: The disciples and their evangelizing activities had a strong hand preserving our earliest impressions of an inspirational Judaic figure from the rural village of Nazareth in Galilee.[29]

How does this attitude match against the historical record? Did the earliest followers living in the Land of Israel support the Nazarene's mission by evangelizing local populations? The synoptic story world in triplicate certainly seemed to think so. Almost all scholars agree on the validity of this basic template.

Verifying these claims, there are several possible tracks to follow. A couple of immediate queries: Did the earliest believers proselytize just to Jews? Or to Gentiles? Or perhaps to both? Or, witnessed on a more suggestively historical stage, did they proselytize at all?

In the *Book of Acts*, readers learn that proselytizing efforts were initially directed at Jewish populations.[30] So first, we should probably take in our best impressions of the late second-temple Judaic psyche.

Were Judaic social groups living in the Land of Israel open to alternate religious forms? And strangers from rural parts unfamiliar to them spreading ideas counter to the Mosaic code?

First off, we have come to understand that the overall Jewish attitude – at least in the first century – was inward looking. Not outward looking. Common Jews were not much concerned about life in Rome. Or the true profile of Alexander the Great.

Even when situated within the diaspora, their reputation did not embrace an outgoing disposition.[31] This attitude was emphasized by historical writers. One example follows:

> The leader of this colony was one Moses, a very wise and valiant man, who, after he had possessed himself of the country, amongst other cities, built that now most famous city, Jerusalem, and the temple there, which is so greatly revered among them. … He made no representation or image of gods, because he considered that nothing of a human shape was applicable to God; but that heaven, which surrounds the earth, was the only God, and that all things were in its power. But he so arranged the rites and ceremonies of the sacrifices, and the manner and nature of their customs, as that they should be wholly different from all other nations; for, as a result of the expulsion of his people, he introduced a most inhuman and unsociable manner of life (Diodorus Siculus, *Bibliotheca Historica*, Book 40.3.3-4).

Whether at home in Israel or in disbursed population groups, during antiquity the Jews considered themselves a culture set apart.[32]

In Palestine, we are led to believe that most would have been little interested in so-called "good news." Even less so delivered by itinerant wanderers in most cases worse off than the disciples' audiences.

The Roman historian Tacitus (*Histories* 5.5.1) claimed, "[T]he Jews feel only hatred and enmity toward every other people (*adversus omnes alios hostile odium*)."[33] Tacitus almost beyond doubt drew this conclusion from a popular impression that the Jews were closed to other social-cultural milieus and the population groups behind them.

From all that we know about the various Judaic Palestinian sects (Sadducees, Pharisees, Essenes, Zealots, and so on), none questioned the credibility or priority of the Mosaic mythos. In fact each of these factions lifted up this cultic ideal to the exclusion of all else. None was searching for a new religious outlet. They were all in hot pursuit of what they perceived as Y-H-V-H's true vision for Israel.

In effect, they were decidedly focused on the *past* with its larger-than-life cultic mythology centered on topics like Temple, Torah, Exodus, Promised Land, Children of Israel, and so on.

Moreover, when we begin to delve into this question of *wandering itinerants* immediate concerns arise. They extend far beyond cultic mythologies and inherently "standoffish" attitudes of local citizenry.[34] On a practical basis, during the late second-temple era, first was the very real, ongoing social problem of roadside "banditry."[35] Especially in Galilee.

Around the time of the Nazarene's birth, in 4 BCE the long reign of Herod from Idumea (i.e. "Herod the Great") ended. The transition fomented enormous social instability across Palestine. The Galilee, especially, emerged as a particularly troublesome hotspot attracting lawbreakers.[36]

This problem was not limited to the Nazarene's home territory, however. The Judaean district experienced its fair share of bandit related unrest.[37] Such circumstances apparently endured for decades beyond the event of Herod's passing.

The problem of renegade highway outlaws cast as "robbers" needs no further description when assessing its impact on the activities of *wandering disciples*. Along with a host of other evidence, in history the two were inevitably incompatible.

So when determining the viability of "wandering itinerants," the Palestinian territorial region manifested a lack of safe connected roadways between population centers. It didn't help matters that road stations (*burganim*) operated by local officials were more times than naught *abandoned* during evening hours due to aggressive highway robbers.[38]

Writing beyond the Land of Israel and decades past the historical setting, religious editors depicting itinerant wanderers had woefully missed the mark. For those of us interested in history, probably most need to reassess some of our standing impressions. Especially concerning violence in first-century Palestinian rural zones.[39]

Adding further pressure to daily living, modern scholars tell us that across the late second-temple period largescale predatory actions were being taken by privileged elites against the disadvantaged. Traces in the canonical stories in fact described such circumstances.[40]

Over time these predatory policies eventually incited mass responses from everyday Jews. Such societal upheaval was sometimes cast as *popular uprisings*.[41] Across the decades of the first century, from time to time local populations had had enough of the Romans and corrupt temple officials.[42] Considering literary records left to us from ancient contemporary sources, it is hard making the case that this point is overstated.

In the timing of Herod's death, fighting engulfed Jerusalem when troops loyal to him turned against the Roman procurator Sabinus. Further, across Palestine at least three genuine uprisings were witnessed during this period: Judas the son of Ezekias; Simon a former slave; and a shepherd named Athronges (Josephus, *Jewish War* 2.3.1-2.5.3; *Antiquities* 17.10.2-17.10.10; Tacitus, *Histories* 5.9 on Simon).[43] This observation was touched upon above.

Over the course of the first century other violent confrontations arose in Palestine. We know there were a number of altercations in Jerusalem itself as well as in the Palestinian countryside leading up to the First Jewish War.

The truth is, across this era the social setting in the Land of Israel was not what most of us typically envision. To repeat the words of Josephus: "At this time there were great disturbances in the country, and that in many places; and the opportunity that now offered itself induced a great many to set up for kings" (Josephus, *War* 2.4.1).

Following is a fairly comprehensive list of troublemakers that spans the post-Herod, Roman era up to the First Jewish War.

2,000 of Herod's veterans in the territory of Idumea (his original home) revolted

Judas, son of Hezekiah (or Ezekias)

Simon a bandit leader active in Perea

Athronges the shepherd from the territory of Judea

Judas the Galilean

The Samaritan Prophet

Eleazar the brigand chief

The Prophet Theudas

The Egyptian Prophet

Jesus, son of Ananias

Sicarii

Other first-century prophets (similar to Theudas)

Simon bar Giora[44]

All of the named individuals, of course, had followings. From the list above, readers can easily discern that the term "popular uprisings" witnessed during the first century is no exaggeration. Palestine was rife with various forms of social unrest. At times, very violent unrest.

Another factor that relates directly to "wandering disciples" is the renowned Roman road system. As most readers know Rome was famous for its roads. For quick troop deployment an elaborate network of connected paved arteries was well-ensconced across the empire.[45]

At the time of Jesus this phenomenon had not taken root in Palestine. This point is indisputable. Archeology has to date determined that the first Roman road was a coastal route constructed around 56 CE. Jesus passed around 30 or perhaps 33 CE (depending on the expert source). Neither alternative speaks to the 56 CE timeframe. In fact, decades prior.

During the first century, near the northwest border of Roman Palestine, the port harbor town of Ptolemais (sometimes called "Acre" or "Acco") was designated by the emperor Claudius (41-54 CE) as a Roman "colony" (probably a veteran settlement).[46] This location was a coastal based point-of-entry into the Land of Israel. We have access to a milestone placard dating to around mid-century that memorializes building a Roman style, paved road connecting Ptolemais with Antioch.

This source tells us that the coastal road to the Land of Israel represented the first official Roman paved road constructed in the Near East.[47] So in their day our alleged wandering itinerants would not have had access to paved roads either. They would have been limited to mostly dirt footpaths.

The greater majority of Roman roads constructed throughout Palestine were built after the Jewish second-temple revolt. Such construction activity seems to have been most concentrated during the reign of the Emperor Hadrian (117 – 138 CE).[48]

We note again that these sometimes archeologically supported dates are all decades after the time of Jesus.[49] Consequently, during the early period that covers the Nazarene's life, throughout Palestine paved roads connecting main population centers were literally *non-existent*.

This incidental actually made a difference living under the rather dependable weather patterns of first-century Palestine. In real terms, throughout the Land of Israel, in inclement weather dirt roads were often impassible.[50] So during Yeshu's lifetime, across the wet season (October thru April[51]) dirt footpaths crisscrossing the landscape would have often been devoid of traffic.[52] In pursuit of the *earliest footprint*, such details would have had unavoidable historical consequences.

All of these factors strongly discourage us from considering the well-attested synoptic theme of wandering disciples. Itinerant missionaries for Jesus.

Rather disconcertingly, the *Fourth Gospel* never addressed the topic of wandering disciples. Consistent with what this study considers *history*, there were no proselytizers in the Johannine memory stream. None whatsoever.

We must remember that, according to the collective synoptic story, the Nazarene's entire missionary program was supposedly accomplished over a *one-year period*. Less breaks in activity for inclement weather. That takes his actual *ministry* down to a period of 8 or 9 months.

That is how the simple math plays out. That is what the synoptic literature wants to tell us. In history this reading is *literally impossible* when remembering poor people *walked* between destination points. Sometimes for many miles and across several days. For the fittest, the one-way trek from Galilee to Jerusalem alone took at least several days. And that would have been accomplished by determined effort.

Within the proselytizing conversation, another extremely difficult logistical obstacle bars our way. This matter relates to a prevailing social attitude. As far as we know, no first-century Israelite willingly followed a path of *homelessness* consistent with images drawn from the synoptic stories. Quite devasting to most readers' current outlook. Nevertheless .... this crucial observation should be *repeated*.

Again: as far as we know, *no first-century Israelite* willingly followed a path of homelessness.[53] Such social behavior was virtually unknown (and would probably have been taken as rather strange) inside the Judaic Promised Land.

The socioeconomic status of "homelessness" was reserved exclusively for the *destitute*. A social stigma no Israelite would willingly adopt. Not even disciples of Jesus. In a time and place setting ruled by "honor and shame" social values, such self-imposed humiliation would have been utterly prohibitive.

If accurate, this one conclusion alone effectively translates to nothing short of a complete reshaping of the synoptic vision. As far as we know, Jesus and his disciples were temple-worshipping Jews. As least on the surface, they would have never voluntarily adopted the negative social stigma of societal outcasts. They would never have invited such damming reputations upon themselves, their villages, or their affiliation with rabbi Jesus.

In a historical light, led by a devout village rabbi, the rustic Galilean band was integrally connected to the prevailing late second-temple social order. Noted in all four canonical texts, the Nazarene was so consecrated to the Mosaic code that he was even remembered teaching inside the Jerusalem temple itself.

> And when he entered the temple, the chief priests and the elders of the people came up to him as he was teaching, and said, "By what authority are you doing these things, and who gave you this authority?" (Mt 21.23, RSV).

> And as Jesus taught in the temple, he said, "How can the scribes say that the Christ is the son of David? (Mk 12.35, RSV).

> And he was teaching daily in the temple. The chief priests and the scribes and the principal men of the people sought to destroy him (Lk 19.47, RSV).

> About the middle of the feast Jesus went up into the temple and taught. ... Early in the morning he came again to the temple; all the people came to him, and he sat down and taught them (Jn 7.14; 8.2, RSV).

Disciples of Jesus adopting an itinerant lifestyle would have been entirely counter-productive. It is difficult imagining Judaic authorities even *allowing* Jesus to teach in the sacred precincts given the social stigma of itinerancy. Or a Judaic audience desiring to listen. In Palestinian society, such a lifestyle was considered the "last straw" in the human drama. Beyond hope. A social situation where crucial *kinship* ties no longer existed.

So there we have it. In late second-temple Palestine, poor roads, village violence, highway robbery, general social unrest, and a natural reluctance to seek out homelessness would seem to work against the theory of traveling itinerants spreading the good news. Not to mention the intense focus on Mosaically inspired devotional tenets. Plus the natural reluctance of the Jewish psyche to engage strangers.

That inside the Land of Israel wandering itinerants would somehow embark on missionary journeys promoting a village rabbi who now stood toe-to-toe with the mysterious, supernatural divine presence would have amounted to a very tall order indeed. In fact, *impossible*!

On this point alone, what we know of the historical backdrop stood at radical variance with clearly delineated portrayals in the synoptic stories. We face the unhappy realization that the problem with the popular synoptic picture (expanded in the *Book of Acts*) is its extreme unlikelihood in history.[54] An empty narrative trail leading nowhere understandably devoid of reliable distance markers.

Still, we have one remaining unanswered question. It is important to address whether Jesus perhaps entrusted his disciples to proselytize local *gentile* populations to the exclusion of Judaic-dominated districts.

If the hypothesis of converting Gentiles (opposed to Jews) was their (i.e. early Jesus followers) mission, a glaring historical factor stands firmly against it. This historical factor relates directly to why the Roman historian Tacitus reported the absence of pictorial images in Judaic public places even in the cities (Tacitus, *Histories* 5.5.4). Why Origen, the early Christian church father, reported that the Jews were not familiar with Greek literature (Origen, *Contra Celsum* 2.34). Why the Jewish Mishnah (*Sotah* 9.14) insisted that Jewish sons not be taught Greek. And why only once in all of canonical literature did the Nazarene reportedly ever refer to actual Greek practices (Mt 6.7). And, vitally, in a *critical* way.[55]

Some readers are well aware most Palestinian torah adherents believed that *ha-goyim* (non-Jews) were steeped in immorality and idolatry.[56] In fact, prior to the First Jewish War, Jews in Palestine – other than scattered urban elites – stridently *resisted* any precursor of assimilation into Hellenism.[57]

If true, we have to ask: how would such contrasting worldviews even interact on a day-to-day basis? Such glaring cultural differences would seem to amount to a major prohibitor in reasonable back-and-forth exchanges. At least in the Land of Israel.

Again, most Judaists living in the Promised Land were not receptive to meeting outsiders. Especially those they deemed ritually, or even morally, "impure." Quite frankly, many would have thumbed their noses at the idea. Rabbis especially.[58] Chances are this attitude to some extent would have included fundamental devotional patterns of at least some disciples.

There is no way to prove this point. But in all honesty we should direct our attention onto what we know of the early movement's inspirational leader. From all sensible indicators, their rabbi-teacher was a pious, observant Jew. It is difficult imagining that Jesus would have promoted recruitment of population groups deemed unworthy of the sacramental "Promised Land." In fact, impossible!

In one well known synoptic tract the Nazarene complained: "It is not fair to take the children's bread and throw it to the dogs" (Mt 15.26; Mk 7.27, RSV). Is it surprising that Jesus was referring explicitly to Gentiles? Pagans? Impure? Unclean?

In history *Yeshu ha-Notzri* was not emboldened to proselytize non-Jews. In that way, he was no different than other late second-temple adherents. And emphasis should be directed on devotional "rabbis," expressly pointed out for their extreme *zealousness* for Torah.

Indeed, his actions would have followed in a long line of united resistance to a uniquely gentile ethos. Even as far back as the Ezra-Nehemiah period, numerous literary tracks associated primary differences characterizing Jews with "purity" and non-Jews with "impurity."[59]

Again, we have already stated that Jesus held the public honorary of "rabbi." Could he have earned this reputation within the late second-temple cult by recruiting pagans to his cause? Given the genuine historical context, such proposals almost sound laughable. So in a real life setting an "affirmative" is highly unlikely. For some knowledgeable experts literally impossible. This study would have to agree.

Most informed Jewish scholars today would likely concur that in a historical sense proactive efforts made by gentiles themselves constituted the main cause for conversion to Judaism. Not proselytizing "Jewish" missionaries. Other than the gospel stories themselves there is no existent literary evidence whatsoever. In any form.[60]

Tracking the historical argument to its logical conclusion, in plain language this position suggests that wherever the synoptic editors got the idea of "proselytizing disciples" it wasn't in Palestine. Certainly not sourced within contemporary Judaic tradition. In first-century Israel amongst faithful temple worshippers the idea of proselytizing to pagans would probably have been taken as an absurd thought. Even as an *insult*!

On top of that the idea of a wise sage with twelve disciples gathered round to master his wisdom sayings was not an original Jewish notion. Most readers will not be familiar with this clear cut idea.

However, the highly recognizable image of the wise "rabbi" dispensing wisdom sayings to his twelve earnest followers was entirely *Hellenistic* in conception and execution.[61] Such notions were not advanced from an original Judaic standpoint. In other words, they did not originate in the Land of Israel.

Hopefully, readers are beginning to see that the more we step into the historical narrative the more ludicrous the idea of wandering disciples *inside geographical Palestine* becomes.

The archaeological evidence strongly suggests that during the first century "some sort of segregation between Judaean cities and Hellenised cities remained."[62] Thus, putting a damper on Jewish disciples traversing pagan urban centers initiating religiously oriented discussions.

One additional note. In the Galilee alone, archaeology reports the first century BCE (just before Jesus) as a time of startling transition. In their private lives many Jews no longer made use of imported cooking vessels.[63]

Population groups also began to practice Judaic forms of immersion purification independently of the temple apparatus. Notably, such changes "all cluster around the Sea of Galilee, from lower Galilee to central Gaulanitis."[64] The physical locations and demographical characteristics would have incorporated the kin of *Yeshu ha-Notzri* and his early disciples. Such transitions reflected the presence of *devotional Jews*.

In fact, during this period in many areas of the Judaic "Promised Land" momentum was apparently moving in exactly the *opposite* direction from receptivity to more liberal social and religious platforms. Under Roman rule, inside the Land of Israel pagan populations were associated by many Jews as *symbols of foreign intervention*.[65]

Probably very difficult for most of us today to grasp, this Judaic *Promised Land* was taken not only as a geographical landmark. But, just as significantly, as a *cultic ideal*. Let us not fall short here of basic understanding.

Such an exclusivist ideal was fully in line with the Exodus stories and their supporting Mosaic myth. Why do we claim that? One simple reason: we know for a fact that at some point during the first century the Israelite mythic story was deemed so vital that a preponderance of Palestinian Jews offered their lives in its defense during the first Roman war.

Right in step, "The Land of Israel" in shared conversation not only represented a geographical domain; but, also, another cultic ideal. And for most Israelites – *a spiritual reality*.

For the Jews, the *Land of Israel* was on identical terms with the *Promised Land*. They were one. In ancient times this shared, religiously oriented, concept was so fundamental to Judaic existence that even the most compassionate adherents like *Yeshu-ha-Notzri* would rebuke perceived territorial threats in harsh, even severe, tones.[66]

Whether we take all of this in, an important point lingers: during antiquity for the Jews the mythical "Promised Land" was as real as milk and honey.[67] Predictably, in the sacred literature, this ideal was represented as such:

[A]nd I have come down to deliver them out of the hand of the Egyptians, and to bring them up out of that land to a good and broad land, a land flowing with milk and honey, to the place of the Canaanites, the Hittites, the Amorites, the Perizzites, the Hivites, and the Jebusites (Ex 3.8, RSV).

But I have said to you, 'You shall inherit their land, and I will give it to you to possess, a land flowing with milk and honey.' I am the Lord your God, who have separated you from the peoples (Lev 20.24, RSV).

And they told him, "We came to the land to which you sent us; it flows with milk and honey, and this is its fruit (Num 13.27, RSV).

Hear therefore, O Israel, and be careful to do them; that it may go well with you, and that you may multiply greatly, as the Lord, the God of your fathers, has promised you, in a land flowing with milk and honey (Deut 6.3, RSV).

For the people of Israel walked forty years in the wilderness, till all the nation, the men of war that came forth out of Egypt, perished, because they did not hearken to the voice of the Lord; to them the Lord swore that he would not let them see the land which the Lord had sworn to their fathers to give us, a land flowing with milk and honey (Josh 5.6, RSV).

[T]hat I may perform the oath which I swore to your fathers, to give them a land flowing with milk and honey, as at this day." Then I answered, "So be it, Lord" (Jer 11.5, RSV).

On that day I swore to them that I would bring them out of the land of Egypt into a land that I had searched out for them, a land flowing with milk and honey, the most glorious of all lands (Ez 20.6, RSV).

And these two alone were preserved out of six hundred thousand people on foot, to bring them into their inheritance, into a land flowing with milk and honey (Sir-Eccl 46.8, RSV).

So to this day there have clung to us the calamities and the curse which the Lord declared through Moses his servant at the time when he brought our fathers out of the land of Egypt to give to us a land flowing with milk and honey (Bar 1.20, RSV).

[A]nd the same number of springs flowing with milk and honey, and seven mighty mountains on which roses and lilies grow; by these I will fill your children with joy (2 Ed 2.19, RSV).

Coinciding with the Roman takeover, across the first century a momentum-building trend was escalating. A general societal attitude was moving from forbearance of the unclean *goyim* to a more defensive posture protective of Israelite cultic mythologies.[68] The following would have represented a nationalistic rallying cry for the life and times:

For you [i.e. those who follow torah] are a people holy to the Lord your God; the Lord your God has chosen you to be a people for his own possession, out of all the peoples that are on the face of the earth (Deut 7.6, RSV).

In support, within the archaeological record, (repeated again) we clearly witness that "household Judaism" across Palestine was on the rise.[69]

Archaeological evidence suggests that under Roman rule during the lifetime of *Yeshu ha-Notzri* at the village level enormous change was in the air. The kind of change that in a uniquely Judaic setting would have strikingly complemented interlinking themes represented by reported baptizing activities performed by John and Jesus (see Jn 3.22-23, 26; 4.1; 10.40).

Yes, these two individuals and their reported cultic activities (in scriptural anecdotes) were placed right in the middle of a widespread cultural transformation. Those brief Johannine threads we read today actually mirrored deeper understanding of the greater historical landscape.

During this era a curious widespread phenomenon emerged in the land of Israel. And, as stated, it is reliably supported in modern archaeology. Strikingly, this singularity was **again** reported in the *Fourth Gospel.* The Johannine tradition supplied a highly plausible *historical* marker in its Cana wedding celebration: "Now six stone jars were standing there, for the Jewish rites of purification, each holding twenty or thirty gallons" (Jn 2.6, RSV).

In 2016 the *Biblical Archaeology Society* reported a 2,000 year old find at *'Einot Amitai* near Nazareth. The location was just south of *Kafr Kanna* often identified as the traditional biblical Cana from the wedding story in the *Fourth Gospel.*[70] The find consisted of a "chalkstone cave" and various other artifacts that would have been found in a first-century *stone vessel* production site.[71]

In modern excavations in Galilee alone the following archaeological sites produced *dining vessels of stone*:

Gamla on the Golan Heights overlooking the Sea of Galilee;

Bethsaida (the traditional birthplace of Peter, Andrew, and Philip) on the shore of the Sea of Galilee near the mouth of the Jordan River;

Capernaum (identified as a location of the later home of Peter) also on the Sea of Galilee;

Yodefat in the Lower Galilee (the region of *Yeshu-ha-Notzri*).[72]

In these geographical locales spread across the general vicinity of the lower Galilee, archaeology tells us that in many family dwellings stone vessels seem to have replaced household goods commonly made of *clay.* Such stone vessels were considered by many Jews to be impervious to impurity.[73] The archaeology is also mirrored in the territory of Judaea.[74]

Prior to the first century many such items had been imported from the Phoenicians. However, a deeper religious sensitivity seems to have inserted itself in the Judaic collective consciousness on a *mass scale*. "In effect they [the Jews] were symbolically making separation from the gentile world an act of worship."[75]

Additionally, in isolated, documented instances open hostility pushed Jews and *goyim* further apart.[76] Several layers of residual evidence codify the claim that local Palestinian Jewish populations resisted – sometimes violently – hellenization.[77] From the ancient world Josephus, archaeology, and authentic antiquarian documents (including Qumran[78]) offer compelling testimony.

When we refocus the lens to a broader sweep of the whole geographical region, the result is startling. We observe that virtually all of the more popular first-century Judaic sects familiar to us – Qumran, Pharisees, (to a lesser degree) Sadducees, Zealots, and Essenes – *bitterly opposed* pagan culture. Qumran rejected both pagans and those Jews who *fraternized* with pagans.[79] Often living in isolated communities, the Essenes "were even more separatist than the Pharisees. They rejected the temple in Jerusalem and all pagan (non-Jewish) culture."[80]

Few casual readers will be familiar with the Judaic sect of the *Essenes* quite active across the late second-temple setting. In some areas they were aligned with what today we might characterize as *ultra-conservative* or *radical* Judaism.

In their mind's eye, the "ultra-conservative" belief system they represented constituted the *real* Israel. Not only that but closer to our drilldown, the Essene sect was overtly hostile to the Roman takeover. Furthermore, their interpretation of the struggle of good versus evil most consistently translated to the struggle of *Jews versus Gentiles!*[81]

During the late second-temple era, each Hebraic sub-group in their own right was intent on reestablishing their place in the world under the banner of a traditional *Israelite* ethos. They would accomplish this end by reinaugurating Mosaic cultic attitudes based on some form of shared awareness instituted and regulated by their deity Y-H-V-H.[82] Thus, we get the strong impression that but for some ruling elites few Israelites were the least interested in hellenized integration.

Large numbers of first-century Judaists who occupied their *Promised Land* were deeply resentful of gentiles. In their eyes these foreign interlopers had imported their detestable idols and uncouth, impure ways into the very heart of G-d's sacred realm (i.e. flowing with *milk and honey*: Ex 3.8, 17; 13.5; 33.3). Many readers will not know that remembered events surrounding the First Jewish War added an extraordinarily violent exclamation point to that narrative claim.

Again, for nearly all observant Jews, regardless of sect, a basic vision was ever in the forefront. In that vision filled with "milk and honey" gentiles were *nowhere* to be seen.

By the time of the First Jewish War, inside the Land of Israel for many the hated, unclean *goyim* had matured into a direct and barbaric threat to their sacred legacy.[83] The historical record ferociously evoked such impressions.

Around this time, across select Palestinian urbanized zones, total social breakdown overwhelmed entire populations. This point is not narrative embellishment. For us today, reimagining such vitriol dominating whole population groups becomes difficult even to contemplate.

Readers might find that many scholars today – both sectarian and non-sectarian – have a habit of *ignoring* the historical record. Such an authentically recalled memory stream discussed herein radically resists many contemporary social-cultural attitudes. Especially in elite academic circles. Consequently, in specialized research such key historical memories are simply set aside.

Nevertheless, if we are in search of the earliest footprint, we are obligated as best we can to accurately assess the era. Josephus records that around the time of the first Jewish War, a broad collapse of basic social structures was in full swing.

In urban settings disbursed across the Palestinian region, open violence of rare magnitude dominated entire populations. In each instance, this study cites the findings of modern scholars who examined the writings of Flavius Josephus:

Caesarea

Gentiles were reported slaughtering upwards of twenty thousand Jews in something like an hour.[84]

Gerasa, Pella, Scythopolis (Bethshan), Gadara, Hippos, (unspecified locales in the) Golan, Kedesh, Ptolemais, Gaba

Violent strife engulfed Jews and Gentiles.[85]

Damascus

Upwards of ten thousand Jews were massacred.[86]

Tiberias

The Gentile population was annihilated.[87]

Batanea

Jews were murdered by pagan overseers.[88]

Antioch

Violent bloodshed between Jews and Gentiles continued even *after* the Roman victory.[89]

Heshbon, Philadelphia, Sebaste, Ascalan, Anthedon, Gaza

Gentile populations were harassed and murdered by Jewish partisans.[90]

As described, an inhuman travesty was brought on largely by opposing social and cultural worldviews. This whole topic can be summarized in the simple cliché: "Pagan" vs "Jew."

Based on memories of *actual historical events*, enormous, uncontrolled hostilities capable of genocide (on both sides) emerged over the years prior to, during, and after the war. Again, according to Josephus, this reality was reported, contextually, in a historical light. There was no comparative "symbolism" involved. Josephus wanted his audience to know that such murderous rampages in fact occurred in real time among disparate population groups.

Suggested above, given our sensitivities in the twenty-first century to *social politics*,[91] especially in academic circles, this historical chapter is not always at the forefront of scholarly discussions. In fact, it is almost never mentioned. Further, our interpretations are dependent on the (sometimes) overwrought memories of traitor-turned-historian, Flavius Josephus.[92]

In every other way, however, such detailed memoirs underline the tremendous widespread resentment and outright hatred expressed between two vested, geographically aligned cultures.

Thus, scholars today who try and filter ancient Judaic populations into the Hellenistic mainstream are probably just *fantasizing*. The facts scream out to us from the first-century historical era. They cannot be set aside. Across this timeframe, with pagan Rome bearing witness, inside the Land of Israel Jews and Gentiles were positioned in a "death grip" to determine cultural and social dominance.

In a narrow window of time two diverse sets of ideologies fought each other to the death. In the end, it was not about wealth. It was not about power. It was not about land. It was not about governance. It was a fundamental difference in perceptions of good versus evil, right versus wrong, acceptable versus unacceptable, tolerable versus intolerable. It was an apocalypse of basic human identity.

We sometimes misremember that why the First Jewish War lasted an extraordinary 7 to 8 years was based largely on Judaic hatred for what a pagan presence symbolized to the late second-temple cultic narrative.[93] In an impartial historical review, there is really no other reliable explanation.

The Jewish homeland was barely a speck on the historical, Near Eastern roadmap. But its Jerusalem temple *physically* dominated the region. And that fact the "Goliath" of Rome could not essentially tolerate.

Thus, back to our original focus, this study strongly suggests that seen in a historical light, deep conflicts arise attempting to place the disciples' evangelizing activities inside the Land of Israel. It is especially true envisioning the synoptic stories pursuing a hypothetical *gentile mission*. For the most part, such hellenistically inspired attitudes were not present in first-century Israel.

We are then faced with a decision. Were the proselytizing stories all made up? Or did the later synoptic editors preserve some form of historical framework? Who did they really envision promoting their Christos-Son-of-God ideology? This study argues that history cancels out the theory of a Palestinian mission. More realistically, is there an alternate view?

In a significant way, the scenario of Paul from Tarsus and his former pagan followers cast as early proselytizing missionaries seems to present a more palatable storyline than wandering Palestinian disciples. And – probably a surprise for readers – aspects of Paul's story are somewhat adaptable to traditional gospel themes.

The *Book of Acts* tracked Paul's adventures collaborating with his gentile companions.[94] They wandered from one hellenistic setting to another.[95] They preached the gospel of a divine figure they named "Christ."[96] They cast out demons.[97] Picked up serpents.[98] They healed.[99] And even claimed to raise the dead.[100] They wrote letters from one congregation to another promoting their "new" faith. They further chastised backsliding believers in the tradition of the synoptic Christ.[101]

Scriptures offered two parallel tracks sharing very similar themes. The *Book of Acts* described Paul and his followers trekking across pagan landscapes preaching the gospel, seeking new converts. They were witnessed performing the same or similar acts as the Nazarene had instructed his disciples in the synoptics. Coincidence? Misreading? Flawed memories? The ultimate effects of a detailed plan drawn by their divine Christos?

According to the synoptic stories, the first "Christian" evangelists were supposedly responsible for promoting the spread of *good news* across territorial Palestine. We know that the apostle Paul later crisscrossed the eastern Mediterranean in response to cosmic visions of the exalted "Kyrios." But some scholars cannot reconcile this behavior with attitudes borne in the Israelite homeland. Certainly not for individuals faithful to second-temple Judaism.

Kyrios means literally "lord" or "master."[102] The term evolved in a theological sense to consider Jesus in light of divine or supernatural symbology.

Modern experts tell us that the term "Kyrios" was enormously popular for Paul and his gentile following.[103] However it may have been unfamiliar to the first Palestinian followers of *Yeshu-ha-Notzri* who most likely would not have been exposed to Paul's hellenized Kyrios thinking.[104]

In gentile municipalities, designating Jesus as Kyrios associated him *directly with pagan deities*. In Hellenic settings, the term directly implied pagan divinities honored by their adherents.[105] In all fairness, other experts today argue against this claim.[106]

Either way it is plausible that the later gospel editors from time to time referred to the term as a descriptor for their Savior's *divine status*. Of course in any historical sense all of these dogmatic characterizations contrasted wildly with the alleged earliest *historical* profile.

There is some further indirect testimony that we might consider. Even beyond Palestine, in the diaspora, time and again during his missionary journeys Paul was confronted by synagogue elders.

One thing is sure. The Apostle Paul *could work a crowd*. Related reports out of the *Book of Acts* are diverse and at times extravagantly measured. But a common theme rings true.

In Antioch of Pisidia, local synagogue officials "incited the devout women of high standing and the leading men of the city, and stirred up persecution against Paul and Barnabas, and drove them out of their district" (Acts 13.50, RSV). Probably an apropos response: what could Paul have possibly said or what form of behavior could procure such extreme reactions from varied, urban, demographic profiles? Were synagogue leaders that influential?

According to the Lucan version, in Iconium synagogue officials again "stirred up the Gentiles and poisoned their minds" against Paul and his companions (Acts 14.2, RSV). Apparently the situation quickly escalated and Paul's group quickly fled the scene upon learning they were to be stoned in the traditional Judaic way (Acts 5-6). This form of sentence was not typical. And implied very extreme behavior. Stoning suggests they had been found guilty of *blasphemy* (see Lev 24.13-16). In the eyes of synagogue leaders, Paul's group had in some way reviled the Hebrew sovereign "Lord."

In Lystra, Jewish synagogue officials arrived from Antioch and Iconium. They, in fact, "stoned Paul and dragged him out of the city, supposing that he was dead" (Acts 14.19, RSV). Consistent with the trend, this is an example of the most severe reaction known to Judaism – blotting out a life. Paul's vitriol must have reached the very core of human emotion. His "Christos" (or the way he presented his beliefs) apparently threatened the status of the Jews' invisible *divine presence*. According to torah faith – the one indefensible sin. There is little alternative to such a conclusion.

In Philippi, a crowd along with city magistrates seized Paul and his follower Silas. They attacked the two tearing away their clothes and beating them with rods. Paul and Silas were deposited in the local jail and their feet were fastened "in the stocks" (Acts 16.24, RSV).

In Thessaloni ca, synagogue officials were again incensed by Paul and Silas. In today's world it is difficult imagining what could have possibly set various synagogues' teeth on edge to want these individuals killed. But the same basic emotional pattern was repeated in Thessaloni ca. Out of precaution, "The brethren immediately sent Paul and Silas away by night to Beroe a" (Acts 17.10, RSV).

In Beroe a, Jewish officials from Thessaloni ca had followed. In short order these Judaic religious authorities were seen "stirring up and inciting the crowds. Then the brethren immediately sent Paul off on his way to the sea" (Acts 17.13-14, RSV). Do readers begin to see a pattern? Entirely from an apparent vitriolic verbal manner alone, the Apostle Paul seemed to have an aptitude for putting people's teeth on edge. Curiously, in diverse geographies and varying social settings.

In Corinth, over another cultic breach, Gallio the (Roman) proconsul of Acha ia got involved by saying he would not pass judgment against *anyone*. Paul's supporters apparently "seized Sos thenes, the ruler of the synagogue, and beat him in front of the tribunal. But Gallio paid no attention to this" (Acts 18.17, RSV). On the local level someone (or some group) sympathetic to Paul was apparently exploiting the bureaucratic state to the detriment of the Jews.

In Ephesus, this time the local pagan population reacted to Paul's view that "gods made with hands are not gods" (Acts 19.26, RSV). After all, *they were pagans*. Paul didn't seem to have much tolerance for others' beliefs. Jews or otherwise. Locals seized both Paul and certain Macedo hians among his followers. A riot was in the making. But the town clerk calmed the situation and "dismissed the assembly" (Acts 19.41, RSV).

Finally, in Jerusalem Paul brought certain Gentile followers (i.e. "Greeks") into the temple itself. This unimaginably shocking and aggressively hostile act should have gotten him killed. At the very least. More like strung up and quartered to simmer emotions. This speculative idea almost ensued. "Then all the city was aroused, and the people ran together; they seized Paul and dragged him out of the temple, and at once the gates were shut" (Acts 21.30, RSV). But Roman officials were notified and Paul was immediately arrested and bound in chains (Acts 21.33).

Within this reading, in every scenario in the *Book of Acts* the Apostle Paul was portrayed as *victim*. They were all after Paul. Pagans and Jews. Between the lines, however, one observes from Paul an almost *maniacal* obsession with religious attitudes that *rejected* simple tolerance. How could Paul from Tarsus possibly have witnessed visions of a former village rabbi who had preached brotherly love and social inclusion?

If we intend to be impartial, we must ask ourselves why Paul would be so aggressively pursued by local populations? In particular, what got into the heads of so many Judaic worshippers (and some pagans as well) in so many diverse locales that after ID'ing Paul's caravan their minds were consumed by murder? What had he said? What had he done?

From available textual sources regarding social unrest and/or riots nine instances in the *Book of Acts* (alone) provide a small catalogue of behaviors from the Apostle Paul that indisputably pointed to confrontation and violence.

Either the Apostle Paul was an unusually ornery fellow. Or his depictions of the supernatural "Christos," according to synagogue Jews living in multiple gentile settings, *radically* conflicted with established sacred norms.

Yes, the confrontations cited above were not mere verbal warnings meant to refocus a drifting devotee. In later written correspondence with the church at Corinth (2 Cor 11.24), Paul reported he had received 40 lashes (less one) *five times* from various Jewish synagogue officials. Virtually an impossible number for one individual in one lifetime to survive. We should note that further details were otherwise left unrecorded in early Christian canon.

If the accounts are somewhat accurate, we know that several times Paul and his companions were driven out of Hellenic municipalities (Acts 17.10, 14; 21.30-31). Once he was stoned, dragged out of the city, and left for dead (Acts 14.19). On another occasion he and his fellows were thrown into prison, chained, and shackled (Acts 16.24).

Again, what could have precipitated such extreme reactions from numerous diasporan communities as well as in the Judaic homeland? The first thought that comes to mind is whatever Paul had to sell, it was roundly rejected on a wide scale by observant Jews. This point is crucial to our discussion. Paul's supernatural "Savior" (Phil 3.20; 2 Tim 1.10; Tit 1.4; 2.13; 3.6) was based on a historical character named *Yeshu ha-Notzri*. A devotional Jew. Acknowledged among his contemporaries as a practicing *rabbi*. A rabbi who taught in the Jerusalem temple.

We need to understand that the connections behind the *Book of Acts* wanted their audiences to understand that it just wasn't *some* of the diasporan synagogue communities that reacted thus. Realistically, for casual readers, from a geographical standpoint, these were religious groups that had found a path to coexistence in a pagan world. Nevertheless, the end result of Paul's Christos evangelizing mission in every instance was that synagogue communities reacted with uncontrolled hostility to his utter rejection of "official" (or institutional) Yahwism.[107]

Perhaps that assessment is too harsh. But whether the question can be answered with any degree of accuracy, in the New Testament writings, out of the 72 references to the term "gospel" (the Greek εὐαγγέλιον) 60 of the 72 are found in Paul's letters.[108] No doubt, aggressive, contrarian proselytizing that depicted a "human-divine" entity ("godman" or "divine man" – a religious concept well embedded in Hellenic pagan culture), was a key to Paul's missionary strategy.[109]

The numbers unmistakably suggest it was Gentile Christianity formed beyond territorial Palestine that first proselytized the familiar gospel message. Not original followers of Jesus. Or worshipping diasporan Jews. At times the later synoptic accounts clearly encapsulated a former pagan (in contrast to an earlier Judaic-Palestinian) vision.

So this study argues that during the life of Jesus, within territorial Palestine, "proselytizing" was a non-factor. Simply didn't exist. Those later stories, as they appear today, were not fashioned for people living in the Land of Israel. But beyond. In the Hellenistic pagan world of the Apostle Paul.

Previously mentioned, out of the canonical texts, only the *Fourth Gospel* recorded no proselytizing accounts at all. None. Among scholars *John's Gospel* bears a reputation for being the last to be inscribed into writing. An odd conclusion when reviewing *historical facts*.

However, even if the Johannine version *was* last, this does not discount the strong possibility that this Gospel preserved thin streams of very old tradition. Original memories. Quite possibly, in this instance, the absence of evangelizing material remembers a very early, primitive voice. Yes, entirely *Judaic* in retention and transmission.

* * *

For readers who have ventured this far the story concludes in the second volume. The final book features a review of so-called Markan "priority," a rendering of the probable earliest oral Gospel, as well as a historically based review of the Resurrection. The work is aptly titled: "Yeshu ha-Notzri."

CHAPTER EIGHT
References

Achtemeir, Paul J. "Gospel Miracle Material and the Divine Man," *Interpretation: A Journal of Bible and Theology*, Volume 26, Issue 2 (1972), 173-197. (Abbr. "Gospel and Divine Man")

Ahlström, Gösta W. *The History of Ancient Palestine*, Edelman, Diana, ed. (Minneapolis, MN: Fortress Press, 1993). (Abbr. "History of Ancient Palestine")

Alexandre, Yardenna. "Karm er-Ras near Kafr Kanna," in *Galilee in the Late Second Temple and Mishnaic Periods, Volume 2: The Archaeological Record from Cities, Towns, and Villages*, Fiensy, David A. and Strange, James Riley, eds. (Minneapolis, MN: Fortress Press, 2015). (Abbr. "Karm er-Ras")

Allison, Dale C. *Jesus of Nazareth: Millenarian Prophet* (Minneapolis, MN: Fortress Press, 1998). (Abbr. "Millenarian Prophet")

Anderson, Paul N. *The Fourth Gospel and the Quest for Jesus: Modern Foundations Reconsidered* (New York, NY: T&T Clark, 2007). (Abbr. "Fourth Gospel Quest")

Andrade, Nathanael. "Ambiguity, Violence, and Community in the Cities of Judaea and Syria," *Historia: Zeitschrift für Alte Geschichte*, Bd. 59, H. 3 (2010), pp. 342-370. (Abbr. "Ambiguity, Violence, Community")

Avshalom-Gorni, Dina and Getzov, Nimrod. "Phoenicians and Jews: A Ceramic Case Study," in *The First Jewish Revolt: Archaeology, History and Ideology*, Berlin, Andrea M. and Overman, J. Andrew, eds. (New York, NY: Routledge, 2002), pp. 74-84. (Abbr. "Phoenicians and Jews")

Bauckham, Richard. "Messianism According to the Gospel of John," in *Challenging Perspectives on the Gospel of John*, Lierman, John, ed. (Tübingen, Germany: Mohr Siebeck, 2006). (Abbr. "Messianism According to John")

Ben-Chorin, Schalom. *Brother Jesus: The Nazarene Through Jewish Eyes*, Klein, Jared S. and Reinhart, Max, eds. and trans. (Athens, GA: University of Georgia Press, 2012). (Abbr. "Brother Jesus")

Berlin, Andrea M. "Jewish Life Before the Revolt: The Archaeological Evidence," *Journal for the Study of Judaism in the Persian, Hellenistic, and Roman Period*, Vol. 36, No. 4 (2005), pp. 417-470. (Abbr. "Jewish Life Before Revolt")

Berlin, Andrea M. "Identity Politics in Early Roman Galilee," in *The Jewish Revolt Against Rome*, Popović, Mladen, ed. (Leiden, The Netherlands: Brill, 2011), pp. 69-106. (Abbr. "Identity Politics").

Betz, Hans Dieter. "Jesus as Divine Man," *in Jesus and the Historian: Written in Honor of Ernest Cadman Colwell*, Trotter, F. Thomas, ed. (Philadelphia, PA: Westminster Press, 1968), pp. 114-133. (Abbr. "Jesus as Divine Man")

Betz, Otto. "The Concept of the So-Called 'Divine-Man' in Mark's Christology," in *Studies in New Testament and Early Christian Literature: Essays in Honor of Allen Wikgren*, Aune, David Edward, ed. (Leiden, The Netherlands: Brill, 1972), pp. 229-240. (Abbr. "Concept So-Called Divine Man")

Bird, Michael F. *Jesus and the Origins of the Gentile Mission* (New York, NY: T&T Clark International, 2006). (Abbr. "Jesus and Origins")

Blackburn, Barry. *Theios Anēr and the Markan Miracle Traditions* (Tübingen, Germany: Mohr Siebeck, 1991). (Abbr. "Markan Miracle Traditions")

Blumell, Lincoln. "Social Banditry? Galilean Banditry from Herod until the Outbreak of the First Jewish Revolt," *Scripta Classica Israelica* 27 (2008): 35 – 53. (Abbr. "Social Banditry")

Borg, Marcus J. *Conflict, Holiness, and Politics in the Teachings of Jesus* (New York, NY: Continuum International Publishing Group, 1998). (Abbr. "Conflict, Holiness, Politics")

Bouchard, Constance Brittain. *Life and Society in the West: Antiquity and the Middle Ages* (San Diego, CA: Harcourt Brace Jovanovich, 1988). (Abbr. "Life and Society")

Bousset, Wilhelm. *Kyrios Christos: A History of the Belief in Christ from the Beginnings of Christianity to Irenaeus*, Steely, John E., trans. (Nashville, TN: Abingdon Press, 1970). (Abbr. "Kyrios Christos")

Braine, David D.C. "The Inner Jewishness of St John's Gospel as the Clue to the Inner Jewishness of Jesus," *Studien zum Neuen Testament und Seiner Umwelt (SNTU)*, Serie A, Band 13, 1988, pp. 101-157. (Abbr. "Inner Jewishness of Jesus")

Bruyneel, Sally and Padgett, Alan G. *Introducing Christianity* (Maryknoll, NY: Orbis Books, 2003). (Abbr. "Introducing Christianity")

Bryan, Steven M. *Jesus and Israel's Traditions of Judgement and Restoration* (New York, NY: Cambridge University Press, 2002). (Abbr. "Judgement and Restoration")

Byrskog, Samuel. *Story as History – History as Story: The Gospel Tradition in the Context of Ancient Oral History* (Tübingen, Germany: Mohr Siebeck, 2000). (Abbr. "Story as History")

Casey, Maurice. *Jesus of Nazareth: An Independent Historian's Account of his Life and Teaching* (New York, NY: T&T Clark International, 2010). (Abbr. "Independent Historian Account")

Chancey, Mark A. *The Myth of a Gentile Galilee* (New York, NY: Cambridge University Press, 2002). (Abbr. "Myth of Gentile Galilee")

Chancey, Mark A. *Greco-Roman Culture and the Galilee of Jesus* (New York, NY: Cambridge University Press, 2005). (Abbr. "Greco-Roman Culture")

Charlesworth, James H. *The Historical Jesus: An Essential Guide* (Nashville, TN: Abingdon Press, 2008). (Abbr. "Historical Jesus Essential Guide")

Charlesworth, James Hamilton. "The Temple, Purity, and the Background to Jesus' Death," *Revista Catalana de Teologia*, [en línia], 2008, Vol. 33, Núm. 2, p. 395-42. (Abbr. "Temple, Purity, Jesus' Death")

Chilton, Bruce. *Rabbi Jesus: An Intimate Biography* (New York, NY: Doubleday, 2000). (Abbr. "Rabbi Jesus")

Choi, Junghwa. *Jewish Leadership in Roman Palestine from 70 C.E. to 135 C.E.* (Boston, MA: Brill, 2013). (Abbr. "Jewish Leadership Roman Palestine")

Clements, Ronald E. *Ezekiel* (Louisville, KY: Westminster John Knox Press, 1996). (Abbr. "Ezekiel")

Cohen, Shaye J. D. *Josephus in Galilee and Rome: His Vita and Development As a Historian* (Leiden, The Netherlands: Brill Academic Publishers, Inc., 2002). (Abbr. "Josephus in Galilee, Rome")

Corrington, Gail Peterson. *The 'Divine Man' – His Origin and Function in Hellenistic Popular Religion* (New York, NY: Peter Lang, 1986). (Abbr. "Divine Man")

Cribbs, F. Lamar. "A Reassessment of the Date of Origin and the Destination of the Gospel of John," *Journal of Biblical Literature*, Vol. 89, No. 1 (Mar., 1970), pp. 38-55. (Abbr. "Origin-Destination John")

Cromhout, Markus. *Jesus and Identity: Reconstructing Judean Ethnicity in Q* (Eugene, OR: Cascade Books, 2007). (Abbr. "Jesus and Identity")

Crossan, John Dominic. "Itinerants and Householders in the Earliest Jesus Movement," in *Whose Historical Jesus?*, Arnal, William E. and Desjardins, Michel, eds. (Waterloo, Ontario, Canada: Wilfrid Laurier University Press, 1997). (Abbr. "Intinerants and Householders")

Culi, Yaakov. *The Torah Anthology: Vol. 4 – Israel in Egypt* (Brooklyn, NY: Moznaim Publishing Corporation, 1978). (Abbr. "Torah Anthology, iv")

Davies, Paul E. "Jesus and the Role of the Prophet," *Journal of Biblical Literature*, Vol. 64, No. 2 (Jun., 1945), pp. 241-254. (Abbr. "Role Prophet")

Dennis, John A. *Jesus' Death and the Gathering of True Israel: The Johannine Appropriation of Restoration and Theology in the Light of John 11.47-52* (Tübingen, Germany: Mohr Siebeck, 2006). (Abbr. "Gathering True Israel")

Dowden, Ken. "Rhetoric and Religion," in *A Companion to Greek Rhetoric*, Worthington, Ian, ed. (West Sussex, United Kingdom: Wiley-Blackwell, 2010), pp. 320-335. (Abbr. "Rhetoric and Religion")

Dunn, James D. G. "Can the Third Quest Hope to Succeed?" in *Authenticating the Activities of Jesus*, Chilton, Bruce D. and Evans, Craig A., eds. (Boston, MA: Brill Academic Publishers, Inc., 2002), pp. 31-48. (Abbr. "Third Quest")

Dunn, James D. G. *Did the First Christians Worship Jesus?: The New Testament Evidence* (Louisville, KY: Westminster John Knox Press, 2010). (Abbr. "First Christians Worshipping Jesus")

Dunn, James D. G. *Jesus Remembered: Christianity in the Making, Volume 1* (Grand Rapids, MI: William B. Eerdmans Publishing Company, 2003). (Abbr. "Jesus Remembered")

Elledge, C. D. *The Bible and the Dead Sea Scrolls*, Vaughn, Andrew G., ed. (Atlanta, GA: Society of Biblical Literature, 2005). (Abbr. "Dead Sea Scrolls")

Evans, Craig A. "Aspects of Exile and Restoration in the Proclamation of Jesus and the Gospels," in *Jesus in Context: Temple, Purity, and Restoration* (Leiden, The Netherlands: Brill, 1997). (Abbr. "Aspects Exile, Restoration")

Evans, Craig A. *Jesus and His World: The Archaeological Evidence* (Louisville, KY: John Knox Press, 2012). (Abbr. "Jesus and His World")

Evans, Craig A. "Jewish Burial Traditions and the Resurrection of Jesus," *Journal for the Study of the Historical Jesus*, Volume 3, Issue 2 (01 Jan 2005), pp. 233-248. (Abbr. "Jewish Burial")

Eve, Eric. *The Jewish Context of Jesus' Miracles* (New York, NY: Sheffield Academic Press Ltd, 2002). (Abbr. "Jewish Context Jesus Miracles")

Faulkner, Neil. *Apocalypse: The Great Jewish Revolt Against Rome AD 66-73* (Glouchestershire, United Kingdom: Amberly Publishing, 2011). (Abbr. "Apocalypse")

Feldman, Louis H. "Conversion to Judaism in Classical Antiquity," *Hebrew Union College Annual*, Vol. 74 (2003), pp. 115-156. (Abbr. "Conversion to Judaism")

Feldman, Louis H. "How Much Hellenism in Jewish Palestine?", *Hebrew Union College Annual*, Vol. 57 (1986), pp. 83-111. (Abbr. "Hellenism in Jewish Palestine")

Feldman, Louis H. *Jew and Gentile in the Ancient World: Attitudes and Interactions from Alexander to Justinian* (Princeton, NJ: Princeton University Press, 1993). (Abbr. "Jew and Gentile")

Ferguson, Everett. *Baptism in the Early Church: History, Theology, and Liturgy in the First Five Centuries* (Grand Rapids, MI: William B. Eerdmans Publishing Company, 2009). (Abbr. "Baptism in Early Church")

Freedman, David Noel, ed. *Eerdmans Dictionary of the Bible* (Grand Rapids, MI: William B. Eerdmans Publishing Company, 2000). (Abbr. "Eerdmans Dictionary the Bible")

Freyne, Sean. *Jesus a Jewish Galilean: A New Reading of the Jesus Story* (New York, NY: T&T Clark, 2004). (Abbr. "Jewish Galilean")

Freyne, Sean. "Jesus and the 'Servant' Community in Zion: Continuity in Text," in *Jesus from Judaism to Christianity: Continuum Approaches to the Historical Jesus*, Holmén, Tom, ed. (New York, NY: T&T Clark, 2007), pp. 109-124. (Abbr. "Jesus and Servant)

Gabriel, Richard A. and Boose, Jr., Donald W. *The Great Battles of Antiquity: A Strategic and Tactical Guide to Great Battles that Shaped the Development of*

War (Westport, Connecticut: Greenwood Press, Inc., 1994). (Abbr. "Great Battles of Antiquity")

Gallagher, Eugene V. *Divine Man or Magician: Celsus and Origen on Jesus* (Chico, CA: Scholars Press, 1982). (Abbr. "Divine Man or Magician")

Garber, Zev. "The Jewish Jewish: Conversation Not Conversion," *Hebrew Studies*, Vol. 56 (2015), pp. 385-392. (Abbr. "Conversation Not Conversion")

Garber, Zev, ed. *The Jewish Jesus: Revelation, Reflection, Reclamation* (West Lafayette, IN: Purdue University Press, 2011). (Abbr. "Jewish Jesus")

Georgi, Dieter. "The Early Church: Internal Jewish Migration or New Religion?", *The Harvard Theological Review*, Vol. 88, No. 1 (Jan., 1995), pp. 35-68. (Abbr. "Internal Jewish Migration")

Georgi, Dieter. *The Opponents of Paul in Second Corinthians*, 2nd ed. (Edinburgh, Scotland: T&T Clark Ltd., 1987). (Abbr. "The Opponents of Paul")

Gibbs, John G. *Creation and Redemption: A Study in Pauline Theology* (Leiden, The Netherlands: Brill, 1971). (Abbr. "Creation and Redemption")

Goldberg, David J. and Rayner, John D. *The Jewish People: Their History and Their Religion* (New York, NY: Penguin Books, 1989). (Abbr. "The Jewish People")

Goodman, Martin. "Galilean Judaism and Judaean Judaism," in *The Cambridge History of Judaism*, vol. III., Horbury, William, et al., eds. (Cambridge: Cambridge University Press, 1999), 596-617. (Abbr. "Galilean Judaism, Judean Judaism")

Goodman, Martin. *Rome and Jerusalem: The Clash of Ancient Civilizations* (New York, NY: First Vantage Books, 2008). (Abbr. "Rome and Jerusalem")

Goodman, Martin. *The Ruling Class of Judaea: The Origins of the Jewish Revolt Against Rome A.D. 66 – 70* (New York, NY: Cambridge University Press, 1987). (Abbr. "Ruling Class")

Grosby, Steven. *Biblical Ideas of Nationality: Ancient and Modern* (Winona Lake, IN: Eisenbrauns, 2002). (Abbr. "Biblical Ideas of Nationality")

Gruen, Erich S. *Diaspora: Jews Amidst Greeks and Romans* (Cambridge, MA: Harvard University Press, 2002). (Abbr. "Jews Amidst Greeks, Romans")

Halpern, Baruch. "The Miraculous Wine in Its Galilean Ceramic Context," in *Confronting the Past: Archaeological and Historical Essays on Ancient Israel in Honor of William G. Dever*, Gitin, Seymour, et al., eds. (Winona Lake, IN: Eisenbrauns, 2006). (Abbr. "Miraculous Wine Galilean Context")

Harrington, Hannah K. *The Purity and Sanctuary of the Body in Second Temple Judaism* (Göttingen, Germany: Vandenhoeck and Ruprecht GmbH and Co. KG, 2019). (Abbr. "Purity and Sanctuary")

Hayes, John H. and Mandell, Sara R. *The Jewish People in Classical Antiquity: From Alexander to Bar Kochba* (Louisville, KY: Westminster John Knox Press, 1998). (Abbr. "Jewish People Classical Antiquity")

Hewitt, J. Thomas. *Messiah and Scripture: Paul's "In Christ" Idiom in Its Ancient Jewish Context* (Tübingen, Germany: Mohr Siebeck, 2020). (Abbr. "Messiah and Scripture")

Hezser, Catherine. *Jewish Travel in Antiquity* (Tübingen, Germany: Mohr Siebeck, 2011). (Abbr. "Jewish Travel in Antiquity")

Hezser, Catherine. *Romanization and Its Consequences: Rabbinic Judaism as a Disaporized Judaism in Late Antiquity – Response to Hayim Lapin, Rabbis as Romans* (Oxford, 2012), Baltimore, MD: SBL Conference (unpublished conference paper), 2013. (Abbr. "Romanization and Its Consequences")

Homolka, Walter. *Jewish Jesus Research and its Challenge to Christology Today* (Leiden, The Netherlands: Brill, 2017). (Abbr. "Jewish Research")

Horsley, Richard A. "Early Christian Movements: Jesus Movements and the Renewal of Israel," *HTS Theological Studies*, Vol 62, No 4 (2006), pp. 1201-1225. (Abbr. "Early Christian Movements")

Horsley, Richard A. "Jesus and Galilee: The Contingencies of a Renewal Movement," in *Galilee Through the Centuries: Confluence of Cultures*,

Meyers, Eric M., ed. (Winona Lake, IN: Eisenbrauns, 1999), pp. 57-74. (Abbr. "Contingencies of Renewal")

Horsley, Richard A. *Jesus and the Spiral of Violence: Popular Jewish Resistance in Roman Palestine* (Minneapolis, MN: Fortress Press, 1993). (Abbr. "Spiral of Violence")

Horsley, Richard A. *Jesus in Context: Performance, Power, and People* (Minneapolis, MN: Fortress Press, 2008). (Abbr. "Jesus in Context")

Horsley, Richard. *The Prophet Jesus and the Renewal of Israel: Moving Beyond a Diversionary Debate* (Grand Rapids, MI: William B. Eerdmans Publishing Company, 2012). (Abbr. "Prophet Jesus")

Horsley, Richard A. and Hanson, John S. *Bandits, Prophets, and Messiahs: Popular Movements at the Time of Jesus* (San Francisco, CA: Harper & Row, Publishers, 1985). (Abbr. "Bandits, Prophets")

Horsley, Richard and Thatcher, Tom. *John, Jesus and the Renewal of Israel* (Grand Rapids, MI: William B. Eerdmans Publishing Company, 2013). (Abbr. "Renewal Israel")

Hvalvik, Reidar. "Paul as a Jewish Believer – According to the Book of Acts," in *Jewish Believers in Jesus: The Early Centuries*, Skarsaune, Oskar and Hvalik, Reidar, eds. (Peabody, MA: Hendrickson Publishers, Inc., 2007), pp. 121-153. (Abbr. "Paul as Jewish Believer)

Johnson, Luke Timothy. *Among the Gentiles: Greco-Roman Religion and Christianity* (New Haven, CT: Yale University Press, 2009). (Abbr. "Among the Gentiles")

Kazen, Thomas. *Jesus and Purity Halakhah: Was Jesus Indifferent to Impurity?* (Winona Lake: Eisenbrauns, 2010). (Abbr. "Jesus and Purity Halakhah")

Keener, Craig S. *The Historical Jesus of the Gospels* (Grand Rapids, MI: William B. Eerdmans Publishing Company, 2009). (Abbr. "Historical Jesus Gospels")

Klausner, Joseph. *From Jesus to Paul*, Stinespring, William F., trans. (New York, NY: The Macmillan Co., 1943). (Abbr. "From Jesus to Paul")

Koester, Helmut. "The Divine Human Being," *The Harvard Theological Review*, Vol. 78, No. 3/4 (Jul – Oct, 1985), pp. 243-252. (Abbr. "The Divine Human Being")

Kohlenberger III, John R., gen. ed. *The Essential Evangelical Parallel Bible – New King James Version, English Standard Version, New Living Translation: The Message* (New York, NY: Oxford University Press, 2004). (Abbr. "Essential Evangelical Parallel Bible")

Köstenberger, Andreas J. "Jesus as Rabbi in the Fourth Gospel," *Bulletin for Biblical Research* 8 (1998): 97-128. (Abbr. "Jesus as Rabbi")

Langton, Daniel R. *The Apostle Paul in the Jewish Imagination: A Study in Modern Jewish-Christian Relations* (New York, NY: Cambridge University Press, 2010). (Abbr. "Paul in Jewish Imagination")

Lee, Bernard J. *The Galilean Jewishness of Jesus: Retrieving the Jewish Origins of Christianity* (Mahwah, NJ: Paulist Press, 1988). (Abbr. "Galilean Jewishness")

Leuchter, Mark. *The Levites and the Boundaries of Israelite Identity* (New York, NY: Oxford University Press, 2017). (Abbr. "Levites and Boundaries")

Levenson, Jon D. *Resurrection and the Restoration of Israel: The Ultimate Victory of the God of Life* (New Haven, CT: Yale University Press, 2008). (Abbr. "Resurrection and Restoration")

Liefeld, Walter L. "The Hellenistic 'Divine Man' and the Figure of Jesus in the Gospels, *Journal of the Evangelical Theological Society (JETS)*, 16: (Fall 1973), pp. 195-205. (Abbr. "Hellenistic Divine Man")

Lizorkin-Eyzenberg, Eli. *The Jewish Gospel of John: Discovering Jesus, King of All Israel* (Tel Aviv, Israel: Jewish Studies for Christians, 2015). (Abbr. "Jewish Gospel")

Longenecker, Richard N. *The Epistle to the Romans* (Grand Rapids, MI: William B. Eerdmans Publishing Company, 2016). (Abbr. "Epistle to the Romans")

Luff, Rosemary Margaret. *The Impact of Jesus in First-Century Palestine: Textual and Archaeological Evidence for Long-standing Discontent* (New York, NY: Cambridge University Press, 2019). (Abbr. "Impact of Jesus")

Maccoby, Hyam. "The Jewishness of Jesus," *European Judaism: A Journal for the New Europe*, Vol. 28, No. 1 (Spring '95), pp. 52-62. (Abbr. "Jewishness of Jesus")

Magee, M. D. *Christianity Revealed: Christianity and the Essenes* (Frome, UK: AskWhy! Publications, 2003), PDF. (Abbr. "Christianity and the Essenes")

Magness, Jodi. "Ossuaries and the Burials of Jesus and James," *Journal of Biblical Literature*, Vol. 124, No. 1 (Spring, 2005), pp. 121-154. (Abbr. "Ossuaries and Burials")

Magness, Jodi. *Stone and Dung, Oil and Spit: Jewish Daily Life in the Time of Jesus* (Grand Rapids, MI: William B. Erdmans Publishing Company, 2011). (Abbr. "Stone, Dung, Oil, Spit")

Malinowski, Francis Xavier. *Galilean Judaism in the Writings of Flavius Josephus* (Ph.D. Diss., Duke University, 1973). (Abbr. "Galilean Judaism")

McCane, Byron R. "'Where no one had yet been laid': The Shame of Jesus' Burial," in *Authenticating the Acts of Jesus*, Chilton, Bruce and Evans, Craig A., eds. (Leiden, The Netherlands: Brill, 1999), pp. 431-452. (Abbr. "Yet Been Laid")

McDonald, Lee Martin. *The Formation of the Biblical Canon: Volume 2: The New Testament: Its Authority and Canonicity* (New York, NY: Bloomsbury, T&T Clark, 2017). (Abbr. "Formation of Biblical Canon")

McGing, Brian C. "Pontius Pilate and the Sources," *The Catholic Biblical Quarterly*, Vol. 53, No. 3 (July, 1991), pp. 416-438. (Abbr. "Pontius Pilate and Sources")

Meier, John P. *A Marginal Jew: Rethinking the Historical Jesus – Volume 2, Mentor, Message, and Miracles* (New York, NY: Doubleday, 1994). (Abbr. "Mentor, Message, Miracles")

Meier, John P. *A Marginal Jew: Rethinking the Historical Jesus – Volume 3, Companions and Competitors* (New York, NY: Doubleday, 2001). (Abbr. "Companions and Competitors")

Metzger, Bruce M. and Coogan, Michael D., eds. *The Oxford Guide to People & Places of the Bible* (New York, NY: Oxford University Press, 2001). (Abbr. "Oxford Guide People Places")

Meyer, Ben F. *The Aims of Jesus* (London, UK: SCM Press, 1979). (Abbr. "Aims of Jesus")

Meyers, Eric M. "The Challenge of Hellenism for Early Judaism and Christianity," *The Biblical Archaeologist*, Vol. 55, No. 2 (Jun., 1992), pp. 84-91. (Abbr. "Challenge of Hellenism")

Millar, Fergus. *The Roman Near East: 31 B.C.-A.D. 337* (Cambridge, MA: Harvard University Press, 1993). (Abbr. "Roman Near East")

Mishkin, David. *Jewish Scholarship on the Resurrection of Jesus* (Eugene, OR: Pickwick Publications, 2017). (Abbr. "Jewish Scholarship")

Moor, Johannes C. de. *The Rise of Yahwism: The Roots of Israelite Monotheism*, Revised and Enlarged Edition (Leuven-Louvain, Belguim: Leuven University Press, 1997). (Abbr. "The Rise of Yahwism")

Murphy, Catherine M. *John the Baptist: Prophet of Purity for a New Age* (Collegeville, MN: Liturgical Press, 2003). (Abbr. "Prophet of Purity")

Murphy, Fredrick James. *The Religious World of Jesus: An Introduction to Second Temple Palestinian Judaism* (Nashville, TN: Abingdon Press, 1991). (Abbr. "Religious World of Jesus")

Oppenheimer, A'haron. *Between Rome and Babylon: Studies in Jewish Leadership and Society* (Tübingen, Germany: Mohr Siebeck, 2008). (Abbr. "Between Rome and Babylon")

Park, Hyung Dae. *Finding Herem?: A Study of Luke-Acts in the Light of Herem* (New York, NY: T&T Clark International, 2007). (Abbr. "Finding Herem")

Pastor, Jack. *Land and Economy in Ancient Palestine* (New York, NY: Routledge, 1997). (Abbr. "Land and Economy")

Payne, Philip Barton, "The Authenticity of the Parables of Jesus," in *Gospel Perspectives: Studies of History and Tradition in the Four Gospels*, Volume II, France, R.T. and Wenham, David, eds. (Eugene, OR: Wipf and Stock Publishers, 2003). (Abbr. "Authenticity of the Parables")

Penner, Todd. *The Epistle of James and Eschatology: Re-reading an Ancient Christian Letter* (Sheffield, England: Sheffield Academic Press, 1996). (Abbr. "The Epistle of James")

Porter, Stanley E. et al., eds., *Journal of Greco-Roman Christianity and Judaism*, Volume 1 (2000) (Sheffield, England: Sheffield University Press, 2004). (Abbr. "Journal Greco-Roman Christianity")

Räisänen, Heikki. *Challenges to Biblical Interpretation: Collected Essays, 1991-2000* (Boston, MA: Brill, 2001). (Abbr. "Challenges to Biblical Interpretation")

Rajak, Tessa. "The Location of Cultures in Second Temple Palestine: The Evidence of Josephus," in *The Book of Acts in Its Palestinian Setting*, Bauckham, Richard, ed. (Grand Rapids, MI: William B. Eerdmans Publishing Company, 1995). (Abbr. "Cultures Second Temple Palestine")

Ramshaw, Gail. *What is Christianity?: An Introduction to the Christian Religion* (Minneapolis, MN: Fortress Press, 2013). (Abbr. "What is Christianity")

Reed, Jonathan L. *Archaeology and the Galilean Jesus: A Re-examination of the Evidence* (Harrisburg, PA: Trinity Press International, 2001). (Abbr. "Re-Examination")

Regev, Eyal. "Christianity in Light of Ancient Greek Practice and Qumranic Ideology," *The Harvard Theological Review*, Vol. 97, No. 4 (Oct., 2004), pp. 383-411. (Abbr. "Christianity in Light")

Riesner, Rainer. "From the Messianic Teacher to the Gospels of Jesus Christ," in *Handbook for the Study of the Historical Jesus, Volume 1: How to Study the Historical Jesus*, Holmén, Tom and Porter, Stanley E., eds. (Boston, MA: Brill, 2011). (Abbr. "Messianic Teacher to Gospels")

Robinson, James M. *The Gospel of Jesus: A Historical Search for the Good News* (San Francisco, CA: HarperSanFrancisco, 2006). (Abbr. "Historical Search")

Rohrbaugh, Richard L. *The New Testament in Cross-Cultural Perspective* (Eugene, OR: Cascade Books, 2006). (Abbr. "NT Cross-Cultural Perspective")

Safrai, Ze'ev. *The Economy of Roman Palestine* (New York, NY: Routledge, 2014). (Abbr. "Economy of Roman Palestine")

Saldarini, Anthony J. *Matthew's Christian-Jewish Community* (Chicago, IL: The University of Chicago Press, 1994). (Abbr. "Matthew's Christian-Jewish Community")

Sanders, E. P. *Jesus and Judaism* (Philadelphia, PA: Fortress Press, 1985). (Abbr. "Jesus and Judaism")

Sanders, E. P. "Jesus and the Kingdom: The Restoration of Israel and the New People of God," in *Jesus, the Gospels, and the Church: Essays in Honor of William R. Farmer*, Sanders, E. P., ed. (Macon, GA: Mercer University Press, 1987), pp. 225-239. (Abbr. "Restoration of Israel")

Sanders, E. P. *The Historical Figure of Jesus* (New York, NY: Penguin Books, 1995). (Abbr. "Historical Figure of Jesus") (Abbr. "Historical Figure of Jesus")

Schiffman, Lawrence H. "Legislation Concerning Relations With Non-Jews in the 'Zadokite Fragments' and in Tannaitic Literature," *Revue de Qumrân*, Vol. 11, No. 3 (43) (1983), pp. 379-389. (Abbr. "Relations Non-Jews Zadokite Fragments")

Schulz, Siegfried. *Die Stunde der Botschaft* (Hamburg, Germany: Furche, 1967). (Abbr. "Die Stunde der Botschaft")

Sim, David C. "Fighting on All Fronts: Crisis Management in the Gospel of Matthew," in *Ancient Jewish and Christian Texts as Crisis Management Literature: Thematic Studies from the Centre for Early Christian Studies*,

Sim, David C. and Allen, Pauline, eds. (New York, NY: T&T Clark International, 2012). (Abbr. "Fighting on All Fronts")

Smith, Morton. "Prolegomena to a Discussion of Aretalogies, Divine Men, the Gospels and Jesus," *Journal of Biblical Literature*, Vol. 90, No. 2 (Jun., 1971), pp. 174-199. (Abbr. "Divine Men")

Sparks, James T. *The Chronicler's Genealogies: Towards an Understanding of 1 Chronicles 1-9* (Atlanta, GA: Society of Biblical Literature, 2008). (Abbr. "The Chronicler's Genealogies")

Stanton, Graham. *The Gospels and Jesus*, Second Edition (New York, NY: Oxford University Press, 2002). (Abbr. "Gospels and Jesus")

Stegemann, Ekkehard W. and Stegemann, Wolfgang. *The Jesus Movement: A Social History of Its First Century*, Dean, Jr., O. C., trans. (Minneapolis, MN, Fortress Press, 1999). (Abbr. "Jesus Movement")

Stein, Robert H. *The Method and Message of Jesus' Teachings*, Revised Edition (Louisville, KY: Westminster John Knox Press, 1994). (Abbr. "Method and Message")

Talbott, Rick F. *Jesus, Paul, and Power: Rhetoric, Ritual, and Metaphor in Ancient Mediterranean Christianity* (Eugene, OR: Cascade Books, 2010). (Abbr. "Rhetoric, Ritual")

Talmon, Shemaryahu. "'Exile' and 'Restoration' in the Conceptual World of Ancient Israel," in *Restoration: Old Testament, Jewish, and Christian Perspectives*, Scott, James M., ed. (Leiden, The Netherlands: Brill, 2001), pp. 107-146. (Abbr. "Exile and Restoration")

Tan, Kim Huat. *The Zion Traditions and the Aims of Jesus* (New York, NY: Cambridge University Press, 1997). (Abbr. "Zion Traditions")

Taylor, Joan E. *The Immerser: John the Baptist Within Second Temple Judaism* (Grand Rapids, MI: William B. Eerdmans Publishing Company, 1997). (Abbr. "Immerser")

Theissen, Gerd. *Sociology of Early Palestinian Christianity*, Bowden, John, trans. (Philadelphia, PA: Fortress Press, 1978). (Abbr. "Sociology Early Palestinian Christianity")

Theissen, Gerd and Merz, Annette. *The Historical Jesus: A Comprehensive Guide* (Minneapolis, MN: Fortress Press, 1996). (Abbr. "Historical Jesus")

Thompson, J. A. *The Bible and Archaeology* (William B. Eerdmans Publishing Company, 1962). (Abbr. "The Bible and Archaeology")

Tilburg, Cornelis van. *Traffic and Congestion in the Roman Empire* (New York, NY: Routledge, 2007). (Abbr. "Traffic and Congestion")

Turner, George A. *Historical Geography of the Holy Land* (Grand Rapids, MI: Baker Book House, 1973). (Abbr. "Historical Geography Holy Land")

Vermès, Géza. *Jesus in His Jewish Context* (Minneapolis, MN: Fortress Press, 2003). (Abbr. "Jewish Context")

Vermès, Géza. *Jesus the Jew: A Historian's Reading of the Gospels* (Philadelphia, PA: Fortress Press, 1981). (Abbr. "Historian's Reading")

Vermès, Géza, *The Religion of Jesus the Jew* (Minneapolis, MN: Fortress Press, 1993). (Abbr. "Jesus the Jew")

Wahlde, Urban C. von. "The First Edition of John's Gospel in Light of Archaeology and Contemporary Literature," in *The Gospel of John in Historical Research*, Charlesworth, James H. and Pruszinski, Jolyon G. R., eds. (New York, NY: T&T Clark, 2019), pp. 99-141. (Abbr. "First Edition John's Gospel")

Wassen, Cecilia. "The Jewishness of Jesus and Ritual Purity," *Jewish Studies in the Nordic Countries Today*, Vol 27 (2016), pp. 11-36. (Abbr. "Jewishness of Jesus")

Webb, Robert L. "Jesus in Relation to John 'The Testifier' and Not 'The Baptizer': The Fourth Gospel's Portrayal of John the Baptist and Its Historical Possibilities," in *John, Jesus, and History, Volume 3: Glimpses of Jesus through the Johannine Lens*, Anderson, Paul N. (Atlanta, GA: SBL Press, 2016), pp. 215-230. (Abbr. "Jesus Relation to John")

Webb, Robert L. "John the Baptist and His Relationship to Jesus," in *Studying the Historical Jesus: Evaluations of the State of Current Research* (Boston, MA: Brill, 1994), pp. 178-229. (Abbr. "John the Baptist")

Webb, Robert L. *John the Baptizer and Prophet: A Socio-historical Study* (Eugene, OR: Wipf and Stock Publishers, 2006). (Abbr. "Socio-historical Study")

Werman, Cana. "Levi and Levites in the Second Temple Period," *Dead Sea Discoveries*, Vol. 4, No. 2 (Jul., 1997), pp. 211-225. (Abbr. "Levi and Levites")

Wilkins, Michael J. *The NIV Application Commentary: Matthew* (Grand Rapids, MI: Zondervan, 2004). (Abbr. "NIV Application Commentary Matthew")

Williams, Travis B. *Good Works in 1 Peter: Negotiating Social Conflict and Christian Identity in the Greco-Roman World* (Tübingen, Germany: Mohr Siebeck, 2014). (Abbr. "Good Works 1 Peter")

Witmer, Amanda. *Jesus, the Galilean Exorcist: His Exorcisms in Social and Political Context* (New York, NY: T&T Clark International, 2012). (Abbr. ("Exorcisms – Social, Political Context")

Yeung, Maureen W. *Faith in Jesus and Paul: A Comparison with Special Reference to 'Faith that Can Remove Mountains' and 'Your Faith Has Healed/Saved You'* (Tübingen, Germany: Mohr Siebeck, 2002). (Abbr. "Faith in Jesus")

Young, Brad H. *Jesus the Jewish Theologian* (Grand Rapids, MI: Baker Academic, 1995). (Abbr. "Jewish Theologian")

Zaslow, David. *Jesus: First-Century Rabbi* (Brewster, MA: Paraclete Press, 2014). (Abbr. "First-Century Rabbi")

Zetterholm, Magnus. The Formation of Christianity in Antioch: A Sociological Approach to the Separation Between Judaism and Christianity (New York, NY: Routledge, 2003). (Abbr. "Formation of Early Christianity").

Zimmermann, Ruban. Puzzling the Parables of Jesus: Methods and Interpretation (Minneapolis, MN: Fortress Press, 2015). (Abbr. "Puzzling the Parables")

CHAPTER EIGHT
Endnotes

1 For background: Klausner 1943, From Jesus to Paul, 441, 528-536, 580-590; Davies 1945, Role Prophet, 241-254; Malinowski 1973, Galilean Judaism Writings Josephus, esp. 66-71; Vermès 1981, Historian's Reading, 19-41; Sanders 1985, Jesus and Judaism; Falk 1985, Jewishness Jesus, 148-161; Feldman 1986, Hellenism Jewish Palestine, 83-111; Braine 1988, Inner Jewishness of Jesus, 101-157; Lee 1988, Galilean Jewishness; Stock 1989, Method and Message Matthew, 57; Feldman 1993, Jew and Gentile, 24-25; Millar 1993, Roman Near East, 347; Vermès 1993, Jesus the Jew, 11-45, 223-224; Saldarini 1994, Matthew's Christian-Jew Community, 75-76; Maccoby 1995, Jewishness of Jesus, 52-62; Young 1995, Jewish Theologian; Witherington III 1997, Jesus Quest, 38; Köstenberger 1998, Jesus as Rabbi, 97-128; Goodman 1999, Galilean Judaism, Judaean Judaism, 596-617; Chilton 2000, Rabbi Jesus, 3-22; Chancey 2002, Myth of Gentile Galilee, 26; Eve 2002, Jewish Context Jesus Miracles; Vermès 2003, Jewish Context; Zetterholm 2003, Formation of Early Christianity, 3; Freyne 2004, Jewish Galilean; Levine 2006, Misunderstood Jew, 17-51; Robinson 2006, Historical Search, 55-88; Charlesworth 2008, Historical Jesus Essential Guide, 17; Casey 2010, Independent Historian Account, 164; Garber, ed. 2011, Jewish Jesus; Bond 2012, Guide for the Perplexed, 80; Ben-Chorin 2012, Brother Jesus; Moore 2014, Jewish Mosaic, 58-81; Zaslow 2014, First-Century Rabbi, 12-32; Garber 2015, Conversation Not Conversion, 385-392; Lizorkin-Eyzenberg 2015, Jewish Gospel; Wassen 2016, Jewishness of Jesus, 11-36; Homolka 2017, Jewish Research, 9-104; Mishkin 2017, Jewish Scholarship, 143.

2 Cribbs 1970, Origin-Destination John, 47; Langton 2002, Dividing It

Right, 134.

3 For thoughtful discussion, see Hvalik 2007, Paul as Jewish Believer, 121-153.

4 See Theissen and Merz 1996, Historical Jesus, 170-171.

5 For a qualified expert's comments on Galilean population growth, see Reed 2001, Re-examination, 82-93.

6 In the last several decades there has been a measurable and sharp decline in people who are willing to claim that they believe in God. See Campbell 2007, Easternization of the West, 70.

7 Magness 2005, Ossuaries and Burials, 143-149.

8 Evans 2012, Jesus and his World, 130.

9 A comprehensive list of experts supports this conclusion. However, the arguments of McCane and Evans stand out as methodically drawn and utterly convincing: McCane 1999, Yet Been Laid, 431-452; Evans 2005, Jewish Burial, 233-248.

10 Charlesworth 2008, Temple, Purity, Jesus' Death, 429.

11 Berlin 2005, Jewish Life Before Revolt, 417-470.

12 Theissen 1978, Sociology Early Palestinian, 1; 8-23; 77-95; Meyer 1979, Aims of Jesus, 128; 197-198; 220-221; Sanders 1985, Jesus and Judaism, 59-119; Sanders 1987, Restoration of Israel, 225-239; Horsley 1993, Spiral of Violence, 167-284; Sanders, 1995, Historical Figure; Theissen and Merz 1996, Historical Jesus, 141-147; Evans 1997, Aspects Exile, Restoration, 263-296; Tan 1997, Zion Traditions; Allison 1998, Millenarian Prophet, 141-145; Borg 1998, Conflict, Holiness, 17-20; 51-72; 123-143; Horsley 1999, Contingencies of Renewal, 57-74; Talmon 2001, Exile and Restoration, 107-146; Meier 2001, Companions and Competitors, 148-154; Stanton 2002, Gospels and Jesus, 295-296; Bryan 2002, Judgement and Restoration, 21-45; Dunn 2003, Jesus Remembered, 350-352; Horsley 2006, Early Christian Movements, 1201-1225; Bird 2006, Jesus and Origins, 26-45; Dennis 2006, Gathering

True Israel, 75-318; Freyne 2007, Jesus and Servant, 110-111; Levenson 2008, Resurrection and Restoration; Horsley 2008, Jesus in Context, 35-55; Casey 2010, Independent Historian Account, 312; Horsley 2012, Prophet Jesus, 67-157; Horsley and Thatcher 2013, Renewal Israel, 34-54; 137-155.

13 Culi 1978, Torah Anthology, iv, 170.

14 Kohlenberger III 2004, Essential Evangelical Parallel Bible, 956.

15 For interesting background on the Levites during the time of Jesus, see Werman 1997, Levi and Levites, 211-225.

16 Sparks 2008, The Chronicler's Genealogies, 156.

17 Leuchter, Levites and Boundaries, 104-105.

18 Sparks 2008, The Chronicler's Genealogies, 156.

19 Clements 1996, Ezekiel, 176.

20 Taylor 1997, Immerser, 315. Also: Dunn 2003, Jesus Remembered, 350-352; Theissen and Merz 1996, Historical Jesus, 196-215; Webb 1994, John the Baptist, 218-223; 226-229; Webb 2016, Jesus Relation to John, 215-230; Meier 1994, Mentor, Message, Miracles, 116-130; Sanders 1985, Jesus and Judaism, 91; Murphy 2003, Prophet of Purity, 59; Stegemann and Stegemann 1999, Jesus Movement, 195-196. For interesting background, Anderson 2007, Fourth Gospel Quest, 154-158.

21 Ferguson 2009, Baptism in Early Church, 111.

22 Bauckham 2006, Messianism According to John, 49.

23 Riesner 2011, Messianic Teacher to Gospels, 422.

24 Mt 10.5-11, 11.1; Mk 3.14; Lk 9.1-6.

25 See Horsley and Thatcher 2013, Renewal Israel, 56-57.

26 Räisänen 2001, Challenges to Biblical Interpretation, 3. Also, Metzger and Coogan, eds., Oxford Guide People Places, 568.

27 Payne 2003, Authenticity of the Parables, 329. Also, Stein 1994, Method and Message, 42; Zimmermann 2015, Puzzling the Parables, 58-75.

28 Mt 10.1, 7-8; Mk 3.14-15; 6.7, 13; 16.16-18, 20; Lk 9.1-2, 6; 24.47-48.

29 Crossan 1997, Itinerants and Householders, 12; Dunn, Third Quest, 2002, 44; Keener 2009, Historical Jesus Gospels, 163; McDonald 2017, Formation of Biblical Canon, ii, 328.

30 Georgi 1995, Internal Jewish Migration, 38.

31 Goodman 1987, Ruling Class, 97-98; Avshalom-Gorni and Getzov 2002, Phoenicians and Jews, 81.

32 Goodman 1987, Ruling Class, 98; Gruen 2002, Jews Amidst Greeks, Romans, 5.

33 Feldman 1993, Jew and Gentile, 227.

34 See Goodman's interesting, related comments (Goodman 1987, Ruling Class, 99-108).

35 Goodman 1987, Ruling Class, 2.

36 Blumell 2008, Social Banditry, 40-49.

37 Pastor 1997, Land and Economy, 157.

38 Safrai 2014, Economy of Roman Palestine, 163.

39 Rohrbaugh 2006, NT Cross-Cultural Perspective, 29.

40 Faulkner 2011, Apocalypse, 62.

41 Murphy 1991, Religious World of Jesus, 308.

42 Wilkins 2004, NIV Application Commentary Matthew, 827.

43 McGing 1991, Pontius Pilate and Sources, 419.

44 Von Wahlde 2019, First Edition John's Gospel, 100-104.

45 Bouchard 1988, Life and Society, 81; Gabriel and Boose 1994, Great Battles of Antiquity, 7; Tilburg 2007, Traffic and Congestion, 39; Goodman 2008, Rome and Jerusalem, 95.

46 Goodman 1987, Ruling Class, 174.

47 Chancey 2005, Greco-Roman Culture, 58.

48 Oppenheimer 2008, Between Rome and Babylon, 204; Safrai 2014, Economy of Roman Palestine, 154.

49 Porter, et al., eds. 2004, Journal Greco-Roman Christianity, 202.

50 Thompson 1962, The Bible and Archaeology, 328.

51 Ahlström 1993, History of Ancient Palestine, 67.

52 Thompson 1962, The Bible and Archaeology, 328; Hezser 2011, Jewish Travel in Antiquity, 34.

53 Hezser 2011, Jewish Travel in Antiquity, 1.

54 Byrskog 2000, Story as History, 70.

55 Dowden 2010, Rhetoric and Religion, 325.

56 Goldberg and Rayner 1989, The Jewish People, 278-279; Andrade 2010, Ambiguity, Violence, Community, 342-370.

57 Feldman 1986, Hellenism in Jewish Paletine, 103-105, 111.

58 Regev 2004, Christianity in Light, 389.

59 Harrington, Purity and Sanctuary, 35. The citation is attributed to scholar Christine Hayes, Gentile Impurities and Jewish Identities: Intermarriage and Conversion from the Bible to the Talmud (New York, NY: Oxford University Press, 2002).

60 Feldman 2003, Conversion to Judaism, 116.

61 Hezser 2013, Romanization and Its Consequences, 2.

62 Yeung 2002, Faith in Jesus, 65.

63 Berlin 2011, Identity Politics, 95.

64 Ibid.

65 Talbot 2012, Love Your Enemy, 27.

66 Bird 2006, Jesus and Origins, 48.

67 Grosby 2002, Biblical Ideas of Nationality, 47.

68 Horsley and Hanson 1985, Bandits, Prophets, 13; Feldman 1986, Hel-

lenism in Jewish Palestine?", 111; Meyers 1992, Challenge of Hellenism, 86; Berlin 2005, Jewish Life Before Revolt, 468-470; Andrade 2010, Ambiguity, Violence, Community, 343-345.

69 Berlin 2005, Jewish Life Before Revolt, 417-470.

70 See Turner 1973, Historical Geography Holy Land, 88-89; Freedman, ed. 2000, Eerdmans Dictionary the Bible, 212; Halpern 2006, Miraculous Wine Galilean Context, 215; Alexandre 2015, Karm er-Ras, 155.

71 See Luff 2019, Impact of Jesus, 86-90. For background, Berlin 2005, Jewish Life Before Revolt, 429; Kazen 2010, Jesus and Purity Halakhah, 84.

72 See Cromhout 2007, Jesus and Identity, 246; Witmer 2012, Exorcisms – Social, Political Context, 84, note 126.

73 Magness 2011, Stone Dung, Oil, Spit, 72.

74 Reed 2001, Re-Examination, 44.

75 Goodman 1987, Ruling Class, 103.

76 See Cohen 2002, Josephus in Galilee, Rome, 181-229; Chancey 2002, Myth of Gentile Galilee, 51, note 117; Park 2007, Finding Herem, 103.

77 Schiffman 1983, Relations Non-Jews Zadokite Fragments, 379-389; Feldman 1986, Hellenism in Jewish Palestine, 95; Meyers 1992, Challenge of Hellenism, 86; Feldman 1993, Jew and Gentile, 43; Andrade 2010, Ambiguity, Violence, Community, 342-370.

78 Penner 1996, The Epistle of James, 39-40, note 1; Elledge 2005, Dead Sea Scrolls, 36; Williams 2014, Good Works 1 Peter, 199-201.

79 Johnson 2009, Among the Gentiles, 30.

80 Bruyneel and Padgett 2003, Introducing Christianity, 37.

81 Magee 2003, Christianity and the Essenes, 11.

82 Meyers 1992, Challenge of Hellenism, 86.

83 On the Jewish side, the one exception was some families among aristocrats. See Webb 2006, Socio-historical Study, 356-357.

84 Hayes and Mandell 1998, Jewish People Classical Antiquity, 186.

85 Feldman 1993, Jew and Gentile, 120; Chancey 2002, Myth of Gentile Galilee, 56; Witmer 2012, Exorcisms – Social, Political Context, 171.

86 Choi 2013, Jewish Leadership Roman Palestine, 124.

87 Rajak 1995, Cultures Second Temple Palestine, 12.

88 Chancey 2002, Myth of Gentile Galilee, 57.

89 Sim 2012, Fighting on All Fronts, 76.

90 Chancey 2002, Myth of Gentile Galilee, 56, note 144.

91 SOCIAL POLITICS: Measuring the differences between population groups based on political beliefs.

92 See Taylor 1997, Immerser, 163.

93 Goodman 1987, Ruling Class, 3.

94 See Horsley 1993, Spiral of Violence, 228.

95 In alphabetical order: Antioch (Acts 15.35); Antioch in Pisidia (Acts 13.14-50); Athens (17.22-34); Beroea (Acts 10.10-13); Corinth (18.1-18); Damascus (Acts 9.10-22); Derbe (Acts 14.6-7, 20-21); Ephesus (Acts 19.10, 18); Iconium (Acts 13.51-14.7); Lystra (Acts 14.6-21; 16.1-3); Macedonia (Acts 16.9-40); Melita (Acts 28.1-9); Philippi (Acts 11.1-15); Rome (Acts 28.16-31); Salamis (Acts 13.5); Thessalonica (17.1-10); Troas (Acts 20.6-12).

96 Acts 8.5; 9.22; 11.26; 16.18; 17.3; 18.5, 28; 20.17-21; 24.24; 26.19-23.

97 Acts 16.16-24; 19.8-21.

98 Acts 28.3-5.

99 Acts 13.11; 14.10; 16.18; 19.11-12; 20.10-12; 28.5, 8.

100 Acts 20.6-12.

101 Rom 16.17-20; 1 Cor 5.1-13; 6.9-11, 15-20; Gal 1.6-10; 2.11-16; Eph 4.25-56; Col 3.5-9; 2 Thess 3.6-12; 1 Tim 1.3-11; 6.2-10.

102 Ramshaw 2013, What is Christianity, 65.

103 Dunn 2010, First Christians Worshipping Jesus, 103.

104 See Bousset 1970, Kyrios Christos, 153.

105 Hewitt 2020, Messiah and Scripture, 14.

106 Gibbs 1971, Creation and Redemption, 33, note 1.

107 "Yahwism must have been the official religion [of Israel] from at least the 9th century B.C. onwards. ... The stele of Mesha confirms that this was the case in the northern kingdom c. 850 B.C." (Moor 1997, The Rise of Yahwism, 12-13).

108 Longenecker 2016, Epistle to the Romans, 61.

109 Schulz 1967, Die Stunde der Botschaft, 54-59, 64-79; Betz 1968, Jesus as Divine Man, 114-133; M. Smith 1971, Divine Men, 174-199; Achtemeir 1972, Gospel and Divine Man, 173-197; Betz 1972, Concept So-Called Divine Man, 229-240; Liefeld 1973, Hellenistic Divine Man, 195-205; Gallagher 1982, Divine Man or Magician; Koester 1985, The Divine Human Being, 243-252; Georgi 1987, The Opponents of Paul; Corrington 1986, Divine Man, 211-275; Blackburn 1991, Markan Miracle Traditions, 97-182. While in general disfavor among scholars today, the "divine man" or "godman" concept constituted a cornerstone of Hellenistic religion. A reasonable semblance of this idea is generously infused across all four canonical texts. Scholars have no credible basis for defending rejection except theological pushback which is often the case.

APPENDIX 'A'

Language Studies

Hebrew Thoughts

Yhvh – יהוה (Strong's #3068)

Lord, YaHVeH

The traditional Jehovah/Yahweh name of God is a confusion of Christian history. The earliest recorded pronunciation of השם *ha-Shem* 'the Name' as 'Jehovah' is 1520 A.D.. Early Greek transliterations of it are *Iabe*, where the 'b' represents a Hebrew 'v' and the 'I' a 'y' for the Greeks had no 'y,j,h,v', and are thus closest to *Ya(h)ve(h)*. The unpointed Hebrew text (i.e., without vowels) recorded the name of God as יהוה *Yhvh*. This could have been read in many ways. When the Massoretic scribes added the later vowel points to the text, more than 600 years after the first century context of Jesus, pre-rabbinic Judaism and Christianity, they played a grammatical trick in the Hebrew text. They did this in order to preserve the sacred name of God from blasphemy and their literal interpretation of the breaking of the second commandment, not to take God's name in vain (Exodus 20:7; Leviticus 24:11).

So, when it came to vowel pointing the consonants of יהוה *Yhvh* 'what was written' was יְהֹוָה *Yehôvâh* or *Jehovah* in English, an impossible, incorrect and meaningless form. However, 'what was read' קרי *qerêy* was אֲדֹנָי *'adhônây*, 'Lord', since the vowels under the word were those of 'adhônây. At first sight the vowels appear slightly different, 'adhônây having a slight 'a' as its first vowel and *Yehôvâh* having a slight 'e'. This is down to the nature of the Hebrew *shevâ* vowel where a guttural letter (as à here) cannot take the simple : but instead takes the augmented form, in this case – :, when this is added to the *yôwdh* of יהוה *Yhvh* it reverts to :.

Before we blame the later Massoretic scribes for this curiosity we should note that they were only acting on existing traditions which chose not to pronounce the name of God. These may go back to before the time of Christ when circumlocutions for God's name were already in use. Indeed, in the Dead Sea scroll of Isaiah (1st century B.C./A.D.) Yhvh is already read as אדני *'adhônây* by placing its consonants, אדני or אדוני (with a full 'ôw'/vâv consonant in place of the 'ô' pointing above the 'd'), above those of יהוה. Earlier still, the Greek Septuagint translation of the Old Testament Hebrew (c. 300 B.C.) already translated all occurrences of the divine name by *ho Kurios* 'the Lord' or אדני *'adhônây* (Adonai). If the biblical text had *Yhvh* next to *Adonai* already they would read it as אֲדֹנָאֱל.הִים *'adhônây 'elôhîym* rather than *Adonai Adonai*. In the earliest biblical times there seems to have been no problem adding *Yah* or *Yahu* to people's names or greeting each other with "YHVH bless you" but by the New Testament period the divine name was only uttered within the temple walls.

יהוה *Yhvh* (Strong's #3068) actually occurs 6519 times in the Hebrew Bible text, the first time in Genesis 2:4 where it is paired with אלהים *'elôhîym*. It doesn't occur on its own until Genesis 4:1 when Eve "gets from God" a son, Cain. Too much should not be read into the differences for in Genesis 4:25 Eve uses אלהים *'elôhîym* rather than יהוה *Yhvh* when she has Seth. A shortened variation appears to be יה *Yâhh* (Strong's #3050, cf. והי Yâhû) which occurs 49 (seven 7's!) times – its first use is in Exodus 15:2 "Yâh is my strength".

יהוה *Yhvh* occurs in a number of significant passages including: Exodus 6:3; Psalm 83:18 [v.19 Heb.]; Isaiah 12:2; 26:4; Genesis 22:14; Judges 6:24. Its origins are assumed to be from either הוה *hâvâh* (Strong's #1933) 'to breathe/live', a rare synonym of היה *hâyâh* (Strong's #1961) 'to be/exist', or from היה *hâyâh* itself.

The apparently awkward verse in Exodus 6:3 which suggests that the patriarchs only knew God as 'God Almighty' and not as *Yhvh* may be solved by inserting a rhetorical question mark after the phrase "and by my name **Yhvh** was I not known to them?", in other words God is the same God of Moses as He is of the patriarchs – hence the continuing validity of the covenant from one age to the next.

FOOTNOTES: F1: Ruth 2:4; Mishnah, Berakôth 9.5, Yoma 3.8; 6.2; Sotah.

Copyright Statement

'Hebrew Thoughts' Copyright 2021© KJ Went. *'Hebrew Thoughts'* articles may be reproduced in whole under the following provisions:

A proper credit must be given to the author at the end of each article, along with a link to:

www.biblicalhebrew.com

AND

https://www.studylight.org/language-studies/hebrew-thoughts.html;

Hebrew Thoughts' content may not be arranged or "mirrored" as a competitive online service.

THIS STUDY GRATEFULLY APPRECIATES KJ Went (copyright holder) associated with *Hebrew Thoughts* authorizing the use of the above expert analysis. In compliance with permission details, appropriate online links are provided above. DANIEL G. SLAWTER, Author.

AUTHOR AND SUBJECT INDEX

Herod from Idumea, made sacrifices in Rome 85
Herod from Idumea, madman 86
Herod from Idumea, murdered family members and rabbis 86
Herod from Idumea, no figure in antiquity more available data 86
Herod from Idumea, prolific builder on grand scale 86
Hewitt, J. 336
Hezser, C. 221, 222, 238, 322, 326
Hirschberg, H. 138
Historical realities 140, 173
Historical realities, social unrest 320
Historical realities, violence 319
Hoff, M. 21
Höistad, R. 218
Homolka, W. 27, 303
Honor and shame values 250
Horbury, W. 174
Horn, C. and Martens, J. 28
Horsley, R. 76, 81, 133, 134, 137, 141, 174, 221, 222, 223, 226, 250, 260, 311
Horsley, R. and Hanson, J. 329
Horsley, R. and Thatcher, T. 311, 314
Household Judaism 329
Household Judaism, stone vessels 330
Household Judaism, stone vessels impervious to impurity 330
Houtart, F. 174
Howson, A. 267
Huller, S. 218
Hull, M. 222
Hutchens, D. 264
Hvalvik, R. 304

I

Indigenous peoples, capable of discerning folklore from myth 260
Individual, role of in ancient society 245
In-group, separation from, loss of hope 248
Instone-Brewer, D. 37, 173

Irwin, W. 116
Isis 111
Israelites, attention and priorities fixed on immediate living groups 247
Israelites, collective reality 247
Israelites, collective reality, generalized about out-groups 247
Israelites, pressured on every side 246
Israelites, survival depended on staying together 247
Israel, no standing militia 80

J

Jacob 101
Jeffers, J. 156, 176
Jeffrey, D. 10
Jensen, M. 85
Jeremias, J. 74
Jerusalem, David's City 70
Jerusalem temple, Jesus dedication 174
Jesus, and ancient prophets 181
Jesus, and divine claims 188
Jesus, and moneylenders 181, 182
Jesus, and Mosaic signs 179, 189, 190
Jesus, as faith healer 131, 173, 184, 186
Jesus, associated with proselytizing a Hellenistic notion 326
Jesus, attended Jewish festivals 78
Jesus, attracted sinners 140
Jesus, cast as mythical character history rejects 218
Jesus, core message Mosaically inspired 248
Jesus, crucified 141, 181
Jesus, dedication 174
Jesus, deeply informed by second-temple Judaism 103
Jesus, derived from village setting 250
Jesus, did not create new religious doctrine 248
Jesus, disturbing seditious behavior 130

Kyrios, referred to Nazarene's divine status 336

L

Laes, C. 156, 176
Land of Israel, cultic ideal 327
Lang, B., ed. 223
Lang, G. 174
Langton, D. 303
Lapide, C. 137
Lawson, R. 28
Leach, T. 111, 113
Lee, B. 27, 303
Lee, G. 138
Lemos, I. 5
Lenski, G., et al. 173
Leonhardt, J. 75
Leuchter, M. 311
Levenson, J. 311
Levine, A. 27, 303
Levine, L. 17, 74, 251
Levites, bore Tabernacle 311
Levites, considered most trustworthy 311
Levites, scattered under Saul's reign 311
Lewis, B. 243
Leyerle, B. 155
Liefeld, W. 341
Linn, D. 241
Linville, J. 117
Litwa, M. 30
Livy 27
Livy, Ab Urbe Cóndita 28
Livy, died extremely old age 28
Livy, greatest Roman narrator of historical events 28
Livy, life of Alexander 28
Lizorkin-Eyzenberg, E. 27, 303
Loader, W. 42, 176, 190
Loewe, M. 3
Long, C. 2
Longenecker, B. 174
Longenecker, R. 341
Lüdemann, G. 15, 23

Luff, R. 141, 330
Lydda 74
Lynch. M. 86

M

Maccoby, H. 27, 38, 303
MacDonald, M. 272
Mack, B. 218
Mackie, D., et al. 245
Magee, M. 331
Magness, J. 173, 174, 306, 330
Maier, P. 81
Maimonides, M. 71
Malamat, A. 79
Malamed, S. 28
Malina, B. 174, 245, 250, 251, 272
Malina, B. and Rohrbaugh, R. 33, 159, 174, 245, 250
Malinowski, F. 27, 303
Mare, W. 173
Marshak, A. 85
Mars, M. 263
Martyn, J. 189
Massey, G. 218
Matilla, S. 251
Mauzy, C. and Camp, J. 5
Maynard-Reed, P. 42, 159, 176
McCabe, E. 111
McCane, B. 308
McDonald, L. 316
McDonough, S. 113
McDowell, S. 138
McGing, B. 319
McIver, R. 130, 151, 159, 176, 190, 245
Meier, J. 135, 185, 311, 312
Memory, cannot be trusted 219
Memory, the nature of 220
Merculieff, I. and Roderick, L. 243, 271
Merlier, O. 189
Metzger, B. and Coogan, M., eds. 314
Meyer, B. 311
Meyers, E. 329, 331, 332
Micah, historical figure 265

Mikalson, J. 7
Millar, F. 27, 303
Minc, L. 241
Minderhout, D. 2
Miriam, one of the oldest threads in
    scriptural tradition 265
Miriam, Qumran tradition 266
Miriam, sister to Aaron and Moses
    265
Mishkin, D. 27, 303
Mishnah, Sotah 324
Mitchell, L. 116
Mojsov, B. 111
Moles, J. 35
Moore, D. 27, 155, 176, 303
Moor, J. 340
Morrill, B. 245, 247, 250
Mortality, 20 to 25 173, 183
Mortality studies, antiquity 27
Moses 101
Mount Scopus, four ancient cave-
    tombs 150
Mount Sinai, also called Mount Horeb
    113
Mournet, T. 221, 225, 240, 260, 271
Mumcuoglu, K. and Hadas, G. 176
Mumcuoglu, Y. and Zias, J. 176
Mumcuoglu, Y., et al. 176
Munich Talmud 173
Murdock, D. 218
Murphy, C. 312
Murphy, F. 319

N

Na'aman 105
Nadel, L. and Sinnott-Armstrong, W.
    220
Nakashima, D., et al. 242
Nel, M. 174
Neufeld, D. and DeMaris, R. 272
Neyrey, J. 174, 250
Nicholls, M. 21
Nicol, W. 189
Noah 101
Nomenology Project 136

Nunn, P. 241
Nussbaum, K. 181
Nyunt, P. 261

O

Oakman, D. 152, 153, 173, 174, 176,
    247
Ogden, D., ed. 3
Oppenheimer, A. 321
Orality, dominated the ancient world
    218
Oral sources, closer to earliest time
    and place settings 218
Origen, Contra Celsum 225, 324
Orlin, E., et al., eds. 155, 176
Otto, W. 33
Out-group, or \ 248
Overman, J. 174

P

Paga, J. 2
Palagia, O. and Spetsieri-Choremi, A.,
    eds. 9
Palestine, banditry 318
Palestine, change was in the air 329
Palestine, first Roman road 320
Palestine, lacked safe roads 318
Palestine, most people were illiterate
    221
Palestine, rainy season 321
Palestine, social instability 175
Papadopoulos, J. 5
Park, H. 331
Parthenon 1, 20, 26
Pastor, J. 318
Paul, all Eastern Mediterranean
    synagogue groups reacted with
    uncontrolled hostility 340
Paul, compared to Jesus 223
Paul, considered himself Jewish 304
Paul, gentile Christianity first prosely-
    tized gospel message 341
Paul, godman concept a key to his mis-
    sionary strategy 341

Paul, often confronted by synagogue officials 337
Paul or Paulus, translates to \ 10
Paul, portrayed as victim in Book of Acts 339
Paul, pursued exalted Kyrios 336
Paul, reportedly received 40 lashes 5 times 340
Paul, sixty of seventy-two references to \ 341
Paul, social setting differed from Galilean setting 251
Payne, P. 315
Peisistratos, tyrant 2
Penner, T. 331
Pericles, \ 9
Pericles, delivered most famous speech in defense of warfare 1
Pericles, son of Xanthippus 1
Pfoh, E. 272
Pharisees, bitterly opposed pagan culture 331
Phillips, C. 1
Philo Judaeus, Philo of Alexandria 83
Pilch, J. 159
Piraeus peninsula 8
Plataea, only Greek city-state to answer Athenian call for help at Battle of Marathon 4
Plato, greatest Western philosopher 1
Plautus, Mostellaria 30
Pliny the Elder 84
Plutarch 29
Plutarch, Clough, H., ed. 29
Poirer, J. 227
Poling, J. 159
Polybius 29
Poor, debt slavery 190
Poor, dedication in temple 174
Poor, focused on miraculous 190
Poor, inadequate harvests 190
Poor, laborers and artisans 174
Poor, land loss 190
Poor, limited personal safety 190
Poor, poor health 190

Poor, popular uprisings 319
Poor, pressing taxation 190
Poor, rural 173
Poor, rural, collectivist attitudes 250
Poor, subsistence living 174
Porphyry of Tyre 15
Porter, S., et al., eds. 321
Preparation Day 80
Promised Land, cultic ideal 327
Promised Land, milk and honey 327
Prophets, and tantrums 182
Pseudo-Clementine Recognitions 224
Pseudo-Clementine Recognitions, mentions Jesus follower literacy 224

Q

Qumran, bitterly opposed pagan culture 331
Qumran, resisted hellenization 331

R

Ra, Egyptian creator-god 111
Räisänen, H. 314
Rajak, T. 333
Ramshaw, G. 336
Reed, J. 155, 157, 158, 159, 173, 174, 176, 187, 304
Regev, E. 325
Reim, G. 189
Retief, F. and Cilliers, L. 186
Reuchlin, A. and Reek, H. 218
Reyes, E. 37, 173
Reynolds, J. 1
Rhoads, D. 222, 251, 260
Rhoads, D. and Dewey, J. 260, 261
Ribbens, B. 83
Richard, C. 28
Richards, E. and James, R. 245, 250
Richardson, P. and Edwards, D. 174
Riesner, R. 314
Rigoglioso, M. 33
Rix, R., ed. 220
Roberts, J. 8